ENCYCLOPAEDIA OF
MULTIMEDIA

ENCYCLOPAEDIA OF
MULTIMEDIA

Kamal Sharma

ANMOL PUBLICATIONS PVT. LTD.
NEW DELHI - 110 002 (INDIA)

ANMOL PUBLICATIONS PVT. LTD.
H.O.: 4374/4B, Ansari Road, Daryaganj
New Delhi - 110 002
Ph.: 23278000, 23261597
B.O.: No. 1015, Ist Main Road, BSK III Stage
III Phase, III Block
Bangalore - 560 085 (India)
Visit us at: www.anmolpublications.com

Encyclopaedia of Multimedia

First Published, 2006

ISBN 81-261-2875-5

PRINTED IN INDIA

Printed at Mehra Offset Press, Delhi.

Preface

The aim of this encyclopaedia is to give definitions and details of terms that are of importance in multimedia. It is an encyclopaedia of multimedia terms, written by specialists, partly for other specialists but more particularly for the man-in-the-street, and for students and interested workers of all kinds and ages: indeed, for all who wish to understand what multimedia is all about.

This Encyclopaedia of Multimedia covers terms related to multimedia and acronyms used by the industry as standard knowledge. It offers detailed definitions of the bewildering array of terms and phrases relating to the Internet, plus short articles to explain more complex topics. Covering graphics, sound and data, new and emerging areas are included such as electronic commerce, security, creating DVD discs, and briefs on new business applications and services. Multimedia is presenting a myriad of applications to professionals and scholars in Computer Science, Information Science, Digital Art, Multimedia, Educational Technology, and Media Arts. Today's digital scholar can use this encyclopaedia as a tool to explore the vast parameters of the applications, problems, and solutions related to digital disciplines. The book has an extensive range of topics for the student who wants to discover and research other areas within the multimedia disciplines beyond their own.

Further to serve the needs of the teacher, student and worker in the field of multimedia science, as well as in related fields, a considerable number of terms have been included from the subject-areas bordering on multimedia, such as applied electronics, internet, web technology etc. The objective of editors and contributors has been the more modest one of providing a book useful as a general reference in multimedia, helpful even to the specialist in regions outside of his domain of specialized knowledge

The aim of this volume is to provide a concise repository of number of major concepts in this field. In preparation of this book, the author has freely consulted large number of books and journals so no authenticity is claimed. Author is especially thankful to M/S Anmol Publications for shaping this book in its final form.Suggestions for further improvement of this book are not only welcome but also greatly appreciated.

Author

A

A frame edit A video edit which starts on the first frame of the 5 video frame (4 film frame) sequence created when 24 frame film is transferred to 30 frame video. The A-frame is the only frame in the sequence where a film frame is completely reproduced on one and only one complete video frame. Here is the full sequence. (The letters correspond to film frames.) A-frame = video fields 1 & 2, B-frame = video fields 1 & 2 & 1, C-frame = video fields 2 & 1, D-frame = video fields 2 & 1 & 2.

A mode edit An editing method where the footage is assembled in the final scene order. Scene 1, scene 2,...

A/V audio/visual As in A/V connections. Most modern TVs have separate sockets for the composite video signal (that's the yellow one) and sound (black or white, or red and white if stereo).

AAC AAC stands for either MPEG2 Advanced Audio Coding or MPEG4 Advanced Audio Coding.

The MPEG2 audio-encoding standard of the format is not backward-compatible with MPEG1 audio. MPEG2 AAC can produce better audio quality than MP3 using less physical space for the files. MPEG4 AAC can produce better quality and smaller files than MPEG2 AAC. AAC is the audio file format used by Apple in their popular iTunes Music Store. Files may appear on your system with the ".M4A" filename extension. View AAC to MP3 or WAV Converter.

AAF(advanced authoring format) A Microsoft multimedia file format for multimedia authoring applications - making it possible to develop a multimedia presentation in one application and edit it in a second application.

A-B test A test by which an observor subjectively compares the performance of two components of the same type; for example, a test between two different speakiers. For the test to be scientifically valid, the inputs, levels, and listening conditions should be matched.

Aberration A term from optics that refers to anything affecting the accuracy of the image when compared with the original scene.

ABX comparatorA device that randomly selects between two components being tested. The listener doesn't know which device is selected.

AC(Alternating current) An electric current that reverses direction regularly. More generally, AC is also used to describe voltage sources in which the polarity of the signal reverses regularly. Power distribution networks use AC because it is relatively easy and cheap to alter the voltage (using transformers) yielding considerable economies for long distance power transmission. All the counties in the world use, it seems, either a 50 or 60 hertz frequency for their power systems. Europe, Australia and India use 50 hertz. The Americas and Japan use 60 hertz.

AC coupled AC coupling passes a signal through a capacitor to remove any DC offset, or the overall voltage level that the video signal "rides" on. One way to find the signal is to remove the DC offset by AC coupling, and then do DC restoration to add a known DC offset (one that we selected). Another reason AC coupling is important is that it can remove large (and harmful) DC offsets.

AC/DC. Usually applied where a power supply can be either Alternating Current or Direct Current.

AC'97, AC'98 These are definitions by Intel for the audio I/O implementation for PCs. Two chips are defined: an analog audio I/O chip and a digital controller chip. The digital chip will eventually be replaced by a software solution. The goal is to increase the audio performance of PCs and lower cost.

AC3 AC3 file, a Dolby Digital audio file, can be found as the standard audio track on Digital Versatile Discs (DVD) and High Definition Television (HDTV). This coder has been designed to take maximum advantage of human auditory masking in that it divides the audio spectrum of each channel into narrow frequency bands of different sizes optimized with respect to the frequency selectivity of human hearing. This makes it possible to sharply filter coding noise so that it is forced to stay very close in frequency to the frequency components of the audio signal being coded. By reducing or eliminating coding noise wherever there are no audio signals to mask it, the sound quality of the original signal can be subjectively preserved.

Academy aspect ratio 1.37:1, the aspect ratio for movies used almost exclusively up to the early 1950s.

Academy sound Fairly soon after the introduction of talkies in the late 1920s, the movie industry settled on using an analogue optical soundtrack on the edge of the film to carry the sound. This was read by the projector and converted to an electrical audio signal. This was a very noisy medium, so in the absence of advanced noise reduction technology such as Dolby A (the cinema equivalent of, and precursor to, the Dolby B and C noise reduction systems on compact cassettes), the situation was eased by sharply cutting the treble response (at around 5kHz). The bass was also cut, which accounts for the characteristic pinched sound of old movies. The recommended system of frequency response tailoring was called 'Academy Sound'.

Access time Length of time required for a hard disk, CD-ROM drive, or other similar device to find the data stored on it. Generally measured in milliseconds (ms).

Accessibility Website accessibility is about designing web pages so people are able to get and use web content. Accessibility is about making content easy to read, navigate and understand for everybody, regardless of their disability or what technology they use to access the internet.

Acid free paper Paper which is pH neutral or slightly alkaline (pH7 or above) at the time of production but not necessarily having an alkaline buffer or reserve.

Acoustics Sound is simply vibrating air. How fast, how much, and when the air is vibrated, determines what we will ultimately hear as sound. The science of this process is called acoustics.

When a speaker cone (or anything else that has the ability to vibrate in the auditory range) moves forward, the air molecules in front of the cone are compressed, causing the molecules to form an accelerating wave forward. This continues to happen until the speaker cone moves in the opposite direction, which causes a rarefaction (or thinning) of the air mass between the speaker and the listener. This is the basic concept of how sound waves are produced.

Acoustical audio signal A series of increasing and decreasing pressure changes in the air which result in sound that you can hear. These pressure changes occur very rapidly and the speed at which they alternate between a positive pressure (one represented by a speaker moving forward toward the listener) and a negative pressure (one represented by a speaker moving away from the listener) determines the pitch of the signal you hear. The frequency of these pressure changes must be between 20 and 20,000 times per second to be heard. An acoustical audio signal differs from an electrical audio signal in that an acoustical audio signal can be heard.

Acoustic coupling The interaction between two or more speakers stacked together in an audio system which may produce a sound different from (and often better than) the sound produced by the individual speakers.

Acoustic feedback A phenomenon where the sound from a loudspeaker is picked up by the microphone or other transducer, like a phono cartridge feeding it, and re-amplifys it through the same loudspeaker only to return to the same microphone to be re-amplified again, etc.. Each time the signal becomes larger until the system runs away and rings, or feeds back on itself producing the characteristic scream or squeal found in sound (mostly, PA) systems. These buildups often occur at particular frequencies called feedback frequencies.

Acoustic signal A method of communicating information using sound which carries the information to its intended destination. Applause is a sort of acoustic signal in that it generally conveys the message "approval" to a performer on stage. A snap of ones fingers can convey the meaning "hurry up" in an audible way. Acoustic signals differ from acoustic audio signals in that the intended purpose of an acoustic signal (when not specifically indicated to be an audio signal) is to convey information.

Acoustic suspension A design for the enclosure of a loudspeaker. With acoustic suspension speakers the enclosure is sealed so that it is air tight, which causes the air within to become a very active part of the woofer's suspension. This raises the resonant frequency of the driver and lowers its compliance. Acoustic suspension speakers tend to be less efficient than bass reflex designs, and begin fading away their bass at a higher frequency. But the rate at which the bass output reduces tends to be less than an equivalent bass reflex speaker, so they frequently produce greater bass extension. Also called infinite baffle.

Acquisition module interface A plug in that allows you import photos from imaging devices such as digital cameras or scanners

Acrobat Adobe Acrobat was the first software to support Adobe Systems' Portable Document Format (PDF). It is mostly described in those entries. The Acrobat Reader program (now just called Adobe Reader) is available as a no-charge download from Adobe's web site, and allows the viewing and printing of PDF files.

Commercial Acrobat programs (of which there are several) allow some minimal editing and adding of features to PDF documents, and come with other modules including a printer driver to create PDF files from Macintosh or Microsoft Windows applications.

Starting

Since the early 1990s, the Acrobat product had several competitors who each used their own document formats, such as:

AnyView from Binar Graphics

Common Ground from No Hands Software

Envoy from WordPerfect Corporation

Folio from NextPage

Microsoft Reader from Microsoft

Replica from Farallon Computing

WorldView from Interleaf

By the late 1990s PDF had become the de facto standard, and the others had become largely historical footnotes. This in turn has led to many more competitors for Adobe Acrobat, both free and commercial.

Today, there are a host of third-party programs that create or manipulate PDF, such as Ghostscript and Nitro PDF. Adobe also allows Acrobat plug-ins to be developed, which can add extra functions within the Acrobat program; popular ones include Enfocus PitStop, ARTS PDF Aerialist and Quite A Box Of Tricks.

Products

Adobe has changed the names of the products in the Acrobat family regularly, also splitting products up, joining them together, or discontinuing members. This causes much confusion, not only about what product to obtain, but even about what product people have.

As of 2006, the current main members of the Adobe Acrobat family are

Adobe Reader 7 (previously Adobe Acrobat Reader); no-charge software to read or print PDF files.

WorldView from Interleaf

Adobe Acrobat Standard 7 and Adobe Acrobat Professional 7; commercial (paid for) software to create PDFs and to manipulate them in various ways. Between version 3 and 5 these were one product simply called Adobe Acrobat.

Adobe has never created a product called either Adobe Writer or Acrobat Writer, although these names seem a natural opposite to the Reader product. Purists and pedants dislike these made-up names. To add more confusion, Acrobat used to include a printer driver called PDFWriter.

History

Version 1 (Released 15 June 1993)

Acrobat Reader 1.0 for DOS, Windows 3.1 and Macintosh. This was not available in single copies and was not initially free. After a while the IRS purchased a right to distribute Reader 1.0, effectively making it seem free to those who obtained it that way.

Acrobat Exchange 1.0 (included PDFWriter printer driver and Acrobat Exchange application).

Acrobat Distiller 1.0. Created PDF from PostScript (no printer driver at this stage).

Version 2 (Released September 1994)

Acrobat Reader 2.0 for Windows and Macintosh. Now free.

Acrobat Exchange 2.0, package as 1.0.

Acrobat Professional 2.0, which included the contents of Acrobat Exchange, plus Distiller.

There were 2.1 updates.

Acrobat Catalog was introduced, using Verity technology to create searchable indexes to PDF files. Searching required a special version of Acrobat Reader, not free, or Acrobat Exchange.

Version 3 (Released 1996)

Acrobat Reader 3.0. The first to display PDF files in-browser, and the first to support form filling.

A free Reader to allow searching was made available, but was not part of the default download.

Acrobat 3.0 – replaced Acrobat Professional 2.1. Included Acrobat Catalog, and a Distiller printer driver.

Updates to 3.01 and 3.02; 3.02 introduced extended forms capabilities and JavaScript.

First release with support for Windows 95 and later. Last release with support for Windows 3.1.

Version 4 (Released April 1999)

Acrobat Reader 4.0.

Acrobat 4.0.

Updates to 4.05.

Introduced Distiller Server 4.0, identical to the regular Distiller but with a multi-user license (Windows, Linux, Solaris).

Acrobat Business Tools 4.0 - a limited version of Acrobat.

Version 5 (Released May 2001)

Acrobat Reader 5.0.

Acrobat 5.0. PDFWriter removed from Macintosh application.

Updates to 5.0.5. Acrobat 5.0.5 was the first to be able to run native in Mac OS X, but also ran in Mac OS 9.

Distiller Server 5.0.

Acrobat Approval 5.0 - a limited version of Acrobat, mainly sold to people who wanted to digitally sign or save fill in forms.

Acrobat Reader 5.1 - supported the Adobe LiveCycle Reader Extensions (e.g. forms saving) (which was then under a different name).

Version 6 (Released April 2003)

Adobe Reader 6.0 (no Linux or Unix versions)

Acrobat Professional 6.0 - replacement for Acrobat 5.0, with new features. Distiller printer driver renamed Adobe PDF. PDFWriter now gone for good. New version of Catalog integrated and not compatible with earlier products for searching.

Acrobat Standard 6.0 - limited version of Acrobat Professional, including Distiller but lacking features including Catalog, form design, prepress support.

Updates to 6.0.1, 6.0.2, 6.0.3 and 6.0.4

Dropped support for Windows 95 and Windows 98 First Edition. Acrobat Professional was Windows NT, 2000, XP only. Dropped support for Mac OS 9 and earlier. First release for Mac OS X.

Distiller Server 6.0.

Acrobat Elements 6.0 - PDF creation only, aimed at the corporate market (minimum 1000 licenses, Windows only)

Acrobat Elements Server 6.0 - client/server version of Acrobat Elements

Technology for "Reader enabling", allowing Reader to save, sign or annotate PDF files if the licensee had enabled the files.

Version 7 (Announced 5 January 2005)

Adobe Reader 7.0

Updates to 7.0.1, 7.0.2, 7.0.3, 7.0.5 and 7.0.7.

Acrobat Professional 7.0 - now includes Adobe LiveCycle Designer 7.0 (Windows only) for XML form design (different and incompatible with previous form support)- Ability to embed 3D object information from the .u3d Universal 3D format. First version to include controversial mandatory Product activation.

Acrobat Standard 7.0

Acrobat Elements 7.0 (now minimum 100 licenses)

Acrobat 3D (Windows only) - includes all of the functionality of Acrobat Professional 7.0 as well as updated support for embedded 3D, tools for capturing 3D content from OpenGL applications, and the Adobe Acrobat 3D Toolkit for converting CAD documents to PDF objects. Also included is a version of the capture tool for installation on Unix.

Windows 2000, XP, Mac OS X only for Acrobat, although Linux and Solaris versions of Adobe Reader have been released.

Other LiveCycle products include LiveCycle Barcoded Forms, LiveCycle Document Security, LiveCycle Reader Extensions (previously Document Server for Reader Extensions and other names), LiveCycle Forms (previously Form Server), LiveCycle Form Manager, LiveCycle Policy Server and LiveCycle Workflow. Some of these are server solutions intended for large businesses. Only LiveCycle Designer is bundled with Acrobat Professional.

Acrobat reader A free product that can be downloaded from the Internet that enables users to view portable document format (.pdf) files.

Act 1) Originally, the major division of dramatic action within a play; on the contemporary stage, the major division of a play on opposite sides of intermission(s); in broadcasting, the major division of a tele- or audio play separated by breaks;

2), to perform a role in a dramatic production;

3), to make a living performing roles in dramatic production; to be an actor.

Action axis Imaginary line drawn between two subjects or along a lone of motion as an aid in maintainging continuity of screen direction.

Action, dramatic Gesture, action or dialogue that advances the plot of a dramatic work.

Action, falling Action following the climax in which tension wanes and loose ends are tied up.

Action, rising Action leading up to the climax characterized by mounting tension.

Actionscript ActionScript is the scripting language of Flash which is derived from ECMA, a European Standard version of JavaScript. ActionScript is a simplified version of ECMA with some additional shortcuts.

Active A word prefacing certain circuits in which the processing is performed by use of transistor or tube juctions, rather than passive componenets such as resistors, capacitors, and coils. Such items as crossovers and equalizers may be constructed either way. Active processing usually affords more more options, and greater precision, albeit at greater cost.

Active loudspeaker A loudspeaker with built-in amplification for all the drivers. Some speakers have an amplifier built-in for bass only, but these are not regarded as active. Most loudspeakers are passive, not active.

Active perl A popular software implementation of the Perl Language from Active State.

Active picture area The part of a TV picture that contains actual image information as opposed to sync or other data. Vertically the active picture area is 486 lines for NTSC and 576 lines for PAL. The inactive area is called blanking.

Active server pages A specification that enables database-driven Web sites. Web pages that have an .asp extension (instead of an .html or .htm extension) are rendered on the spot using updated information from the database. This enables "on the fly" updating and easier content management, but it can also present security problems because it opens "holes" in security to enable information to be accessed and viewed in real time. Ensuring security with active server pages is possible, but it requires specialized Web site development skills to create secure Web sites.

Active subwoofer A subwoofer with built-in amplification. Most subwoofers are active, not passive.

Active video The part of the video waveform that contains picture information. Most of the active video, if not all of it, is visible on the display.

Activemovie Microsoft's architecture for the control and processing of streams of multimedia data and software that uses this architecture to play digital video and sound. It is intended to supersede Video for Windows.

ActiveX A set of technologies developed by Microsoft based on Object Linking and Embedding (OLE) which allows running aplications on the users machine.

Actor One who acts, variously called bum, comedian, mummer, player, talent Thespian (after Thespis, the legendary inventor of Greek tragedy), tragedian; an often infuriating, ultimately likable, neurotic – plagued by narcissistic disorders that compound a hopeless addiction to an impossible profession.

Actuality Unrehearsed or documentary sound, speech or music recorded in the field.

Adaptive differential pulse code modulation (ADPCM) An audio-compression technique.

Adaptive reception A circuit that provides adjustable delay such that the time at which a sound wave is produced from various signal channels can be changed. This allows synchronization for each channel of a multi-channel output device, so that sound waves from multiple speakers will converge at approximately the same time at a single point in space (the listener).

ADC (Analog-to-digitalconverter) "Recording" feature of sound cards that converts the analog/ sound waveforms to digital format, i.e. bits and bytes. This digital representation can then be stored, edited, processed and transferred between media. To playback sound files, the sound card uses a DAC (Digital-to-Analog Converter). The ADC samples the audio at very fast intervals ("sampling rate"), producing a stream of snapshots. When played back by the DAC at the same pace, the samples are perceived as sound. Animation, path - the animation software lets you specify a beginning position and an ending position, then calculates the positions in between.

Additive color Artificially created color.

Color hues cannot be substracted on electronic devices that are used for displaying color. On these devices color ghues are added to one another.

The primary additive colors are: red, green, blue. Secondary additive colors are obtained by mixing primary colors in a 1:1 ratio. The absence of light results in black, while adding all three primary additive colors result in white. Adding the three primary substractive colors in equal ratios would result in brown.

Adjustment layer A layer that is designed to experiment with adjustments and colors for a certain layer without perminantly modifying the image.

Ad-lib Unrehearsed spontaneous act of speaking.

Adobe Acrobat A product that enables you to convert documents to portable document format (.pdf). You would convert files to .pdf if you wanted to post them on your Web site or to send them via e-mail while preserving the format, the look and feel, of the documents. Acrobat enables people to view the files even if they don't own the software you used to create them, and Acrobat has features that can ensure against copying or tampering with the document.

Adr studio, adr room A studio designed for "automated dialog replacement," the process of recording a new vocal performance by an actor to replace an existing performance acoustically flawed but visually acceptable. In the U.S. where audio drama rooms do not exist, ADR studios are often acoustically right for audio drama.

ADSL (Asymmetric digital subscriber line) ADSL is a broadband technology, where data travels downstream faster than it travels upstream (hence asymmetric). Specifically ADSL is a method of moving data over regular phone lines. An ADSL circuit is much faster than a regular phone connection.

An ADSL circuit must be configured to connect two specific locations, similar to a leased line.

AES Audio engineering society

AES/EBU (Audio engineering society/ european broadcasting union) A digital audio communication standard most commonly seen in professional audio applications. Electrically it is only subtly different to the consumer-oriented S/PDIF standard, the main variation being a different method of handling the clocking signal, and it generally being carried by balanced connections. Nevertheless implementations are seen that seem to be fully compatible with unbalanced S/PDIF.

Affiliate A station accepting programs or services under contract from, but not owned by, a national or regional network .

AFM The American Federation of Musicians; the musicians' union.

AFP(appletalk file protocol) A newtork protcol that allows file sharing to work across an AppleTalk Network. AppleTalk was commonly from Mac OS 6 through Mac OS 9.

AFTRA The American Federation of Television and Radio Artists; the talent union that has jurisdiction over radio and audio.

AGC(Automatic gain control) A section in an electronic circuit that has feedback and regulates the output voltage level to fall within predetermined margins. Often used in acamera to give a constant one volt peak-to-peak video output, when light levels reduce after the lens' auto iris is fully open.

Agent, literary A licensed professional who represents writers before publishers and producers.

Agent, talent A licensed professional who helps actors get work. A theatrical agent specializes in dramatic television, film, and theater; a commercial agent handles TV and radio commercials and voice-overs.

AGMLib The Adobe Graphics Manager library file which Adobe Photoshop requires

AHG Ad hoc group (MPEG) A group of people established to address a specific ic.

AIFF Short for Audio Interchange File Format, a file format for storing and transmitting sampled sound. It was developed by Apple Computer and is the standard audio format for Macintosh computers. Files are 8-bit mono or stereo and generally end with a .AIF or .IEF extension. Normal AIFF does not support data compression so files tend to be large, but another format called AIIF-Compressed (AIFF-C or AIFC) does support compression.

Air check A recording of a program made by the broadcaster during broadcast for archival or legal purposes.

Air gap In a speaker's motor section, the space between the top plate and the pole piece. This is where the magnetic flux field is concentrated and where the voice coil interacts with it.

Algorithm In mathematics and computer science, an algorithm is a procedure (a finite set of well-defined instructions) for accomplishing some task which, given an initial state, will terminate in a defined end-state.

Informally, the concept of an algorithm is often illustrated by the example of a recipe, although many algorithms are much more complex; algorithms often have steps that repeat (iterate) or require decisions (such as logic or comparison). In most higher level programs, algorithms act in complex patterns, each using smaller and smaller sub-methods which are built up to the program as a whole. In most languages, they are isomorphic to functions or methods.

The concept of an algorithm originated as a means of recording procedures for solving mathematical problems such as finding the common divisor of two numbers or multiplying two numbers. The concept was formalized in 1936 through Alan Turing's Turing machines and Alonzo Church's lambda calculus, which in turn formed the foundation of computer science.

Most algorithms can be directly implemented by computer programs; any other algorithms can at least in theory be *simulated* by computer programs.

The word *algorithm* comes from the name of the 9th century Persian mathematician Abu Abdullah Muhammad bin Musa al-Khwarizmi. The word *algorism* originally referred only to the rules of performing arithmetic using Hindu-Arabic numerals but evolved via European Latin translation of al-Khwarizmi's name into *algorithm* by the 18th century. The word evolved to include all definite procedures for solving problems or performing tasks.

The first case of an algorithm written for a computer was Ada Byron's notes on the analytical engine written in 1842, for which she is considered by many to be the world's first programmer. However, since Charles Babbage never completed his analytical engine the algorithm was never implemented on it.

The lack of mathematical rigor in the "well-defined procedure" definition of algorithms posed some difficulties for mathematicians and logicians of the 19th and early 20th centuries. This problem was largely solved with the description of the Turing machine, an abstract model of a computer formulated by Alan Turing, and the demonstration that every method yet found for describing "well-defined procedures" advanced by other mathematicians could be emulated on a Turing machine (a statement known as the Church-Turing thesis). Nowadays, a formal criterion for an algorithm is that it is a procedure that can be implemented on a completely specified Turing machine or one of the equivalent formalisms.

Formalization

Algorithms are essential to the way computers process information, because a computer program is essentially an algorithm that tells the computer what specific steps to perform (in what specific order) in order to carry out a specified task, such as calculating employees' paychecks or printing students' report cards. Thus, an algorithm can be considered to be any sequence of operations which can be performed by a Turing-complete system.

Typically, when an algorithm is associated with processing information, data is read from an input source or device, written to an output sink or device, and/or stored for further use. Stored data is regarded as part of the internal state of the entity performing the algorithm. The state is stored in a data structure.

For any such computational process, the algorithm must be rigorously defined: specified in the way it applies in all possible circumstances that could arise. That is, any conditional steps must be systematically dealt with, case-by-case; the criteria for each case must be clear (and computable).

Because an algorithm is a precise list of precise steps, the order of computation will almost always be critical to the functioning of the algorithm. Instructions are usually assumed to be listed explicitly, and are described as starting 'from the top' and going 'down to the bottom', an idea that is described more formally by *flow of control*.

So far, this discussion of the formalization of an algorithm has assumed the premises of imperative programming. This is the most common conception, and it attempts to describe a task in discrete, 'mechanical' means. Unique to this conception of formalized algorithms is the assignment operation, setting the value of a variable. It derives from the intuition of 'memory' as a scratchpad.

Some writers restrict the definition of *algorithm* to procedures that eventually finish. Others include procedures that could run forever without stopping, arguing that some entity may be required to carry out such permanent tasks. In the latter case, success can no longer be defined in terms of halting with a meaningful output. Instead, terms of success that allow for unbounded output sequences must be defined. For example, an algorithm that verifies if there are more zeros than ones in an infinite random binary sequence must run forever to be effective. If it is implemented correctly, however, the algorithm's output will be useful: for as long as it examines the sequence, the algorithm will give a positive response while the number of examined zeros outnumber the ones, and a negative response otherwise. Success for this algorithm could then be defined as eventually outputting only positive responses if there are actually more zeros than ones in the sequence, and in any other case outputting any mixture of positive and negative responses.

Standardised notation

Algorithms in computer science suffer somewhat by the proliferation of computer languages each with their own syntax and basic methods. As a result, the usual standard is to write code either in C or pseudo-code. In both cases annotation usually accompanies the code in the form of an accompanying document for longer algorithms, or in the form of C style comments embedded in the code.

Some algorithms are built for purpose and it makes sense to use a more specific language. In such cases it is usual to formalise the algorithm by defining all of it's basic functions, constants and variables before the algorithm.

Implementation

An algorithm is a set of steps to perform a computation. Most algorithms will be implemented as computer programs. They can be expressed in any notation including English for documenting and research purposes. A more preferred way is to embody (or sometimes called *codify*) an algorithm by writing of its pseudocode. Pseudocode representation avoids ambiguities that are common in English statements. The pseudocode can also be translated into particular programming language more straightforwardly. Algorithms are implemented not only as computer programs, but often also by other means, such as in a biological neural network (for example, the human brain implementing arithmetic or an insect relocating food), in electric circuits, or in a mechanical device.

Example

One of the simplest algorithms is to find the largest number in an (unsorted) list of numbers. The solution necessarily requires looking at every number in the list, but only once at each. From this follows a simple algorithm, which can be stated in English as

1. Let us assume the first item is largest.

2. Look at each of the remaining items in the list and make the following adjustment.

a. If it is larger than the largest item we gathered so far, make a note of it.

3. The latest noted item is the largest in the list when the process is complete.

Algorithm analysis

As it happens, most people who implement algorithms want to know how much of a particular resource (such as time or storage) is required for a given algorithm. Methods have been developed for the analysis of algorithms to obtain such quantitative answers; for example, the algorithm above has a time requirement of $O(n)$, using the big O notation with n as the length of the list. At all times the algorithm only needs to remember two values: the largest number found so far, and its current position in the input list. Therefore it is said to have a space requirement of *O(1)*. Different algorithms may complete the same task with a different set of instructions in less or more time, space, or effort than others. For example, given two different recipes for making potato salad, one may have *peel the potato* before *boil the potato* while the other presents the steps in the reverse order, yet they both call for these steps to be repeated for all potatoes and end when the potato salad is ready to be eaten.

The analysis and study of algorithms is one discipline of computer science, and is often practiced abstractly (without the use of a specific programming language or other implementation). In this sense, it resembles other mathematical disciplines in that the analysis focuses on the underlying principles of the algorithm, and not on any particular implementation. The pseudocode is simplest and abstract enough for such analysis.

Classes

There are various ways to classify algorithms, each with its own merits.

Classification by implementation

One way to classify algorithms is by implementation means.

Recursion or **iteration** A recursive algorithm is one that invokes (makes reference to) itself repeatedly until a certain condition matches, which is a method common to functional programming. Iterative algorithms use repetitive constructs like loops and sometimes additional data structures like stacks to solve the given problems. Some problems are naturally suited for one implementation to other. For example, towers of hanoi is well understood in recursive implementation. Every recursive version has an equivalent (but possibly more or less complex) iterative version, and vice versa.

Serial or **parallel** Algorithms are usually discussed with the assumption that computers execute one instruction of an algorithm at a time. Those computers are sometimes called serial computers. An algorithm designed for such an environment is called a serial algorithm, as opposed to parallel algorithms, which take advantage of computer architectures where several processors can work on a problem at the same time. Parallel algorithms divide the problem into more symmetrical or asymmetrical subproblems and pass them to many processors and put the results back together at one end. The resource consumption in parallel algorithms is both processor cycles on each processors and also the communication overhead between the processors. Sorting algorithms can be parallelized efficiently, but their communication overhead is expensive. Recursive algorithms are generally parallelizable. Some problems have no parallel algorithms, and are called inherently serial problems. Those problems cannot be solved faster by employing more processors. Iterative numerical methods, such as Newton's method or the three body problem, are algorithms which are inherently serial.

Deterministic or **random** Deterministic algorithms solve the problem with exact decision at every step of the algorithm. Randomized algorithms as their name suggests explore the search space randomly until an acceptable solution is found. Various heuristic algorithms generally fall into the random category.

Exact or **approximate** While many algorithms reach an exact solution, approximation algorithms seek an approximation which is close to the true solution. Approximation may use either a deterministic or a random strategy. Such algorithms have practical value for many hard problems.

Classification by design paradigm

Another way of classifying algorithms is by their design methodology or paradigm. There is a certain number of paradigms, each different from the other. Furthermore, each of these categories will include many different types of algorithms. Some commonly found paradigms include:

Divide and conquer A divide and conquer algorithm repeatedly reduces an instance of a problem to one or more smaller instances of the same problem (usually recursively), until the instances are small enough to solve easily. One such example of divide and conquer is merge sorting. Sorting can be done on each segment of data after dividing data into segments and sorting of entire data can be obtained in conquer phase by merging them. A simpler variant of divide and conquer is called decrease and conquer algorithm, that solves an identical subproblem and uses the solution of this subproblem to solve the bigger problem. Divide and conquer divides the problem into multiple subproblems and so conquer stage will be more complex than decrease and conquer algorithms. An example of decrease and conquer algorithm is binary search algorithm.

Dynamic programming When a problem shows optimal substructure, meaning the optimal solution to a problem can be constructed from optimal solutions to subproblems, and overlapping subproblems, meaning the same subproblems are used to solve many different problem instances, we can often solve the problem quickly using *dynamic programming*, an approach that avoids recomputing solutions that have already been computed. For example, the shortest path to a goal from a vertex in a weighted graph can be found by using the shortest path to the goal from all adjacent vertices. Dynamic programming and memoization go together. The main difference between dynamic programming and divide and conquer is, subproblems are more or less independent in divide and conquer, where as the overlap of subproblems occur in dynamic programming. The difference between the dynamic programming and straightforward recursion is in caching or memoization of recursive calls. Where subproblems are independent, there is no chance of repetition and memoization does not help, so dynamic programming is not a solution for all. By using memoization or maintaining a table of subproblems already solved, dynamic programming reduces the exponential nature of many problems to polynomial complexity.

The greedy method A greedy algorithm is similar to a dynamic programming algorithm, but the difference is that solutions to the subproblems do not have to be known at each stage; instead a "greedy" choice can be made of what looks best for the moment. Difference between dynamic programming and greedy method is, it extends the solution with the best possible decision (not all feasible decisions) at an algorithmic stage based on the current local optimum and the best decision (not all possible decisions) made in previous stage. It is not exhaustive, and does not give accurate answer to many problems. But when it works, it will be the fastest method. The most popular greedy algorithm is finding the minimal spanning tree as given by Kruskal.

Linear programming When solving a problem using linear programming, the program is put into a number of linear inequalities and then an attempt is made to maximize (or minimize) the inputs. Many problems (such as the maximum flow for directed graphs) can be stated in a linear programming way, and then be solved by a 'generic' algorithm such as the simplex algorithm. A complex variant of linear programming is called integer programming, where the solution space is restricted to all integers.

Reduction It is another powerful technique in solving many problems by transforming one problem into another problem. For example, one selection algorithm for finding the median in an unsorted list is first translating this problem into sorting problem and finding the middle element in sorted list. The goal of reduction algorithms is finding the simplest transformation such that complexity of reduction algorithm does not dominate the complexity of reduced algorithm. This technique is also called *transform and conquer.*

Search and enumeration Many problems (such as playing chess) can be modeled as problems on graphs. A graph exploration algorithm specifies rules for moving around a graph and is useful for such problems. This category also includes the search algorithms and backtracking.

The probabilistic and heuristic paradigm Algorithms belonging to this class fit the definition of an algorithm more loosely.

1. Probabilistic algorithms are those that make some choices randomly (or pseudo-randomly); for some problems, it can in fact be proven that the fastest solutions must involve some randomness.

2. Genetic algorithms attempt to find solutions to problems by mimicking biological evolutionary processes, with a cycle of random mutations yielding successive generations of "solutions". Thus, they emulate reproduction and "survival of the fittest". In genetic programming, this approach is extended to algorithms, by regarding the algorithm itself as a "solution" to a problem. Also there are

3. Heuristic algorithms, whose general purpose is not to find an optimal solution, but an approximate solution where the time or resources to find a perfect solution are not practical. An example of this would be local search, taboo search, or simulated annealing algorithms, a class of heuristic probabilistic algorithms that vary the solution of a problem by a random amount. The name "simulated annealing" alludes to the metallurgic term meaning the heating and cooling of metal to achieve freedom from defects. The purpose of the random variance is to find close to globally optimal solutions rather than simply locally optimal ones, the idea being that the random element will be decreased as the algorithm settles down to a solution.

Classification by field of study

Every field of science has its own problems and needs efficient algorithms. Related problems in one field are often studied together. Some example classes are search algorithms, sort algorithms, merge algorithms, numerical algorithms, graph algorithms, string algorithms, computational geometric algorithms, combinatorial algorithms, machine learning, cryptography, data compression algorithms and parsing techniques.

Some of these fields overlap with each other and advancing in algorithms for one field causes advancement in many fields and sometimes completely unrelated fields. For example, dynamic programming is originally invented for optimisation in resource consumption in industries, but it is used in solving broad range of problems in many fields.

Classification by complexity

Some algorithms complete in linear time, and some complete in exponential amount of time, and some never complete. One problem may have multiple algorithms, and some problems may have no algorithms. Some problems have no known efficient algorithms. There are also mappings from some problems to other problems. So computer scientists found it is suitable to classify the problems rather than algorithms into equivalence classes based on the complexity.

Aliased imaging This is a technique, commonly applied to Direct Digital Synthesis (DDS), for using intentional aliasing as a source of high-frequency signals.

Aliasing In a sampled data system, the analog input must be sampled at a rate of FS>2FA in order to avoid loss of data (Nyquist Theorem). Adhering to the Nyquist Theorem prevents in-band "alias" signals, which are beat frequencies between the analog signal and the sampling clock that inherently occur at FS-FA. As the Nyquist limit is exceeded, the aliased signals move within the band of the analog input (DC - FS/2) and create distortion. Likewise, high-frequency noise can also be aliased into the input signal range, which mandates low-pass filtering, or anti-alias filtering, on the input of a sampled system.

Alliteration The purposeful repetition of sounds, particularly the beginning consonants of words. "The fickle finger of fate."

Alpha channel The alpha channel is used to specify an alpha value for each video sample. The alpha value is used to control the blending, on a sample-by-sample basis, of two images.

new pixel = (alpha)(sample A color) + (1 - alpha)(sample B color)

Alpha typically has a normalized value of 0 to 1. In a graphics environment, the alpha values can be stored in additional memory. When you hear about 32-bit frame buffers, what this really means is that there are 24 bits of color, 8 each for red, green, and blue, along with an 8-bit alpha channel.

Alpha mix This is a way of combining two images. How the mixing is performed is provided by the alpha channel. The little box that appears over the left-hand shoulder of a news anchor is put there by an alpha mixer. Wherever the little box is to appear, a "1" is put in the alpha channel. Wherever it doesn't appear, a "0" is used. When the alpha mixer sees a "1" coming from the alpha channel, it displays the little box. Whenever it sees a "0", it displays the news anchor. Of course, it doesn't matter if a "1" or a "0" is used, but you get the point.

Alphanumeric video generator (also text inserter or character generator). A device for providing additional information,normally superimposed on the picture being displayed; this can range from one or two charactersto full-screen alphanumeric text. Such generators use the incoming video signal sync pulses as areference point for the textinsertion position, which means if the video signal is of poor quality,the text stability will alsobe of poor quality.

Also The relative sensitivity to the reception of RF signals in a tuner measured in dBf. The lower the number the better. Normal is now 10 to 14 dBf.

Alternating current (AC) An alternating current (AC) is an electrical current whose magnitude and direction vary cyclically, as opposed to direct current, whose direction remains constant. The usual waveform of an AC power circuit is a sine wave, as this results in the most efficient transmission of energy. However in certain applications different waveforms are used, such as triangular or square waves.

Used generically, AC refers to the form in which electricity is delivered to businesses and residences. However, audio and radio signals carried on electrical wire are also examples of alternating current. In these applications, an important goal is often the recovery of information encoded (or modulated) onto the AC signal.

William Stanley Jr designed one of the first practical coils to produce alternating currents. His design was an early precursor of the modern transformer, called an induction coil. The system used today was devised by Nikola Tesla, George Westinghouse, Lucien Gaulard, John Gibbs, and Oliver Shallenger from 1881 to 1889. These systems overcame the limitations imposed by using direct current, as found in the system that Thomas Edison first used to distribute electricity commercially.

The first long-distance transmission of alternating current took place in 1891 near Telluride, Colorado, followed a few months later in Germany. Thomas Edison strongly advocated the use of direct current (DC), having many patents in that technology, but eventually alternating current came into general use. And through the use of alternating current, Charles Proteus Steinmetz of General Electric was able to solve many of the problems associated with electricity generation and transmission.

AC voltage can be stepped up or down by a transformer to a different voltage. High-voltage, direct current electric power transmission systems contrast with the more common alternating-current systems as a means for the bulk transmission of electrical power. However, these tend to be more expensive and less efficient than transformers, or did not exist when Edison, Westinghouse and Tesla were designing their power systems.

Use of a higher voltage leads to more efficient transmission of power. The power losses in a conductor are a product of the square of the current and the resistance of the conductor, described by the formula $P = I^2R$. This means that when transmitting a fixed power on a given wire, if the current is doubled, the power loss will be four times greater. It is advantageous when transmitting large amounts of power to distribute the power with extremely high voltages (sometimes as high as hundreds of kilovolts). However, high voltages also have disadvantages, the main ones being the increased danger to anyone who comes into contact with them, the extra insulation required, and generally increased difficulty in their safe handling. In the power plant the voltage is generated on three phase low voltage, with a frequency of either 50 or 60 hertz, and stepped up to a high voltage for distribution and stepped down, with a neutral, to a relatively low level for the consumer, generally around 200 V to 500 V between phases and 100 V to 250 V between each phase and the neutral.

Three-phase electrical generation is very common and is a more efficient use of commercial generators. Electrical energy is generated by rotating a coil inside a magnetic field, in large generators with a high capital cost. However, it is relatively simple and cost effective to include three separate coils in the generator stator (instead of one). These sets of coils are physically separated and at an angle of 120° to each other. Three current waveforms are produced that are 120° out of phase with each other, but of equal magnitude.

Three-phase systems are designed so that they are balanced at the load; if a load is correctly balanced no current will flow in the neutral point. Also, even in the worst-case unbalanced (linear) load, the neutral current will not exceed the highest of the phase currents. For three-phase at low (normal mains) voltages a four-wire system like this is normally used, reducing the cable requirements by one third over using a separate neutral per phase. When stepping down three-phase, a transformer with a Delta primary and a Star secondary is often used so there is no need for a neutral on the supply side.

For smaller customers (just how small varies by country and age of install) only a single phase and the neutral or two phases and the neutral are taken to the property. For larger installs all three phases and the neutral are taken to the main board. From a three-phase main board both single and three-phase circuits may lead off (and in some cases also circuits with two phases (not to be confused with two-phase) and a neutral are led off).

Three-wire single phase systems, with a single centre-tapped transformer giving two live conductors, is a common distribution scheme for residential and small commercial buildings in North America. A similar method is used for a different reason on construction sites in the UK. Small power tools and lighting are supposed to be supplied by a local center-tapped transformer with a voltage of 55V between each power conductor and the earth. This significantly reduces the risk of electric shock in the event that one of the live conductors becomes exposed through an equipment fault whilst still allowing a reasonable voltage for running the tools.

A third wire is often connected between non-current carrying metal enclosures and earth ground. This conductor provides protection from electrical shock due to accidental contact of circuit conductors with the case of portable appliances and tools.

Frequencies

The frequency of the electrical system varies by country; most electric power is generated at either 50 or 60 Hz. Some countries have a mixture of 50 Hz and 60 Hz supplies.

Very early AC generating schemes used arbitrary frequencies based on convenience for steam engine, water turbine and generator design, since frequency was not critical for incandescent lighting loads. Frequencies between 16 2/3 Hz and 133 Hz were used on different systems, with lower frequencies favoured where loads were primarily composed of motors, and higher frequencies preferred to reduce lighting flicker. For example, the city of Coventry, England, in 1895 had a unique 87 Hz single-phase distribution system that was in use until 1906. Once induction motors became common, it was important to standardize frequency for compatibility with the customer's equipment. Standardizing on one frequency also, later, allowed interconnection of generating plants on a grid for economy and security of operation.

It is generally accepted that Nikola Tesla chose 60 hertz as the lowest frequency that would not cause street lighting to flicker visibly. The origin of the 50 hertz frequency used in other parts of the world is open to debate but seems likely to be a rounding off of 60 Hz to the 1-2-5-10 structure, called a set of preferred numbers, popular with metric standards.

Other frequencies were somewhat common in the first half of the 20th century, and remain in use in isolated cases today, often tied to the 60 Hz system via a rotary converter or static inverter frequency changer. 25 Hz power was used in Ontario, Quebec, the northern USA, and for railway electrification. In the 1950s, much of this electrical system, from the generators right through to household appliances, was converted and standardised to 60 Hz. Some 25 Hz generators still exist at the Beck 1 and Rankine generating stations near Niagara Falls to provide power for large industrial customers who did not want to replace existing equipment; and some 25 Hz motors in New Orleans' floodwater pumps.

A low frequency eases the design of low speed electric motors, particularly for hoisting, crushing and rolling applications, and commutator-type traction motors for applications such as railways, but also causes a noticeable flicker in incandescent lighting and objectionable flicker of fluorescent lamps. 16.7 Hz power (approx. 1/3 of the mains frequency) is still used in some European rail systems, such as in Austria, Germany, Norway, Sweden and Switzerland (until 1995 the frequency was 16.67 Hz).

Off-shore, textile industry, marine, computer mainframe, aircraft, and spacecraft applications sometimes use 400 Hz, for benefits of reduced weight of apparatus or higher motor speeds.

AC-powered appliances can give off a characteristic hum at the multiples of the frequencies of AC power that they use. Most countries have chosen their television standard to approximate their mains supply frequency. This helps prevent powerline hum and magnetic interference from causing visible beat frequencies in the displayed picture. Unless specified by the manufacturer to operate on either 50 or 60 Hz, appliances may not operate efficiently or even safely if used on other than the intended supply frequency.

For direct current, where the current is a constant, the current uniformly flows throughout the cross section of the conductor (wire) which carries the current. When the current oscillates, as is the case for alternating current (regarless of frquency), the current tends to concentrate more towards the edge of the wire, and less in the center. For very high frequencies (over a GHz, or a billion oscillations per seconds), the current effectively flows on the surface of the wire, within a thickness called the skin depth.

Because at very high frequencies, the current essentially flows *on* the conductor, rather than *in* the conductor, energy which is supposed to be carried by the wire is lost to electromagnetic radiation (in other words, the wire acts as an antenna). Therefore, techniques must be implemented to reduce the radiation loss.

At frequencies below 1 GHz, wires are paired together in cabling to form a twisted pair in order to reduce losses due to electromagnetic radiation. The idea behind the twisted pair is that the current flowing in (on) one wire is cancelled by the current flowing in (on) the other wire, as the two wires carry currents that are equal in magnitude, but opposite in direction (and hence, the total current flow equals zero).

At frequencies greater than 1 GHz (AKA microwave frequencies), wires are not applicable. Instead, currents are carried by coaxial cables or waveguides. A Coax cable has a conductive wire inside a conductive tube, so the current carried by the wire is completely cancelled by the equal and opposite current that flows on the outer tube, and hence, no radiation loss. Coaxial cables are appropriate (i.e. losses are not too excessive) for frequencies less than 20 GHz.

For frequencies greater than 20 GHz, the ohmic losses for the dielectric inside the coaxial cable (which separates the inner wire from the outer tube) becomes too large, making waveguides a more attractive medium for transmitting energy. With waveguides, the energy is no longer carried by a flow of an electric current, but by an electromagnetic field.

Alternator whine A siren-like whining that appears as the rotational speed of an engine increases. The noise is usually the result of a voltage differential created by more than one ground path or a poor ground path to the affected equipment.

Always on A key feature of the broadband technology which means that users do not need to dial up to log on to the Internet. Broadband gives users instant Internet access 24 hours a day.

AM (Amplitude modulation) A method of impressing a signal onto a sine wave for its transmission or storage. A constant frequency sine wave has its amplitude increased or decreased from moment to moment to correspond with the signal. The sine wave, called a carrier, must be of considerably high frequency than any component of the signal. AM radio is an application of this technique. Very simple AM receivers (consisting of little other than a crystal and a coil) can be implemented very easily to receive these signals, although of course more sophisticated circuits can produce higher quality results.

Ambience A sound bed used in lieu of scenery to indicate environment or setting. Also called atmosphere.

Ambience track A track devoted to atmospheres.

Ambient noise Natural background noise.

America online (AOL) A commercial organization that offers subscribers a connection to the internet.

Amino-acid Organic acid derived from ammonia; part of the constituent of protein

Amperes (A) Ampere is a unit measurement of current of electrical energy equal to one coulomb of charge per second. Most DC applications refer to positive current current which flows from a positive potential to a more negative potential, with respect to a reference point which is designated as zero or neutral potential (usually ground).

The electrons in a circuit flow in the opposite direction as the current itself. Ampere is commonly abbreviated as "amp", not to be confused with amplifiers, of course, which are also commonly abbreviated "amp". In computation, the abbreviation for amperes is commonly, "I".

Amplification classes All sound is a sinosoidial waveform. It has alternating peaks and valleys. The center point of each wave is the zero, or switching point that separates the positive (top) from the negative (bottom) portion of each wave. When a tube or transistor amplifier operates in Class A, the output tubes or transistors amplify the entire waveform without splitting it into positive and negative halves. In Class AB, used in the overwhelming majority of amplifier designs, the signal is split into two halves, positive and negative, and each half is sent to a tube or transistor circuit for amplification. Both sides work in tandem, and the two halves are recombined at the output section to reconstruct the whole signal. This technique increases the amount of power that can be applied, but increases distortion. Class A amps usually provide lower, often imperceptable distortion, but at the expense of reduced power output.Class D or High Current operation is essentially rapid switching, hence the term switching power amplifier. Here the output devices are rapidly switched on and off at least twice for each cycle. Theoretically, since the output devices are either completely on or completely off they do not dissipate any power. If a device is on there is a large amount of current flowing through it, but all the voltage is across the load, so the power dissipated by the device is zero; and when the device is off, the voltage is large, but the current is zero. Consequently, class D operation (often, but not necessarrily digital) is theoretically 100% efficient, but this requires zero on-impedance switches with infinitely fast switching times — a product yet to be made; meanwhile designs do exist with efficiencies approaching 90%. This is a design that is increasimgly popular for use in bass systems, where maximum power is necessary, and slightly elevated levels of distortion are easily tolerated.

Amplifier A component or module of a component that increases the amplitude of an electrical signal. Voltage amplifiers and current amplifiers are optimised to provide amplification for specific purposes.

Amplitude The strength or intensity of an AC signal applied by the amplifiers output to a speaker's input. Also, a measure of the relative power of any variable recurring phenomenon. Typically, measurements are made in Decibels.

AMS(Automatic music search) A feature that allows a CD or cassette mechanism to skip forward or backwards to another track.

Anagnorisis In drama, a character's self-revelation or self-discovery, especially one that precipitates a turning point in the action.

Analogue An analogue signal in an electrical facsimile of the item being represented. For example, when playing a stereo DVD, the analogue audio outputs of a DVD player trace an electrical curve that is identical, other than in sheer power, to the electrical curve that the amplifier will deliver to the speakers and this, in turn, is identical to the pattern of sound waves the speaker will create, except for distortions that creep into the system. An analogue signal can have any value within set limit, while a digital signal is constrained to a set of discrete values.

Analog camcorder Portable device for recording live-motion video and audio to a magnetic videocassette (VHS, S-VHS, 8mm, Hi-8, etc.).

Analog digital conversion The method of converting analog data to digital data.

Analog ground In high-speed data acquisition applications, system ground is generally physically separated into "analog" and "digital" grounds in an attempt to supress digital switching noise and minimize its effect on noise-sensitive analog signal processing circuitry. Input signal conditioners, amplifiers, references, and A/D converters are usually connected to analog ground.

Analog recording The common form of magnetic recording where the recorded wave-form signal maintains the shape of the original wave-form signal. An example of this is a video tape.

Analog signal A representation of some event in way the mimicks the original in a unique way. For example, an audio signal consists of air pressures changing from higher than normal to lower than normal, again and again, back and forth. A turntable playing a record uses a needle to rest inside of a groove that gets deeper and shallower. The deeper the oscillations of the groove go, the louder the sound reproduced becomes. The record is an analogy of the air pressures produced by the acoustic instruments played during the recording of it.

Analog signals differ from digital signals in that they can convey a continuum of information with no apparent limitation on the resolution of the data they convey. The medium used to convey the information is what determines any limit on how much information an analog signal can carry. In the case of a vinyl record, the level of valid information obtainable as an acoustical audio signal is limited by the fact that the record contributes unwanted additional information (noise) which covers up, or interferes with the recovery of some of the original signal.

A laser, on the other hand, can be modulated (changed) in a way that very accurately represents its source signal with minimal interference. The recovery and retranslation of the signal at the receiving end of the laser produces a faithful replica of the original signal.

Analog switch A hardware-oriented switch that only passes signals that are faithful analogs of transducer parameters.

Analog video A video signal that represents an infinite number of smooth gradations between given video levels. By contrast, a digital video signal assigns a number for each level. The Macintosh video board converts computer-created (or digital) video to an analog signal for output to a monitor.

Anamorphic Also known as '16:9 enhanced' or 'widescreen enhanced'. This means stretching a picture out of shape, making the images tall and skinny. Many widescreen movies have been filmed on standard Academy aspect ratio cameras and film stock. This can be done either by wasting a lot of film between each frame, or making use of the full frame by using an anamorphic lens to horizontally squeeze the picture together. If a single frame is looked at, the characters will be as mentioned. When the film is shown, a reverse form of the anamorphic lens widens the picture again so that everything appears as it should. On DVDs an anamorphic widescreen picture is encoded to use all the vertical lines of resolution available (576 for PAL and 480 for NTSC). When played back on a widescreen TV it is horizontally stretched so that the picture contents are shaped normally, but with the benefit of DVD's full resolution. If played back on a 4:3

TV (that does not have a widescreen mode), the DVD player's set up menu must be told so that the DVD player can convert the anamorphic picture to a letterboxed picture for the TV. More.

Anamorphic lens A lens whose optical magnification properties are different along different radii so that an image seen through the lens is distorted. These lenses are used to translate images from one aspect ratio to another.

Anchor An anchor in a markup language is a technical term for what is popularly known as a "link" between web documents, or between locations within the same document (in which case it is identified by a fragment identifier).

Source Anchor : where the linked anchor starts. In HTML the Source Anchor is specified with the href attribute.

Destination Anchor : where the link must go to. In HTML the Destination Anchor is specified with the name attribute, and in XHTML with the id attribute. An anchor in a document such as a DTP document is a fixed point to which a containing box is referenced for layout purposes. For example, the box containing an image in text may be offset at a certain coordinate point from the of a page. Its anchor point can be measured from this point to the position in which it actually occurs.

Ancillary timecode BT.1366 Defines how to transfer VITC and LTC as ancillary data in digital component interfaces.

Anechoic chamber A special room that is constructed without acoustically reflective surfaces, such that it is without echoes, or an-echo-ic. This experimental setup enables engineers to more precisely measure the acoustical properties of many types of equipment. A real life anechoic situation is experienced by skydivers. However, they may be a bit distracted from the experience by the approaching ground.

Angled (box or enclosure) A type of speaker enclosure wherein the woofers, or Drivers, are situated in a box that is angled on one side. This is usually done to facilitate a more direct coupling of the upper part of the speaker's range to the listening environment.

Animated GIF (graphics interchange format) An animated GIF is a graphic image on a Web page that moves. It also contains within the single file a set of images that are presented in a specified order. An animated GIF can loop endlessly or it can present one or a few sequences and then stop the animation.

Animatic A limited animation used to work out film or video sequences. It consists of artwork shot on film or videotape and edited to serve as an on screen storyboard. Animatics are often used to plan out film sequences without incurring the expense of the actual shoot.

Animation Animation is the optical illusion of motion created by the consecutive display of images of static elements. In film and video production, this refers to techniques by which each frame of a film or movie is produced individually. These frames may be generated by computers, or by photographing a drawn or painted image, or by repeatedly making small changes to a model unit, and then photographing the result with a special animation camera. When the frames are strung together and the resulting film is viewed, there is an illusion of continuous movement due to the phenomenon known as persistence of vision. Generating such a film tends to be very labour intensive and tedious, though the development of computer animation has greatly sped up the process.

Graphics file formats like GIF, MNG, SVG and (SWF) Flash allow animation to be viewed on a computer or over the Internet.

Animation techniques

Traditional animation began with each frame being painted and then filmed. Cel animation, developed by Bray and Hurd in the 1910s, sped up the process by using transparent overlays so that characters could be moved without the need to repaint the background for every frame. More recently, styles of animation based on painting and drawing have evolved, such as the minimalist Simpsons cartoons, or the roughly sketched The Snowman.

Computer animation has advanced rapidly, and is now approaching the point where movies can be created with characters so lifelike as to be hard to distinguish from real actors. This involved a move from 2D to 3D, the difference being that in 2D animation the effect of perspective is created artistically, but in 3D objects are modeled in an internal 3D representation within the computer, and are then 'lit' and 'shot' from chosen angles, just as in real life, before being 'rendered' to a 2D bitmapped frame. Predictions that famous dead actors might even be 'brought back to life' to play in new movies before long have led to speculation about the moral and copyright issues involved. The use of computer animation as a way of achieving the otherwise impossible in conventionally shot movies has led to the term "computer generated imagery" being used, though the term has become hard to distinguish from computer animation as it is now used in referring to 3D movies that are entirely animated.

Computer animation involves modelling, motion generation, followed by the addition of surfaces and then rendering. Surfaces are programmed to stretch and bend automatically in response to movements of a 'wire frame model', and the final rendering converts such movements to a bitmap image. It is the recent developments in rendering complex surfaces like fur and clothing textures that have enabled stunningly life-like character models, including surfaces that even ripple, fold and blow in the wind, with every fibre or hair individually calculated for rendering. However, that actually has little to do with the animation itself. Animation is the process of bringing a lifeless puppet to life through the use of motion. Many people confuse fancy effects and high-res textures with animation, but in fact life-like motion can be created using the simplest of models. Pixar's work is a testament to this. The goal of an animator is not simply to "copy" the real world, but to enhance and to take the essence of the motion that is there, and this is how animation can be elevated to the level of art.

There is a large misconception in the public mind that computers create animation today. This couldn't be further from the truth. A computer is nothing more (though also nothing less) than a very expensive fancy pencil, and has to be treated as such for any quality work to be achieved. The choices a computer makes when interpolating motion are almost always the wrong ones, because the computer does not know what you are trying to create. Even if a complex physics system were created complete enough to exactly mimic the real world, the end result would not be the desirable one, because a large part of animation concerns the choices an animator makes. When a computer tries to make the choices for you, disaster is the general result.

History

The major use of animation has always been for entertainment. However, there is growing use of instructional animation and educational animation to support explanation and learning.

The "classic" form of animation, the "animated cartoon", as developed in the early 1900s and refined by Ub Iwerks, Walt Disney and others, requires up to 24 distinct drawings for one second of animation. This technique is described in detail in the article Traditional animation.

Because animation is very time-consuming and often very expensive to produce, the majority of animation for TV and movies comes from professional animation studios. However, the field of independent animation has existed at least since the 1950s, with animation being produced by independent studios (and sometimes by a single person). Several independent animation producers have gone on to enter the professional animation industry. Bill Plympton is one of the most well known independent animators today.

Limited animation is a way of increasing production and decreasing costs of animation by using "short cuts" in the animation process. This method was pioneered by UPA and popularized (some say exploited) by Hanna-Barbera, and adapted by other studios as cartoons moved from movie theaters to television.

Annotations Comments, in either a text or audio fashion, which you can attach to a photoshop file.

Anode The electrically positive pole of an electronic device such as a semiconductor. A diode, for instance, has a positive and a negative pole; these are known as the anode and the cathode.

Anonymous Refers to a generic account username that any user can enter to log-in to a FTP file archive.

ANSI (American national standards institute) An organization that defines standards in the information technology industry and participates in defining network protocol standards. ANSI is a member of ISO. The ANSI characters are characters that when preceded with the ESC (Escape) character they function as a command. ANSI escape sequences are used to send commands to monitors or keyboards.

ANSI lumens (American national standards institute lumens) A measure of brightness for projectors under standards set by this body. This specifies an average brightness produced on a screen of known reflectivity using a particular test image, or images. A specification war is underway with each projector claiming a higher and higher ANSI lumens rating. The amount of brightness required for a good job from a projector requires three things to be taken into account, in order of increasing importance: the reflectivity of the projection surface, the size of the projected image, and the amount of ambient light in the room. High output projectors (> 1,000 ANSI lumens) are important for making presentations, class room work and the like. But for home theatre use, look for something lower, preferably under 700. It will generally give you a longer lamp life and darker black areas, which are more important for delivering a good quality image. If the projector has an 'economy mode', try using this. If it doesn't throw out the colour balance too much, it may well deliver a better home theatre image.

Antagonist A character whose dramatic function is to oppose the protagonist the bad guy. . A minor climax or drop in dramatic tension, which, depending on how it's used, can enhance the climax, dilute it, and produce numerous wanted or unwanted effects.

Antenna A device, such as a rod or wire, which picks up a received radio frequency signal or radiates a transmitted RF signal.

Anti aliasing Anti-aliasing is the manipulation of the edges of an image, graphic or text, to make them appear smoother to the eye. On close inspection, anti-aliased edges appear blurred, but at normal viewing distance, the apparent smoothing is dramatic. Anti-aliasing is important when working with high quality graphics for television use.

Anti-alias filter A lowpass filter used to bandwidth-limit a signal to less than one-half the sampling rate.

Anti-skating A device on a turntable's tonearm to counteract skating. This sometimes consists of an adjustable spring-loaded device near the tonearm's pivot, but is better implemented as a weight on a string (since the torque applied by this arrangement remains constant throughout the range of travel).

Apache A public domain web server package that was developed by a group of volunteers. This server is free with sophisticated features and excellent performance.

APD (Avalanche photo diode) A type of detector used in fibre optic receivers.

Aperature priority An exposure mode that allows the camera's user to set the desired aperature and the camera will select the appropriate shutter speed

Aperiodic Refers to a type of bass-cabinet loading. An aperiodic enclosure type usually features a very restrictive, (damped), port. The purpose of this restrictive port is not to extend bass response, but to yeild a smoother response pattern by lowering the Q of the system and reducing the impedance peak at resonance. Most restrictive ports are damped with quantities of sound absorbtive material.

Aperture A measure of the width of the opening allowing light to enter a camera. Higher apertures allow more light to enter a camera, hence darker scenes can be recorded. Conversely, lower apertures allow less light to enter, but have the advantage of creating a large depth of field.

Aperture delay Aperture delay is the time from an edge of the input clock of the ADC until the time the ADC actually takes the sample. The smaller this number, the better.

Aperture grille A part of a CRT TV tube. This is a barrier within the tube, placed between the electron guns at the narrow end and the phosphor screen at the wide end. It consists of a series of vertical wires or fine slats. The geometric arrangement permits the electrons emitted for each colour gun to activate only its matching colour phosphors. This alternative to the shadow mask was developed by Sony and marketed under the name 'Trinitron'.

Aperture jitter Uncertainty, or sample-to-sample of variation, in the aperture delay time. Aperture jitter is a source of error in a sampling system, and it determines the maximum slew rate limitation of the sampled analog input signal for a given system resolution.

API (application programming interface) Set of routines/functions that an application program uses to request and carry out lower-level services performed by the operating system. For Windows, for example, API's help manage icons, windows, menus and other GUI elements.

Apostilb A photometric unit for measuring luminance where, instead of candelas, lumens are used to measure the luminous flux of a source. One Apostilb = 0.318309886183791 candela/m^2.

Apple macintosh Introduced in 1984, the Apple Macintosh was the first mass-market computer with a graphical user interface. Often shortened to just "Mac", this type of computer is popular with designers and journalists. Macs have their own operating system, known as Mac OS, which is similar to the Windows operating system.

Applet A Java code program. You can use small Java programs without having to know anything about their code. A Java applet such as Zoom or Ptviewer (by Helmut Dersch) allows you to avoid having viewers having to download plugins to view a panoramic image. To use this you need to learn how to setup a folder with your images and the applet somewhere in your website.

Application Another way of saying "computer program.

Application layer The OSI model linterface layer that establishes communication rights to other applications and can initiate a connection between two applications.

Application sharing Videoconferencing applications that enable conference participants to run the same applications at the same time.

Archetype The first, prototypical, and quintessential expression of a theme, character type, style, genre etc.

Archie An older brother of search engines oni the Internet allowing searches of ftp sites.

Archival file An archival file is a "master copy" of a piece of digital media. It is usually either uncompressed or only slightly compressed. Because of this, archival files are usually too large to distribute. Generally media is created in an archival format so that the master copy is as high-quality as possible. Then smaller, more compressed, lower quality copies can be converted from this archival master as needed. One archival master can be used to create any number distribution copies in different formats and sizes as the need arises.

Archive A collection of stored files not often used, but nevertheless available. In practice there is no difference between files of current web sites and those in the archive. Both are equally accessible.

Argument A summary or short statement of the plot or subject of a literary work.

Aria In opera, a solo number; hence, in drama, any long speech that suspends the flow of dramatic action, especially a long, reflective soliloquy .

ARIB (Short for association of radio industries and businesses) A standards oganization in Japan. The ARIB provides several specifications that form the core of the ISDB digital television system used in Japan.

Arib std-B10 Japan ISDB-S and ISDB-T digital television service information specification.

Arib std-B20 Japan ISDB-S (satellite) digital television system specification.

Arib std-B21 Japan ISDB-S and ISDB-T digital television receiver specification.

Arib std-B24 Japan ISDB-S and ISDB-T digital television data broadcasting specification.

Arib std-B25 Japan ISDB-S and ISDB-T digital television access control specification.

Arib std-B31 Japan ISDB-T (terestrial) digital television system specification.

Arib std-B32 Japan ISDB-S and ISDB-T digital television video coding, audio coding and multiplexing specification.

Arib std-B38 Japan ISDB-S and ISDB-T digital television home server specification.

Aristotle Among his achievements, this Greek philosopher (384-322 BC) was the first dramatic theorist of the Western World. His Poetics, apparently written as lecture notes, describes Greek Tragedy and attempts to explain how it moves an audience. Aristotelian terms and principles, such as hubris, puerility, catharsis, are still useful to critics and dramatists.

ARP(address resolution protocol) This protocol is broadcast from an internet server and all TCP/IP devices on the local network can hear it. When the machine with the appropriate IP address hears it, it responds to the ARP request.

Each hardware card (.ie. each NIC, Network Interface Card) has a unique hardware address. It is also possible to assign a software address to the card (which would be an IP address). Hardware address information is obtained from the ARP.

Each host has an ARP table that contains software (IP) addresses mapping to hardware (NIC) addresses. ARP looks for a hardware address for a given IP address (the opposite of RARP).

ARPA (advanced research projects agency) ARPA is an alliance formed in the 1970s between computer manufacturers and universities to develop communication standards for networks. It designed a protocol that became the basis for TCP/IP.

ARPANET (Advanced research projects agency network) The precursor to the Internet, ARPANET a large wide area network, developed by the US Defence Department in the late 60s and early 70s.

Arpanet The granddaddy of The Internet. This was the original experimental network funded by the US government to determine the feasibility of such a network.

Art, audio A type of audio production akin to "performance art," which may or may not include dramatic elements.

Artifacts In the video domain, artifacts are blemishes, noise, snow, spots, whatever. When you have an image artifact, something is wrong with the picture from a visual standpoint. Don't confuse this term with not having the display properly adjusted. For example, if the hue control is set wrong, the picture will look bad, but this is not an artifact. An artifact is some physical disruption of the image.

Artificial light Man Made light source such as a bulbs, headlamps, etc.

Artistic distance A psychological distance between fictive events of a literary or dramatic work and the life experience of the audience, theoretically necessary before the work can be appreciated as art. If a work relates too personally to the audience, the audience will lose its aesthetic objectivity.

ASCII American standard code for information interchange) This is a character set suited for the characters of a particular language. ASCII is a subset of the UCS (Universal Character Set). As the computer revolution started in the USA ASCII became the standard code set, although there are some systems (such as IBM's EBCDIC) that use a different configuration. Originally ASCII consisted of code for 128 characters, and later this was extended to 256 codes (the extended character set). This extended set included European characters that are not found in English, such as ê é ô and graphic signs such as ¦. Each key on a computer keyboard has an ASCII code and the keyboard can be set to use different configurations of character sets. Languages that use different kinds of alphabets have different kinds of character sets.

More technically, the smallest information unit used by computers are bits, that make up larger units called bytes. There are 8 bits to one byte in an 8-bit system. Using this system there are 128 codes available to represent characters. Some of the codes are reserved for control keys such as the ENTER and space bar keys. There are thus not enough keys on a particular keyboard for all the characters of all the languages of the world. For this reason the language characters are divided into character sets.

The ASCII system is based on the 8-bit system, but the first digit is used for checking and control purposes. ASCII is represented in binary format on the machine level. This table shows how ASCII is represented in the alphanumeric and binary systems:

alphanumeric

binary 1

00110001 2

00110010 3

00110011 4

00110100 5

00110101 6

00110110 7

00110111 a

01000001 b

01000010 c

01000011 d

01000100 e

01000101 f

01000101 g

01000111 Asymmetric Digital Subscriber Line.

ASCII based characters Acronym for the American Standard Code for Information Interchange. ASCII is a code for representing English characters as numbers, with each letter assigned a number from 0 to 127. Computers use ASCII codes to represent text, which makes it possible to transfer data from one computer to another.

ASF ASF stands for Advanced Streaming Format.

ASF is a highly compressed file format that contains streaming video, audio. When an ASF file is palyed back, content is deliverd to you as a continuous flow of data. You no longer have to wait for the whole video and audio file to fully download before you start to view them. So, this file format is specially designed to run on networks. When an AVI file is compressed and converted to an .asf file, the file begins playing after only a few seconds. ASF files can be played back with the Windows Media Player (provided the appropriate codecs are installed), streamed with Windows Media Services or optionally packaged with Windows Media Rights Manager.

Aside A dramatic convention in which a character speaks his inner thoughts aloud to himself; or speaks in a stage whisper to another character or the audience, as if the other characters in the scene can't hear him/her. In radio, asides are often distinguished from regular speech by a change of sound quality, mike position, or filter, rather than by a stage whisper.

ASP.net A Microsoft server-side web technology to develop web pages.

Aspect ratio The ratio of the width of a film frame to its height. Now often 1.85 to 1, in the "studio era" it was 4 to 3 (the 1.33:1 "Academy ratio" still used for TV). Wider ratios like Panavision (2.2:1) and Cinemascope (2.55:1) are closer to what our eyes actually see, but need increasingly anamorphic lenses for photography and projection, and are difficult to translate to television. (The usual "solutions" to this problem are either to chop off the sides of the widescreen frame or, during the credits, where all the words are necessary, to use an anamorphic lens to squeeze them in; this lens stretches the height of the images we see—for example, the horses and riders in the opening credits of video versions of The Wild Bunch).

Aspherical lens A lens that has an aspherical (not spherical) surface. It is harder and more expensive to manufacture, but it offers certain advantages over a normal spherical lens such as a lower F number.

Aspiration The vocal sound made by turbulent airflow preceding or following vocal fold vibration, as in "ha" or "ah."

Assemble editing Adding new material to the end of a previously recorded portion of a videotape that involves writing a completely new signal (including the control track) onto the tape. Performing an assemble edit in the middle of an existing program will introduce an undesirable glitch on the tape caused by an abrupt change in the sync information of the video signal.

Assembly The first part of the editing process in which outtakes are removed from the masters and the remaining keepers are placed in broadcast order.

Asset The components, such as video, audio, and scripts, that are used as part of a multimedia project.

Assistive listening device A transmitter connected to a sound system which provides hearing enhancement to a receiver.

Assistive technology Sometimes called enabling technology, assistive technology allows people with disabilities or special needs to fully take part in activities that would otherwise be difficult or impossible.

Association Refers to a certain file type which is directly associated with a certain program.

PSD files for examples are directly associated with Photoshop and Photoshop Elements.

AST(Automatic scan tracking) Ampex technology which provides "slow motion" capability on professional VTRs and DTVRs.

Astigmatism The uneven foreground and background blur or horizontal / vertical blur that is in an image. It is caused by distortions in the lens surface.

ASX ASX stands for Advanced Stream Redirector.

An asx file is used to store information on servers and media files for streaming video and audio over the Internet, such as multimedia web sites. The .asx file is a simple text file that contains server and media information, so you can easily find out the name of the file and server address of the streaming content with a text editor.

Asymmetrical digital A digital communications application that allows for up to 7 MBPS of Subscriber Line data transmission capacity over conventional twisted pair telephone lines. ADSL is a contender for a major piece of the "information highway" pie and it promises to deliver telephone, TV, and data services to your home over the existing telephone line.

Asynchronous A multiplexing and switching technique that organizes information Transfer Mode into fixed-length cells consisting of an identification header field and an information field. The transfer rate is asynchronous in that the recurrence of cells depends on the instantaneously required bit rate.

Asynchronous communication Users communicate/ interact, but at different times. These interactions may occur using e-mail, listservs or discussion boards.

Audio sound, either synthesized or digitized, for playback with a computer. File formats: .WAV - Windows, .AU - Unix, playable on both Macs and Windows machines with the right players.

ATM(Asynchronous transfer mode) This is a method used for high bandwidth data transfer, made possible by hardware switches that create a temporary direct path between two points. This ATM is not to be confused with the Automatic banking machines encountered in shopping malls.

Atmosphere 1) The prevailing mood (calm, mysterious, gay, etc.) of a play or other work of fiction; 2) (television) extras, supernumeraries, walla.

ATRAC A system for compressing digital audio using perceptual encoding techniques. This was developed by Sony to allow the full contents of a CD to fit onto a Minidisc, which offers considerably less storage space. In recent years a new version, called ATRAC3, has been introduced which permits greater levels of compression than the original version. This permits ATRAC-based solid state players. The bit rates used by ATRAC3 are 132 and 66 kb/s. The ATRAC compression system also forms the basis of Sony's cinema sound system SDDS.

ATSC (Advanced television systems committee) They defined the HDTV standards for the United States. Other countries are also adopting the ATSC HDTV standard.

ATSC A/100 This DTV Application Software Environment (DASE) defines a software layer (middleware) that allows programming content and applications to run on a common ATSCATSC receiver.

ATSC A/49 Defines the ghost cancellation reference signal for NTSC.

ATSC A/52 Defines the (Dolby Digital) audio compression for ATSC HDTV.

ATSC A/53, A/54 Defines ATSC HDTV for the USA.

ATSC A/57 Defines the program, episode, and version ID for ATSC HDTV.

ATSC A/64 Defines the transmission measurement and compliance for ATSC HDTV.

ATSC A/65, A/69 Defines the program and system information protocol (PSIP) for ATSC HDTV.

ATSC A/70 Defines the conditional access system for ATSC HDTV.

ATSC A/80 Defines a standard for modulation and coding of ATSC data delivered over satellite for digital television contribution and distribution applications.

ATSC A/81 Defines the transmission system for ATSC Direct-to-Home (DTH) satellite broadcast system.

ATSC A/90, A/91 Defines the data broadcast standard for ATSC HDTV.

ATSC A/92 Defines the IP multicast standard for ATSC HDTV.

ATSC A/93 Defines the transmission of synchronized data elements, and synchronized and asynchronous events for ATSC HDTV.

ATSC A/94 Defines an Application Reference Model (ARM) including a binding of application environment facilities onto the ATSC A/90 data broadcast standard.

ATSC A/95 Defines the ATSC Transport Stream File System (TSFS) standard for delivery of hierarchical name-spaces, directories and files. It builds on the ATSC A/90 data broadcast standard.

ATSC A/96 Defines a core suite of protocols to enable remote interactivity in ATSC television environments.

Attack To begin a scene, line or action; 2) The beginning of a scene, line or action; an approach or concept for the production of a drama, writing of a script, playing of a role, or reading of a line.

Attenuate The act of reducing the Amplitude or intensity of a signal. In speaker systems, high frequency drivers are commonly more efficient than low frequency drivers. This creates a need to adjust the driver levels to create a uniform overall frequency response. L-pads are commonly used for many passive systems.

Attenuation The decrease in magnitude of a wave, or a signal, as it travels through a medium or an electric system. It is usually measured in decibels (dB).

Attenuator A circuit that provides reduction of the amplitude of an electrical signal without introducing appreciable phase or frequency distortion.

Attribute Markup language An attribute is a markup command used together with SGML elements that allow more control over the element. In HTML 4 there are more than 120 attributes. Attribute specify characteristics of specific elements and cannot be used with any element. DTDs specify which attributes can be used with which elements.

Image An attribute is a property of an image - such as its color, or texture, each of which is an attribute of the image.

AU An audio file format for UNIX systems. AU is SUN Microsystem's proprietary format. Probably the most commonly used sound format on the Web.

Audio 1. Of, or relating to, humanly audible sound, i.e., audio is all the sounds that humans hear.

2. a. Relating to the broadcasting or reception of sound. b. Relating to high-fidelity sound reproduction.

Audio dub Result of recording over pre-recorded videotape soundtrack without affecting the video track.

Audio effects board The audio effects board is like the switcher, and acts as the main router and mixer for source audio. Here audio levels are adjusted, mixed, and filtered. Usually audio effects are kept to a basic level in a video editing session. More complex audio work is usually performed with a digital audio workstation.

Audio frequency spectrum The band of frequencies extending roughly from 20 Hz to 20 kHz and encompassing the full range of normal human hearing.

Audio mixer Device with user-adjustable controls used to blend multiple sound inputs into desired composite output.

Audio modulation Refers to modifying an audio subcarrier with audio information so that it may be mixed with the video information and transmitted.

Audio scrubbing Moving within an audio file or tape to locate a particular section.

Audio Subcarrier A specific frequency that is modulated with audio data.

Audiobook A commercial sound recording, usually on cassette or compact disk, of a narrator reading a literary work aloud; hence, any commercial recording of dramatic or narrative speech.

Audiophile A person who places, or would like to place if circumstances permitted, a high priority on having an audio system that performs very highly. They have generally trained themselves to be very discerning about the sound of audio systems. Some audiophiles stray into a purely subjective realm.

Audiovisual Any information that combines sound (audio) - for example music, voices and sound effects - with images (visual). As such, a television, DVD player or video recorder can be described as audiovisual equipment.

Auteur A producer or director of a dramatic production, who creates such a strong and pervasive artistic vision over a stage, optisonic or audio production, often contributing decisively to the script, that s/he is for all intents and purposes, the production's author, no matter how many other creative persons contribute to it. The term is rarely used in the theater, because a production most often needs to be fixed and definitive before it can be said to have an auteur. American radio drama auteurs include Norman Corwin, Arch Oboler, and Orson Welles, also a cinema auteur.

Authentication A process for verifying the correctness of a piece of data.

Author / web author A web author is a person who writes the markup (HTML) for web documents. Note that a distinction should be made between a Web Author (who writes the HTML markup code), the Web Graphics Designer (who designs a web page artistically), a Web Designer (who designs the information and information technology of the website; this term is also popularly used for the person responsible for all the authoring aspects mentioned here) and a Web Copy Writer (who writes the text of the document. In some cases these functions may be performed by the same individual, but they are different functions demanding different skills.

Authoring software Programs used to create full, multimedia productions, such as simulations and tutorials. Although most of these programs have some point-and-click features to simplify development, most require some knowledge of programming language concepts. Popular authoring software packages include Asymetrix ToolBook, Microsoft Visual Basic, Macromedia Director and Authorware. FAQ's - Authoring Packages.

At the "lower" end, presentation software, like Microsoft PowerPoint, provide simpler ways to put multimedia into presentations. HyperStudio, sits somewhere in the middle: It provides more interactive capabilities than presentation software, but cannot do all that a fully-robust authoring package can do.

Typical authoring systems:

Macromedia Authorware and Macromedia Director (Mac & Windows)

Asymetrix's Multimedia Toolbook/ Assistant/Librarian (Windows)

Apple's Hypercard (Mac & Windows)

HyperStudio (Mac & Windows)

Microsoft Visual Basic (Windows)

Authoring system Software that helps developers design interactive applications, titles, or courseware more easily than with conventional programming language.

Authoring tool An Authoring Tool is a program that enables a multimedia author to create a multimedia product. Authoring tools typically write many of the functions withou the developer having to know the technicalities of programming in a programming language. In its simplest form, an HTML Authoring Tool, for example, automatically completes end tags. A Multimedia tool may simplify ways in which objects are placed on a timeline.

Auto assemble If all the editing decisions are made off-line, and the EDL is loaded into the CMX the actual editing is automatic, executing one event after another. This is called auto-assemble mode. During auto-assembly, the editor monitors video and audio levels, but does not need to control each edit. Loading the EDL into the CMS is typically done manually, however, some Macintosh programs can create CMX disks. The EDL generated by computer based editing systems like the Digital F/X and Avid Media Composer are usually perfectly accurate, therefore, they make auto-assembly a breeze since the opportunity for errors in entering the EDL by hand are eliminated.

Auto iris (AI) An automatic method of varying the size of a lens aperture in response to changes in scene illumination.

Auto memory A tuner feature that automatically finds the strongest stations in the local area, and places them in preset memories.

Auto slate A "silent" digital version of movie clap sticks.

Autocorrelation Multiplication of a signal with a time-delayed replica of itself.

Auto-focus (AF) A camera setting that will automatically focus the image on a certain section (usually a small square in the center of the camera's view).

Automatic content distribution Replicates and dispatches content to local workgroup servers, localizing bandwidth consumption and enabling scalability.

Automatic frequency control (AFC) A technique to lock onto and track a desired frequency.

Automatic frequency sweep An implementation of DDS where the output frequency is automatically swept across a band of frequencies. This is particularly useful in radar applications.

Automatic gain control (AGC) A circuit that has a constant output amplitude, regardless of the input amplitude.

Autoreply/autoresponse An e-mail message automatically sent in response to an incoming message. Most current e-mail management software has the ability to allow you to create one or more autoreply, and many House and Senate offices are using them to indicate to e-mailers that their messages have been received and will be answered promptly. Some offices are also using them in conjunction with sophisticated filters and rules to respond to e-mail on certain issues or to indicate to non-constituents that their message will not be answered and that they should contact their own Representative or Senators.

Avatar An icon, usually graphically generated, representing a real person in cyberspace. They can be used to play games, as a tour guide around a site, to simulate walking, speaking, etc.

Average or apparent power The result of multiplying the rms value of the voltage by the rms value of the current in an electronic circuit. It is expressed in watts (W) for resistive loads and in voltamperes (VA) for reactive loads. The real power is usually less because of losses when the power factor is accounted.

AVI AVI stands for Audio Video Interleaved and developed by Microsoft.

An AVI file can use different codecs and formats so there is no set format for an AVI file unlike for example standard VCD video which sets a standard for resolution, bitrates, and codecs used. Most commonly used video codecs that use AVI structure are M-JPEG and DivX.

A-weighting A system of adjusting signal to noise ratio measurements to take into account the differing sensitivity of the human ear to different frequencies. Thus an A-weighted signal to noise ratio more accurately reflects how a system's noise performance will be perceived than an unweighted measure.

AWG(American wire gauge) A wire diameter specification based on the American standard. The smaller the AWG number, the larger the wire diameter. Alternatively :- the measure of the diameter of a conductor. AWG is the U.S. standard measuring gauge for certain conductors, including copper. The higher the AWG number the thinner the wire. This measure stems from the fact that the original measurement represented the number of times the wire was run through a wire machine which thus reduced the diameter of the wire. Thus a 24-guage wire was thinner than an 18-guage wire because it was run through a wire machine 6 more times than the 18-guage wire, reducing the overall diameter.

B

B mode edit An editing method where the footage is assembled in the order it appears on the source reels. Missing scenes are left as black holes to be filled in by a later reel. Requires fewer reel changes and generally results in a faster edit session.

B'-Y' The blue-minus-luma signal, also called a color difference signal. When added to the luma (Y') signal, it produces the blue video signal.

Back A script indication signaling that a sound or voice is in the background. Usually applied to outdoor sounds.

Back light In receivers, a display may be lit from the rear to create better visibility under a wide range of ambient light conditions.

Back plate The part of the woofers metal Basket or frame on which the Magnet structure is mounted.

Back porch 1. The portion of a video signal that occurs during blanking from the end of horizontal sync to the beginning of active video.

2. The blanking signal portion that lies between the trailing edge of a horizontal syncpulse and the trailing edge of the corresponding blanking pulse. In CCIR and PAL it is 5.8μs long. Chroma burst is located in the back porch.

Back projection A technique in which action is projected on a screen behind live actors. A popular early use of back projection was to simulate out-of-control car rides.

Back story Background information on the characters or events of a drama that need to be revealed during the action so that the ramifications of the action can be fully exposed.

Back time To determine the length of a program fragment, or to line up two production elements, such as selected lines and a musical bed, by timing them backwards from their end points.

Backbone The term backbone refers to a main data transmission line, or trunk line. The backbone is the larger transmission line that carries calls and data gathered from the smaller lines that connect with it. In terms of the Internet, backbone is one or more data transmission lines (predominantly optic fibre but can also be based on microwave technology) that local data networks connect to at points called nodes. Local networks connect to the infrastructure backbone to achieve long distance data transmission.

Back-focus A procedure of adjusting the physical position of the CCD-chip/lens to achieve the correct focus for all focal length settings (especially critical with zoom lenses).

Background In an image document refers to the lowest layer which all other layers appear on top of. In many applications this layer is locked

Badge A symbol in the corner of a QuickTime movie window which is pressed to bring the standard QuickTime movie controller into view.

Baffle A plate surrounding a driver in a loudspeaker. The lower the frequency of the sound produced by the vibrating cone of a driver, the more apt it is to simply cause air to rush from one side of the cone to the other, rather than produce the compression waves that constitute sound. By adding a baffle around the driver, this increases the length of the path that air must travel, lowering the frequency at which this destructive interference takes place. In most loudspeakers, the enclosure forms a baffle. In the case of infinite baffle enclosures, the enclosure is sealed (thus 'infinite') while with bass reflex speakers a port is carefully tuned to allow energy from the back of the cone to supplement that from the front at selected bass frequencies. In regular talk, the baffle is the front panel of the loudspeaker.

Balanced Balanced analog audio connectors use an extra condutor which helps eliminate electromagnetic interference that might otherwise be picked up in a length of cable. This interference can appear in the audio signal as background hum. Professional equipment will often use balanced jacks and cables while consumer equipment generally does not. Interconnecting balanced and unbalanced audio devices can be tricky and generally requires special adapters. Balanced audio usually uses either XLR-type or 2-condutor 1/4" phono connectors for each channel of balanced audio. It is easy to mistake a balanced mono phono connector for a unbalnced stereo one, as the jacks and cables are the same.

Balanced signal In CCTV this refers to a type of video signal transmission (or data transmission) through a twisted pair cable. It is called balanced because the signal travels through both wires in anti-phase, with no reference to Earth, thus being equally exposed to the external interference, common mode interference is cancelled out. It needs a differential receiver.

Balanced wiring Audio line signals require two conductors. In an unbalanced line, the shield is one of those. In a balanced line, there are two internal wires plus the shield. For the system to be balanced requires output transformers and usually employs XLR connectors. Balanced lines are less apt to pick up external noise. This is usually not a factor in home or car audio, but is a factor in professional audio requiring hundreds or even thousands of feet of cabling.

Balun This is a transformer used to match or transform an unbalanced coaxial cable to a balanced twisted pair system, or visa versa.

Banana jacks & plugs A set of connectors in which 4 spring contacts are wrapped vertically around a central pin like a banana peel. When inserted into the receptacle jack it maintains a strong and consistent contact. This type of connector is highly regarded as an excellent and reliable interconnector for cables between amplifiers and speakers.

Bandpass (box or enclosure) An enclosure that is specifically tuned to give maximum energy to a very limited range of frequencies, usually the lowest. In this arrangement, the woofers are fully enclosed in the box with the sound pressure being vented through one or more ports.

Bandpass filter A filter that has a finite passband, neither of the cutoff frequencies being zero or infinite. The bandpass frequencies are normally associated with frequencies that define the half power points, i.e. the -3 dB points. In multi-driver speaker systems, the Midrange driver may be fed by a bandpass filter.

Band-limiting filters A low-pass and a high-pass filter in series, acting together to restrict (limit) the overall bandwidth of a system. Many audio amplifiers and processors, having switches labeled as "Rumble" or "Hiss," are filters of this type.

Bandpass gain The increase (or decrease) in efficiency of loudspeakers, due to the enclosure size and tuning. This is measured by the midband sensitivity of the speaker as a whole.

Bandwidth Bandwidth is a measure of frequency range, measured in hertz, of a function of a frequency variable. Bandwidth is a central concept in many fields, including information theory, radio communications, signal processing, and spectroscopy. Bandwidth also refers to data rates when communicating over certain media or devices. According to the Shannon-Hartley theorem, the data rate of reliable communication is directly proportional to the frequency range of the signal used for the communication. In this context, the word bandwidth can refer to either the data rate or the frequency range of the communication system (or both).

Bandwidth is a key concept in many applications. In radio communications, for example, bandwidth is the range of frequencies occupied by a modulated carrier wave, whereas in optics it is the width of an individual spectral line or the entire spectral range

There is no *single* universal precise definition of bandwidth, as it is vaguely understood to be a measure of how wide a function is in the frequency domain. For different applications there are different precise definitions. For example, one definition of bandwidth could be the range of frequencies beyond which the frequency function is zero. This would correspond to the mathematical notion of the support of a function (i.e., the total "length" of values for which the function is nonzero). Another definition might not be so strict and ignore the frequencies where the frequency function is *small*. Small could mean less than 3 dB below (i.e., less than half of) the maximum value, or it could mean below a certain absolute value. In short, as with any definition of the *width* of a function, there are many definitions available, which are suitable for different applications.

Analog systems

For analog signals, which can be mathematically viewed as a function of time, bandwidth is the width, measured in hertz, of a frequency range in which the signal's Fourier transform is nonzero. This definition can be relaxed where the bandwidth would cover the range of frequencies where the signal's Fourier transform has a power above a certain amplitude threshold, say 3 dB within the maximum value, in the frequency domain. Bandwidth of a signal is a measure of how rapidly it fluctuates with respect to time. Hence, the greater the bandwidth, the faster the variation in the signal may be. The word bandwidth applies to signals as described above, but it could also apply to *systems*. In the latter case, to say that a system has a certain bandwidth is a short-hand for saying that the transfer function of the system has a certain bandwidth.

As an example, the 3 dB bandwidth of the function depicted in the figure is $f_2 - f_1$, whereas other definitions of bandwidth would yield a different answer.

The fact that real baseband systems have both negative and positive frequencies can lead to confusion about bandwidth, since they are sometimes referred to only by the positive half, and one will occasionally see expressions such as $B = 2W$, where B is the total bandwidth, and W is the positive bandwidth. For instance, this signal would require a lowpass filter with cutoff frequency of at least W to stay intact.

The bandwidth of an electronic filter is the part of the filter's frequency response that lies within 3 dB of the response at the center frequency of its peak.

In signal processing and control theory the bandwidth is the frequency at which the closed-loop system gain drops to -3 dB.

In photonics, the term bandwidth occurs in a variety of meanings:

the bandwidth of the output of some light source, e.g., an ASE source or a laser; the bandwidth of ultrashort optical pulses can be particularly large

the width of the frequency range that can be transmitted by some element, e.g. an optical fiber

the gain bandwidth of an optical amplifier

the width of the range of some other phenomenon (e.g., a reflection, the phase matching of a nonlinear process, or some resonance)

the maximum modulation frequency (or range of modulation frequencies) of an optical modulator

the range of frequencies in which some measurement apparatus (e.g., a powermeter) can operate

the data rate (e.g., in Gbit/s) achieved in an optical communication system

Digital systems

In a digital communication system, bandwidth has a dual meaning. In the technical sense, it is a synonym for baud rate, the rate at which symbols may be transmitted through the system. It is also used in the colloquial sense to describe channel capacity, the rate at which bits may be transmitted through the system. Hence, a 66 MHz digital data bus with 32 separate data lines may properly be said to have a bandwidth of 66 MHz and a capacity of 2.1 Gbit/s — but it would not be surprising to hear such a bus described as having a "bandwidth of 2.1 Gbit/s." Similar confusion exists for analog modems, where each symbol carries multiple bits of information so that a modem may transmit 56 kbit/s of information over a phone line with a bandwidth of only 12 kHz.

In discrete time systems and digital signal processing, bandwidth is related to sampling rate according to the Nyquist-Shannon sampling theorem.

Bandwidth is also used in the sense of commodity, referring to something limited or something costing money. Thus, communication costs bandwidth, and improper use of someone else's bandwidth may be called bandwidth theft.

CD (Compact disc)

A compact disc (or CD) is an optical disc used to store digital data, originally developed for storing digital audio. It is the standard playback format for commercial audio recordings today.

A standard compact disc, often known as an "audio CD" to differentiate it from later variants, stores audio data in a format compliant with the red book standard. An audio CD consists of several stereo tracks stored using 16-bit PCM coding at a sampling rate of 44.1 kHz. Standard compact discs have a diameter of 120 mm, though 80 mm versions exist in circular and "business-card" forms. The 120 mm discs can hold 74 minutes of audio, and versions holding 80, 90 or even 99 minutes have been introduced. The 80 mm discs are used as "CD-singles" or novelty "business-card CDs". They hold about 20 minutes of audio. Compact disc technology was later adapted for use as a data storage device, known as a CD-ROM.

The design of the CD was originally conceived as an evolution of the gramophone record, rather than primarily as a data storage medium. Only later did the concept of an 'audio file' arise, and the generalising of this to any data file. As a result, the original CD format has a number of limitations; no built-in track names or disc naming for example. Online services such as CDDB were developed to work around these shortcomings in the computer age.

Starting

In the early 1970s, using video Laserdisc technology, Philips' researchers started experiments with "audio-only" optical discs, initially with wideband frequency modulation FM and later digitized PCM audio signals. At the end of the 1970s, Philips, Sony, and other companies presented prototypes of digital audio discs.

In 1979 Philips and Sony decided to join forces, setting up a joint task force of engineers whose mission was to design the new digital audio disc. Prominent members of the task force were Kees Immink and Toshitada Doi. After a year of experimentation and discussion, the taskforce produced the "Red Book", the Compact Disc standard. Philips contributed the general manufacturing process, based on the video Laserdisc technology. Philips also contributed the Eight-to-Fourteen Modulation, EFM, which offers both a large playing time and a high resilience against disc handling damage such as scratches and fingerprints; while Sony contributed the error-correction method, CIRC. The Compact Disc Story, told by a former member of the taskforce, gives background information on the many technical decisions made, including the choice of the sampling frequency, playing time, and disc diameter. According to Philips, the Compact Disc was thus "invented collectively by a large group of people working as a team."

The Compact Disc reached the market in late 1982 in Asia and early the following year in other markets. This event is often seen as the "Big Bang" of the digital audio revolution. The new audio disc was enthusiastically received, especially in the early-adopting classical music and audiophile communities and its handling quality received particular praise. The far larger popular and rock music industries were slower to adopt the new format, especially in the huge consumer markets in Europe and the United States. This "highbrow niche" status of the CD format changed dramatically in May, 1985, when UK rock band Dire Straits, then under contract by Philips' Polygram, released the album *Brothers in Arms.* One of the first all-digital rock recordings and the first by a major act, *Brothers in Arms* played to the strengths of the CD by offering more and longer tracks, running ten minutes longer than the album's concurrent LP and cassette releases. It spurred the sale of compact disc players like no other recording before it, helped to drive down the price of players, induced other acts and record labels to release more music on CD and firmly established the format in the mind of the average consumer.

From its origins as a music format, Compact Disc has grown to encompass other applications. Two years later, in 1985, the CD-ROM (read-only memory), developed by Sony and Philips, was introduced. With this it was now possible to disseminate massive amounts (for the time) of computer data instead of digital sound. A CD can store around 640 megabytes of data, several hundred times as much as the most popular software distribution medium of the time, the floppy disk. A user-recordable CD for data storage, CD-R, was introduced in the early 1990s, and it became the de facto standard for exchange and archiving of computer data and music. The CD and its later extensions have been extremely successful: in 2004 the annual worldwide sales of CD-Audio, CD-ROM, and CD-R reached about 30 billion discs.

Compact discs are made from a 1.2 mm thick disc of polycarbonate plastic coated with a much thinner layer of Super Purity Aluminium (or rarely, gold, used for its data longevity, such as in some limited-edition audiophile CDs) layer which is protected by a film of lacquer. The lacquer can be printed with a label. Common printing methods for compact discs are silkscreening and offset printing. CDs are available in two sizes. By far the most common is 120 mm in diameter, with a 74-minute audio capacity and a 650 MB data or an 80-minute audio capacity and a 700 MB data. Such a standard disc weighs 15 grams. 80 mm discs are also available, a format which is mainly used for audio CD singles in some regions (e.g. Japan), much like the old vinyl single. Each such "miniCD" or "Maxi CD" can hold 21 minutes of music, or 180 MB of data (this form factor has also been called "CD3", since it is about three inches across).

Other unique shapes and smaller form factors have also been sold or given away as promotional items. Examples include Business Card CDs in the shape of a rectangular card and CDs shaped like the map of a country etc, although such discs are not always compatible with all CD players — they will work with any machine where the disc is inserted by manually clipping it onto the spindle (the mechanism used in virtually all portable CD players), but may not necessarily be inserted into drives which load the disc from a tray, or pull it into a slot. Irregularly shaped, non rotationally symmetric discs with an offset centre of mass may also cause damaging vibration if played in computer CD drives, which can operate at a much higher rotational velocity than stand-alone audio CD players. Some irregularly shaped discs will work with tray loading CD drives if they include a circular ridge on their underside which centers them on the part of the tray designed to hold 80 mm CDs, assuming the tray has such a feature.

There is a 15 mm hole in the centre of the disc, usually used by some form of clamp or clip device within the player to hold it in place and allow it to be rotated by a motor. The Diameter of this hole was agreed upon eventually as the same diameter as a 10 dutch cent coin as this being a denominating currency of dutch based company Philips.

The information on a standard CD is encoded as a spiral track of *pits* moulded into the top of the polycarbonate layer. (The areas between pits are known as *lands.*) Each pit is approximately 100 nm deep by 500 nm wide, and varies from 850 nm to 3.5 ìm long. The spacing between the tracks is 1.6 ìm. To grasp the scale of the pits and land of a CD, if the disc is enlarged to the size of a stadium, a pit would be approximately the size of a grain of sand. The spiral begins at the center of the disc and proceeds outwards to the edge, which allows the different size formats available.

A CD is read by focusing a 780 nm wavelength semiconductor laser through the bottom of the polycarbonate layer. The difference in height between pits and lands is one quarter to one sixth of the wavelength of the laser light, leading to a half-wavelength or less phase difference between the light reflected from a pit and from its surrounding land. The destructive interference thus reduces the intensity of the reflected light compared to when the laser is focused on just a land. By measuring this intensity with a photodiode, one is able to read the data from the disc. The pits and lands themselves do not represent the zeroes and ones of binary data. Instead a change from pit to land or land to pit indicates a one, while no change indicates a zero. This in turn is decoded by reversing the Eight-to-Fourteen Modulation used in mastering the disc, and then reversing the Cross-Interleaved Reed-Solomon Coding, finally revealing the raw audio data stored on the disc. Data CDs, unlike Audio CDs, require the removal of a third layer of Error Correcting Code, before the data is accessible in a useful format. This is because computer software could be rendered non-functional by a single incorrect bit, which is not the case for audio data.

Manufacturing Process

Mastering Process First, in a clean room, a glass master is prepared by coating a perfectly flat piece of half inch thick circular glass with a layer of nickel. The nickel is transferred by exciting the nickel to a plasma state whereupon a thin layer of nickel will adhere to the glass. The glass is coated with an emulsion. Source material is encoded into the appropriate format whereupon a computer controlled machine "burns" the pits into the emulsion layer of the glass master. The glass master produced is quality checked before it moves to the next stage.

Stamper Process Next the glass master is used to create nickel stampers using an electroplating technique. Multiple stampers can be made from one glass master. Each stamper is quality checked. This process is also done in a clean room environment.

Pressing Each stamper is mounted in an injection moulding machine. Melted polycarbonate resin is injected into the chamber and the CD is pressed using up to 40 tons of pressure. The chamber opens and a robotic arm grabs the disc and transfers it to the next stage. At this point the disc is clear, so a coating of aluminum is applied to the disc for reflectivity. A laquer is spin coated onto the disc and the disc is tranfered to a spindle. The discs are sampled by QC to ensure quality product.

Printing and Packaging: The label is printed onto the disc using a one to six color process (in the case of silk screening), then the printed discs are loaded into a packaging machine that combines a jewel box, tray card, the disc, and booklet. The finished assembly has security stickers applied, and is shrinkwrapped with marketing stickers applied. Sometimes the spindle of 150 discs are shrinkwrapped together in bulk. Bulk packaging can be done before or after printing.

Audio format

The format of the audio disc, known as the "Red Book" / Sony standard, was laid out by Sony and Philips in 1981. Philips is responsible for the licensing program of the intellectual property pertinent to the Compact Disc including the "Compact Disc Digital Audio" logo that appears on the disc. In broad terms the format is a two-channel (four-channel sound is an allowed option within the Red Book format, but has never been implemented) 16-bit PCM encoding at a 44.1 kHz sampling rate. Reed-Solomon error correction allows the CD to be scratched to a certain degree and still be played back.

The sampling rate of 44.1 kHz is inherited from a method of converting digital audio into an analog video signal for storage on video tape, which was the most affordable way to get the data from the recording studio to the CD manufacturer at the time the CD specification was being developed. A device that turns an analog audio signal into PCM audio, which in turn is changed into an analog video signal is called a PCM adaptor. This technology could store six samples (three samples per each stereo channel) in a single horizontal line. A standard NTSC video signal has 245 usable lines per field, and 59.94 fields/s, which works out at 44,056 samples/s. Similarly PAL has 294 lines and 50 fields, which gives 44,100 samples/s. This system could either store 14-bit samples with some error correction, or 16-bit samples with almost no error correction. There was a long debate over whether to use 14 or 16 bit samples and/or 44,056 or 44,100 samples/s when the Sony/Philips task force designed the compact disc; 16 bits and 44.1 kilosamples per second prevailed. The Sony PCM-1610 and PCM-1630 are well known examples of PCM adaptors used in conjunction with the Sony U-matic VCR.

During develpment the target storage capacity for the CD was sufficient for one hour of audio content, and a disc diamter of

11.5 cm was sufficient. However, according to Philips, Sony vice-president Norio Ohga suggested extending the capacity to 74 minutes to accommodate a complete performance of Beethoven's 9th Symphony on a single disk. The extra playing time required changing to a 12 cm disc.

According to a Sunday Times' interview the story is slightly more involved. At that time (1979) Philips owned Polygram, one of the world's largest distributors of music. Polygram had set up a large experimental CD disc plant in Hanover, Germany, which could produce huge amounts of CDs having, of course, a diameter of 11.5cm. Sony did not yet have such a facility. If Sony had agreed on the 11.5cm disc, Philips would have had a significant competitive edge in the market. Sony was aware of that, did not like it, and something had to be done. The long-playing time of Beethoven's Ninth imposed by Ohga was used to push Philips to accept 12cm, so that Philips' Polygram lost its edge on disc fabrication.

The 74-minute playing time of a CD, being more than that of most long-playing vinyl albums, was often used to the format's advantage during the early years when CDs and LPs vied for commercial sales. CDs would often be released with one or more bonus tracks, enticing consumers to buy the CD for the extra material. However, attempts to combine double LPs onto one CD occasionally resulted in an opposing situation in which the CD would actually offer fewer tracks than the LP equivalent.

The main parameters of the CD are as follows:

Scanning velocity: 1.2–1.4 m/s (constant linear velocity) - Equivalent to about 500 rpm at the inside of the disc, or about 200 rpm at the outside edge.

Track pitch: 1.6 ìm.

Disc diameter 120 mm.

Disc thickness: 1.2 mm.

Inner radius program area: 25 mm.

Outer radius program area: 58 mm.

The program area is 86.05 cm^2, so that the length of the recordable spiral is 86.05/1.6 = 5.38 km. With a scanning speed of 1.2 m/s, the playing time is 74 minutes, or around 650 MB of data on a CD-ROM. If the disc diameter were 115 mm, the maximum playing time would have been 68 minutes, i.e., six minutes less. A disc with data appearing slightly more densely is allowable. Using a linear velocity of 1.2 m/s and a track pitch of 1.5 micrometre leads to a playing time of 80 minutes, or a capacity of 700 MB. This is the limit for most conventional audio CDs today.

Another technique to increase the capacity of a disc is store data in the lead out groove that is normally used to indicate the end of a disk, and an extra minute or two of recording is often possible. However, these discs can cause problems in playback when the end of the disc is reached.

CD capacities are always given in binary units. A "700 MB" (or "80 minute") CD has a nominal capacity of about 700 MiB, but DVD capacities are given in decimal units. A "4.7 GB" DVD has a nominal capacity of about 4,489 MiB.

Data structure

Under a microscope, all that is visible is a series of various-sized pits arranged in a long spiral, starting near the inner hole. As bit-times are counted off, a transition (pit-to-land, or land-to-pit) is interpreted as a "1" bit, while a constant region (all-land or all-pit) is interpreted as a "0" bit. Each 14 consecutive bits are grouped and decoded using Eight-to-Fourteen Modulation to get a byte. Each 14-bit EFM word alternates with a 3-bit merging word.

The smallest entity in the CD audio format is called a *frame*. A frame can accommodate six complete 16-bit stereo samples, i.e.

2×2×6 = 24 bytes. Data in a CD-ROM are organized in both frames and sectors. A frame comprises 33 bytes, of which 24 are audio bytes (six full stereo samples), eight error correction, CIRC-generated, bytes plus one subcode byte. The eight bits of a subcode byte are available for control and display. In total we have 33*(14+3) = 561 channel bits. A 27-bit unique synchronization word is added, so that the number of channel bit in a frame totals 588. The synchronization word cannot occur in the normal bit stream, and can thus be used to identify the beginning of a frame.

A CD-ROM *sector* contains 98 frames, and holds 98×24 = 2352 bytes. The CD-ROM is in essence a data disc, which cannot rely on error concealment, and it requires therefore a higher reliability of the retrieved data. In order to achieve improved error correction and detection, a CD-ROM has a third layer of Reed-Solomon error correction. Note that the CIRC error correction system used in the CD audio format has two interleaved layers. A Mode-1 CD-ROM, which has the full third layer error correction capability, contains a net 2048 bytes of the available 2352 per sector. In a Mode-2 CD-ROM, which is mostly used for video files, there are 2336 user-available bytes per sector. The net byte rate of a Mode-1 CD-ROM is 44.1k×2048/(6×98) = 153.6 kB/s. The playing time is 74 minutes, or 4440 seconds, so that the net capacity of a Mode-1 CD-ROM is 682 MB.

A 1x speed CD drive reads 75 consecutive sectors per second.

A CD-ROM (data) sector contains 2352 bytes:

12 bytes: sync

4 bytes: sector ID

2 048 bytes: user data

4 bytes: error detection

8 bytes: null

276 bytes: error correction

An audio CD has a very different structure:

Subcode

Besides digital audio, a CD contains digital data called "subcode", which is multiplexed with the digital audio. The data in a CD are arranged in frames. A frame comprises 33 bytes, of which 24 are audio bytes (six full stereo samples), eight error correction, CIRC-generated, bytes plus one subcode byte. The eight bits of a subcode byte are available for control and display. The eight bits are used as eight different subcoding channels, and given letters designating their usage: *P*, *Q*, ..., *W*. Thus each channel has a bit rate of 7.35 (=44.1/6) kbit/s.

In each sector there are 2352 bytes (24×98) of audio content data and 96 bytes of subchannel data.

The 96 bytes of subchannel information in each sector contain four packets of 24 bytes apiece:

1 byte for command, 1 byte for instruction, 2 bytes for parityQ, 16 bytes for data, and 4 bytes parityP.

Each of the 96 subchannel data bytes can be thought of as being divided into eight bits. Each of these bits corresponds to a separate stream of information.

Channel	P	Q	R	S	T	U	V	W
Bit	7	6	5	4	3	2	1	0

Channel *P* is a simple pause/music flag, which can be used for low-cost search systems. Quite a few players ignore it in favor of the *Q* Channel.

Channel *Q* is used for control purposes of more sophisticated players. It contains positioning information, the Media Catalog Number (MCN), and International Standard Recording Code (ISRC). The ISRC is used by the media industry, and contains information about the country of origin, the year of publication, owner of the rights, as well as a serial number, and some additional tags:

Data

This track contains Data (rather than audio). Can be used for muting in audio CD players.

Copy Flag

Used by the Serial Copy Management System to indicate permission to digitally copy the track.

Four Channel Audio

The track uses four channel audio. This is very rarely used on Compact Discs.

Pre-Emphasis

The audio track was recorded with pre-emphasis. Used very rarely on Compact Discs.

Channels *R...W* are unused by Red-Book compliant CDs, and have been used for extensions to the standard.

CD-Text

CD-Text is part of the CD+G extension to the Red Book standard for audio CDs. It allows for storage of additional information (e.g. album name, song name, and artist) on a standards-compliant audio CD. The information is stored in the lead-in area of the CD, where there is roughly five kilobytes of space available, or in the *R* through *W* Subchannels on the disc, which are not used by strict Red Book CDs. About 31 megabytes of information can be stored there. The text is stored in a format usable by the Interactive Text Transmission System (ITTS). ITTS is also used by Digital Audio Broadcasting or the MiniDisc.

Note that the CD+G or "karaoke" extension also uses the R-W subchannels or subcodes to store low resolution graphics.

Three-Letter Codes

DDD digital tape recorder used during session recording, mixing and/or editing, and mastering (transcription).

ADD analog tape recorder used during session recording, digital tape recorder used during subsequent mixing and/or editing and during mastering (transcription).

DAD digital tape recorder used during session recording, analog tape recorder used during subsequent mixing and/or editing, digital tape recorder used during mastering (transcription).

AAD analog tape recorder used during session recording and subsequent mixing and/or editing, digital tape recorder used during mastering (transcription).

CD-ROM

For its first few years of existence, the compact disc was purely an audio format. However, in 1985 Yellow Book CD-ROM standard was established by Sony and Philips, which defined a non-volatile optical data storage medium using the same physical format as audio compact discs, readable by a computer with a CD-ROM drive.

Recordability

Injection moulding is used to mass produce compact discs. A "stamper" is made from the original media (audio tape, data disc, etc.) by writing to a glass disc (referred to as a glass master) coated with a photosensitive dye with a laser. This dye is then etched, leaving the data track. It is then plated to make a positive version of the CD. Polycarbonate is liquified and injected into the mold cavity where the stamper transfers the pattern of pits and lands to the polycarbonate disc. The disc is then metallized with aluminum and lacquer coated.

Recordable compact discs are injection molded with a "blank" data spiral. A photosensitive dye is then applied, and then the discs are metallized and lacquer coated. The write laser of the CD recorder changes the characteristics of the dye to allow the read laser of a standard CD player to see the data as it would an injection molded compact disc. CD-R recordings are permanent. The resulting discs can be read by most CD-ROM drives and played in most audio CD players.

CD-RW is a re-recordable medium that uses a metallic alloy instead of a dye. The write laser in this case is used to heat and alter the chemical properties of the alloy and hence change its reflectivity. A CD-RW does not have as great a difference in the reflectivity of lands and bumps as a pressed CD or a CD-R, and so many CD audio players cannot read CD-RW discs, although the majority of standalone DVD players can.

Copy protection

The Red Book audio specification does not include any copy protection mechanism. *Ripping* is the process by which the contents of an audio disc is copied out verbatim to a duplicate disc or re-encoded into some other format, such as MP3 or Ogg Vorbis.

An error-correcting code is included with Red Book audio to deal with small scratches or defects on the disc media. Where error correction fails on larger defects, audio CD players are expected to apply interpolation algorithms to conceal the loss of audio data.

Starting in early 2002, attempts were made by record companies to market "copy-protected" compact discs. Some of these deliberately introduced error patterns into audio tracks severe enough to defeat the error-correcting code (and hence defeat most CD-ROM drives attempting to copy the tracks as data), but not so disruptive as to prevent interpolation from working (hence allowing the same tracks to be played in audio mode without overly affecting fidelity). These discs are said to be more sensitive to disc pollution or surface damage (typically in the form of scratches) because they partially exhaust the error-correction thresholds incorporated into the Red Book standard right from the time of production.

Another copy protection method places a data track (usually containing bonus software for computer users) at the end of the disc and gives it an invalid size in the disc's table of contents. This is intended to prevent the data track from being ripped, but can be defeated by ignoring the table of contents and reading the disc sector by sector.

Philips has stated that such discs are not permitted to bear the trademarked *Compact Disc Digital Audio* logo because they violate the Red Book specification. It also seems likely that Philips' new models of CD recorders will be designed to be able to record from these "protected" discs. However, there has been great public outcry over copy-protected discs because many see it as a threat to fair use. For example, audio tracks on such media cannot be easily added to a personal music collection on a computer's hard disk or a portable (non-CD) music player. Also, many ordinary CD audio players, e.g. in car radios, have problems playing copy-protected media, mostly because they use hardware and firmware components also used in CD-ROM drives. The reason for this reuse is cost efficiency.

Other systems developed are Macrovision CDS-200 and Mediamax CD-3.

In any case, even if a disc cannot be directly ripped, it can still be played in audio mode, and the audio thence captured. Any loss of sound quality caused by this method is generally considered negligible. This is commonly referred to as the analog hole.

As stated above, a CD is made up of a layer of about 1.2mm of polycarbonate plastic which has been moulded from a master with pits burnt into it. The height difference between pits and lands is similar to that of oil on water, and something approaching the wavelength of visible light. When light hits a CD a small amount will be reflected off the outmermost plastic layer, with the rest being allowed through. When this light hits the metallic reflective layer it will bounce back off the different layers. The light reflecting off the different heights (as well as the sides of the "pits") will be out of phase. These phases will either interfere with each other (constructively or destructively), or have an in-between result. This has a similar effect to that of oil on water and like oil on water, the CDs are not exactly uniform in their shape (always at least very slightly warped) and hence different colors and reflectivness are produced.

Some commercially released audio discs have a "secret" bonus track. These may be an extension of the last audio track or a separate track hidden from the disc's table of contents. Either way, the hidden portion is heard when the disc is played to the end.

Other discs hide the extra material at the beginning of the disc. On most discs, the location of the first track listed in the table of contents immediately follows the table of contents itself. In this case, the hidden track is an unlisted track sandwiched between the two. To hear the hidden track, the listener must usually "rewind" the player past the beginning of the first listed track. Not all players allow this.

Barium ferrite A speaker magnet material made from an alloy with iron and barium for improved magnetic strength.

Barn doors Hinged doors mounted on a light, which may be positioned to direct or block off light.

Base The support for a carrier. Examples include the clear film that holds a film or magnetic tape emulsion, the aluminium plate that is coated with lacquer to make an instantaneous disc.

Base station The central transmitter in a communications system that acts as the cell hub for communicating with handsets and/ or mobile units.

Baseband When applied to audio and video, baseband means an audio or video signal that is not modulated onto another carrier (such as RF modulated to channel 3 or 4 for example). In DTV, baseband also may refer to the basic (unmodulated) MPEG stream.

Baseline JPEG A compression scheme used for JPEG images which displays the image in line by line passes.

Basket The metal frame structure of a standard dynamic loudspeaker. In larger, heavier speakers, this may be made of cast metal for extra strength and rigidity. All the other elements of the speaker are mounted on this structure.

Bass The portion of the audible sound spectrum that contains the lowest frequencies. These frequencies have the longest wavelength and require considerably greater electrical power to render them at their original strength. In a good modern speaker system, the bass portion of the response curve extends from as high as 500 hertz, down to 20 Hz.

Bass boost/enhancer circuit An active low pass amplifier section added to some receivers, equalizers, and amplifiers that allows as much as an 18 decibel boost to be applied to an audio signal in the low frequency 35 to 90 Hertz range.

Bass extension An imprecise term concerning how low in frequency a loudspeaker or subwoofer can still operate to produce usable output. A typical bookshelf-sized speaker may manage a bass extension of 80 hertz (say, at -10dB), a good floorstanding speaker may manage 30 or 40 hertz, an inexpensive subwoofer 40 hertz, a middling one 25 to 30 hertz, an expensive one 16 hertz.

Bass management A facility in home theatre receivers that permits some of the speakers in a 5.1 channel system to be specified as 'small' rather than 'large'. 'Large' speakers receive the entire signal for their respective channel, but 'small' speakers have the bass stripped off and sent elsewhere. If a subwoofer is attached, this bass goes to it, otherwise it goes to the front main speakers (you will notice that most systems will not permit you to select 'small' for the front stereo pair if you have the subwoofer set to 'off'). Some home theatre receivers permit you to choose the crossover frequency for bass management, but many use a standard value of 80 hertz.

Bass reflex A design for the enclosure of a loudspeaker. With bass reflex speakers the enclosure has a port that permits air to flow between the interior and exterior of the cabinet. The port is a hole, usually backed by a tube. The dimensions of the port are carefully calculated so that it permits bass at a selected frequency to be produced from the interior of the enclosure (driven by the back of the woofer's cone). This arrangement permits a bass reflex speaker to generally achieve greater efficiency than an acoustic suspension speaker, and it extends the depth at which bass may be produced without significant attenuation. However for frequencies below the band produced by the port, the output drops off quite rapidly.

Batch capture The ability of computer based editing suites to automatically capture whole lists or batches of clips from source videotapes.

Batch processing Allows you to apply a certain change such as resizing to a group of images all at once.

Bathos Excessive pathos, often unintentionally funny.

Baud rate The speed at which data is transmitted measured in symbols-per-second.

Baud The rate at which data is transferred. Named after Maurice Emile Baud. The Baud rate is equivalent to bits per second in cases where each data event represents exactly 1 bit. To communicate the baud rates of the equipment must be set the same. Note the baudrateandbit rate in a system can be different.

BBC British broadcasting corporation.

BBE 1 & 2 processing A signal processing circuit that provides improvements in imaging and spatial realism by altering the frequency and phase characteristics of portions of the input signal.

BBS(Bulletin board system) The father of newsgroups. A BBS allows one to 'paste' messages on an electronic bulletin board. The FTP service is usually also available on BBS's berkeley internet name domain.

Beat A stage direction indicating a brief pause the length of one stroke in the rhythm of the scene, signified by the expression beat or an ellipsis (. . .); the smallest unit of dramatic action; it is sometimes handy for preparation, rehearsal or taping purposes to divide scenes into beats or French scenes .

Bed Sound or music playing continuously under speech, as a musical bed for announcements, or a sound bed (ambience) under a scene.

Bel Abbr. b, B Ten decibels. (In honor of Alexander Graham Bell.) The Bel was originally a unit measure of the amount a signal dropped in level over a one-mile distance of telephone wire.

Belt Sometimes the loop of material that is used to transmit rotational energy from motor to record platter on a turntable. Here, we are referring to a set of extreme audio system tweaks popularised in the 1980s and beyond by Peter Belt in the United Kingdom. These tweaks, for the most part, have no measurable effect on the sound produced by the system and there is no rational reason why they would affect, let alone improve, the sound of the system. They include such ideas as placing an extra sheet of paper in all books within the listening room, to ensure that there are an odd number of leaves in each book, placing a sheet of paper 'twixt the floor and just one leg of your listening chair and, more recently, freezing and then defrosting your CDs. Try not to laugh. Some subjective reviewers have, over the years, sworn by these measures.

BER (Bit error rate) The ratio of received bits that are in error relative to the total number of bits received bit stream. The BER is expressed as a powers of 10 (usually multiples of 3 ie k, M etc) eg, a 1 bit error in 1 million bits is a BER of 10-6.

Bessel alignment A particular crossover configuration which offers superior phase coherence in exchange for slightly lower output level match.Bessel: A design that places emphasis on phase and transient response over reducing ripple.

Beta or betamax The first widely-used consumer-level video recording system on the market. Developed by Sony in the late 1970s, it eventually lost out to the rival VHS system, which came to market about a year later, primarily because of shorter playing and recording times.

Betacam An analog videotape format using 12.5mm tape developed by Sony and derived from the earlier Betamax. Also includes Betacam SP (Superior Performance), and digital versions Digital Betacam and Betacam SX.

Bi-Amplification Some speaker systems with multiple drivers do not contain a crossover network, and they require a separate amplifier for each frequency range. The bi-amplified system still requires an active crossover network to send the proper frequency band to each amplifier and speaker, but it is in the circuit preceding the amplifier and speaker and does not handle the power output.

Bi directional prediction A form of compression in which the Indeo video 4 codec uses information not only from frames that have already been decompressed, but also from frames yet to come. The codec looks in two directions: ahead as well as back. This helps avoid large spikes in data rate caused by scene changes or fast movement, improving image quality.

Bias An ultrasonic tone that an analogue tape recorder inserts on the tape while recording, to prevent sound distortion. Different types and brands of tapes require different biases during recording. Distortion may result when one type of tape is used for recording on a machine biased for another type.

Bible A treatment for a dramatic serial, series, or soap showing the continuity over a number of episodes.

Bibliographic description A set of formalised data elements describing a publication.

Bibliographic record A discrete bibliographic description stored either manually or electronically.

BIF (Broadband innovation fund) A Victorian Government initiative to encourage innovative use of broadband within Government. BIF aims to accelerate the rollout of broadband to government facilities such as schools and hospitals, which will also deliver improved broadband access to communities and businesses.

Billboard 1) The opening announcements to a program;

2) To make or record these announcements.

Billing The order and manner of publishing or announcing the names of the artists involved in a particular production; hence top billing, the artist mentioned most prominently.

Binary A base 2 numbering system using the two digits 0 and 1 (as opposed to ten digits [0-9] in the decimal system). In computer systems, the binary digits are represented by two different voltages or currents, one corresponding to zero and another corresponding to one, positive logic uses a positive voltage to represent binary 1 and zero volts to represent binary 0.

Binary file A file that can only be read with special software, such as word processors or image viewers. Binary files contain special, embedded codes (i.e. program commands) that create bold or underlined text, for example. Text files, on the other hand, contain no embedded codes.

Binaural sound A method of recording in conventional stereo that gives the listener the impression, not only of right and left, but also up and down, forward and back. The listener must wear earphones to perceive the binaural effect.

BIND (Berkeley internet name domain) BIND is an Internet Domain Name Service allowing aliasing of IP numbers (such as 197.45.67.176) to human recognizable names

Binhex Mac OS encoding scheme which converts normal computer files into ASCII (text) characters for transmission over the Internet. Binhexed files normally end with ".hqx" and must be returned to their binary format prior to use.

Bipole A loudspeaker designed to offer well-dispersed sound by firing its high frequencies, and in some models its full frequency range, in two opposing directions. Unlike dipole speakers, the sound is in phase from all the drivers.

Bipolar transistor A older but still effectively used transistor type that contains two p or n junctions or diodes between two layers of opposite polarity material (emitter and collector) . In handling large power, mostly replaced by MOSFET types.

Bit binary digit A bit is the smallest unit that is measured in digital computing systems. The bit relates to the on/off status of a processor. Eight bits make up one byte. The architecture of early personal computers was such that they could handle larger units than bits, namely eight bits at a time. This larger unit is called a byte. The early computers were thus 8-bit or 1-byte machines. Later machines could handle 16-bits or 2-bytes. The technology is now at the stage where PCs can handle 32-bit words and larger Unix-based systems 64-bits.

Bit depth The size of the number that records each digital sample. Since the system is digital, the number relates to powers of two. The compact disc uses a bit depth of 16, which allows 65,536 different levels to be used to track the analogue source signal. DVDs usually also use 16, but may also use 20 bits (which gives over a million levels) or 24 bits (which gives more than 16.7 million levels). The greater the bit depth, the lower the harmonic distortion and quantization noise, and the more storage space required for the signal.

Bit rate The number of digital bits a system transfers per second. In general, the higher the bit rate, the higher the quality of the signal. In every case, the higher the bit rate, the more data space required. With audio bit rates are measured in the hundreds of kilobits per second (kb/s). With DVD video, they are measured in megabits per second (mb/s).

Bit stream A continuous series of bits.

BITC (Burned-in time code) The timecode information is displayed within a portion of the picture, and may be viewed on any monitor or TV.

Bitmap Most common medium for images like photographs because they have subtle gradations. Examples include JPEG images. They are resolution dependent, meaning you cannot enlarge the image without a loss of quality.

Bitmap graphic A bitmap graphic is a pixel-based model for displaying images on display units such as computer and TV screens. A bitmap graphic contains data about the color and coordinates of each pixel that needs to be triggered on the computer screen. Strictly speaking bitmap graphics are not bitmaps, but pixelmaps.

Bitmap images Files that use a grid of pixels to display the image. The pixels are each assigned a secific location and color value.

Bitmaps on computer screens Bitmap graphic files are typically huge, so for better computer network transport they are compressed. The most typical bitmap compression methods on the Web are GIF, JPEG and PNG.

Another method for displaying images on computer screens is vector graphics.

Bitrate used to measure information flow, this indicates the number of bits (pieces of computer information) per given time interval. Digital audio is often measured in kbps (kilobits per second)

Bits per channel A measurement that specifies how many tones each color channel can contain

Bitstream The digital audio output of a DVD player, when switched to outputting the DVD's native digital audio format. Most DVD players can be switched to output a Dolby Digital bitstream, or convert the digital output to PCM.

BL (measured in Tesla meters) The product of a speaker driver's gap flux density and the length of the voice coil conductor in the gap.

Black box A term used to describe a piece of equipment dedicated to one specific function, also called dedicated hardware.

Black burst Black burst is a composite video signal with a totally black picture. It is used to synchronize together video equipment so the video outputs are aligned. Black burst tells the video equipment the vertical sync, horizontal sync, and the chroma burst timing.

Black level A part of the video signal, close to the sync level, but sometimes slightly above it (usually 20 mV - 50 mV) in order to be distinguished from the blanking level. This is called a pedestal. It electronically represents the black part of an image, whereas the white part is equivalent to 0.7 V from the sync level.

Blank skip A cassette feature that automatically detects blank areas of the tape over a set number of seconds in length and activates Fast Forward, until either the end of the tape, or audio information is reached.

Blank verse A type of verse popular in verse drama because it approximates the rhythm of natural prose speech in English. It is unrhymed iambic pentameter — that is, lines of five iambs, metrical feet consisting of one unstressed syllable followed by a stressed syllable, as in "The rose is in the garden of the king."

Blanking The portion of the video signal that is off, or black, during the retrace interval of the scan. Blanking occurs between each horizontal line and during the vertical retrace between each field.

Blanking is important in broadcast production situations since there are strict FCC rules defining the blanking periods. Not all video products for the Macintosh conform to this aspect of the NTSC broadcast standard. Discuss this issue with vendors if broadcast quality is required.

Related to composite sync, this signal has both horizontal and vertical components and is at its negative level whenever video is to be blanked or turned off.

Bleeding Video image imperfection characterized by blurring of colors.

BLOB(Binary large object) Which is a collection of binary data stored as a single entity in a database management system (DBMS). BLOBs are used to hold multimedia objects such as images, videos, and audio, but they can also store programs and code elements. Not all DBMSs support BLOBs.

Block To design the flow of movement and traffic patterns of objects (such as vehicles) and characters in a play, such as the placement of their entrances, exits and crosses hence, to teach the blocking to, or work it out with, the performers during rehearsal.

Blooming This is an effect, sometimes caused when video becomes whiter-than-white, in which a line that is supposed to be nice and thin becomes fat and fuzzy on the screen.

Blue book CD designed for laserdisc use.

Blue-ray A high capacity development of the DVD which uses higher frequency (blue) rather than red light frequencies for reading the disc. The combination of shorter wavelengths and other enhancements bumps up the maximum capacity from 8.5GB for a dual layer DVD to around 27GB, allowing the storage of high definition video.

BMP Bitmap file The official file format for Microsoft Windows images. BMP is an RGB-only format; it supports Indexed 256 colors, Grayscale and 24-bit RGB documents; does not support CMYK documents.

BNC BNC stands for Bayonet-Neil-Concelman connector, and it is the "standard" connector in CCTV and broadcast TV for transmitting a basic bandwidth video signal over a coaxial cable. It can also be used as abbreviations for British Naval Connector or Bayonet Nut Connector.

Board, mixing The dashboard of the sound studio. Also called console or board.

Bob One of several strategies used in deinterlacing video. Bobbing is where each alternate video scan line is shifted horizontally so that vertical lines are not displayed in a jagged fashion. This is useful for video sourced material, in which the two interlaced fields constituting the full video frame were actually captured at slightly different times from each other, causing a combed effect on vertical lines. Compare weave.

Bonus group A Group on a DVD Audio to which access can be gained only through entering a four digit numeric password. Rarely, if ever, used for any actual content.

Book rate The prices that a commercial sound studio publishes for its services. The book rate may have no relationship to real prices, except as a starting point for haggling.

Bookmarks Tags used by some Web browsers for marking and recalling frequently used URLs. These can also be called Favourites.

Boom channel (Also called "low frequency effects.") Very low frequency sounds that are fed only to a subwoofer.

Boom A hand-operated mechanical "arm," in a wide array of sizes, to assist in holding a device (such as a microphone) at a desired point where an arm is not possible or practical.

Boom microphone A pole-like device used to project the microphone over a set, and out of camera range, to pick up the sound of dialogue. It can be quickly lengthened or shortened according to need, and pointed in any direction as required. May also be called a fishpole or fishpole boom.

Boomy Usually refers to excessivly reverberant bass response, or a peak in the bass response of a recording, playback, or sound reinforcement system.

Booth The control room of a studio.

Bottlenecks Points on the network at which data transfer rates slow because of inadequate routers, switches, cables, or other equipment. Because of the tremendous amount of data they involve, video and audio can be especially prone to bottlenecking. The slowed data transfer rates associated with bottlenecking are sometimes referred to as network congestion.

Bounce To move the signal from one track or recording to another.

Bowser Odetics video browsing system that allows the viewer to track and view the material database

Box Another, and common name for a standard speaker enclosure. There are many variations in type, which are basically compromises between size, power handling, cost, frequency response, and many other considerations.

Boy The youthful male love interest in a play; an actor playing the role or specializing in such roles.

B-picture Bi-directionally predictive coded picture; an MPEG term for a picture that is coded using motion compensated prediction from a past and/or future reference picture.

BPS (bits per second) Bits per second refers to the number of bits transferred per a second through a medium. This unit of measurement is used to determine the bandwidth of the medium.

Bracketing The practice of taking more than one photograph of an area to ensure proper exposure. It's useful to do when multiple images overlapping each other must be blended together to create a panoramic immersive image.

Braid A number of metallic strands interwoven to form a tubular structure that may be applied over one or more wires or flattened to form a strap.

Breadcrumb trail A breadcrumb trail is a useful way of navigating a website. Taken from the children's fairy tale of Hansel and Gretel, a breadcrumb trail allows you retrace your steps through the website by a series of links at the top of the page that show where you currently are in the website.

Break 1) An interruption in the program for announcements such as commercials and station I.D.s;

2) to interrupt a program in this way.

Break key In Media Control Interface (MCI), a keystroke that interrupts a wait operation. By default, MCI defines this key as CTRL+BREAK. An application can redefine this key using the MCI_BREAK command message.

Breakdown/breakdowns (The singular and plural are used interchangeably.) Written project description used for casting purposes, of which the most important parts are thumbnail descriptions of the cast of characters.

Break-up A distortion of sound caused by over-modulation in which the sound becomes fuzzy or intermittent.

Breezeway That portion of the video waveform between the trailing edge of horizontal sync and the start of color burst.

BRI(basic rate interface) (ISDN) 3 digital signals over a single pair of copper wires: 2 voice (B) channels and 1 signal (D) channel. (e.g. voice and fax on a single pair of wires).

Bridge Bridge is a network related term.

A bridge operates on the Data Layer of the OSI model. A bridge keeps a record of each connected network segment. Bridges can be used for different protocols and serve as a filtering mechanism. Because the filter of a bridge can be configured to allow or disallow certain types of information, it forwards or ss frames for pre-determined network segments.

Bridge mounted (2 & 3-way speakers) In combined 2 and 3-way speakers, which have woofers together with a Tweeter, or a Tweeter and a Midrange Driver, the smaller drivers are attached to the woofer by either one of two standard mountings.

The bridge-mount method has a metal or plastic bridge running from one side of the woofer's outer perimeter to the other. The smaller driver or drivers, together with the Crossover network, is then mounted on the bridge. The advantage of this arrangement is that the woofer is left intact with no exposure of the voice coil or other internal elements. On the negative side, there is more covered surface area that marginally reduces the output at certain frequencies, and makes it a little more difficult to mount the unit.

The post-mount method provides a post that is attached to the center of the inner magnetic pole, to which the other drivers are then mounted. It has a reduced obstruction to woofer dispersion, but it does require a hole in the Dust Cover/Cap that can give environmental access to the woofer's inner workings. This creates the possibility in some less well designed units of operational degradation from airborne particles over time.

Bridged power Bridging an amplifier, combines the power output of two channels into one channel. Bridging allows the amplifier to drive one speaker with more power than the amp could produce for two speakers. Because of this high power output, bridging is the best way to drive a single subwoofer.

If the amp is bridgeable, the owner's manual will have directions that tell you how. Usually, an amp is bridged by connecting the speaker leads to the positive (+) terminal from one channel and the negative (-) terminal from the other channel. However, be sure to consult your owner's manual before attempting to bridge your amp!

Also, keep in mind that most amplifiers need to see a 4-ohm load when bridged to mono operation. When bridging an amplifier, use one 4-ohm speaker or, if you prefer multiple woofers, connect two 8-ohm speakers in parallel. Again, consult your manual before operating your amp in bridged mode.

Brightness 1. The luminance of the video signal, or the level of brightness on the scale from black to maximum white. One of the three determinants (with hue and saturation) of the color of an image, and the only one of the three that affects a monochrome image.

2. The brightness of a monitor or video projector measured in lumens.

Broadband Broadband is a term used describe high speed, high bandwidth internet connections that are "always on". A broadband connection allows you to use the internet at the same time as the telephone. Dial-up modems, where the modem has to dial a number to connect to the internet, are called "narrowband".

Broadcast Refers to signals intended for delivery over the television system, as well as network delivery to a wide audience.

Broadcast quality An NTSC composite video signal conforming to FCC rules concerning signal properties like video and sync levels, timing, and blanking. Devices providing NTSC signals do not necessarily meet FCC broadcast standards. This is important if the video signal or videotape being recorded is going to be used in a broadcast situation.

Browser A browser is a software program that interprets markup documents (such as HTML) and renders them visually on computer screens. At present the most common way to access The Internet is by means of a visual browser. With the advent of other media devices a browser is merely one of the ways used for accessing The Internet. As The Internet can be accessed by means of other media, such as audio, and in future smelling and touching, it is technically more correct to rather speak of a User Agent than of a browser. There are many browsers other than Netscape or Internet Explorer available for PCs, and there are "browsers", i.e user agents, for other types of visual devices, such as handheld devices, projection screens and others.

A parser (which is a part of a browser) investigates the elements and their relationships and determines the structure of the document. This is done on the bases of marked document objects. For example, in HTML paragraphs are marked as such with the <p>...</p> tag set. The parser then passes that information along to a rendering engine which manipulates the content, typically using associated style sheets to determine how the content is to be rendered. The most typical manipulation is to display the content graphically on a computer screen, but it could also be manipulated to be rendered on other types of devices, such as speech synthesizers or tactile devices (eg Braille devices).

Browser window This is the window on the screen where your internet browser displays the contents of a website document. One browser can have several windows open at once.

BS.707 This ITU recommendation specifies the stereo audio specifications (Zweiton and NICAM 728) for the PAL and SECAM video standards. Purchase the specification.

BSDI berkeley software distribution, inc BSDI is a flavor of Unix originally developed at the University of California, Berkeley Campus.

BSI British standards institute

BT.1119 Defines the widescreen signaling (WSS) information for NTSC and PAL video signals. For (B, D, G, H, I) PAL systems, WSS may be present on line 23, and on lines 22 and 285 for (M) NTSC.

BT.1124 Defines the ghost cancellation reference (GCR) signal for NTSC and PAL.

BT.1197 Defines the palplus standard, allowing the transmission of 16:9 programs over normal PAL transmission systems.

BT.1302 Defines the transmission of 16:9 BT.601 4:2:2 YCbCr digital video between pro-video equipment. It defines a parallel interface (8-bit or 10-bit, 36 MHz) and a serial interface (360 Mbps).

BT.1303 Defines the transmission of 16:9 BT.601 4:4:4:4 YCbCrK and RGBK digital video between pro-video equipment. Two parallel interfaces (8-bit or 10-bit, 36 MHz) or two serial interfaces (360 Mbps) are used.

BT.1304 Specifies the checksum for error detection and status for pro-video digital interfaces.

BT.1305 Specifies the digital audio format for ancillary data for pro-video digital interfaces.

BT.1358 720 x 480 (59.94 Hz) and 720 x 576 (50 Hz) 4:2:2 YCbCr pro-video progressive standards.

BT.1362 Pro-video serial interface for the transmission of BT.1358 digital video between equipment. Two 270 Mbps serial interfaces are used.

BT.1364 Specifies the ancillary data packet format for pro-video digital interfaces.

BT.1365 Specifies the 24-bit digital audio format for pro-video HDTV serial interfaces.

BT.1366 Specifies the transmission of timecode as ancillary data for pro-video digital interfaces.

BT.1381 Specifies a serial digital interface-based (SDI) transport interface for compressed television signals in networked television production based on BT.656 and BT.1302.

BT.1618 This ITU recommendation specifies a data structure for DV-based audio, data and compressed video at data rates of 25 and 50 Mbps.

BT.1620 This ITU recommendation specifies a data structure for DV-based audio, data and compressed video at data rates of 100 Mbps.

BT.470 Specifies the various NTSC, PAL, and SECAM video standards used around the world.

SMPTE 170M also specifies the (M) NTSC video standard used in the United States. BT.470 has replaced BT.624.

BT.601 720 x 480 (59.94 Hz), 960 x 480 (59.94 Hz), 720 x 576 (50 Hz), and 960 x 576 (50 Hz) 4:2:2 YCbCr pro-video interlaced standards.

BT.653 Defines the various teletext standards used around the world. Systems A, B, C, and D for both 525-line and 625-line TV systems are defined.

BT.656 Defines a parallel interface (8-bit or 10-bit, 27 MHz) and a serial interface (270 Mbps) for the transmission of 4:3 BT.601 4:2:2 YCbCr digital video between pro-video equipment.

BT.709 This ITU recommendation specifies the 1920 x 1080 RGB and 4:2:2 YCbCr interlaced and progressive 16:9 digital video standards. Frame refresh rates of 60, 59.94, 50, 30, 29.97, 25, 24, and 23.976 Hz are supported.

BT.799 Defines the transmission of 4:3 BT.601 4:4:4:4 YCbCrK and RGBK digital video between pro-video equipment. Two parallel interfaces (8-bit or 10-bit, 27 MHz) or two serial interfaces (270 Mbps) are used.

BT.809 This ITU recommendation defines Programme delivery control (PDC) system for video recording of PAL broadcasts.

BTL Bridged, transformer less. A circuit design wherein two small Integrated Circuit (IC) amplifier channels are bridged together to provide a single, larger output circuit. These circuits are limited by their current capabilities and the amount of heat they generate.

BTM Best tuning memory A feature in which the tuner selects radio stations by signal strength, and assigns them to presets in numerical order, according to their frequency value.

BTSC This EIA TVSB5 standard defines a technique of implementing stereo audio for NTSC video. One FM subcarrier transmits a L+R signal, and an AM subcarrier transmits a L-R signal.

Buffer Temporary storage area of data enabling the central processing unit (CPU) of a computer to manipulate data before transferring it to a device. Because the process of reading and writing data to a disk can be slow, many programs keep track of data changes in a buffer and then copy it to a disk.

Bug An error in a computer program. Also something that bites you on a camping trip.

Build 1) To increase the emotional level of a speech, sequence, scene, or act; 2), the increase thus made; 3), to overdub.

Built-in crossovers Frequently used to limit the high-frequencies reaching a subwoofer, a low-pass filter crossover allows only frequencies below the crossover point to be amplified. A high-pass crossover allows only frequencies above the crossover point to be amplified – used to keep destructive low bass away from small speakers, so they can played safely. Crossovers may be variable or selectable. Continuously Variable means the crossover circuit can be adjusted to any frequency between the listed end points. Selectable means that any of several preset crossover points can be chosen to accomodate variuous driver (speaker) designs.

Bullet horn (tweeter) A type of tweeter in which the radiator has a large passive, bullet-shaped device above its center that extends the nominal dispersion angle of the sound, thus allowing it to cover a greater area with high frequency radiation

Bump up Making a copy from one recording medium onto a second medium which is more suitable for post-production purposes due to it's higher bandwidth and/or timecode capability. For example, material shot on Hi8 is usually "bumped-up" to 3/4-inch SP or Betacam SP for editing purposes since these formats feature higher resolution, less generation loss, a more robust tape, timecode, better frame-accuracy and faster shuttle speeds.

Bumped & vented Many higher power speakers have a vent hole in the center Pole Piece of the magnet. When viewed from the back, there is usually a screen over the hole to prevent debris or particles from falling into the voice coil gap. But it does allow for greater ventilation of the motor section, and this in turn provides for higher power inputs by permitting greater heat dissipation for the voice coil assembly.

Bumped A method of woofer construction in which the rear suspension system is anchored a little further back by designing the back plate so that it is press stamped, or cast, outward. This allows greater Excursion of the voice coil, and prevents "bottoming out," which is very destructive to the coil form when large signals move the voice coil beyond its range limits. This technique does not eliminate the problem, but does help to reduce it.

Burn Term used to describe the process of writing data to a CD or DVD.

Burned in time code Time code numbers that are superimposed on the picture. Also called window bum.

Burst (colour burst or chroma burst) Ten cycles (PAL) or seven to nine cycles (NTSC) of sub-carrier placed near the end of horizontal blanking to serve as the phase (colour) reference for the modulated colour sub-carrier. It enables the monitors' Phase Locked Loop tosynchronize and track the change of phase during every line of video.

Burst gate This is a signal that tells a video decoder where the color burst is located within the scan line.

Buss or bus A signal-carrying conductor or electrical pathway designed to carry multiple signals. A mixing console auxiliary bus may carry signals derived from several channels on that console. The term is sometimes used to refer to a power distribution circuit, or "mains".

Butt splice 1) In editing, to join cues tightly together;

2) a splice so made.

Butterworth crossover A type of crossover circuit utilizing low-pass filter design characterized by having a maximally flat magnitude response, i.e., no variation in the amplitude response in the domain of the passband.

Button A method of input on a website. Often used to submit a form or activate a command.

Byte Is 8 binary bits (ones and zeroes). The greater multiples of bytes are shown below

Kilobyte (1,024 bytes)

Megabyte (1,024 kilobytes, 10488576)

Gigabyte (1,024 Megabytes 1073741824 bytes)

Terabyte (1,024 Gigabytes 1099511627776 bytes)

Petabyte (1,024 Terabytes 11258999 06842624 bytes)

Exabyte (1,024 Petabytes 11529215 04606846976 bytes)

Zettabyte (1,024 Exabytes 11805916 20717411303424 bytes)

Yottabyte (1,024 Zettabytes 120892581 9614629174706176 bytes)

C

C HTML (compact hypertext markup language) W3C NOTE 09 Feb 1998.

Small devices (such as cell phones and PDAs) have hardware restrictions such as small memory, low power CPU, small or no secondary storage, small display, mono-color, single character font, and restricted input method (no keyboard and mouse). These devices therefore cannot handle traditional HTML web pages. c-HTML was introduced as a scaled-down version of HTML, containing what is regarded as core HTML. Apart from scaling down the variety of typical HTML features, the following HTML features are excluded from c-HTML:

Table

JPEG image

Image map

Multiple character fonts and styles

Background color and image

Frame

Style sheet

c-HTML has been replaced by XHTML, which is a modular XML-compliant version of HTML.

C web Community Web: 'Community' = a set of people who share some common objectives and, more importantly, share common background knowledge. To reach their common objective, community members will increase and modify this common body of knowledge.

Cabin gain A low frequency boost normally obtained inside a vehicle interior when woofers are optimally in phase, and with the proper enclosures.

Cable equalization The process of altering the frequency bands of a video signal to compensate for the loss of high frequency in a cable. The video equivalent to a graphic equalizer in a stereo system.

Cable modem A device that allows computer data to be transferred through the cable wire common in most households. Cable modems allow for fast transfer rates in comparison to traditional (28.8, 56k, and even ISDN) modems.

Cable telephony This is the idea of using digital communications techniques to provide enhanced home telephone service via the exisiting home cable-TV connections. The bandwidth of cable is high enough to simultaneously support interactive cable-TV, telephone communications, and on-line data services. In this scenario, the cable connection becomes the primary link to the information highway vs. twisted pair telephone wire or a wireless connection.

Cache Caching (pronounced "cash-ing") is a technique used by computers to save memory and speed up access to files that are frequently opened. Web browsers cache web pages that have been recently downloaded on to your local hard drive, so they can be accessed quickly without having to download the file again from a distant server.

Cache file File that is used for virtual memory which can speed the performance of the running application.

Cadence 1)A falling inflection of the voice, as at the end of a sentence;

2) General inflection or modulation of the voice.

Calibration A process of making your monitor, printer and other devices ensure that they are all using accurate and similar color values.

Call The time and date at which one or more production personnel are scheduled to begin a casting, rehearsal, taping, or posting session. "My call tomorrow is for 6 in the morning, but Tiffany doesn't have to show up 'til noon."

Call, cattle. An audition session, in which actors are herded in and out as quickly as possible, so that they have only a few minutes to show what they can do.

Cameo A secondary or tertiary role in a dramatic work, sometimes lasting no more than one scene, that is played by a name who normally accepts only major roles.

Cameo lighting Directional lightling focused on a subject while standing in front of a black background.

Camera angle The angle at which a scene is photographed. The terms "high angle," "low angle," and "wide angle" are based on an imaginary norm which roughly corresponds to a 35mm camera with a 2-inch lens pointed at a scene from about eye level with the actors.

Camera crew The group of crew members who, variously, set up, load, operate, assist, focus, and move the camera.

Camera operator The person who operates the camera. Works closely with the director, and sometimes is the director himself.

Can, in the Finished, recorded. "The tracks are in the can."

Candela [cd] (or candle power) A unit for measuring luminous intensity. The modern definition is the candela is the luminous intensity, in a given direction, of a source that emits monochromatic radiation of frequency 540×10^{12} hertz and that has a radiant intensity in that direction of 1/683 watt per steradian. The frequency chosen is that to which the eye is most sensitive. This frequency is normally referred to as the corresponding wavelength: 555 nanometer. The strange choice of the number 683 is to make the value identical to that obtained with the previous version of the unit: the emission from 1 square centimeter of glowing, solidifying platinum. The old definition is :- One candela is approximately equal to the amount of light energy generated by an ordinary candle. Since 1948 a more precise definition of a candela has become: "1/60 of the light emitted from 1cm2 of the surface of a blackbody radiatorheld at the temperature at which platinumconverges from a liquid state to a solid (i.e. freezes)."

CANDP (Customer access network demonstrations program) The Customer Access Network (CAN) Demonstrations Program is a Victorian Government program that provides financial support to pilot alternative CAN telecommunications infrastructure in rural, regional and remote Victoria. The program is designed to improve the availability of technical, financial and commercial information on alternative CAN infrastructure technologies and business models to help promote investment in broadband telecommunications across the State.

Canned Removed or recorded, not benefiting from the synergetic interaction of spectators and performers sharing the same space, said of performance media such as video, cinema, and audio; prerecorded, as canned laughter.

Canon/cannon Brand name of multipoint connector used for professional audio equipment. Also known as XLR connectors.

Cantilever The thin rod within a turntable's cartridge that transmits the movement of the stylus in response to a record's groove to the interior components of the cartridge that generate the electrical signal.

Canvas In image editing suites this is your image workspace.

Capacitance The property of an electric device that permits the storage of energy as a result of electric displacement when opposite surfaces of conductive plates are maintained at a difference of potential. In a capacitor, capacitance is the measure of the property (the amount of charge that can be stored) equal to the ratio of the charge on either surface to the potential difference between the surfaces. Capacitance is measured in Farads, and micro, or pico-farads for smaller units.

Capacitor (power audio) Power stabilizing capacitors store the necessary power amplifiers need to punch larger bass notes while limiting clipping. They store energy during intervals when it is not required, which is most of the time, and release it when demand exceeds what is available from the car's power system. The amount of capacitance to be used is half (.5) farad per 500 watts of available RMS power. Capacitors are not used with amplifiers that supply less than 300 watts RMS in total.

Capex Also referred to as capital spending or capital expense. Capex is the money spent to acquire or upgrade physical assets.

Capture card A circuit board installed into a PC expansion card slot, which enables the user to record digital or analog video from an external source.

Capture, video Video capture cards let you record/digitize pictures for use with a computer. The pictures may be still-images or movies. Once captured, the picture data is compressed using a CODEC, with playback requiring CODEC-decompression. Intel's Smart Video Recorder board, an excellent capture card, can compress video real-time, or "on the fly", provided you have a fast machine and lots (and lots) of defragmented storage.

Cardioid "Heart" shaped pickup pattern characteristic of some microphones which reduces sensitivity to sounds from the sides and back.

Carrier A sine wave which may be modulated by a signal to form an AM signal. The frequency of the carrier must be significantly higher than that of the modulating signal. In practice, the carrier is usually a radio frequency sine wave, and so is two orders of magnitude higher in frequency than the signal.

Cart 1) A cartridge containing tape that can be instantly cued;

2) to transfer a recording to cart.

Cartridge The device that converts the movements of a stylus in the grooves of an LP to electrical signals. The cartridge is a small, light-weight device secured to the end of a turntable's tonearm by means of two screws mounted 12.5mm apart. The movements of the stylus are transmitted through a cantilever to some form of electrical generating device. The two main types of cartridge are ceramic and magnetic. The latter is further subdivided into moving magnet and moving coil types.

Cascading style sheet Instructions included in the HTML code of a Web site that describe how a browser should render any instance of a particular element on the page. For example, you can provide one-time instructions for how all of the hypertext or headings on a page should look. Cascading Style Sheets (CSS) are basically shorthand that makes HTML editing faster and easier. They are less important if you are using a WYSIWYG editor, though they can ensure consistency.

Case sensitivity If there is a difference between whether a word or letter needs to be entered in upper case (ABC) or lower case (abc) the system is said to be case sensitive. Usernames and passwords are often case sensitive, so it important you remember this information exactly.

Cast In Film and TV "cast " is used for the actors and extras. In Macromedia Director "cast" includes all the objects (i.e. text, graphics, sound, video, or Lingo scripting behaviors) used in a production. An object needs to be identified as a cast member before it can be used.

In terms of function the Director cast is similar to the Flash symbol library.

Catharsis (from a Greek word meaning purgation) The effect narrative and musical art sometimes have on an audience of purging it of or purifying its emotions, especially the emotions of fear and pity.

CAV(Constant angular velocity) As opposed to CLV. A method of spinning a disc or disk carrying a signal. CAV means that the rate of spin remains unchanged regardless of where the reading device is on the surface. An LP is an example (which is part of the reason why the outer tracks tend to sound better than the inner ones). While CDs are designed to be operated at a CLV, fast CD-ROM drives actually run them with a CAV.

C-band A range of microwave frequencies, 3.7~4.2 GHz, commonly used for satellite communications.

CBR(Constant bit rate) As opposed to variable bit rate. The signal (video or audio) is digitally encoded so that a fixed amount of data flows each second. This has the advantage of making the space requirements for the signal easy to calculate. DTS and Dolby Digital are both CBR systems, as are the earlier versions of MPEG audio and video compression. Most MP3 files are CBR encoded, although the format does support VBR as well.

CCD(Charge coupled device) A "bucket brigade" shift register device which when combined with photodiodes is the modern imaging device, replacing the old tubes. When first invented in the 1970s, it was designed to be used as a memory device, as an analogue shift register. Most often used in cameras, but also in telecine, fax machines, scanners, etc.

CCD Iris A term used by some manufacturers to describe automatic shutter control, to compensate for changes of lighting in a scene, without having any moving parts.

CCIF (Coordinated communications infrastructure fund) A Commonwealth Government program that supports health, education and other sectors to work together to secure broadband access and services in regional Australia.

CCIR 601 An international standard (renamed ITU 601) for component digital television that was derived from the SMPTE RP1 25 and EBU 3246E standards. ITU 601 defines the sampling systems, matrix values and filter characteristics for Y, Cr, Cb and RGB component digital television. It establishes a 4:2:2 sampling scheme at 13.5 MHz for the luminancechannel and 6.75MHz for the chrominance channels with eight bit digitizing for each channel. These sample frequencies werechosen because they work for both 525 line 60Hz and 625 line 50Hz component videosystems. The term 4:2:2 refers to the ratio of the number of luminance channel samples to the number of chrominance channel samples; for every four luminance samples, the two chrominance channels are each sampled twice.

CCITT (Committée consultatif internationale de telegraphique et telephonique) The CCITT, now known as the ITU-T (for Telecommunication Standardization Sector of the International Telecommunications Union), is the primary international body for fostering co-operative standards for telecommunications equipment and systems. It is located in Geneva, Switzerland.

CCTV camera A unit containing an imaging device that produces a video signal in the baseband form, usually with synchronization pulses and colour information (composite video).

CCTV (Closed circuit television) A television system intended as a "closed" system, rather than broadcast, to be viewed by only a very limited number of viewers e.g. 1 camera to 1 monitor in its simplest form.

CCTV installation A CCTV system, or an associated group of systems, together with all necessary hardware, auxiliary lighting, etc., located at a site to be monitored.

CCTV system An arrangement comprising of a camera and lens with all ancillary equipment required for the surveillance of a specific area.

CCVE(closed circuit video equipment) An alternative acronym for CCTV created by a manufacturer.

CD (Compact disc) The most popular format for conveying music and data currently available. It is among the first digital media to take over from the analog formats of phonograph records and tapes; coming to the market in the early 1980's. Developed by Phillips, Sony, and Pioneer, it records information on the now familiar shiny discs by deforming the inner metal foil on the disc with tiny micro pits burned in by a laser. These pits taken together, form a binary digital code, which when converted to bits, then bytes, can recreate the original information, such as audio. It's superiority as a format, consists of the fact that the process gets around such problems as: noise, hiss, pops, transducer irregularities, and other audible problems that made analog carriers a less than fully high fidelity mode. Dynamic range exceeds 100 decibels, a sufficient soft/loud difference to make the reproduction very lifelike. Frequency response is at the theoretical limits of human hearing and unwanted aural artifacts are generally below the threshold of perception. The only significant improvement is the DVD borne addition of multiple channels, to recreate the original sonic environment. In short, it's the best thing to come along since Mozart sat down at the piano.

CD burner Another term for CD Recorder.

CD Changer Separate units that may allow the user to hear any of 3 to 120 discs, or more in whatever order they wish to program them, or to skip from one track to another, or from one disc to another. Many of these come with separate controller units that allow for user operation and programming. Some are built to take advantage of controller systems built in to many receivers expressly for that model. Many also have a device called an FM modulator that permits connection to any standard FM stereo radio. The signal can be heard on whatever unused frequency the radio is tuned to. Most changers also permit direct audio outputs to any standard RCA high impedance, line level, input. This is the preferred input to avoid noise and distortion that may occur with radio usage.

CD Receiver Multiple function receivers are most commonly configured with radio and CD player capabilities in standard car receiver (head end) units. These may include cassette tape decks as well, and may also have high power amplifiers (over 15 watts RMS) installed in them. Some units may even have mini 3 to 5 disc changers in them. Among common and desirable features are:

Four speaker outputs with a fader control to balance front and back; Bass and Treble controls; Left right balance; 12 or more presets for AM & FM stations; Random play for the CD; digital clock. FM mono sensitivity should be at least 13dBf. Preamp outputs are desirable: minimum output voltage should be at least 1.8 volts. Also, audio line inputs for the CD changer you may want later. Remember that RMS output power is usually no more than half of the "peak power" rating.

CD-ROM "hybrids" CD-ROM's with embedded Internet links. Although the Web can provide current information, i.e. timely updates and corrections, it lacks the bandwidth to deliver large multimedia files quickly. The "Internet-enabled" CD-ROM, or "cybrid," is being touted as a software solution that will use the strengths of both technologies. The parts of a program that can slow down access time if downloaded from the Internet (multimedia, index searches) are kept on the CD-ROM for faster loading. The Internet side of the equation is used for providing, and for adding new features without the need to send out a new CD-ROM disc. In the near future, look for hybrid DVD's.

CD+G Compact Disc plus Graphics is a format that includes limited video graphics capabilities in a CD-DA format. Mostly used in Karaoke (sing-along) devices.

CDA CDA stands for CD Audio.

You can play .cda files only from a CD-ROM. The tracks however, can be ripped to your HDD as a digital audio format like WAV, wma, or MP3 files.

CD-DA Compact Disc Digital Audio, or CD-DA, contains musical or audio information that is encoded digitally. CD-DA is the standard format used by the music industry.

CDFS CD-ROM file system.

CD-I Compact disc-interactive, developed by Phillips/Sony, includes audio, full-screen video and interactive capabilities. Follows ISO's "Green book" standard.

CDMA Code-division multiple access, or a digital cellular technology applying what is called "spread-spectrum techniques". This differs from GSM, for example, which does not assign a specific frequency to each user. Instead, every channel uses the full available spectrum.

CDs A generic term used to represent all optical laser compact disc formats including, but not limited to CD-DA, CD-i, CD-ROM, Video CD, and CD+G. Typically, a CD is 4.72" in diameter.

Cellulose The main structural material of plants, the fibres of which are used for textiles, paper and synthetic resins.

Celsius The Systeme Internationale (SI) unit of temperature equivalent to the Centigrade scale. It does not use the prefix "degrees".

Center channel In home theater, a signal sent to a speaker mounted in front of the listener, specially designed to enhance voices and sound effects associated with center stage action from a movie soundtrack. Sometimes used in car audio to help offset skewed stereo imaging due to seating positions in the automotive environment.

Ceramic cartridge A cartridge that produces an electrical signal through a piezoelectric effect. Such cartridges are rarely used in high fidelity applications because they require a relatively high tracking weight (usually upwards of 10 grams), have a low compliance and produce an uneven frequency response. However they do have the advantage of producing a rather higher output voltage than magnetic cartridges, and their frequency response characteristics approximate the RIAA equalization curve, allowing simpler circuitry to be used with the signal.

CERN (conseil européen pour la reserche nucléaire) The European Laboratory for Particle Physics is the birthplace of the World Wide Web, the institution where Tim Berners-Lee served as consultant when he created HTTP and HTML. CERN httpd was written by Ari Luotonen, Henrik Frystyk and Tim Berners-Lee.

Certificate Sometimes reffered to as a digital certificate. An attachment to an electronic message used for security purposes.

Certification authority (CA) A trusted third party organization or company that issues digital certificates.

CFA (Colour filter array) A set of optical filters (usually individual pixel sized) used in single chip colour CCD cameras to produce the colour components of a video signal.

CG Acronym for character generator.

CGI (common gateway interface) Server-side programs, running at the request of the client, that typically perform interactive Web actions. Normally, servers "serve" the content of static files (html, images, movies, sounds). In CGI, clients request a program to be executed and its results to be returned, as in database or search applications. All form-processing requires CGI. (in-depth look).

CGMS-A Copy Generation Management System - Analog (CGMS-A).

Channel Common name for a complete amplifying stage in any audio amplifier. Most amplifiers are denominated as 1, 2, 4, 5, or 6 channel units. Each of these is a discrete audio amp on its own, capable of taking a small line signal input and amplifying it sufficiently to be heard on an appropriate speaker. Some amplifiers are capable of bridging two channels together, to form one channel of double the power of each separately. The manufacturer's instructions differ widely on how to accomplish this, and each must be followed exactly.

Channel map A channel map, provided by the MIDI Mapper, that can redirect Musical Instrument Digital Interface (MIDI) messages from one channel to another.

Chaoji videoCD Another name for Super VideoCD.

Chapter The divisions within a Title on a DVD Video. Navigation is most easily achieved by using the forward and reverse 'skip' keys of the DVD player's remote control.

Character generator A character generator (CG) is a video device found in on-line editing suites used for titles and credits. A CG is simply a high-end word processor for video with a wide variety of fonts and sizes available. The most common character generator is the Chyron.

Character man/woman An actor or actress specializing in mature roles or roles that call for great skill with superficial detail, such as regional accents and physical quirks.

Character set There are tens of thousands of characters used in human writing systems. Unicode lists about 40'000 of these characters. On 8-bit PCs only 128 characters can be mapped to machine code, definitely not enough to handle all these characters. The Unicode characters are divided into sets of characters. A PC needs to be set up to use a particular set. Documents that are distributed over the internet need to specify in which character set they are written so that devices that receive them can render them correctly by first adapting to the specified character set.

Charge coupled device (CCD) A sensor that will convert a light value passing through a cameras lens into an electronic equivalent of the color.

Chebyshev filter A filter that has some ripple in the pass-band but has an initial attenuation slope which is steeper than a Butterworth filter.

Checksum An error-detecting scheme which is the sum of the data values transmitted. The receiver computes the sum of the received data values and compares it to the transmitted sum. If they are equal, the transmission was error-free.

Chip An integrated circuit in which all the components (resistors capacitors and semiconductors) are micro-fabricated on a tiny piece of silicon or specialist material (silicon on sapphire). Often used to refer to the detector in a CCD camera.

Chip rate In spread spectrum systems, this is the rate at which the pseudo-random noise code is applied. In frequency hopping systems, chip rate is the inverse of the dwell time which the output frequency occupies a single carrier frequency. Also called "chipping rate".

Chirp Pulsed frequency modulation scheme in which a carrier is swept over a wide frequency band during a given pulse interval.

Chord A combination of two or more notes played simultaneously.

Chorus 1. A narrator, as in the Elizabethan theater;

2. the group of singers and dancers of the ancient Greek theater who performed choral odes commenting on the action between scenes, and who, singly and as a group, interacted with the actors during the scenes;

3. the singing and dancing ensemble of a musical theater production;

4. any character or characters in a dramatic work whose dramatic function is to comment on the action.

Chroma bandpass In a NTSC or PAL video signal, the luma (black and white) and the chroma (color) information are combined together. If you want to decode an NTSC or PAL video signal, the luma and chroma must be separated. A chroma bandpass filter removes the luma from the video signal, leaving the chroma relatively intact. This works reasonably well except in images where the luma and chroma information overlap, meaning that we have luma and chroma stuff at the same frequency. The filter can't tell the difference between the two and passes everything. This can make for a funny-looking picture. Next time you're watching TV and someone is wearing a herringbone jacket or a shirt with thin, closely spaced stripes, take a good look. You may see a rainbow color effect moving through that area. What's happening is that the video decoders thinks that the luma is chroma. Since the luma isn't chroma, the video decoder can't figure out what color it is and it shows up as a rainbow pattern. This problem can be overcome by using a comb filter.

Chroma Chroma is also known as saturation or intensity, and refers to how much of the same hue is present in a color. It refers to the "brightness" of a color. When a primary color is added to, or substracted from itself, its chroma is changed. A color is fully saturated when no other color, no white or no black is added to it.

The primary color blue becomes peacock blue if its chroma is increased, while it becomes navy when its chroma is reduced.

Chroma crawl An artefact of encoded video, also known as dot crawl or cross.

Chroma demodulator After the NTSC or PAL video signal makes its way through the Y/C separator, the colors must be decoded. That's what a chroma demodulator does. It takes the chroma output of the Y/C separator and recovers two color difference signals (typically I and Q or U and V). Now, with the luma information and two color difference signals, the video system can figure out what colors to display.

Chroma gain (chroma or colour, saturation) In video, the gain of an amplifier as it pertains to the intensity of colours in the active picture.

Chroma key This is a method of combining two video images. An example of chroma keying in action is the nightly news person standing in front of a giant weather map. In actuality, the person is standing in front of a blue or green background and their image is mixed with a computer-generated weather map. This is how it works: a TV camera is pointed at the person and fed along with the image of the weather map into a box. Inside the box, a decision is made. Wherever it sees the blue or green background, it displays the weather map. Otherwise, it shows the person. So, whenever the person moves around, the box figures out where he is, and displays the appropriate image.

Chroma trap In a NTSC or PAL video signal, the luma (black and white) and the chroma (color) information are combined together. If you want to decode the video signal, the luma and chroma must be separated. The chroma trap is one method for separating the chroma from the luma, leaving the luma relatively intact. The NTSC or PAL signal is fed to a trap filter. For all practical purposes, a trap filter allows certain frequencies to pass through, but not others. The trap filter is designed with a response to remove the chroma so that the output of the filter only contains the luma. Since this trap stops chroma, it's called a chroma trap. The sad part about all of this is that not only does the filter remove chroma, it removes luma as well if it exists within the frequencies where the trap exists. The filter only knows ranges and, depending on the image, the luma information may overlap the chroma information. The filter can't tell the difference between the luma and chroma, so it traps both when they are in the same range. Using a comb filter for a Y/C separator is better than a chroma trap or chroma bandpass.

Chrominance-to-luminance intermodulation (crosstalk, cross-modulation) An undesirable change in luminance amplitude caused by superimposition of some chrominance information on the luminance signal. Appears in a TV picture as unwarranted brightness variations caused by changes in colour saturation levels.

Chunk The basic building block of a Resource Interchange File Format (RIFF) file, consisting of an identifier (called a chunk identifier), a chunk-size variable, and a chunk data area of variable size.

CIE Commission internationale de l'eclairagé This is the International Committee for Light, established in 1965. It defines and recommends light units.

CIE Model A colour model based on human perception developed by the CIE (Commission Internationale de l'Eclairage) committee. While widely regarded as the most accurate colour model, CIE is unsuitable for many technologies, including colour printing and colour monitors. Consequently, these systems need to use other colour models, such as CMYK and RGB. There is a growing trend, however, to make all colour models relative to the CIE model. This would make it easier to translate from one model to another.

CIF(Common intermediate format) A video format used in videoconferencing systems that easily supports both NTSC and PAL signals. CIF is part of the ITU H.261videoconferencing standard. It specifies a data rate of 30 frames per second (fps), with each frame containing 288 lines and 352 pixels per line. A related standard, QCIF (Quarter CIF), transfers one fourth the amount of data and is suitable for videoconferencing systems that use telephone lines.

Cinch plug Another name, used by companies that presumably don't like to use the opposition's brand name in their own literature, for RCA plug.

Cinematographer (director of photography or dp, first cameraman or lighting cameraman) The artist or technician in charge of photography. His or her expertise with lights, lenses, cameras, film stock and processing establishes the "look" and "mood" of a film. He or she typically works in close consultation with the Director.

Cinepak A video compression CODEC developed by Apple for use in QuickTime movies and often used for web-based delivery. Though Cinepak can create highly compressed files, it sometimes results in annoying artifacts.

CIP Cataloguing-in-publication records, created using information supplied pre-publication by the publisher.

Circuit breaker An electrical switch that automatically breaks a circuit if the current through it is higher than its rating. Once tripped it can be manually reset. Performs the same function as a fuse, but eliminates the need for replacement after activating.

Cladding The outer part of an optical fibre cable, which is also glass but with a different refractive index to the central core. It enables "total internal reflection" so that the light transmitted through the central core stays, inside that core.

Clamping (DC) The circuit or process that restores the DC component of a signal. A video clamp circuit, usually triggered by horizontal synchronizing pulses, re-establishes a fixed DC reference level for the video signal. DC clamping can, in some cases remove of low-frequency interference, especially mains hum.

Class A/B A power amplifier in which a certain amount of DC bias voltage is applied to the power transistors so that, at low power outputs, the output signal operates entirely in the positive or negative part of the cycle, avoiding crossover distortion. Thus, at low outputs, a Class A/B amplifier operates in Class A mode. At higher outputs the signal does cross over the zero point, effectively entering Class B territory. This design is a compromise between the efficiency of Class B amplifiers (in which there is no DC bias) and the elimination of crossover distortion in Class A designs. The DC bias is filtered out before being fed to the speakers.

Claymation Animation where a picture is taken of a model, usually made out of clay, and then manipulated so that there is a small difference in the shape of the model, then a second picture is taken and the whole process is repeated. Also called Stop Motion Animation.

Clean list (clean EDL) An EDL which does not contain any overlapping or redundant edits. Typically during the off-line editing process changes are made which result in edits that overlap or become redundant. Most computer-based editing systems can clean an EDL automatically. Compare dirty list.

Clean speech A take in which all dialogue was performed without error.

Client A client is a device that receives data or programs from a server. This device may be a different computer, or a 'virtual' computer inside a physical computer.

Client application Any application or compiled object intended to run on a client computer.

Client script Sometimes called cleint-side scripts which are embedded into an HTML document and are run by the web browser.

Client/server computing The model or scheme underlying programs running on the Internet as well as other network and database software. In this design, the work of an application is divided between two programs - the client (or "front end") and the server (or "back end"). The client program handles the work of connecting to the server and requesting files or information, and the server handles the work of finding and "serving up" the information (or of providing some other service such as directing documents to be printed to a printing device).

Client/server Set of computer applications (programs) in which two or more computers work together. Server(s) store data and programs, which they deliver on request to clients. Part of the processing is done on the client, while the server concentrates on storing and delivering the data to be processed. This interaction between the client and server occurs in the background, so users are typically unaware which computer handles what.

Cliff effect Where the degradation of a signal's reception does not gradually increase with a reduction in signal quality or strength, but maintains full quality until some threshold, at which point the signal collapses into incoherence. Analogue transmissions tend to degrade gradually. Digital transmissions in modern systems (with error correction built in) tend to maintain full quality, but then cut out completely at the threshold.

Climax The highest point of tension in the dramatic action.

Clip 1) To cut off the beginning or end of a syllable, sound or musical note, usually by accident, as in a bad edit or improper setting of a sound-processing device, such as a gate;

2) to rush; to top.

Clip art Collections of pictures/photographs. Many application programs, such as PowerPoint, contain built-in clipart.

Clipboard A temporary holding area for information that has been previously copied using the Copy or Cut commands.

Clip or video clip A segment of a larger video. A clip is typically that portion of a full video or movie that will be used to create another digital project using a digital movie-making program such as MovieShop™. A professionally produced full-length movie can consist of hundreds or thousands of clips.

Clipping A signal that results from an amplifier that is either overloaded or underpowered relative to the signal Amplitude it being asked to generate. A clipped waveform is one in which the gently rounded peaks and valleys of the AC audio wave are instead sliced off or clipped, to yield what looks a lot like a square or alternating DC wave. When DC is applied to a speaker, the voice coil has no means of propelling itself relative to a constant magnetic field. Instead, it can only convert the incoming current to heat, and ultimately burns up. The effect of alternating DC on speakers is remarkable, irritating, painful, and short. If you are able to hear evident Distortion at high volume levels, or smell smoke, reduce the volume. It may already be too late for your speakers, but at least you may be able to save the amplifier.

Clipping level An electronic limit to avoid overdriving the video portion of the television signal.

Clipping logic A circuit used to prevent illegal conversion. Some colors can exist in one color space but not in another. Right after the conversion from one color space to another, a color space converter might check for illegal colors. If any appear, the clipping logic is used to limit, or clip, part of the information until a legal color can be represented. Since this circuit clips off some information and is built using logic, it's not too hard to see how the name "clipping logic" was developed.

Clocking signal A signal used to synchronise items of equipment which are communicating digital audio or video signals to each other. The lack of a suitable clocking signal would allow their timing to drift apart from each other since their internal clocking signals would generally not be identical, so digital samples would be lost.

Cloning The process of copying pixels from one part of an image and pasting it into another part.

Close up (CU) A tight shot that close enough to show an actor's head and upper torso.

Closed captioning A service which decodes text information transmitted with the video signal and displays it on the display. For NTSC, the caption signal may be present on lines 21 and 284. For PAL, the caption signal may be present on lines 22 and 334.

For MPEG-2 video, including ATSC and DVB, the closed caption data are multiplexed as a separate data stream within the MPEG-2 bitstream. It may use the picture layer user_data bits as specified by EIA-708, or in PES packets (private_stream_1) as specified by ETSI EN 301 775.

For DVD, caption data may be 8-bit user_data in the group_of_pictures header (525/60 systems), a digitized caption signal (quantized to 16 levels) that is processed as normal video data (625/50 systems), or a subpicture that is simply decoded and mixed with the decoded video.

Close-mike To track each actor with his or her individual microphone, which requires close proximity of actor and mike . Close-micing adds warmth to the voice (called the proximity effect) and reduces the signal to noise ratio.

Cloth ears A purported characteristic of a person, the possession of which is alleged to account for his or her inability to notice differences in the sound quality produced by different pieces of equipment. Those so accused, assuming they have taken care to listen carefully to the demonstration, should forthrightly reject the allegation.

CLV (Constant linear velocity) As opposed to CAV. A method of spinning a disc or disk carrying a signal. CLV means that the rate of spin varies in order to maintain a constant velocity of the track at the point where the reading device is on the surface. A CD playing back in an audio CD player is an example of this, because the CD player runs at about 500rpm at the start of the CD (where the inner grooves are being read), gradually reducing speed to about 200rpm as the track nears the outer edge.

Cmap files Files that are used to access character sets in double-byte fonts such as Japanese.

C-mount adaptor An adaptor used to convert a CS-mount camera to C-mount to accommodate a C-mount lens. It is simply a ring 5 mm thick, with a male thread on one side and a female on the other side. It has a 1" diameter and 32 threads/inch, as the cameras and lenses. It often comes packaged with the newer type (CS-mount) of cameras. CMYK. A 4 colour encoding system used by many computer printers, in which colours are expressed by the "subtractive primaries" (cyan, magenta and yellow) plus black (called K). The black layer is added to give increased contrast and range.

C-mount cine mount The first standard for CCTV lens screw mounting. It is defined with the thread of 1" (25.4 mm) in diameter and 32 threads/inch, and the back flange-to-CCD distance of 17.526 mm (0.69"). The C-mount description applies to both lenses and cameras. C-mount lenses can be put on both, C-mount and CS-mount cameras, but must use a C-mount adaptor when used on a CS-mount camera. If a C adaptor is used on a C-mount camera the image will only focus at very short range, it can then be considered as an economy macro adaptor.

CMS In the context of the web, it's an abbreviation for Content Management System. The content of a website is stored in a database on a server and the HTML is generated on the fly when a visitor accesses a page. Content is changed and created using a web browser allowing users to update their site from remotely.

CMX The most commonly used editing computer. The EDL is loaded into it and it executes the edits and effects by controlling all of the required video machines. Actually, it may not control all of them. Certain operations may need to be done manually. Most editing computers use the CMX language, which has become an industry standard.

CMYK (cyan, magenta, yellow, k (for black)) The CMYK color scheme is a substractive color scheme where a color is substracted from white light. This scheme is commonly used for devices such as printers because printer inks can be easliy manipulated by removing some hue. By combining certain color hues, the resulting color is absorbed, and thereby prevent it from being reflected by white.

Cyan (a turquoise-like, or blue-green color hue) absorbs red from white and transmits blue plus green. Cyan is derived from the Greek word kyanos, which means blue.

Magenta (a pinkish color hue, also known as hot pink or fuchsia) absorbs green, so it is red plus blue. Magenta is named after the town Magenta in northwest Italy.

Yellow absorbs blue, so it is red plus green.

Black absorbs all the above colors, but in practice it is easier to print with a separate black color rather than mixing these three colors.

Coax, coax cable A high capacity copper-wire cable that carries audio and video signals and radio frequency (RF) energy, consisting of an outer conductor concentric and inner conductor, separated from each other by insulating material. It has more bandwidth than twisted pair, but less bandwidth that fiber-optic cable.

Coaxial digital The digital audio output signal of a DVD player in an electrical format, rather than optical. The data format accords with the S/PDIF specification.

Code (1) A set of symbols for representing something. E.g. most computers use ASCII codes to represent characters.

(2) Written computer instructions. The term code is colloquial.

Codec Compressor and decompressor. An algorithm to reduce the size of audio or video data General purpose multimedia file formats, such as AVI and Quicktime rely on external codecs to do the compression and decompression – the algorithms are not part of the file format. This means that if you compress a file with a given codec, the user viewing the file must have the same codec installed to decompress it .

For video, we recommend using one of the following codecs for distribution.

RealVideo (codec included in RealPlayer)

Sorenson (codec included in Quicktime 3 Player and above)

MPEG-4 (codec included in Quicktime 6 Player and above)

MPEG-1 (codec included in most video players)

Some codecs are free and/or bundled with poular operating systems and media players. Others must be purchased and can be fairly expensive. Be sure your target audience will have access to the appropriate codec in order to decompress your movie.

Coded description MPEG-7 A Coded Description is a Description that has been encoded to fulfil relevant requirements such as compression efficiency, error resilience, random access, etc.

Coded orthogonal frequency division multiplexing Coded orthogonal frequency division multiplexing, or COFDM, transmits digital data differently than 8-VSB or other single-carrier approaches. Frequency division multiplexing means that the data to be transmitted is distributed over many carriers (1,705 or 6,817 for DVB-T, as opposed to modulating a single carrier. Thus, the data rate on each COFDM carrier is much lower than that required of a single carrier. The COFDM carriers are orthogonal, or mutually perpendicular, and forward error correction ("coded") is used.

Coder Also referred to as Encoder and is that portion of the CODEC that digitizes the analog signals to be placed on the digital fiber optic network.

COFDM A multiplexing technique rather than a modulation technique. One of any of the common modulation methods, such as QPSK, 16-QAM or 64-QAM, is used to modulate the COFDM carriers.

Collagen Proteineous substance yielding gelatine.

Colloquy An extended passage of dialogue between two characters in a play.

Color The physics of color is made up of a subset of the electromagnetic spectrum which, when combined, shows as white. Human eyes are physiologically adapted to view such rays, when they are reflected from objects, as colors.

On CRT screens (such as computer or TV screens) electron beams light phosphors of three different frequencies: red, green and blue. The color palette is divided into hues of red, green and blue (RGB).

Color bars This is a test pattern used to check whether a video system is calibrated correctly. A video system is calibrated correctly if the colors are the correct brightness, hue, and saturation. This can be checked with a vectorscope.

Color burst A waveform of a specific frequency and amplitude that is positioned between the trailing edge of horizontal sync and the start of active video. The color burst tells the color decoder how to decode the color information contained in that line of active video. By looking at the color burst, the decoder can determine what's blue, orange, or magenta. Essentially, the decoder figures out what the correct color is.

Color correction In imaging, this refers to the process of matching the colors in a digital reproduction of an image to an analog original, such as a photograph. Adobe Photoshop is the standard application for color-correcting images. In film, this refers to adjusting the final print so that colors match from shot to shot, regardless of the film stock and camera used.

Color depth or bit depth, refers to the number of bits used to describe the color of a pixel. The color depth of 24-bit color would be 24 bits.

Color map / color palette / indexed color

A color map or color pallete is a predefined list of colors with their values. This method is used when colors do not exceed 256 colors. For more colors the palatte becomes too large, and a direct color method is preferred.

1-bit color (21 = 2 colors) monochrome (for black and white)

2-bit color (22 = 4 colors) CGA

4-bit color (24 = 16 colors) as used by the least common denominator VGA standard

8-bit color (28 = 256 colors)

Color difference All of the color spaces used in color video require three components. These might be R'G'B', Y'IQ, Y'UV or Y'(R' - Y')(B' - Y'). In the Y'(R' - Y')(B' - Y') color space, the R' - Y' and B' - Y' components are often referred to as color difference signals for obvious reasons. They are made by subtracting the luma (Y') from the red and blue components. I and Q and U and V are also color difference signals since they are scaled versions of R' - Y' and B' - Y'. All the Ys in each of the Y'IQ, Y'UV and Y'(R' - Y')(B' - Y') are basically the same, although they are slightly different between SDTV and HDTV.

Color edging Extraneous colors that appear along the edges of objects, but don't have a color relationship to those areas.

Color encoder The color encoder does the exact opposite of the color decoder. It takes two color difference signals, such as I and Q or U and V, and combines them into a chroma signal.

Color frame A sequence of four fields (2 frames) of NTSC video. Since the phase of the color subcarrier reverses every frame in NTSC (which makes the color information essentially invisible on a black-and-white receiver) two complete frames are required to carry a complete sequence of color information.

Color key This is essentially the same thing as chroma key.

Color killer A color killer is a circuit that shuts off the color decoding if the incoming video does not contain color information. The color killer looks for the color burst and if it can't find it, it shuts off the color decoding. For example, let's say that a color TV is going to receive material recorded in black and white. Since the black and white signal does not contain a color burst, the color decoding is shut off. Why is a color killer used? Well, in the old days, the color decoder would still generate a tiny little bit of color if a black and white transmission was received, due to small errors in the color decoder, causing a black and white program to have faint color spots throughout the picture.

Color mode A setting that will determine the color scheme to be used in your images such as Grayscale or RGB.

Color palette Available color selections, ranging from 16 colors to 16.7 million. Color resolution comparison. There are often color shifts from machine to machine that can have "unfortunate" results.

Color purity This term is used to describe how close a color is to the theoretical. For example, in the Y'UV color space, color purity is specified as a percentage of saturation and +/-q, where q is an angle in degrees, and both quantities are referenced to the color of interest. The smaller the numbers, the closer the actual color is to the color that it's really supposed to be. For a studio-grade device, the saturation is +/-2% and the hue is +/-2 degrees. On a vectorscope, if you're in that range, you're studio quality.

Color separation A process in which colors are separated into four primary colors for printing purposes. The four colors used for most ink printing are cyan, magenta, yellow, and black. After a graphic is separated into the four basic ink colors, it can be printed one color at a time, one layer at a time to produce the best and most efficient results. Most professional printers require four-color separation to complete a print request.

Color space A color space is a mathematical representation for a color. No matter what color space is used – RGB, Y'IQ, Y'UV, etc. – orange is still orange. What changes is how you represent orange. For example, the RGB color space is based on a Cartesian coordinate system and the HSI color space is based on a polar coordinate system.

Color subcarrier The color subcarrier is a signal used to control the color encoder or color ecoder. For (M) NTSC the frequency of the color subcarrier is about 3.58 MHz and for (B, D, G, H, I) PAL it's about 4.43 MHz. In the color encoder, a portion of the color subcarrier is used to create the color burst, while in the color decoder, the color burst is used to reconstruct a color subcarrier.

Color table A table of colors referenced by the pixels in an image.

Color temperature Color temperature is measured in degrees Kelvin. If a TV has a color temperature of 8,000 degrees Kelvin, that means the whites have the same shade as a piece of pure carbon heated to that temperature. Low color temperatures have a shift towards red; high color temperatures have a shift towards blue.

The standard for video is 6,500 degrees Kelvin. Thus, professional TV monitors use a 6,500-degree color temperature. However, most consumer TVs have a color temperature of 8,000 degrees Kelvin or higher, resulting in a bluish cast. By adjusting the color temperature of the TV, more accurate colors are produced, at the expense of picture brightness.

Coloration A term used to describe levels of audio Distortion that cause serious departures from a true High Fidelity rendition of the original signal.

Colorstream, colorstream Pro, colorstream HD The name Toshiba uses for the analog YPbPr video interface on their consumer equipment. If the interface supports progressive SDTV resolutions, it is called ColorStream Pro. If the interface supports HDTV resolutions, it is called ColorStream HD.

Colour bars A pattern generated by a video test generator, consisting of eight equal width colour bars. Colours are white (75%), black (7.5% setup level), 75% saturated pure colours red, green and blue, and 75% saturated hues of yellow, cyan and magenta (mixtures of two colours in 1:1 ratio without third colour). The colours appear in the order White, Yellow, Cyan, Green, Magenta, Red, Blue, Black.

Colour carrier The sub-carrier frequency in a colour video signal (4.433619 MHz for PAL & 3.58MHz for NTSC) that is phase modulated with the colour information. The colour carrier frequency is chosen soits spectruminter leaves with the luminance spectrum with minimum interference. This signal is superimposed on the luminance level. The amplitude of the colour sub-carrier represents saturation and phase angle represents hue.

Colour difference signal A video colour signal created by subtracting luminance and/or colour information from one of the primary colour signals (red, green or blue). In the Betacam colour difference format, for example, the luminance (Y) and colour difference components (R-Y and B-Y) are derived as follows:

Y = 0.3 Red + 0.59 Green + 0.11 Bluealso (Y)

R-Y = 0.7 Red - 0.59 Green - 0.11 Blue also (U)

B-Y = 0.89 Blue - 0.59 Green - 0.3 Red also (V)

The G-Y colour difference signal is not created because it can be calculated from the other three signals. The colour difference signals are, sometimes, wrongly referred to as component video signals. That term is reserved for the RGB colour components.

Colour difference These are two of the three components of a colour video signal. One is the Red colour difference signal, called variously Y-R or CR while the other is the Blue colour difference signal (Y-B or CB). They are created from the original RGB signal by creating a luminance signal (Y) and then subtracting this from the red and blue respectively (thus the name, colour 'difference'). When combined with the luminance signal the original three RGB signals can be recreated with very little degradation. The two colour difference signals and the luminance signal are, together, known as component video.

Colour phase The timing relationship in a video signal that is measured in degrees and keeps the hue of a colour signal correct.

Colour temperature Indicates the hue of the colour. It is derived from photography where the spectrum of colours is based upon a comparison of the hues produced when a black body (as in Physics) is heated from red through yellow to blue, which is the hottest. Colour temperature measurements are expressed in Kelvin (not degrees Kelvin).

Colouration An unwanted alteration in the character of audio. Significant colouration of sound can make instruments and voices sound unrealistic. It may be caused by harmonic distortion, vibrations of component parts (for example, the panels of an inadequately braced loudspeaker enclosure) or, most commonly, through an uneven frequency response.

Comb filter An electrical filter circuit that passes a series of frequencies and rejects the frequencies in between, it combs out the frequencies. Used on a composite video signal, to separate the chrominance signal and reject the luminance signal, or to select the luminance signal and reject the chrominance signal. This filter is found in S-VHS VCRs to separate the chrominance and luminance so that a composite video input can be recorded in S-VHS format. These filters can also be found in some multiplexers to give a Y - C output for recording on an S-VHS recorder.

Comb filter effect This acoustical and electronic effect occurs when two signals interact in such a way as to produce an irregular spiked and choppy response pattern. When graphed on paper, this pattern looks like the teeth of a comb, hence the name. This effect is frequently the product of overlapping outputs from the various drivers in the system. It can develop in either a single speaker between the individual drivers, or between unmatched sets of speakers. This same effect can also be produced by wall reflections and other room anomalies. The usual remedy for this, if it becomes objectionable, (not every instance is even perceived as such) is to make sure the Crossover set points are appropriate for the drivers being used, or that the crossover is operating correctly. Obviously, one should also use only compatible speaker sets.

Comedian 1) A performer of any kind specializing in comedy;

2) an actor specializing in comedy; 3) (poetic or archaic) an actor, even one who performs serious plays.

Comet tailing Smear of light resulting from inability of a camera's pickup to bright objects.

Command key Also know as the Apple key, the command key is a key on the Apple Macintosh computer. It is used as a shortcut for common commands in a similar way to the Control (Ctrl) key on a PC.

Command message In media control interface (MCI), a symbolic constant that represents a unique command for an MCI device. Command messages have associated data structures that provide information a device requires to carry out a request.

Command Refers to any menu item or shortcut used in a program to perform a specific function.

Command string In media control interface (MCI), a null-terminated character string that represents a command for an MCI device. The text string contains all the information that an MCI device needs to carry out a request. MCI parses the text string and translates it into an equivalent command message and data structure that it then sends to an MCI device driver.

Commedia del' arte A popular, long-lived and seminal theatrical genre originating in Renaissance Italy, typified by stereotyped characters played by actors wearing masks, improvisation, recurring gags, and physical humor; it profoundly influenced Molière, Chaplin, Buster Keaton, the early Marx Brothers, burlesque and vaudeville comedy, Punch and Judy Shows, mime, circus clowns, and contemporary improvisational comedy.

Commercial sound studio A sound studio that hires out its facilities, equipment and engineers to ad agencies, producers, and others, but produces little, if anything of its own.

Common gateway interface (CGI) A specification for transferring information between a program on a web server and a client.

Compact camera Any small camera with the basic features. Also known as a point and shoot camera and generally comes with zoom lens capabilities.

Compact cassette A neatly packaged magnetic tape recording and playback system for audio introduced in the 1960s. This uses a narrow plastic tape with four tracks running at a speed of 28.6mm/s (1 1/8 inches per second), contained in a sturdy plastic enclosure. In consumer equipment, only two of the tracks are accessible at any one time, providing stereo recording and playback. The tape is turned over (or an auto-reverse transport moves the recording and playback heads sideways) to access the other two tracks.

Some semi-professional four track recording systems allow all four tracks to be recorded and played back at once, or even separately to permit multi-track recording. All cassette decks capable of recording (some are playback-only) have at least two heads: a record/playback head and an erase head. Some better decks include three heads, with separate record and playback heads to allow close-to real-time monitoring of the recorded material directly from the tape, and allowing the heads to be optimised for their different functions. While initially very low in fidelity, in the early 1970s tremendous advances were made in tape formulations, first with Chromium Dioxide magnetic materials and then later with 'Metal' tapes, which extended the high frequency response and improved their saturation characteristics. The addition of Dolby B noise reduction (and later Dolby C) reduced the inherent problem of high noise levels due to the low tape speed.

Compander compressor/expander A noise-reduction system that works by compressing the dynamic range of the audio before recording, and expanding it again by an equivalent amount during playback. An example of this was the dbx system.

Comparator On chip comparator allows square wave generation for clocking purposes.

Compelling conveyance To use appropriate content and data type to communicate with maximum impact on an audience.

Compliance The degree of 'springiness' in a mechanical system. For example, the cone of a loudspeaker driver with a soft suspension which can move to and fro relatively easily is more compliant than one with a stiff suspension. The stylus of turntable cartridge with a high compliance tends to follow the excursions of the groove more easily than a that of a cartridge with low compliance.

Complication A factor in the dramatic action that intensifies the conflict or a previous complication.

Component object model (COM) A specification developed by Microsoft for building software components that can be assembled into programs.

Component system This term is used in relation to speaker systems, to indicate a system in which separate mounting arrangements are provided for each component of the system. In a typical car system you might see a woofer in a box in the rear, midranges at the side and tweeters mounted on the dash panel. This compares to the typical integrated speaker enclosure in which all the Drivers are mounted in the same box.

Composite video A single video signal that contains brightness, color, and timing information. If a video system is to receive video correctly, it must have several pieces of the puzzle in place. It must have the picture that is to be displayed on the screen, and it must be displayed with the correct colors. This piece is called the active video. The video system also needs information that tells it where to put each pixel. This is called sync. The display needs to know when to shut off the electron beam so the viewer can't see the spot retrace across the CRT display. This piece of the video puzzle is called blanking. Now, each piece could be sent in parallel over three separate connections, and it would still be called video and would still look good on the screen. This is a waste, though, because all three pieces can be combined together so that only one connection is needed. Composite video is a video stream that combines all of the pieces required for displaying an image into one signal, thus requiring only one connection. NTSC and PAL are examples of composite video. Both are made up of active video, horizontal sync, horizontal blanking, vertical sync, vertical blanking, and color burst. RGB is not an example of composite video, even though each red, green, and blue signal may contain sync and blanking information, because all three signals are required to display the picture with the right colors.

Composite video signal CVS A signal in which the luminance and chrominance information have been combined using one of the coding standards NTSC, PAL, Secam,etc.

Compositing Combining two or more video or electronic images into a single frame or display.

Compositing layering Multiple pictures on top of each other. A cutout or matte holds back the background and allows the foreground picture to appear to be in the original picture. Used primarily for special effects.

Composition Visual makeup of a video image including all of its variables such as balance, subjects, depth of view, etc.

Compound device A Media Control Interface (MCI) device that requires a device element, usually a data file. An example of a compound device is the MCI waveform audio driver.

Compression (video) Process which reduces the number of bytes required to store/ transmit digital video. Typical schemes involve comparing frames and coding-out, or eliminating, inter-frame and intra-frame redundancies. The compression may be done by software, hardware or a combination of the two. On playback, the data is decompressed.

Why compress video data? To reduce storage space and to playback faster. A full-screen (640 x 480 pixels) image with 16.4 million colors takes up 1 Mb of memory. For full-motion, the computer needs to display 30 pictures/frames per second, thus requiring it to "shuffle" 30 Mb of data every second. Storing 10 seconds of video would require 300 Mb.

Compression (audio/video files A process of temporarily or permanently reducing audio data for more efficient storage or transmission. A temporary reduction in file size is called 'non-lossy' compression, and no information is lost. A permanent reduction in file size (such as with mp3 files) is called 'lossy' compression, and involves discarding (supposedly) unnecessary information which is irretrievably lost.

Compression Process that reduces the number of bytes required to store/transmit digital video. Typical schemes involve comparing frames and coding-out, or eliminating, inter-frame and intra-frame redundancies. The compression may be done by software, hardware or a combination of the two. On playback, the data is decompressed.

Why compress video data? To reduce storage space and to playback faster. A full-screen (640 x 480 pixels) image with 16.4 million colors takes up 1 Mb of memory. For full-motion, the computer needs to display 30 pictures/frames per second, thus requiring it to "shuffle" 30 Mb of data every second. Storing 10 seconds of video would require 300 Mb.

Compression driver Compression drivers are usually dynamic; that is, with a magnet and interacting coil arrangement, and a small diaphragm as the main transducer. These are the motor parts, also known as the driver, of a compression horn tweeter or compression horn general-purpose speaker, such as those used for Public Address (PA) purposes. These drivers are usually coupled to the throat of an exponential horn. Such an arrangement enables this type of tweeter to have very high directional characteristics, which allows them to be especially effective in situations requiring a very wide sound field. In typical home and car stereo near-field applications, large horns can be a bit too narrowly directional to be practical. For this reason, compression horn systems are usually found only in special purpose speakers used in mid and wide field applications such as PA systems or the sound systems installed in large theaters.

However, some specialized horns have small apertures and very shallow horns, and can be quite suitable for close spaces.

Compression ratio Compression ratio is a number used to tell how much information is squeezed out of an image when it has been compressed. For example, suppose we start with a 1 MB image and compress it down to 128 KB. The compression ratio would be:

1,048,576 / 131,072 = 8

This represents a compression ratio of 8:1; 1/8 of the original amount of storage is now required. For a given compression technique - MPEG, for example - the higher the compression ratio, the worse the image looks. This has nothing to do with which compression method is better, for example JPEG vs. MPEG. Rather, it depends on the application. A video stream that is compressed using MPEG at 100:1 may look better than the same video stream compressed to 100:1 using JPEG.

Compression wave A wave propagated by means of the compression of a fluid, such as a sound wave in air. To create sound, the opposite state of rarification alternates with the crest of every compression.

Compression-lossy Form of compression that sacrifices more data to produce better compression. MPEG-4 is a lossy compression that can keep high quality but can reduce the amount of space a video file needs tremendously.

Compressor A type of dynamic range processor which reduces the gain of audio signals which are over an adjustable 'threshold' level, therefore reducing the dynamic range. Generally allows the operator control over threshold, ratio, attack and release times. Both analogue and digital types are available.

Concave lens A lens that has negative focal length, i.e., the focus is virtual (in front of the lens) and it reduces theobjects. A concave lens cannot project an image.

Concert pitch A standard for the tuning of musical instruments, internationally agreed in 1960, in which the note A above middle C has a frequency of 440 Hz.

Condenser microphone A mike that depends on an external power supply or internal battery to electrostatically charge capacitor plates, one of which is subjected to sonic motion. Also called a 'Capacitor' microphone.

Conditional access This is a technology by which service providers enable subscribers to decode and view content. It consists of key decryption (using a key obtained from changing coded keys periodically sent with the content) and descrambling. The decryption may be proprietary (such as Canal+, DigiCipher, Irdeto Access, Nagravision, NDS, Viaccess, etc.) or standardized, such as the DVB common scrambling algorithm and OpenCable. Conditional access may be thought of as a simple form of digital rights management.

Two common DVB conditional access (CA) techniques are SimulCrypt and MultiCrypt. With SimulCrypt, a single transport stream can contain several CA systems. This enables receivers with different CA systems to receive and correctly decode the same video and audio streams. With MultiCrypt, a receiver permits the user to manually switch between CA systems. Thus, when the viewer is presented with a CA system which is not installed in his receiver, they simply switch CA cards.

Conductor Materials along which electrons will flow, making them suitable for use as connecting links in electrical circuits. Also, persons who guide symphony orchestras or streetcars.

Conduit A passage (pipe or tunnel) that electric wires or other cabling run through.

Cone The cone-shaped diaphragm of a speaker. This is directly attached to the voice coil motor which actions produces the pulsation's of air that the ear detects as sound. Also useful for holding ice cream.

Confidentiality If you send information about yourselves to us we guarantee that your data will be handled sensitively and not passed to other departments or organisations without your prior consent.

Conflict A factor or person that opposes the protagonist and causes tension.

Conforming The process of doing the final editing of a video using an off-line edited master as a guide.

Connection A link between two or more computers, process, applications, devices, etc.

Conservation Active intervention by specialists to inhibit further deterioration of an object and to stabilise it in its present condition.

Console window An application of the operating system that allows you to type commands and communicate with operating system with a keyboard.

Constant bit rate Constant bit rate (CBR) means that a bitstream (compressed or uncompressed) has the same number of bits each second.3.

Constant directivity (CD) horn A horn-loaded high frequency driver that exhibits more or less constant distribution of high-frequency sound in the horizontal direction. This is done by using one of several special dual shaped horn designs created to solve the traditional problem of horn-loaded driver output varying with frequency. All CD horns exhibit a high frequency roll-off of approximately 6 dB/octave beginning somewhere in the 2 kHz to 4 kHz area.

Constructive interference Where two signals, added together, act in sympathy with each other to boost the signal level. For example, bass from a subwoofer may, at certain frequencies, bounce from a nearby wall and that reflected signal may interfere with bass still coming directly from the subwoofer to effectively increase the output at that frequency. But it is also likely, at other frequencies, to result in destructive interference.

Consumer equipment "Consumer" Audio and video equiment typically means equipment sold to home users for amateur or home use. Most electronics found in department stores of chain electronics stores is considered "Consumer". The other categories of equipment are "Pro-sumer" and "Professional" . Consumer equipment typically costs less than pro-sumer or professional equipment, but also has fewer features and is less rugged.

Content In this context, content refers to all types and forms of information, including, text, HTML, interactive and/or dynamic Web pages, images, animation, video and sound files. Content however is more than just information on a web page; the way it is delivered, organised, and shown together also form content.

Content type Content type is a technical term (following RFC2045 and RFC2046) used for describing the content of a web document so that a user agent can handle the content properly.

Web documents can be sent via different protocols such as HTTP or email (SMTP).

In the Web environment the term Mime type is used.

Continuous audio The audio connection for a switched video network which allows all connected endpoints to speak at the same time, in the same manner as an audio bridge.

Continuous branching A program that enables the user to modify the presentation at any point rather than at specific branch points.

Contouring This is an image artifact caused by not having enough bits to represent the image. The reason the effect is called "contouring" is because the image develops vertical bands of brightness.

Contrast A video term referring to how far the whitest whites are from the blackest blacks in a video waveform. If the peak white is far away from the peak black, the image is said to have high contrast. With high contrast, the image is very stark and very "contrasty", like a black-and-white tile floor. If the two are very close to each other, the image is said to have poor, or low, contrast. With poor contrast, an image may be referred to as being "washed out" — you can't tell the difference between white and black, and the image looks gray.

Contrast ratio The ratio between the darkest blacks (ie. the pixels in the area are fully shut off) and the brightest whites (pixels fully on) capable of being produced on-screen by a projector or other display device. For quality home entertainment work, this is a far more important than the ANSI lumens rating. LCD projectors typically have a specified contrast ratio of between 500:1 and 1,100:1. DLP projectors tend to start around 1,000:1 and the newer models can reach as high as 3,500:1. CRT projectors, noted for being the best at producing black blacks, are up around 15,000:1.

Control track A signal recorded on video tape to allow the tape to play back at a precise speed in any VTR. Analogous to the sprocket holes on film.

Control track editing Editing videotape with equipment that reads the control track information in order to synchronize the editing between two decks. Frame accuracy is not certain as the VTRs can go slightly out of sync during pre-roll. Compare time code editing.

Controller Portion of the QuickTime Movie Playback window with which you interactively control the direction and rate of playback.

Convention A stereotype artifice that an audience agrees to accept, as, in drama, an aside, or, in audio drama, a three-legged horse, a musical bridge or, for that matter, background music.

Convergence 1. The beam-position accuracy of the red, green, and blue beams of a color monitor or projector. Color systems require exact accuracy of beams, both for position and speed, to properly produce the desired colors from their phosphors.

2. The adjustment of the red, green, and blue electron beams in a monitor or video projector to align the red, green and blue images.

Convex lens A convex lens has a positive focal length, i.e., the focus is real (behind the lens). It is usuallycalled magnifying glass, since it magnifies the objects. It can be used to project an image.

Cookie A "cookie" is a small piece of information, a virtual "sticky note", sent by a Web server to be stored, by your browser, on your hard drive. The cookie stores information about you and can be retrieved by the Website each time you visit there. Without them, sites would not be able to retain information about individual visits; thus, cookies store "state information." Cookies are passive files, typically used in .asp (Active Server Page) programming, and should not be confused with server-side databases that collect personal information you've voluntarily (or unwittingly) submitted.

Copy Text, as in "announce copy," the text the announcer is to read.

Copyright A legal protection of an artistic or literary intellectual property, such as a script or audio production, against unauthorized use; to legally protect an intellectual property, especially by registering a published work with the Copyright Office of the Library of Congress.

Copyright, common law A legal protection of an unpublished intellectual property, created when an author (or producer) mails the property to him/herself and keeps the sealed mailing container, the cancellation date of which provides the protection. Once a fairly common practice, common law copyrighting has diminished since the revamping of the U.S. copyright law in the 1980s.

Core A hub around which recording tape or film is wound for storage, to save money by conserving reels.

Correspondence management system Database programs specifically designed to help House and Senate offices record, process, track, and manage their constituent correspondence. Almost all House and Senate offices use correspondence management system (CMS) databases to manage the thousands of postal letters, e-mail messages, phone calls, and faxes they receive from and send to constituents each year.

Corruption A change in data such that the data content received is not what was originally sent.

Coulomb An amount of electrical charge which contains 6.24 x 1018 of electrons. So there!

Counter firing A method for reducing harmonic distortion at low frequencies that involves the use of a secondary coil in a woofer or mid bass driver to cancel non-fundamental wave elements not found in the original signal. The signal from the coil is used by the amplifier to refine it's damping control over the cone motion. This proprietary servo-feedback technology was originally developed by Velodyne in the early '90s.

Counter 1) In the studio, a device, somewhat like a timer, to count the expenditure of tape as it winds on the take-up reel;

2) in theater, to make as an actor an unmotivated movement on stage that balances the stage picture, hence, in a radio drama, to pan a voice or sound to balance the stereo field. movement that an actor makes to balance the stage .

Cover, In stage parlance, to position oneself on stage so that your back is mostly or completely to the audience. One is thus said to be in a covered position.

CPU(central processing unit) The processor chip in a computer.

CPU intensive Used to describe processes that require large amounts of processor time. CPU-intensive processes usually slow down other processes running on the same computer, and may not run very well, if at all, on slower computers.

Creepy crawlies Yes, this is a real video term! Creepy-crawlies refers to a specific image artifact that is a result of the NTSC system. When the nightly news is on, and a little box containing a picture appears over the anchorperson's shoulder, or when some computer-generated text shows up on top of the video clip being shown, get up close to the TV and check it out. Along the edges of the box, or along the edges of the text, you'll notice some jaggies "rolling" up (or down) the picture. That's the creepy-crawlies. Some people refer to this as zipper because it looks like one.

Crisis A minor or major point in the dramatic action in which the risk arising from conflict or complication requires a response from the protagonist.

CRON A system level command found in Unix based operating systems (example: Mac OS X, Linux) used to schedule commands to run at specific times. The tasks performed are ofteh, generically, referred to as a cron-job or CRONJOB or cronjob. A cronjob might be a system level maintenance task just as removing cache files.

Crop To select out an area of an image. Once an image is cropped, save the cropped version with a different name, retaining the original image.

Cross 1) To move across the stage or, in radio theater, across the stereo field;

2) a movement thus made.

Cross color A defect characteristic of NTSC composite video that manifests itself as spurious rainbow patterns on highly textured objects like the one found on a striped shirt or tweed jacket. Cross-color defect is attributed to the make-up of the signal which mixes the high luminance and chrominance information in the same composite baseband spectrum. Johnny Carson used to wear ties with designs specifically designed to create this effect.

Cross-correlation The degree of agreement between two unlike signals.

Crossfade 1) The simultaneous reduction of one sound, set of sounds or scene and simultaneously raising of another;

2) to make a crossfade.

Cross luminance A defect characteristic of NTSC composite video that appears as a dot pattern crawling up or hanging on the edges of color areas. This is a result of the signal structure where the color information leaks into the luminance signal. Also referred to as dot crawl.

Cross modulation A condition when one signal erroneously modulates another signal.

Cross platform Files usable/executable with different operating systems. For example, Virtus WalkThrough, a 3-D animator program, can produce "cross-compatible" animation files for Macintosh and DOS/ Windows machines. "Power" Mac's let you change to the PC work-mode; "power" PC's can handle Macintosh software/files.

Crosstalk Where a signal (particularly audio) leaks from one channel to another. Thus a voice may be intended to be entirely in the left channel of a stereo recording, but some portion of it appears in the right, dragging the apparent position of the voice somewhat towards the centre of the sound stage. Normally specified by the inverse of crosstalk: separation.

Crossover A device or passive circuit used in systems with separate tweeter and/or midrange Drivers. It Rolls Off frequencies above and below certain points in the range, to allow the sound to be tailored for the specific driver to which it is sent. Most speakers have crossovers that consist of passive elements such as capacitors, coils, and resistors to separate the various frequencies. In a bi-amped or multi-amped system, the crossover is an active device that feeds the various frequency bands to the inputs of the amplifiers that operate the individual drivers.

Crossover distortion A small discontinuity (or, at least, nonlinearity) in a signal when a transistor-based amplifier circuit switches from positive to negative operation. This is addressed by Class A and Class A/B designs. Sometimes called 'zero cross distortion'.

Crossover frequencies The frequencies at which a passive or electronic crossover network divides the audio signals, which are then routed to the appropriate amplifiers or speakers.

Crossover network The set of components in a loudspeaker that divides up the incoming signal, sending the bass to the woofer, the treble to the tweeter and, sometimes, the middle frequencies to a midrange driver. The crossover network uses resisters, capacitors and inductors (coils) to divide up the signal. Some high end systems use active crossover networks. In such cases, the division is made before the signal is amplified, so a separate amplifier is required for each driver.

Crossover slope The rate at which a crossover circuit attenuates the blocked frequencies. Slope is expressed as decibels per octave. A 6dB per octave crossover reduces signal amplitude level by 6dB in every octave starting at the crossover point. This means that every time the frequency of the audio signal is changed by a factor of 2 (one octave), the level of the audio signal is attenuated by 6dB. For example, if a low-pass crossover is set at 60Hz with a 6dB slope, you'll see a drop in level of 6dB at 120Hz. With slopes of 12dB and higher, the output beyond the crossover point will be reduced to below the level of audibility.

CRT (cathode-ray tube) A CRT screen is a display unit of which the phosphorous surface is lit by an electron beam in different frequencies resulting in three different color hues: red, green and blue. This is typically the method used for creating images on a computer or TV screen.

Other methods are used for LED (Light Emission Display) and plasma screens.

Cryptography A general term for the encryption and decryption methods used for data transmission and protection.

CS-Mount cine short mount The newer standard for lens mounting. It uses the same physical thread as theC-mount, but the back flange-to-CCD distance is reduced to 12.5 mm. The lenses are smaller, more compact and less expensive. CS-mount lenses can only be used on CS-mount cameras.

CU seeme A leading desktop videoconferencing software package.

Cue 1) To give a beginning signal, as when the director points to the actor or the studio cue light goes on; hence, to deliver a line, effect or musical passage that signals another line, effect or musical passage;

2) a beginning signal such as in the above examples;

3) the beginning or end of a sound, musical passage or line of dialogue.

Cue in The first line, sound or music of a program or tape.

Cue out The sound or line that ends the tape or program, and that cues the live station engineer or announcer to go on with whatever is next.

Cue, operative The operative cue is the word or phrase in a line that motivates another character to speak or perform an action, even though it is not the final word or phrase of the speech.

Current The volume or quantum of the flow of electrons through a conductor, as opposed to voltage, which is the measure of the intensity or velocity of the electrical flow.

Curtain line The last line of an act or play, usually, in the former instance, giving the audience a sense of anticipation for the next act, or, in the latter, giving a sense of finality; so-called because, on stage, it is the line that cues the curtain to fall.

Curtain The final punctuation mark of a major division in a dramatic work; in theater, a black out, fade-out or lowering of the stage curtain; in audio drama, a fade-out, musical passage, or ring-out of a sound effect.

Custom file A feature package that provides intuitive and safe source management for an audio and A/V system. Examples include Disc Memo, Selection, Station Memo, and Memo List.

Custom shapes A shape that is added to an image as a vector graphic.

Cut A stop in the action, or, in editing, the place where one shot moves to another. The completed version of a film is sometimes called a "cut." "Cross-cutting" refers to parallel action that is edited together to represent action happening simultaneously in different places or from different angles.

Cut and paste A simple way of moving items or data between different documents or software. For example you might select and then "cut" a piece of text from one text document and then "paste" it into another document. This will remove the object from the first document and place it in the second document. If you want to keep the object in the first document as well as the second you can use the "copy" command.

Using the Control (Ctrl) key on a PC with the "x" key is a common shortcut for cutting an object. Ctrl + "c", copies the object and Ctrl + "v" will paste the object.

Cut to To transition instantly from one scene to another.

Cutoff frequency filters The frequency at which a signal falls off by 3 dB (the half power point) from it's maximum value. Also referred to as the -3 dB points, or the corner frequencies.

CVBS (Composite video baseband signal) In broadcast television this refers to the video signal, including the colour information and syncs.

Cyber advocacy The use of the Internet and e-mail to mobilize people to express their views on the issues that matter to them.

Cyberculture "A collection of cultures and cultural products that exist on and/or are made possible by the Internet, along with the stories told about these cultures and cultural products."

Cyberspace A word or metaphor used to describe the non-physical 'space' linking one computer system to another.

D

DVHS DVHS is a digital recording and playback format for High Definition material. It's based on the existing 1/2" VHS-sized cassettes.

D/A converter (also D/A or DAC) Short for digital-to-analog converter, this is a device that changes a digitally-coded word into its "equivalent" quantized analog voltage or current. Just like the A/D device, there are very high-speed D/A's available, capable of converting at data rates up to 1 GHz.

D1 Digital video tape format using the CCIR 601 standard to record 4:2:2 component video on 19mm tape. Currently the highest quality video tape format generally available. The first digital video tape format, hence D1.

D2 Digital video tape format using the 4fsc method to record composite digital video. Uses 19mm tape and a cassette similar to D1. The second digital video tape format, hence D2.

D3 Digital video tape format using 4fsc composite signals like D2, but recorded on 12.5 mm (1/2-inch) tape. The third digital video tape format.

D4 Does not exist. The number 4 is considered unlucky in Japan.

D5 Digital video tape format using CCIR 601, 4:2:2 video. Uses the same cassette as D3. Bet you can guess why it's called D5.

Damping As Newton observed, an object once set in ,motion will keep on moving unless a restrictive counterforce is applied. Damping is that force at work in the mechanical resistance that is applied to a speaker cone to keep it from resonating in the absence of an input signal. It is also the factor that is applied as a control voltage by the amplifier for the same purpose. These measures help reduce or dampen Harmonic Distortion. This also improves bass accuracy.

Damping factor A specification for power amplifiers which suggests the degree of control that the amplifier exercises over a connected loudspeaker. It is the ratio of the nominal impedance of the speaker (and is typically quoted for eight ohms) to the internal impedance of the output stage of the amplifier. A high internal impedance for the amplifier means that its frequency response will vary with real-world speakers since their impedance varies across their frequency range. It also means that the driver, which wants to do its own thing under the influence of air, its suspension and so forth, rather than what the signal is telling it to do, will face a relatively high impedance to the voltage it is generating back into the amplifier. Consequently it will be freer to do its own thing, rather than what the amplifier is telling it to do. However the damping factor quoted for amplifiers does not take into account the impedance of the wiring between amplifier and loudspeakers, nor the impedance of the speakers' own voice coils. Consequently there is only a modest performance gain between a damping factor of, say, 60 and one of 600.

Dark current Leakage signal from a CCD sensor in the absence of incident light.

Dark noise Noise caused by the random (quantum) nature of the dark current.

DARPA (defense advanced research projects agency) DARPA (originally known as ARPA) is a branch of the American Defense Department that funds advanced research. The Internet originated as an ARPA project.

DAT (Digital audio tape) A compact tape developed in the late 1980s by Sony which stores audio in PCM format. The tapes look very similar to the MiniDV tapes used in digital video cameras, but are somewhat larger, measuring 71mm wide by 53mm deep and 10mm thick. The reading part of the tape is protected by the casing. In order to pack sufficient capacity on, the tape is read using a helical scan head in the same way as a VCR. The default format for DAT is a 48 kHz sampling frequency and 16 bits of resolution, but they can also be switched to 44.1kHz.

Data projector Used to project a computer's image onto a screen. Commonly used in conjunction with a presentation graphics program such as Microsoft's PowerPoint.

Data rate An attribute assigned to a media file by a compression utility. It is a measure of the amount of digital information transmitted in a given unit of time—usually a second. Thus, a video could be encoded to play back at a rate of 500 kb/s. The data rate set for a file is usually influenced by the limitations of the target delivery medium. CDs, for instance, generally have a maximum transfer rate of 300 kb/s.

Data rate limiting A function of some media editing applications that allows you to ensure even data transfer rates by placing a ceiling on the data rate for a media file.

Data rate spiking Media files—especially uncompressed ones—generally have uneven data rates in that some areas of the file are more complex and require more bytes of digital storage. This means that a processor needs to work harder to play back those areas, and sometimes can't keep up. These denser areas of digital information that sometimes hamper performance are called data rate spikes.

Data source name (DSN) A piece of information that links an embedded database query to a specific database on the server.

Database (DB) A computer Program for entering, storing and retrieving items of information in a structured fashion.

Database server A computer system used to process database queries.

Dataflowa Transfer of data between a sender and a recipient.

Datagram Datagram is also known as Data Packet or Network Message.

Datagram is a unit of information that, apart from the data, also contains address information, which tells the network where the data must be sent and who the sender is. The datagram is thus like an addressed envelope with its contents.

DAVIC Abbreviation for digital audio visual council. It's goal was to create an industry standard for the end-to-end interoperability of broadcast and interactive digital audio-visual information, and of multimedia communication. The specification is now ISO/IEC 16500 (normative part) and ITR 16501 (informative part).

DBM Measure of power in communications. 0 dBm = 1 mW, with a logarithmic relationship as the values increase or decrease. In a 50-ohm system, 0 dBm = 0.223 volts.

DBS Direct broadcast satellite Broadcasting from a satellite directly to a consumer user, usually using a small aperture antenna.

DBSPL Decibel - sound pressure level A measure of sound intensity. This is a logarithmic measure. To increase the sound level by three decibels, it is necessary to double the power output. A 10dB increase in sound level roughly equates with a perceived doubling of volume level. A figure of around 120-130dB is normally considered to be the threshold of pain. dB is sometimes loosely used as a synonym.

DBw Decibels referenced to 1 watt.

Dbx A brand name for a device that reduces unwanted noise in an analog recording.

DC Direct current An electric current that retains its level and direction, at least in the short term. More generally, DC is also used to describe voltage sources that deliver this kind of current. DC is generally used at low voltages within electronic equipment. Batteries deliver DC. Compare with AC.

DC Restoration DC restoration is what you have to do to a video signal after it has been AC-coupled and has to be digitized. Since the video waveform has been AC-coupled, we no longer know absolutely where it is. For example, is the bottom of the sync tip at -5v or at 1v? In fact, not only don't we know where it is, it also changes over time, since the average voltage level of the active video changes over time. Since the ADC requires a known input level and range to work properly, the video signal needs to be referenced to a known DC level. DC restoration essentially adds a known DC level to an AC-coupled signal. In decoding video, the DC level used for DC restoration is usually such that when the sync tip is digitized, it will be generate the number 0.

DC/DC Converter Since 12 volts limits the amplitude of an audio signal, a group of components within an amplifier converts battery voltage (DC) into AC so that it can be increased by swetching devices and a transformer, and converted back to DC (rectified). This provides higher voltage to drive the amplification stage to higher power. Also called the Power Supply circuit.

DCC Digital compact cassette An attempted replacement for the compact cassette introduced by Philips in the late 1980s, early 1990s. This recorded audio in digital format, but used a lossy compression system. It failed to make headway since Sony's Minidisc had the advantage of direct access and, more recently, the recordable CD provides convenient and cheap recording with higher quality.

DCR A Shockwave audio format used in Shockwave movies. Requires the Shockwave plug-in.

DCT Discrete cosine transform Mathematical algorithm used to generate frequency representations of a block of video pixels. The DCT is an invertible, discrete orthogonal transformation between time and frequency domain. It can be either forward discrete cosine transform (FDCT) or inverse discrete cosine transform (IDCT). It is part of the JPEG compression algorithm.

DD Direct drive A method of controlling one form of auto iris lens (the other is video iris), where the electronic has been removed from the lens and is built into the camera. To use a DD lens with a camera, the camera must have a DD output.

DDE (dynamic data exchange) Windows' process that supports exchange of commands and data between two application. OLE is a DDE enhancement.

DDL (description definition language) The DDL is a language that allows the creation of new Description Schemes. Description Schemes can be modified and extended using the DDL.

DDR digital disk recorder A digital video recording device based on high speed computer disk drives. Commonly used as a means to get video into and out from computers and for editing.

Dead. Lacking reverberation and overtones, said of an acoustical environment.

Dead room A studio with neutral acoustics used to record outdoor scenes.

Deal memo In show business and elsewhere, a summary of contract stipulations, sometime used in lieu of a contract, but most often as a preliminary document.

Decay The time of reduction of the level of a signal immediately after its cessation

Decibel or dB .

One tenth of a Bel. This is a measurement of the comparative strength of two powers, and can be applied when measuring any signal in the audio, video, and electromagnetic spectrum. If two powers differ by one Bel, there is a difference of 10 times the power. If comparing amplifiers, where one is rated at 10 watts while the other is 100 watts, then we have a difference of 10 decibels, or one Bel. Decibels should be understood as ratios, not fixed quantities.

Decibels are the preferred method and term for representing the ratio of different audio levels. It is a mathematical shorthand that uses logarithms (a shortcut using the powers of 10 to represent the actual number) to reduce the size of the number. For example, instead of saying the dynamic range is 32,000 to 1, we say it is 90 dB [the answer in dB equals 20 log x/y, where x and y are the different signal levels]. Being a ratio, decibels have no units. Audiologists generally assert that 1 decibel is the smallest difference in volume that can be heard by the average person. The term is derived as an honor to Alexander Graham Bell, who invented the telephone, and did much of the preliminary work in the modern science of acoustics.

Decibel abbreviation db A logarithmic measure of ratio. To determine the decibel relationship of, for example, two voltages you use the formula dB=20*log(V1/V2). If the result is negative, V1 is less than V2. If positive, then V1 is greater than V2. For power the formula is dB=10*log(P1/P2). dB is often used loosely as shorthand for dBSPL.

Decimation filter A decimation filter is a lowpass filter designed to provide decimation without the aliasing artifacts associated with simply throwing data away.

Decimation When a video signal is digitized so that 100 samples are produced, but only every other one is stored or used, the signal is decimated by a factor of 2:1. The image is now 1/4 of its original size, since 3/4 of the data is missing. If only one out of five samples were used, then the image would be decimated by a factor of 5:1, and the image would be 1/25 its original size. Decimation, then, is a quick-and-easy method for image scaling.

Decimation can be performed in several ways. One way is the method just described, where data is literally thrown away. Even though this technique is easy to implement and cheap, it introduces aliasing artifacts. Another method is to use a decimation filter, which reduces the aliasing artifacts, but is more costly to implement.

Decoder A device used to recover the component signals from a composite (encoded) source.

Decoders are used in displays and in various processing hardware where component signals are required from a composite source.

Decompress The process of converting video and audio data from its compact form back into its original form in order to play it.

De-emphasis Also referred to as post-emphasis and post-equalization. Deemphasis performs a frequency-response characteristic that is complementary to that introduced by pre-emphasis.

De-emphasis network A circuit used to restore a frequency response to its original form.

Deep focus An effect in which objects both near to and far away from the camera are in sharp focus. It is achieved through small apertures in the camera lens. Orson Welles and his cinematographer Gregg Toland pioneered this effect in Citizen Kane.

Deep link This is a link from one website that links to a page of specific and appropriate content within a second website, rather than to the second website's homepage.

Disability Discrimination Act 1995 (DDA)

The DDA aims to stop discrimination against people with disabilities. The DDA gives people with disabilities equal rights and access to employment, education, property, transport and goods, facilities or services. The DDA says that service providers, employers and similar are not allowed to treat disabled people less favourably because of their disability.

Degauss To demagnetize or randomize magnetic particles in a tape.

Deinterlace The conversion of an interlaced video signal to a progressive video signal. Two common systems are weaving and bobbing.

Delay A signal processing device or circuit used to delay one or more of the output signals by a controllable amount. This feature is used to correct for loudspeaker drivers that are mounted such that their points of apparent sound origin (not necessarily their voice coils) are not physically aligned. Good delay circuits are frequency independent, meaning the specified delay is equal for all audio frequencies (constant group delay). Delay circuits based on digital sampling techniques are inherently frequency independent and thus preferred.

Delay line A device designed to delay the video signal for a specific length of time. Required when switching between different types of devices or cameras with significantly different cable lengths.

Delivery 1) The affective speaking of lines by an actor – the employment of cadence, timbre, quality, volume, etc. to imbue lines with meaning, emotion, beauty, and interest;

2) the method or system by which a program or product is put before audiences or consumers; delivery system.

Delta frame A frame containing only the data that has changed since the last frame. Delta frames are an efficient means of compressing image data.

Demand aggregation The process of identifying and accumulating potential and existing demand for telecommunications, and matching that demand with a provider.

Demand registers Some carriers have established ADSL demand registers that nominate the number of potential customers required to rollout broadband in specific areas. Once the trigger level has been met by a community, the carrier will typically seek confirmation of interest and assess available and existing infrastructure in the area before determining whether the exchange will be broadband enabled (there is no guaranteed time frame or rollout of services).

Demodulate To recover the information being transmitted by a modulated signal. For example, a conventional TV receiver demodulates an incoming broadcast signal to convert it into the luminance and chrominance information displayed by the CRT and the sound emitted by the speaker. Compare modulate.

Demodulator In NTSC and PAL video, demodulation is the technique used to recover the color difference signals.

Denouement (from Fr., "end") Dramatic action following the climax that resolves the plot; the falling action.

Deposit of publications A system in operation in many countries, usually legally enforced, whereby publishers must deposit one or more copies of every publication with nominated libraries. Often referred to as Legal Deposit.

Depth of field The amount of the picture (in terms of distance from the camera) which is in focus. For landscape shots typically the depth of field is maximum so as to get the entire scene all the way to the horizon in sharp focus. For portrait photography the depth of field is normally very small so that the subject is in focus and all of the unwanted background is thrown out of focus (the effect is to emphasize the subject). Depth of field is affected by the aperture set when taking a picture: for large depth of field the aperture should be small (e.g. F22) and for portrait work, etc., it should be large (e.g. F4).

Descriptor A Descriptor is a representation of a Feature. It defines the syntax and semantics of Feature representation. A single Feature may take on several descriptors for different requirements.

Example The color feature may be described in terms of a color histogram, the average of the frequency components, the motion field, the text of the title, etc.

Descriptor value A Descriptor Value is an instantiation of a Descriptor for a given data set, or subset thereof.

Designer, sound An audio engineer who assumes principal artistic responsible for composing and orchestrating sounds, music and voices in a production.

Desktop publishing Using the functions of a personal computer or office workstation (computer linked to a network) to produce (commercial) quality printed material.

Desktop video This system is based on a desktop computer on which a small camera is mounted on top of the monitor. Software to allow image display, voice transmission, and other functions of the system resides in the computer. These systems are designed for one-on-one interaction, but can accommodate two or three people on each station if necessary. Desktop systems also include software for sharing control of programs, documents and other files, and are designed to facilitate collaboration.

Desktop viewing The ability to use the computer screen to view the output of a project of in interpersonal and corporate communication.

Dessimation The loss of lines of data in a movie window as the size of the frame is reduced. Lack of data for certain lines causes undesirable artifacts during movie playback.

Destructive interference Where two signals, added together, act in opposition to each other and reduce the signal level. For example, bass from a subwoofer may, at certain frequencies, bounce from a nearby wall and that reflected signal may, if arriving back out of phase, interfere with bass still coming directly from the subwoofer to effectively reduce the output at that frequency. But it is also likely, at other frequencies, to result in constructive interference.

Detachable face Occasionally referred to as 'Removable Panel' or 'Theft Deterrent Faceplate', or some variation. This is a physical method for foiling receiver thieves.

The idea is that you take just the front panel with the controls with you when you leave the car. A thief cannot buy a new face for a unit unless he has a receipt for it. Some manufacturers makes sets with rotating faces called Mask.

Deus ex machina (from Gr., "God out of the Machine") An improbable or inorganic plot contrivance to resolve the various complications of the dramatic action, such as the cavalry coming to the rescue, an unexpected inheritance, or a sudden remission.

Device Any machine or component that attaches to a computer.

Device driver Software to enable a computer to access or control a peripheral device, such as a printer.

Device element Data required for operation of Media Control Interface (MCI) compound devices. The device element is generally an input or output data file.

Device interface A converter box which separates the RGB and sync signals in order to display computer graphics on an RGB video monitor. Vendors include Covid and Extron.

DHTML (dynamic hypertext markup language) An extension of HTML supported only by 4.0 and later browsers that allows for interactivity and more advanced presentation of web pages.

Dial-in service A method of obtaining access to the services provided by a computer by establishing a connection over the telephone system.

Dialog normalization In Australian, 'dialog normalisation'. Frequently called 'dialnorm'. A metadata indication in a Dolby Digital bitstream of the volume level of the dialog in an audio signal. Dolby Digital decoders can use this 'flag' to adjust the volume level of the whole audio stream, so that the dialog levels of different program sources remain the same. Most DVD movies have this flag set to '27', which means -27dBFS. If the decoder is set to act upon this, it will reduce the level of the signal by 4dB because it means that the dialog is set 4dB higher than the calibration level of -31dBFS. It is important to note that this volume adjustment is made not just to the dialog, but to the entire sound track. It is also important to note that it does nothing to the sound other than adjust the overall volume level. Whether or not the dialog normalization feature actually works as hoped — in the sense of bringing the voice levels of all programs into line with each other — depends entirely on the engineers who mix the sound setting the dialog to the appropriate level in the first place. Dolby Digital encoders typically default to the value of 27, and must be explicitly changed for a different value. Many home theatre receivers report dialog normalization with reference not to 0dBFS, but to -31dBFS (the calibration level), and so a level of -27dBFS is reported as -4dB.

Dialogue The words uttered in a play; the lines given actors to speak.

Diaphragm This term describes the sound-producing element in a tweeter, or Horn. This is the surface that produces the sound you actually hear. The motor that drives it can be any of several technologies including Piezo, conventional dynamic, or ribbon types. Diaphragms do not produce low and low midrange frequencies well, so they are not usually found in that application.

Die cast (basket) A type of speaker basket or frame that is cast as a single piece of relatively thick, rigid metal. This contrasts with a Stamped frame that is shaped by pressure, much like a car body fender. Cast metal is heavier and more rigid, and thus less likely to "ring" at certain frequencies, and will hold its shape somewhat longer against the pull of gravity. This is mainly advantageous in the larger woofers of 12" or greater. Smaller drivers will likely not benefit perceptibly from being cast.

Dielectric An insulating (non-conductive) material usually when used in a capacitor or specific insulating situation such as in a coaxial cable.

Differential gain (DG) and differential phase (DP) The distortion characteristics of the chrominance signal expressed as a numerical value which indicates to what degree the amplitude (differential gain as a percentage) and phase (differential phase in degrees) are distorted from the beginning and end of one horizontal scanning line.

Differential nonlinearity (also DNL) In an ideal D/A and A/D converter, any two adjacent digital codes should result in measured output (or input) values that are exactly one LSB apart. Any positive or negative deviation in the measured "step" from the ideal differences is called differential non-linearity. It's expressed in (sub) multiples of 1 LSB. DNL errors more negative than -1 LSB can result in a non-monotonic response in a D/A and missing codes in an A/D.

Differential phase Differential phase is how much the hue changes when the luma level changes (it isn't supposed to). For a video system, the better the differential phase – that is, the smaller the number specified – the better the system is at figuring out the correct color.

Diffraction A change in the direction and velocity of a wave front that is caused by the wave moving past an obstacle.

Diffuser Gauzy or transparent material that alters the quality of light passing through it to soften shawdows and produce less intense lighting.

Digital As opposed to analogue. It is a method of representing real-life signals (which are generally effectively infinitely variable) by using discrete numbers, usually binary numbers (a pattern of 1s and 0s). Holding discrete values, rather than the infinite number of intermediate levels used by analogue, makes digital signals relatively resistant to distortion and noise. The reason is that if any inaccuracy creeps in, unless very severe it will not affect the signal enough to throw it off. Consider a binary system. If all data is represented as either 0 volts or 1 volt, then it doesn't matter if some interference causes the 1 volt level to be sometimes 1.1 volts, sometimes 0.9 volts. The receiving module will regard any voltage as greater than 0.5 volts as 1 volt and treat it accordingly.

Digital 8 Digital 8 compresses video using standard DV compression, but records it in a manner that allows it to use standard Hi-8 tape. The result is a DV "box" that can also play standard Hi-8 and 8 mm tapes. On playback, analog tapes are converted to a 25 Mbps compressed signal available via the i-Link digital output interface. Playback from analog tapes has limited video quality. New recordings are digital and identical in performance to DV; audio specs and other data also are the same.

Digital audio workstations Computer-based systems for editing and manipulating digital audio. The audio can be synchronized with video for video post-production applications. Some common systems based on the Macintosh include Dyaxis, Pro Tools, Synclavier, and Dawn.

Digital betacam Digital video tape format using the CCIR 601 standard to record 4:2:2 component video in compressed form on 12.5mm (1/2-inch) tape.

Digital composite video Digital video that is essentially the digitized waveform of NTSC or PAL video signals, with specific digital values assigned to the sync, blank, and white levels.

Digital compositing A technique whereby separately filmed or digitally generated components are combined through digital editing. Contrast with Optical Printing.

Digital disk recorder A recorder much like a videotape recorder which uses large digital disk memories instead of tape. They can record and play back in single frame steps (with no pre-roll, since there is no tape involved), at variable speeds or at 30 fps. Digital disk recorders are available as both component and composite machines. Very, very, expensive.

Digital disk recorders can usually mix an incoming video signal with a stored one and record the net result simultaneously. Since everything is digital, this mix can be performed repeatedly, producing layer upon layer of moving images.

Digital downconversion (also direct IF to digital conversion) This refers to a demodulation technique for sampling an intermediate frequency (IF) signal with a wide-bandwidth A/D whose sampling rate is equivalent to the local oscillator frequency (< IF frequency). In this super-Nyquist application, the A/D serves as the mixer stage and its digital output data is a beat frequency; the modulation data can be recovered with a DSP stage.

Digital editing Editing a portion of a movie by digitizing one or more frames and altering them electronically or combining them with other digitized images, and then printing the modified frame.

Digital filtering The process of smoothing, spectrally shaping, or removing noise from a signal has traditionally been accomplished with analog components. With the advent of high-speed DSP products, now filtering can effectively and economically be accomplished in the digital domain. Digital filters are basically mathematical functions that are performed on the digital data stream and their characteristics can be altered under software control, which adds to their overall flexibility. Finite Impulse Response (FIR) and Infinite Inpulse Response (IIR) are examples of digital filter functions.

Digital image A computer file which, when used in conjunction with the proper software, displays a picture on the computer screen or prints to a digital device such as a laser printer or imagesetter.

Digital rights management (DRM) Digital rights management (DRM) is a generic term for a number of capabilities that allow a content producer or distributor to determine under what conditions their product can be acquired, stored, viewed, copied, loaned, etc.

Digital signal A series or stream of impulses (normally electrical) characterized by the ON and OFF nature of its pulses. This means that a digital signal can exist in only one of two states at any given time: ON or OFF.

A lightswitch is a sort of digital input device because it receives one of two possible inputs: ON or OFF. The light, itself, is a sort of digital output device in that it conveys one of two possible meanings, or outputs: ON or OFF. If you were to operate the lightswitch ON and OFF repeatedly in a way that conveyed meaning to someone observing it, then you would be producing a digital signal. This is the basis for Morse Code, a language of flashing light patterns that represent letters of the alphabet. Morse code can also be transmitted along electrical wires as an electrical signal and it is just as much a digital signal going this way as it is going through the atmosphere as a visible signal.

The word "digital" does not necessarily mean "electrical", "visible", or "audible" as the previous example illustrates. In fact, "digital" simply refers to an encoding scheme used to convey information. Digital signals differ from analog signals in that there is no inherent way of recovering the information stored digitally without some key to knowing what the digital ON and OFFs mean.

Digital signal processor A separate processor, built into some sound cards, that offloads/ relieves audio processing from the computer's CPU.

Digital signatures Special code that can be attached to e-mail messages that is unique to a specific individual. Digital signatures do not protect messages from being altered. Like handwritten signatures, they simply provide one way of verifying the identity of an e-mailer. They can be combined with a variety of security and encryption features to help protect e-mail. Unfortunately, digital signatures are still not very user-friendly, so they do not make sense for widespread use, at present.

Digital subscriber line A type of high-speed Internet connection. Digital subscriber lines (DSL) are sophisticated technology that enables data to be "packed" and sent over regular telephone wires. Unfortunately, the technology is not available to everyone because the packed data breaks up if it must travel more than about 20,000 feet between a home or office to the telephone switching station. Consequently, DSL is not available in all areas.

Digital technology Human beings directly process information in an analog format. That is, our senses directly convey information to the brain in the form of constantly varying amplitudes and frequencies that approximate the impact of outside stimuli upon the receptors (eyes and ears, etc.) of the organs involved.

Digital technology is a method of translating this same information in the form of packets (bytes and bits) of numerically equivalent values. This enables input transducers (microphones, cameras, chemical sensors, etc.) to produce differential waveforms that can be reduced, down to the smallest differences, to a number. This number is transmitted to a receiver with a digital to analog converter that allows the original analog information to be reconstructed for the benefit of our human brains. This is of course an egregiously simplified explanation of the most significant technology of the present time. We invite you to explore more this topic deeply, not just for audio/video, but to understand the new world we have entered.

Digital theatre systems (DTS) A digital soundtrack standard that competes with Dolby digital and SDDS.

Digital transmission content protection (DTCP) An encryption method (also known as "5C" and "DTCP") developed by Sony, Hitachi, Intel, Matsushita and Toshiba for IP, USB and IEEE 1394 interfaces.

Digital VCR Digital VCRs are similar to analog VCRs in that tape is still used for storage. Instead of recording an analog audio/video signal, digital VCRs record digital signals, usually using compressed audio/video.

Digital vertical interval timecode DVITC digitizes the analog VITC waveform to generate 8-bit values. This allows the VITC to be used with digital video systems. For 525-line video systems, it is defined by SMPTE 266M. BT.1366 defines how to transfer VITC and LTC as ancillary data in digital component interfaces.

Digital video A video signal represented by binary numbers describing a finite set of colors and luminance levels. In accordance with "CCIR 601," the international digital video standard for sampling, the conversion from analog to digital suffers virtually no loss.

With current technology, the cost of using digital video to represent the range of levels and colors easily handled by analog videotape is prohibitive. Digital video requires more bandwidth than analog video to produce the same results, unless fancy compression techniques are used. As digital memory capacity and processing speeds become more economical, digital video will eclipse analog video. Standards such as QuickTime, DVI, MPEG, and JPEG for video make digital manipulation of video information possible on today's personal computers.

Note: consumer "digital" televisions and camcorders use the term to refer to the use of digital frame buffers for effects or signal processing. The output of these buffers is still converted back into analog signals for display and storage.

Digital video effects (DVEs) A real-time frame buffer that can zoom in and out, reposition, and freeze frame in real time. Some can also warp video frames into trapezoids, cylinders, and spheres to create a variety of special effects. Common trade names include ADO, Encore, Mirage, and Pinnacle.

Digital watermark A pattern inserted into a digital image, audio or video file identifying the file's copyright information (author, rights, etc.). The name comes from the faint watermarks imprinted on stationery which identify a manufacturer of stationery. The purpose of digital watermarks is to provide copyright protection for intellectual property. Unlike print watermarks, which are supposed to be visible, digital watermarks are designed to be completely invisible.

Digitize To convert analog (wave-based) media into digital format (zeros and ones) so that they can be understood by computers. Also known as "capturing," and sometimes "encoding." Digitization of video is usually accomplished with add-on devices for computers known as "Video Capture Cards," although firewire ports, which are increasingly becoming a standard on out-of-the-box systems for both Mac's and PCs, can perform this function. Audio can normally be digitized through standard sound cards that come with most computers.

.doc File extension that is associated with digital documents created in Microsoft Word. If you have or are given a file with this extension on it (for example, BusinessLetter.doc), it is likely the document was originally created in Microsoft Word.

Digitizing tablet Pen-based input system, resembling a sketch pad. The pressure of the pen on the tablet is translated in electronic dot patterns. Many delivery companies, such as UPS, use tablet technology to record signatures upon package receipt. President Clinton used a Wacom graphics tablet and pen to sign the Telecommunication Reform Act of 1996.

D-ILA (Direct drive digital image light amplifier) A projection technology used by JVC. It uses three reflective Liquid Crystal on Silicon panels which control light representing the signals for the three different colours.

DIN Acronym for Deutsche Industrie Norm (Deutsches Institut fuer Normung), the German standardization body. A world reference standard for the mounting parameters of many common receivers (Head ends) as well as other types of cables and equipment. Single DIN is the standard face size for receivers, and measures 7-3/8"wide by 2-1/4" high. DIN+1/2 measures 7-3/8"wide by 3-3/8"high. Double DIN measures 7-3/8"wide by 4-1/2" high.

Diplophonic. A diplophonic voice is one in which two simultaneous pitches are perceived.

Dipole A loudspeaker designed to offer a diffuse, non-directional sound by firing its high frequencies in two directions, out of phase with each other, so that a listener receives few aural clues as to their exact location. To make such speakers work optimally, they should be placed so that the axis running through the front and rear tweeters is at 90 degrees to a line drawn from the speaker to listener. This will maximise the cancellation of direct radiation from the speaker to the listener's position.

Direct color When 256 or less colors are used to be rendered on a computer's screen, a Color map / color palette / indexed color is typically used, but when more colors need to be described such a palette becomes too large. The Direct color method is used. In this method a specific value is assigned to a color hue. For computer screens RGB color model is used which directly encodes relative brightnesses of red, green, and blue to specify a color.

16-bit (Hi-Color) uses 16 bits to create colors, with a total of 65'536 colors.

This is sometimes called 15-bit color, as red, green, and blue components often take up 5 bits each ($2^5 = 32$ levels)

The extra bit is either left empty, or sometimes used for one of the colors. When used, green is the most commonly used color.

24-bit color values can represent 16'777'216 distinct colors. Each component is 8 bits deep (2^8 = 256 levels).

32-bit color consists of 24-bit color plus an additional 8 bits used either as empty padding space or to represent an alpha channel .

Direct digital synthesis (DDS) A process by which you can digitally generate a frequency-agile, highly-pure sinewave, or arbitrary waveform, from an accurate reference clock. The digital output waveform is typically tuned by a 32-bit digital word that allows sub-Hz frequency agility. The DDS's frequency output is normally reconstructed with a high-speed, high-performance D/A to generate an analog output signal. The ability to add internal functions such as phase modulation, amplitude modulation, digital filtering, and I&Q outputs, are making DDS devices attractive for digital communication applications. They serve in capacities such as modulators, local oscillators, and clock detect/recovery circuits.

Direct sound field A speaker system in which the great majority of the sound that you hear is coming directly from the loudspeakers, and very little from reflections from surfaces within the listening space. Direct sound field speakers tend to deliver a more accurate reflection of the source, and sharper stereo imaging, than reverberant sound field speakers. Direct sound field sound can be achieved by choosing speakers with restricted dispersion and placing them close to you.

Direct sound Sound that arrives at the listeners ear first.. Sound reaching the listening location without reflections, i.e., sound that travels in the most direct path from the source to the listener.

Direct view A display device in which you look directly at the component which produces the picture. Thus a standard CRT TV is a direct view device, as is a plasma or LCD display. An RPTV and a front projection system are not direct view since you are looking at an image projected onto a screen.

Direction The guidance and instructions of the director, as in the phrase "to take direction," meaning to follow the director's orders, something actors are not equally capable of doing.

Director In American theater, television, cinema, and audio drama, the person who conducts performances and rehearsals and who supervises, defines, and gives unity to the performances; called, in Britain and elsewhere, the producer.

DirectX 3D graphic programming API written by Microsoft. Allows programs to interface with and use built in high speed 3D graphic routines on graphic cards. Built into Windows 95 and 98.

Dirty list (dirty EDL) An EDL containing overlapping or redundant edits.

Discrete cosine transform (DCT) A DCT is just another way to represent an image. Instead of looking at it in the time domain — which, by the way, is how we normally do it — it is viewed in the frequency domain. It's analogous to color spaces, where the color is still the color but is represented differently. Same thing applies here — the image is still the image, but it is represented in a different way.

Why do JPEG, MPEG, H.261, and H.263 base part of their compression schemes on the DCT? Because it is more efficient to represent an image that way. In the same way that the Y'CbCr color space is more efficient than RGB in representing an image, the DCT is even more efficient at image representation.

Discrete output devices A separate active unit in an amplifier, capable of performing a single essential function within the output circuit. There are three basic types of output devices found on car audio amplifiers —

integrated circuits, bipolar transistors, or MOSFETs. Integrated Circuits (or IC)are found only on relatively low-wattage (20 watts RMS per channel or less) amplifiers and receivers. An IC incorporates many functional devices and thus is not considered a discrete output device. Most cannot handle more than 25 watts RMS.

Bipolar transistors and MOSFETs are found on the output stages of high powered amplifiers. They are fast enough and can handle enough current to provide power in excess of 20 watts per channel to speakers. Both of these types of transistors are considered discrete output devices. Usually there are two per channel, but some amps feature as many as eight per channel.

Discrete time oscillator (DTO) A discrete time oscillator is a digital version of the voltage-controlled oscillator.

Disk (as in hard or floppy disc) A flat circular plate, coated with a magnetic material, on which data may be stored by selective magnetization of portions of the surface, representing binary ones or zeroes. May be a flexible, floppy disc or rigid hard disk. It can also be a plastic sandwich of a metal to be optically read by reflection or scattering of laser light eg. a compact disc (CD) or Digital Versatile Disc (DVD).

Disk cache A part of RAM that is set aside to temporarily hold data which is to be read from, or written to, a disk.

Dispersion The extent to which a sound emitter yields acoustic radiation over a given area. This is a particular concern in tweeters and midranges whose portion of the audio spectrum has a much more directional character than woofers. Many Horn tweeters, while very energetic, have a more limited area of dispersion within which their effect can be fully perceived. Generally, Dome tweeters can be heard over a much wider area, all other factors being equal. But each particular example must be assessed individually for this factor. Some radiator designs are better than others.

Displace action To call attention to an unimportant production element at the expense of an important one; to upstage.

Displacement The measurement of cubic volume that an item (such as a speaker or port) takes away from the internal volume of an enclosure. When designing an enclosure, this figure must be added to the enclosure volume.

Display adapter (aka: video adaptor) A card (or board) that plugs into the computer and converts data to be displayed on the monitor. Display adaptors generally conform to video standards, such as VGA, DVI, XGA and others.

Dissolve An editing transition in which one shot fades out as the next fades in, so that both are briefly superimposed. In a lap (or overlap) dissolve, different parts of the frame dissolve at different times.

Distance education/learning Instruction that takes place when the student and instructor are separated by physical space and/or time. Correspondence courses provide one type of "distance learning". Networked computers, especially those linked into the Internet, provide many remote education opportunities. In fact, you can now obtain a degree from a "virtual university."

In North Carolina, there are three major "forces" in distance learning: 1.NCIH (North Carolina Information Highway) the entire statewide 2-way interactive network.

2. NC-REN (NC Research and Education Network) - the protion of NCIH connecting the state's 19 teaching hospital research centers and public universities.

3. MCNC (Microelectronics Center of NC) - Research Triangle organization which functions as a technical resource and central scheduling facility of the NCIH.

Distortion Any departure from a true and accurate reproduction of the original waveform. It can include Noise, Clipping Distortion, Harmonic, and Intermodulation Distortion. These last two forms are fairly common in loudspeaker reproduction and can be reduced but not entirely eliminated in the existing technology. It would be fair to say that modern amplifier design fairly eliminates nearly all forms of inherent perceived distortion, leaving only that caused by inappropriate user settings and overloading.

Distortion is the name given to anything that alters a pure input signal in any way other than changing its size. The most common forms of distortion are unwanted components or artifacts added to the original signal, including random and hum-related noise. Distortion measures a system's linearity or nonlinearity. Anything unwanted added to the input signal changes its shape (skews, flattens, spikes, alters symmetry or asymmetry). A spectral analysis of the output shows these unwanted components. If a circuit is perfect, it does not add distortion of any kind. The spectrum of the output shows only the original signal nothing else no added components, no added noise nothing but the original signal.

It's rather amusing to see amplifier manufacturers making great claims about the advantage of the extra .001 % Distortion they've wrung out of their products, while most speakers are considered very good if they can keep such distortions below 5 %. It's true that the reduction of any distortion anywhere is a positive contribution to the goal of high fidelity, but the disparity between the two technologies in this regard points up the largely subjective nature of many such claimed advantages.

Dither pattern The matrix of color or gray-scale values used to represent colors gray shades in a display system with a limited color palette.

Dithering A technique for alternating the values of adjacent dots or pixels to create the effect of intermediate values. In printing color or displaying color on a computer screen, the technique of making adjacent dots or pixels different colors to give the illusion of a third color. For example, a printed field of alternating cyan and yellow dots appears to be green. Dithering can give the effect of shades of gray on a black-and-white display, or more colors on a color display.

Diversity tuner An FM tuning method which employs two antennas. The tuner can switch between the two antennas in order to attain better reception.

Division type The technique used to represent the time between musical instruments digital interface (MIDI) events in a MIDI sequencer.

DIVX It is video encoding technology, released by company called DivXNetworks. The DivX codec is based on the MPEG-4 compression standard. This codec is so advanced that it can reduce an MPEG-2 video (the same format used for DVD or Pay-Per-View) to ten percent of its original size.

DLL (dynamic link library) A Windows' code module that is loaded and linked at runtime, then unloaded when it has finished executing.

DLP(Digital light processor) A type of projector based on the DMD. Most DLP projectors use a single DMD, so to derive the three necessary colours they have a spinning wheel with colour filter windows, carefully synchronised with the signal driving the DMD. High end DLP projectors use three DMD panels, avoiding the need for the spinning wheels. This is likely to remove the Rainbow Effect that afflicts many DLP projectors. The main advantages of DLP projectors over LCD-based ones is that the narrower band of electronics around each active pixel on the DMD's surface reduces the screen door effect, and they produce significantly darker blacks (or, more correctly, they are better at stopping light from coming out the lens when a pixel is supposed to be black).

DMD (Digital micromirror device) A technology available (until the patents run out, it seems) only from Texas Instruments. This is used in DLP projectors and controls the transmission of light by means of hundreds of thousands of microscopic mirrors on its surface which physically swing through ten or twelve degrees in accordance with the signal. They come in a range of resolutions, from SVGA (800 by 600) through XGA (1,024 by 768) in the 4:3 aspect ratio, and 1,024 by 576 (woo hoo! A real PAL-optimised one!) to 1,280 by 720 in the latest Mustang HD2 DMD.

DMF (Digital media fund) A suite of programs, funded by Multimedia Victoria (MMV) and administered by Film Victoria, that supports the creation and exhibition of digital content.

DMG A Mac OS X Disk Image File that may be mounted on your Desktop which behaves much like a traditional hardware disk such as a CD, DVD or hard drive volume. The Disk Image may contain files and folders which can be copied from the disk image to your computer. To access the contents of a disk image, double click it's icon on your Desktop.

DNS (domain name system) The domain name is a human language name for a website at which web documents are kept. The domain name is the human friendly website address. This human friendly name, is mapped to an IP address (such as 149.98.45.241) – computers do not directly work with names, but with numbers. When a web user types in an address such as www.user.com, a nameserver looks up the IP address (in numbers) and sends the requests there. DNS's are very important in the internet environment. A web address typically consists of a domain name that needs to be resolved to an IP address (i.e. the numerical address, such as 215.145.09.189). The server IP and domain does not necessarily have to be linked to a unique physical machine – the mapping may be to a unique virtual machine, which means that many different domain names and IP addresses may reside on the same physical server machine.

DNTSC Technique developed by Dotcast for data broadcasting within the NTSC video signal. It supports up to 4.5Mbps per analog TV channel.

Docudrama or documentary drama A presentation combining elements of theater and documentary; either a dramatization of historical or current events that makes, or purports to make, extensive use of authentic elements, or a purely fictive work, the documentary elements of which contribute to a sense of realism and immediacy.

Document 1. The combination of a medium and the information recorded on or in it which may be used as evidence or for consultation

2. A single record or item. Examples include: a sheet of paper with writing; an E-Mail message; a film with images; a magnetic tape with a sound recording.

Document camera A camera used to take digital images of documents/transparencies to be projected on a screen using a data projector. This technology serves the purpose of, and will eventually replace, standard overhead projectors.

Document type declaration (DTDecl) You should rather not use the abbreviation DTD for the Document Type Declaration.

The Document Type Declaration calls on the DTD (either internal or external) to be used with its related document. The Document Type Declaration thus contains the DTD; it declares which document definition is to be used with the document.

The DTDecl consists of two parts: the FPI and the URI where the FPI can be found.Example Here is an example of declaring the document type in an HTML document. the first line is the FPI, the second line the URI where the DTD can be found.

Documentary The term documentary was first used in 1926 by John Grierson (the British pioneer of non-fiction film) to mean "the creative treatment of actuality." In general, we use the word "documentary" for films intended to describe and explain their subjects, and to inform the audiences.

Dolby The most common shared logo or feature between all brands is the Dolby labs' 'double D' symbol. Named after audio engineer, Ray Dolby, it represents a number of sound processing technologies that are incorporated in a diverse number of products since the early 1970's.

Dolby digital Dolby digital is an encoding scheme invented by Dolby Laboratories as a way of compressing digital audio so that it uses a lot less data space. It is also known as AC-3. Originally developed as an audio compression system for US digital television, it achieved prominence by allowing multiple channel sound tracks to fit onto standard 35mm cinema film prints (in between the sprocket holes on the film!), it has become the de facto standard for DVD. The compression system uses perceptual encoding, similar to DTS, MPEG audio (including MP3) and Sony's SDDS and ATRAC. It can carry up to 5.1 channels of sound, but does not necessarily have that many. Dolby Digital 2.0 (that is, stereo) can be encoded with Dolby Pro Logic surround sound. The Dolby Digital bitstream can also carry codes (metadata) to control playback parameters in the Dolby Digital decoder. Dolby Digital apparently supports bit rates of up to 640kb/s, but on 5.1 (or higher) channel DVDs the bit rates actually used at 384kb/s and 448kb/s. (Note, the 'k' here stands for 1,000, not 1,024). Dolby Digital bitstreams also include metadata for controlling the operation of the decoder.

Dolby digital EX 6.1 A new surround sound standard which provides the usual 5.1 channels plus an additional channel: the centre rear channel. Unlike DTS ES 6.1 Discrete the additional channel is not carried discretely but is encoded into the two rear channels in a similar way to the front centre channel is encoded into a Dolby Pro Logic sound track. Movies prepared for Dolby EX 6.1 presentation in cinemas should have the same encoding on DVD. However EX 6.1 is compatible with 5.1 channel systems in the same way that Dolby Pro Logic is compatible with stereo systems. More correctly, this should be termed LucasFilm THX 6.1 since it was developed by them, but the name above seems to have come into common currency.

Dolby HX dolby headroom extensioin Not to be confused with the various sorts of Dolby noise reduction, Dolby HX is a process that improves the high frequency, high level recording performance of magnetic tape, particularly compact cassettes. In order to provide reasonable performance linearity, magnetic tape needs to have a 'bias' signal applied to it during recording. This is an ultrasonic sine wave. Magnetic tape also has limits to the level at which it will record a signal. The problem is tape 'saturation'. You can only make the particles so magnetic, then they won't magnetise any further. Tape saturation tends to afflict higher frequencies more than mid and low frequencies. That is why many good quality cassette decks will maintain a flat frequency response all the way to 20,000 hertz at an indicated -20dB recording level, but roll off badly before that frequency at 0dB. Some proportion of a tape's signal-holding capacity is used by the bias signal. The Dolby HX system monitors the frequency and level content of the signal during the recording and when these reach certain levels, the system reduces the level of the bias signal, consequently allowing higher recording levels, particularly at high frequencies, to be reached before tape saturation. It relies on the signal to be self-biasing.

Dolby noise reduction It was the invention of an effective noise reduction circuit by Ray Dolby in the 1960s that got Dolby Laboratories onto the road to where it is today. This circuit was developed into Dolby Type A noise reduction, which became very widely used for professional analogue recording onto tape, prior to the advent of digital recording. Most analogue recording media produce background noise, typically like white noise. The simple solution would be to boost the middle and upper frequencies during recording, then cut them on playback, thus also cutting the hiss. But this causes overloading problems. Dolby noise reduction systems rely on the masking effect of sounds. If the signal was loud, the hiss would be largely inaudible anyway. So Dolby's system tracked the level of the signal, leaving it unaltered when it was strong, but introducing the boost/cut system when the signal was low. Dolby noise reduction later made it onto consumer equipment in the form of Dolby B, C and S noise reduction systems which all work along similar lines. It was Dolby B, in particular, that allowed the compact cassette to become an established media. Dolby HX, which also appears on recent cassette decks, is not to be confused with the noise reduction systems.

Dolby surround The home equivalent of Dolby Stereo. This was the original system for decoding sound tracks for surround sound in the home, usually from video cassette. Dolby Surround sound tracks carry three channels of sound, matrixed into two channels. The Dolby Surround decoder extracts the additional channel, known as the surround channel, and sends it to a pair of rear or surround speakers. This surround channel is limited in frequency range to 100-7,000 hertz.

Dolly shot A shot taken by a camera mounted on a mobile platform, or dolly. The dolly may move on rubber wheels or on a special track set up for the scene. It may dolly in for a close-up or dolly out by rolling away from the subject. Or it may simply roll alongside a moving character, in what is often called a tracking shot. Today stabilized hand-held steadicams can achieve a smoothness almost as good as a dolly's.

DOM (document object model) The DOM is an API (Application Programming Interface) for markup documents such as XML and HTML. A document is considered to consist of objects. A paragraph would be a typical object, although not all objects may be visible to the browser. The relationships between document objects can be represented in a tree diagram. Objects are thus related just as human family members would be: there are parents, children and siblings. By manipulating this tree, the objects can be manipulated. The manipulation typically occurs by means of a scripting language, such as JavaScript. It is thus possible, for example, to change the order in which objects appear in a document. To make the scripting of such manipulation easier, scripting languages have built-in and pre-defined processes to operate on DOM.

Note that there are various flavors of DOM. For example, the HTML and XML DOM's are not exactly the same, and neither is the JavaScript DOM exactly the same as these.

Domain name system (DNS) An internet service that translates names into IP addresses.

Domain The name of an entity on the Internet. Domain names can be suffixed with the two-digit code that indicates nationality eg, uk. They can also be suffixed to indicate that the entity is of the government, a company, an educational institution, etc.

Dome tweeter Tweeters come in several different types; cones, horns and domes being the most popular. Dome types are heavily favored in many standard applications. They are efficient, and have low Distortion and wide dispersion. There is a choice between hard and soft dome materials, but all have relatively low mass and high power handling capabilities.

This same design in a larger form is quite effective as a midrange Driver also, and for many of the same reasons.

Doppler effect An apparent pitch change that takes place as a sound approaches (getting higher) or recedes (getting lower) from a sound receiver.

DOS(Disk operating system) A software package that makes a computer work with its hardware devices such as hard drive, floppy drive, screen, keyboard, etc.

Dot matrix display A display type that employs regularly spaced patterned grids of point-source lighting elements. As a result, characters displayed have greater resolution than a segmented display.

Dot pitch The distance in millimeters between centres of individual phosphor dots on a monitor screen. The smaller the dot pitch the better, since it allows for more dots to be displayed per inch and thus better resolution. The dot pitch defines the resolution of a monitor.

Dot space The horizontal distance between dot centers. This distance depends on the character pitch in effect.

Dot.Mac A fee based online internet service offered by Apple Computers composed of various components incluidng email, web pages, file sharing pages, web blogs and several other services.

Dots per inch (DPI) DPI is a count of the number of pixels (in a displayed image or scanner) or dots of ink (in a printed image or printer) per linear inch. The horizontal (h) and vertical (v) DPI of an image or device can be different. If you know an image's size and resolution, you can determine the DPIs.:

DPI(h) = resolution(h) x size(h); DPI(v)=resolution(v) x size(v)

DPI does not measure the amount of information in an image as resolution does, it measures how densly the image's information will be displayed. For example, a low resolution image could have a high DPI if it is displayed very small.

Double buffering As the name implies, you are using two buffers – for video, this means two frame buffers. While buffer 1 is being read, buffer 2 is being written to. When finished, buffer 2 is read out while buffer 1 is being written to.

Double click To click a button, typically on a mouse, twice in quick succession. Usually clicking a button twice will perform a different task to a single click: for example, single clicking on a word in a text editor will place the cursor at the point where you clicked, while double clicking will highlight the whole word. In this case, triple clicking will select the whole line or sentence that contains the word.

Double stacked (magnet) Two magnets overlaying each other to increase the overall magnetic field. In some designs for home theater applications the polarity is reversed which provides the effect of "shielding," inhibiting the size of the magnetic field radiation, thus allowing the speakers to be used next to a television without creating Distortions on the picture tube. This is achieved without a detrimental effect on the normal power handling capabilities of the speaker.

Downconverter A circuit used to change a high-frequency signal to a lower frequency.

Downlink Transmission of a signal from a satellite to a receiver on Earth.

Download The process of "pulling" information from one computer onto another. For example, when you access a Web site, the code and graphics must be downloaded from a remote onto your computer before you can see the Web site. The time it takes to do this depends on the of your connection to the Internet. Encryption Translating data or documents into a code that cannot be read without a "key." Encryption is the best way to ensure that e-mail is not intercepted and tampered with between the time it is sent and the time it is received, but the technology is not yet user friendly enough to warrant everyday use. Encryption also does not offer any protection once the document has been decrypted by the recipient, since it can be altered at that point. is currently the most commonly-used encryption software.

Dragging Holding the mouse button down while moving the mouse to move the pointer on the screen.

Drama (as opposed to theater : 1) The field of performance art concerned with the acting out of a story from a written script primarily using speech and movement; especially as pertains to the substantive and literary aspects of such performance art; 2) a type of play, serious in tone, but lacking the elevation and fatalism of tragedy.

Drama, audio Drama for the ear, whether performed live before an audience or transmitted via radio, cable audio, cassettes, compact disks, or other media; distinguished from play readings by its reliance on the electronic amplification, homogenization and manipulation of music, sound effects, and voices.

Drama, closet A type of play written to be read rather than performed, or a narrative poem cast as a play but meant to be read, e.g. Milton's Samson Agonistes, Goethe's Faust, Ibsen's Peer Gynt.

Drama, remote Dramatic performance employing technology to reach an audience physically removed from the performance space, and sometimes removed in time as well; the most far-reaching theatrical innovation of the twentieth century.

Dramatic literature The body of written drama, especially that which possesses literary merit as well as, or more than, theatrical merit; drama considered as a branch of literature.

Dramatist, audio (or radio dramatist) A sonic auteur: one who writes, produces and directs audio drama professionally; a great unsung and persecuted benefactor of mankind.

Dramatization A dramatic work adapted from non-dramatic source or sources.

Dress The arrangement of signal leads and wiring for optimum circuit operation, cosmetic appeal, and protective routing.

Driver The moving part, or parts, of a loudspeaker. These are usually woofers (bass drivers), tweeters and midrange drivers. There are a number of different driver designs. Virtually all woofers use the traditional speaker cone (some light material, often paper pulp or polypropylene) held in place by a suspension and backed by a coil inserted into the magnetic field of a strong permanent magnet. The amplifier's signal is fed into the coil, generating its own magnetic field, causing the coil and the attached cone to move. Midrange drivers, which are relatively rare these days, usually use either cones or domes (often polypropylene or a light metal such as magnesium), although there are some ribbon midrange drivers. Tweeters are most commonly domes (often polypropylene, silk or some other textile, or a light metal such as aluminium or titanium), but cheaper ones use cones. Some use inverted domes (that is, they are concave rather than convex), while some expensive speakers use ribbon tweeters. There was even, for a while, a 'plasma' tweeter where the high frequencies were generated by a pulsating ball of superheated air. Some speakers do not use what could be conventionally called drivers, for example electrostatic speakers.

Driver volume The amount of enclosure airspace that is displaced by the speaker itself.

DRM DRM stands for digital rights management.

DRM doesn't mean just basic copy-protection of digital content (like ebooks, MP3s or DivX videos), but it basically means full protection for digital content, ranging from delivery to end user's ways to use the content. somehow DRM system needs to know when the copying is allowed and when not — users also have rights to make copies to their closest relatives, etc. So, normally this has been solved by allowing "hops" — original file can be copied, but the copy of the original file cannot be copied any further. Obviously this also causes problems, if user accidentally deletes the original file, but still has the legal copy of the file.

Drop field scrambling This method is identical to the sync suppression technique for scrambling analog TV channels, except there is no suppression of the horizontal blanking intervals. Sync pulse suppression only takes place during the vertical blanking interval. The descrambling pulses still go out for the horizontal blanking intervals (to fool unauthorized descrambling devices). If a descrambling device is triggering on descrambling pulses only, and does not know that the scrambler is using the drop field scrambling technique, it will try to reinsert the horizontal intervals (which were never suppressed). This is known as double reinsertion, which causes compression of the active video signal. An unauthorized descrambling device creates a washed-out picture and loss of neutral sync during drop field scrambling.

Drop frames To fail to play every frame in a video file, usually because of performance limitations of the systems playing the video.

Drop out Missing information from magnetic tape caused by dust, lack of oxide, and so forth. Especially noticeable with a format such as Hi8 which packs a tremendous amount of information onto a tiny and fragile tape.

Dropdown menu Dropdown menus are used in many computer programs and on websites, for example in toolbars or dialogue boxes. When you click on an item, a list of further choices 'drops down' from the original item.

Dropped frames In digitial video, when the computer cannot keep pace with the displayed images, it drops frames in an attempt to catch up.

Dry. Lacking sound processing, especially equalization and reverb, said of a recording signal .

DS (description scheme) A DS specifies the structure and semantics of the relationships between its components, which may be noth Descriptors and Description Schemes.

A Descriptor and a Description Scheme differs as follows:

A Descriptor contains only basic data types, as provided by the Description Definition Language; a Descriptor does not refer to another Descriptor, or sub-Description Scheme.

DS-0/DS-3 Designations given to circuits of different bit rates. A DS-0 circuit has a bit rate of 56 KBs (actually, the full width is 64 KBs, but the rest is used for overhead associated with the transfer). A single digital telephone circuit uses a DS-0. A DS-3 has a bit rate capability of 45 Mbs, which is equivalent to 28 T1 circuits, or 672 DS-0 circuits.

DSD Direct stream digital The digital audio format used in the SACD. Unlike the PCM system normally used, DSD uses a stream of single bits of information. The momentary level of the analogue wave form being represented by the bitstream is determined by the density with which the bits are 'on' rather than 'off'. It is modified by using noise shaping to increase the effective dynamic range in the main audible band. DSD uses for each channel a bit rate of 2,822,400 bits per second.

DSL (digital subscriber line or digital subscriber loop) A technology that allows using copper telephone lines for the high-speed transmission of digital data.

DSP Digital signal processor A computer-type processing unit optimised to perform 24 or 32 bit floating-point operations on digital audio signals. This allows it to perform Fast Fourier Transforms and other complicated operations in real-time to apply frequency response adjustments, generate reverberation and even split-out certain frequency bands into separate channels. Many home theatre receivers incorporate DSP programs to generate ambient multichannel sound from stereo sources.

DSS Digital satellite system.

DSSSL (document style semantics and specification language) DSSSL is an ISO standard for SGML documents' style sheet specifications. Just as SGML is the granny of HTML and XML, DSSSL is the granny of CSS. The conventions of CSS look similar to DSSSL statements. DSSSL is more powerful than CSS because it supports style programming, while CSS contains just a list of properties.

DST Ampex automated library archive system for broadcast video server applications. DST Systems include tape drives and robotic libraries designed to provide near on-line storage for video servers.

DTD This abbreviation could be confusing as it is sometimes incorrectly used for two different but related phrases: DTD and DTDecl.

Document type definition (DTD)

The Document Type Definition defines a particular application of SGML, such as HTML or XML. It states which element, attribute and entity types and other components are permitted in the particular document. These statements are written as markup declarations and specify among other things inheritence (e.g. that an element called A can or cannot be a child of an element called B).

In XML only documents with DTDs are valid documents.

Example Here is an HTML 4.1 example of the DTD fragment for a paragraph (i.e. the definition of the HTML 4 paragraph). It states that a paragraph is an inline element.

<!ELEMENT P - O (%inline;)* — paragraph —>

The HTML DTDs do not comply 100% to the syntax of SGML DTDs (as indicated by the O above - for Optional). This has been rectified in XHTML. Here is the XHTML DTD fragment for a paragraph.

<!ELEMENT p %Inline;>

DTE Data terminal equipment.

D-terminal A video connection that delivers component video, along with useful ancilliary data. Despite the 'D', don't confuse it with any digital video standards such as DVI. The video signals are the same as component video (with up to 1080i high definition supported), while additional signals indicate the resolution of the video signal, whether it is progressive or interlaced, and its aspect ratio. The display device can use this information to set itself appropriately.

DTMF (Dual tone multi frequency) Is the dialling signal that you generate when you press an ordinary telephone's keys. It is known as "Touchtone" phone (formerly a registered trademark of AT&T). With DTMF, each key you press on your phone generates two tones of specific frequencies. So that a voice can't imitate the tones, one tone is generated from a high-frequency group of tones and the other from a low frequency group. It is sometimes used as a telemetry control signalling system.

DTS (Digital theatre system) A high quality digital surround sound compression format capable of carrying multiple channels of audio. While using perceptual encoding like many other systems, it uses much lower levels of compression. DTS claims that it first uses non-lossy compression techniques to reduce or eliminate the need for perceptual encoding. Many users consider that it produces higher quality sound than Dolby Digital . DTS sound tracks come on DVD encoded at either 768kb/s or 1,536kb/s. (Note, the 'k' here stands for 1,000, not 1,024). The principle advantage of DTS over Dolby Digital is the implementation of DTS in the cinema. Rather than the digital data being optically recorded onto the film itself, DTS audio is recorded on a CD. Special CD players attached to the cinema's film projector keep the audio and film synchronised by means of time sync signals on the film. The advantage lays in the fact that in distributing foreign language sound tracks, only the CD needs to be different for each language, not the film.

DTS ES 6.1 matrix A 6.1 channel version of DTS where a centre-rear channel is encoded into the two normal surround channels in a similar way to that employed by Dolby Pro Logic to hold a centre channel encoded into the two front channels. DTS ES 6.1 DVDs are backwards compatible with standard DTS decoders.

DTS Neo:6 A processing system that endeavours to extract an engaging 6.1 channel surround experience from two channels of audio. Unlike Dolby Pro Logic, this is not an encode/decode system, but more like a DSP system to generate something new.

Dual channel or dual voice coil (speaker) A woofer with two voice coils mounted to a common cone, which can be connected to separate amplifiers, to produce a common bass output. Since bass has a non-directional character, this still permits the optimum reproduction of the stereo image via other speakers. Care should be taken in making connection, to observe proper polarities, however. Failure to do so can result in the quick extinction of the Driver if the amplifiers are pulling the cone in different directions at once.

Dual layer A type of DVD in which there are two physical data layers on the disc. The outermost one is semi-transparent, so a DVD player can focus its laser through this layer to extract data from the bottom layer. Such a disc has, in single-sided format, a capacity of 8.5GB, rather then the 4.7GB of a single layer DVD.

Dual platform Hardware/software that operates on either Mac or Windows machines.

Dual-cone Many factory installed auto speakers are of the dual cone type. Sometimes also referred to as a "full-range" speaker, it uses an inexpensive, efficient design. The small "whizzer" cone in the center of the woofer reproduces high frequencies, but not with the dispersion, range, or intensity of a separate tweeter.

Dub 1) To copy recorded material;

2) a copy so made; hence, dubbing, the copying of recorded material; sometimes refers to the process of mixing.

Dublin core A metadata format being discussed internationally to define a minimal information resource description for use in a WWW environment. The term "Dublin" is used as Dublin, Ohio is the location of OCLC's headquarters.

Dump In digital recording, to save or store a sound file on a dat or another medium, in order to free computer memory and disk space.

Duotone files A grayscale file that supports two colors that use custom inks.

Duplex A communication system that can carry information in both directions, at the same time is called a duplex system. In CCTV, duplex is often used to describe the type of multiplexer that can perform two functions simultaneously, recording in multiplex mode and playback in multiplex mode. It can also refer to duplex data communication between a matrix switcher and a telemetry receiver.

Duration The length or persistence of a signal in time. Compare frequency.

Dust cover/cap A rigid cardboard or plastic dome placed over the opening to the voice coil cylinder in a dynamic cone driver. The main purpose is to prevent dust from falling into the voice coil-magnet gap and causing problems. In some units it may have a slight ancillary function in extending slightly the midrange/ high response. Occasionally the dome may be inverted in such a manner as to extend the inner surface of the woofer and provide a very slight improvement in the smoothness of low frequency to midrange roll-off.

Dutch angle, canted angle shot, dutch tilt A shot composed with the horizon not parallel with the bottom of the frame. Used extensively and frequently by Orson Welles.

DV and Mini-DV camcorders Portable device for recording live-motion video and audio as binary digits (rather than analog) that can be easily uploaded to a computer. Some DV (digital video) camcorders can also play 8mm and Hi-8 tapes that were recorded with an analog camcorder.

DV type-1 method The native DV interleaved stream that is produced and consumed in I/O with a DV device contains DV compressed video and pulse code modulated (PCM) audio data. This single interleaved stream can be stored in an AVI file as "ivas" stream (for interleaved video/audio stream). Microsoft refers to this format as a type-1 DV AVI file.

Because the type-1 format stores data as a single AVI stream, type-1 DV AVI files are not compatible with VfW. DirectShow, however, easily handles type-1 data streams by routing the streams to a DV Splitter filter that produces a DV-encoded video stream and one or more PCM audio streams for playback or subsequent processing.

DV type-2 method Interleaved DV data can also be split into a single video stream and one to four audio streams within an AVI file. Microsoft refers to this format of storing DV data as type-2. This format has the advantage of being backward compatible with VfW, because it contains a standard video stream and at least one standard audio stream.

The type-2 file format requires a small amount of additional processing to split and multiplex the DV stream during the functions of capture and transmit to IEEE 1394 DV devices.

DVB (Digital video broadcast) A method of transmitting digital audio and video (SDTV or HDTV resolution), based on MPEG-2. There are several variations: DVB-T for terrestrial broadcasting (ETSI EN 300 744), DVB-S for satellite broadcasting (ETSI EN 300 421), and DVB-C for cable broadcasting (ETSI EN 300 429). MPEG-2, Dolby Digital and DTS compressed audio are supported.

DVB-S uses the QPSK modulation system to guard against errors in satellite transmissions caused by reduced signal-to-noise ratio, with channel coding optimized to the error characteristics of the channel. A typical set of parameter values and 36 MHz transponder gives a useful data rate of around 38 Mbps.

DVB-C uses Quadrature Amplitude Modulation (QAM), which is optimized for maximum data rate since the cable environment is less prone to interference than satellite or terrestrial. Systems from 16-QAM up to 256-QAM can be used, but the system centers on 64-QAM, in which an 8 MHz channel can accommodate a physical payload of about 38 Mbps. The cable return path uses Quadrature Phase Shift Keying (QPSK) modulation in a 200 kHz, 1 MHz, or 2 MHz channel to provide a return path of up to about 3 Mbps. The path to the user may be either in-band (embedded in the MPEG-2 Transport Stream in the DVB-C channel) or out-of-band (on a separate 1 or 2 MHz frequency band).

DVC digital video cassette A digital tape recording format using approximately 5:1 compression to produce near-Betacam quality on a very small cassette. Originated as a consumer product, but being used professionally as exemplified by Panasonic's variation, DVC-Pro, and Sony's variation DVCam.

DVCAM Digital video tape format developed by the Sony Corporation.

DVCPro Digital Video tape format developed by Panasonic.

DVD DVD is a media format for storing digital information. There are several kinds of DVD disks:

DVD-Video (often referred to as simply DVD) to hold pre-recorded video.

DVD-Audio to hold pre-recorded audio.

DVD-ROM to hold pre-recorded computer data and programs.

DVD-R for home recording of video or storage of computer data and programs.

DVD-RW for storage ofcomputer data.

DVD+R for home recording of video or storage of computer data and programs. DVD+RW for storage of computer data and programs.

DVD-RAM to store computer progams and data.

Not all players or drives can play or record all types disks. A DVD can hold from 4.7 to 17.0 Gigabytes of information depending on how many sides and layers it has. DVD-Video disks and DVD-R's that are used to hold video for playback in set-top DVD players use MPEG-2 video compression to encode the digital video.

The PRESENT has DVD-RW burners. This burner will record DVD-R or DVD-RW discs. This is the format supported by Apple, Pioneer, Gateway and Compaq. The DVD+RW format supported by Phillips, Sony, Dell and HP is not available in the PRESENT.

DVD +R DL A write-once (ie. once recorded, it cannot be overwritten) high-capacity recordable DVD. Unlike the competing formats, this version (announced 2003, product availability in 2004) is dual layer, allowing it to store up to 8.5GB of data rather than the 4.7GB of the other formats. This format is supported by the DVD+RW Alliance.

DVD 10 DVD-10 is a double sided single layer DVD. Video DVD, DVD-R/W and DVD+R/W support this format. Effectively this means that DVD-10 is a dual-sided DVD-5 and can hold 8.75 gigabytes of data with 4.38 gigabytes on each side. Two-sided discs need to be flipped over in order to access the other data side. Unfortunately many blank DVD media advertisers mislead customers to believe that these discs are actually blank DVD-9 discs in hope that they could copy their dual-layer discs directly to blank discs.

DVD 18 DVD-18 is a double sided dual layer DVD which can fit up to 17 GB or 15.9 computer GB which some commercial video DVDs are using today (a DVD-18 is basicly four pressed plastic DVD-5s pressed together, they are not burned). Video DVD supports this format but DVD-R/W and DVD+R/W does not support this format.

DVD 5 DVD-5 is a single sided single layer DVD that stores up to about 4.7 GB = 4 700 000 000 bytes and that is 4.38 computer GigaBytes where 1 kilobyte is 1024 bytes(4 700 000 000B/1024 = about 4 589 843KB/1024 = about 4485MB/1024 = about 4.38GB) . Video DVD, DVD-R/W and DVD+R/W supports this format. Often referred to as "single sided, single layer".

DVD 9 DVD-9 is a single sided dual layer DVD which can fit up to 8.5 GB or 7.95 computer GB which many commercial video DVDs are using today (a DVD-9 is basicly two pressed plastic DVD-5s pressed together, they are not burned). Video DVD supports this format but DVD-R/W and DVD+R/W does not support this format.

DVD audio DVD-Audio is music disc, aimed to replace regular audio CD within next few years. DVD-Audio disc can contain 4 - 18 GBs of data, depending on how many layers and sides of the disc are used. Regular DVD-Audio disc contains various copy-protection methods and obviously the audio data itself — audio can be stored in various formats, including uncompressed (L)PCM format (in frequencies from 44.1kHz upto 192kHz) with bitrates as high as 9.8Mbit/sec. Other formats allowed include Dolby Digital 5.1, MPEG-1 (stereo, audio layers II and III), MPEG-2 (multichannel), DTS and SDDS.

DVD-Audio discs can't be played with regular DVD-Video players — the player has to be so-called "Universal DVD" player in order to support DVD-Audio (but if your player has DVD-Audio logo, it supports these discs).

DVD burner Another term for DVD Recorder.

DVD Dynamic HTML/DHTML A set of recent technologies (HTML, layers, Cascading Style Sheets, Javascript) which, togehter, enable richer, more interactive content.

DVD MP3 This type of disc is created when MP3 audio files are burned on a DVDR/W disc. Some DVD Players can play these discs, but many so far cannot.

DVD recorder A consumer electronics device which uses one or more of several different types of recordable DVD media as storage for video and audio material. It acts as a replacement for the VCR, offering significant improvements in picture quality, plus the usual DVD playback conveniences of fast access, chapter breaks and the like. DVD recorders typically incorporate an analogue TV tuner for direct-from-broadcast recording, plus external inputs. One of the external inputs is often a DV port which accepts a digital signal from a digital video camera. However DVD recorders do not use the DV compression system for their video storage. They use MPEG2 the same as commercial DVDs for broad compatibility with DVD players. DV input is converted to MPEG2. They usually record sound using Dolby Digital 2.0, but some also offer PCM. There are two different kinds of media for making recordings which cannot be over-written: DVD-R and DVD+R. There are three different kinds of media which can be re-used: DVD-RW, DVD+RW and DVD-RAM. An increasing number of DVD recorders are multi-format, capable of recording to four different kinds of media. Most support only single layer recordable DVDs and thus offer a capacity of 4.7GB, however some are appearing with support for dual layer discs. DVD recorders permit different recording times, with longer times trading off for poorer quality. Very good quality recordings of two hours duration are achievable with a 4.7GB disc, while some offer six or more eight at low quality. Some premium DVD recorders incorporate a computer-style hard disk drive upon which recordings can be made, then edited, before being dubbed (at high speed) to a black disc.

DVD R drive (digital versatile disc-recordable drive) A device capable of recording audio, video, text and other information to an optical disc identified as a DVD-R (Digital Video Disc-Recordable). A DVD-R drive cannot write to a DVD-RW. Typically, a DVD-R drive can read CD's, CD-R's, CD-RW's, DVD's, DVD-R's and DVD-RW's. There are several types of DVD-R drives available on the market. Consult the documentation included with the computer or DVD drive for specifics.

DVD-RAM A rewritable (ie. recorded material can be erased or over-written) recordable

DVD. This format is supported by the DVD Forum. It should noted that DVD-RAM has very limited compatibility with standard DVD players (although recent Panasonic models support it), because it uses significantly different technology to the other types of recordable DVDs. In particular, it offers true random access writing to identified sections of the disc, which has allowed Panasonic DVD recorders to implement a 'time-slip' feature (continuous recording, and the ability to rewind and watch recorded material, even while recording continues). It is also said to support a higher order of magnitude of re-write cycles than either DVD-RW or DVD+RW.

DVD ROM (digital versatile disc, read only memory) Small optical disc similar to a CD-ROM; however, a DVD-ROM is capable of holding up to 133 minutes of high quality audio and video in MPEG-2 format. Data on a DVD-ROM cannot be erased; however, it can be viewed or copied to another location.

DVD ROM Drive (digital versatile disc, read only memory drive) A device connected to a computer capable of reading both DVD's and CD's. DVD-ROM drives are not capable of recording to a DVD; however, some DVD drives, for example a DVD-ROM/CD-RW drive, are capable of recording to a CD-R or CD-RW or both. Consult the documentation included with the computer or drive for specifics.

DVD RW Drive (digital versatile disc-rewritable drive) A device capable of recording audio, video, text and other information to an optical disc identified as a DVD-RW (Digital Video Disc-ReWritable). Typically, a DVD-RW drive can read CD's, CD-R's, CD-RW's, DVD's, DVD-R's and DVD-RW's. There are several types of DVD-RW drives available on the market. Consult the documentation included with the computer or DVD drive for specifics.

DVD+R DL (DVD+Recordable dual layer) A recordable DVD format. A DVD+R DL is similar to a DVD+R disc, in that it can only record data once and then the data becomes permanent on the disc, and cannot be recorded onto a second time. However, a DVD+R DL has two layers, in which the disc can hold up to 8.5 GB of video or computer data. A DVD+R DL formats are supported by Philips, Sony, Hewlett-Packard, Dell, Ricoh, Yamaha and others.

DVD+VR The recording mode provided for DVD+RW and DVD+R discs on consumer DVD recorders. While somewhat different to the standard DVD-Video mode used with commercial discs, it still provides for good compatibility with standard DVD players. On DVD+RW discs it allows significant levels of editing of recordings, while still retaining that good compatibility, and eliminating the need to 'finalise' the disc (DVD+R discs must still be finalised).

DVD-Authoring The process by which already-encoded video files are transferred onto a DVD. DVD authoring usually involves using separate DVD authoring software that allows users to create menus, chapters, music, etc to the disc's layout in addition to the actual video files and transfer this structure to a filesystem that can then be burned to a DVD.

DVD-Interactive DVD-Interactive provides additional interactive capability for users by being able to access additional content on the DVD and/or Web sites on the Internet.

D-VHS A new standard proposed by JVC for recording digital signals on a VHS video recorder.

DVI, DVI-D, DVI-I, DVI-A Abbreviation for digital visual interface. This is a digital RGB video interface to a display. The EIA-861 standard specifies how to include data such as aspect ratio and format information. The VESA EEDID and DI-EXT standards document data structures and mechanisms to communicate data across DVI.

DVI-D is a digital-only connector; a DVI-I connector handles both analog and digital. DVI-A is available as a plug (male) connector only and mates to the analog-only pins of a DVI-I connector. DVI-A is only used in adapter cables, where there is the need to convert to or from a traditional analog VGA signal.

DWDM(Dense wavelength division multiplexing) A recently introduced system for increasing the number of channels in a fibre optic system. The spacing between wavelengths can be as little as 10nm.

DXF File type (.dxf) which is the industry standard 3D format. Used by CAD-based software and hardware.

Dynamic HTML/DHTML A set of recent technologies (HTML, layers, Cascading Style Sheets, Javascript) which, togehter, enable richer, more interactive content.

Dynamic power In some respects dynamic power is a similar measure to PMPO, but remains far more realistic. It is quoted in conjunction with continuous power outputs and shows how much power the amplifier or receiver can deliver for a very brief instant, such as when a crescendo is played in music. An amplifier with a reasonably low continuous power output can often sound quite good at reasonably high levels if it has a high dynamic power rating.

Dynamic range control A facility in Dolby Digital to the reduce the dynamic range of the audio content in order to allow the entire program to be heard in adverse conditions. It does this by reducing the loudness of the parts of the program which are louder than the level set by the dialog normalization setting, and boosting those parts quieter than that setting. The parameters for reductions are carried in Dolby Digital metadata. This feature is useful for appreciating movies without disturbing neighbours, and when the audio from a DVD is being heard through a limited sound system. In particular, if DRC is available on a DVD player, it should always be switched on if a TV's speakers are being used to listen to the program.

Dynamic range suppression A signal compression technique which raises the level of lower passages without affecting overall volume. Especially useful with high noise levels, such as a moving vehicle.

Dynamic range The ratio of the loudest (undistorted) signal to that of the quietest (discernible) signal in a unit or system as expressed in decibels (dB). Dynamic range is another way of stating the maximum S/N ratio. With reference to signal processing equipment, the maximum output signal is restricted by the size of the power supplies, i.e., it cannot swing more voltage than is available. While the minimum output signal is determined by the noise floor of the unit, i.e., it cannot put out a discernible signal smaller than the noise. Professional-grade analog signal processing equipment can output maximum levels of +26 dBu, with the best noise floors being down around -94 dBu. This gives a maximum dynamic range of 120 dB pretty impressive numbers, which coincide nicely with the 120 dB dynamic range of normal human hearing (from just audible to uncomfortably loud).

Dynamics When used in music, refers to the varying degree of loudness and softness in a musical performance.

Dynamic tracking The ability for a video head to "bend" back and forth enough to find an adjacent track and follow it. This allows true freeze-frame rather than only freeze-field display. It also allows for variable speed playback, including playing in reverse, which otherwise is not possible.

E

Ear candy Sound elements added for aural richness, but that do not significantly alter the dramatic story-line (bird ambience as opposed to a car crash, for instance).

Earth An electrical connection to the earth, which represents 0 volts or 'ground potential' by way of a metal or conductive rod.

Easter egg A surprise "extra" coded into DVD's, computer programs or web pages that is accessed by an undocumented keystroke combination or hidden link.

EBP Efficiency bandwidth product A parameter that helps determine the suitability of a driver for a sealed or ported enclosure. An EBP of less than 50 indicates the driver should be used in a sealed box, 50 90 indicates flexible design options including bass reflex, over 90 indicates the need for a ported enclosure. EBP = Fs / Qes.

Echo chamber An acoustic environment that enhances reverberation.

Echo The effect of a sound and a delayed version of that same sound. A 'Slap-Back Echo' is the original sound plus a single repeat; "Multiple Echo" is the original sound plus several repeats with the identical delay spacing and decay times.

ECMA Script ECMAScript 1.0 (ECMA-262) is the JavaScript standard of the European Computer Manufacturers Association.

E commerce This is the technical name for something like a Shop, which sells products or services through a website. Ecommerce sites often have secure areas and will encrypt (or encode) the information that you enter in that secure area to protect you from fraud.

Edge numbers Code numbers printed on the edge of 16 and 35mm motion picture film every foot which allow frames to be easily identified in an edit list.

EDI (Electronic data interchange) The exchange of structured data messages to enable automated transactions between application systems.

EDIFACT (EDI for administrations, commerce and transport) The international EDI standard messaging syntax under the responsibility of the UN, for trading transactions in all industries. Also known as UN-EDIFACT.

Edit decision lists (EDL) The Edit Decision List, or EDL, is the data controlling the editing computer during an on-line session. It lists "in-points" and "out-points" for both the source playback decks and the record deck. These "events" can be for video, audio, or both. The EDL may control all sources, various effects machines (for fades and dissolves, for example) and the record deck. An EDL may be created manually after the off-line editing is complete or it may be generated by the edit controller used in more sophisticated off-line systems. Computer based editing systems including the Digital F/X and Avid Media Composer will automatically generate an EDL.

Editing The selecting and joining together of shots in the way they will appear on the movie screen. The work progresses from assembly to rough cut, then fine cut, at which point the sound editor is usually brought in.

Effects Effects involve any manipulation or processing of the video or audio signal. Though they are often used for gratuitous gimmickry, they can also be used for valid functional and aesthetic design purposes. Video effects seem to change annually, and are heavily technology-driven. Since they sometimes cannot be simulated in an off-line environment, the best way to prepare to use them is to look over the free demos available from various video facilities and vendors. Off-line systems like the Avid Media Composer allow you to preview most of the standard video effects.

Effective piston area (Sd) (measured in square inches or meters) The active radiating area of a speaker cone, including that part of the surround which displaces sufficient air to produce a measurable acoustic output.

Efficiency The ability of an audio system to convert electrical energy (watts) into mechanical energy (Decibels of acoustical energy). This ratio is usually given as the amount of energy measured in Decibels at a distance of one meter from the input of one watt of electrical energy. In most speakers, the greater the efficiency rating, the louder the unit will play in response to the same setting of the volume control, in comparison to less efficient types. The overall efficiency for most speakers systems is under 20 percent. Typical speakers can be rated at anywhere from 85 to 110 dB. Keep in mind, of course, that efficiency is only one parameter of a speaker's overall quality.

EI Electronic iris Electronic circuits in a camera that enable the camera shutter mode to be automatically controlled to vary the output video level, much as an auto iris in the lens would do. It enables manual iris lenses to be used where light levels vary.

EIA Electronic industries association Which changed in 1997 to Electronic Industries Alliance, which has recommended the television standard used in the US, Canada and Japan, based on 525 lines interlaced scanning.Formerly known as RMA or RETMA. It also specifies the RS data standards.

EIA-516 United States teletext standard, also called NABTS.

EIA-608 United States closed captioning and extended data services (XDS) standard. Revision B adds Copy Generation Management System - Analog (CGMS-A), content advisory (v-chip), Internet Uniform Resource Locators (URLs) using Text-2 (T-2) service, 16-bit Transmission Signal Identifier, and transmission of DTV PSIP data.

EIA-708 United States DTV closed captioning standard. EIA CEB-8 also provides guidance on the use and processing of EIA-608 data streams embedded within the ATSC MPEG-2 video elementary transport stream, and augments EIA-708.

EIA-744 NTSC "v-chip" operation. This standard added content advisory filtering capabilities to NTSC video by extending the EIA-608 standard. It is now included in the latest EIA-608 standard, and has been withdrawn.

EIA-761 Specifies how to convert QAM to 8-VSB, with support for OSD (on screen displays).

EIA-762 Specifies how to convert QAM to 8-VSB, with no support for OSD (on screen displays).

EIA-766 United States HDTV content advisory standard.

EIA-770 This specification consists of three parts (EIA-770.1, EIA-770.2, and EIA-770.3). EIA-770.1 and EIA-770.2 define the analog YPbPr video interface for 525-line interlaced and progressive SDTV systems. EIA-770.3 defines the analog YPbPr video interface for interlaced and progressive HDTV systems. EIA-805 defines how transfer VBI data over these YPbPr video interfaces.

EIA-775 EIA-775 defines a specification for a baseband digital interface to a DTV using IEEE 1394 and provides a level of functionality that is similar to the analog system. It is designed to enable interoperability between a DTV and various types of consumer digital audio/video sources, including settop boxes and DVRs or VCRs.

EIA-775.1 adds mechanisms to allow a source of MPEG service to utilize the MPEG decoding and display capabilities in a DTV.

EIA-775.2 adds information on how a digital storage device, such as a D-VHS or hard disk digital recorder, may be used by the DTV or by another source device such as a cable set-top box to record or time-shift digital television signals. This standard supports the use of such storage devices by defining Service Selection Information (SSI), methods for managing discontinuities that occur during recording and playback, and rules for management of partial transport streams.

EIA-849 specifies profiles for various applications of the EIA-775 standard, including digital streams compliant with ATSC terrestrial broadcast, direct-broadcast satellite (DBS), OpenCable™, and standard definition Digital Video (DV) camcorders.

EIA-805 This standard specifies how VBI data are carried on component video interfaces, as described in EIA-770.1 (for 480p signals only), EIA-770.2 (for 480p signals only) and EIA-770.3. This standard does not apply to signals which originate in 480i, as defined in EIA-770.1 and EIA-770.2. The first VBI service defined is Copy Generation Management System (CGMS) information, including signal format and data structure when carried by the VBI of standard definition progressive and high definition YPbPr type component video signals. It is also intended to be usable when the YPbPr signal is converted into other component video interfaces including RGB and VGA.

EIA-861 The EIA-861 standard specifies how to include data, such as aspect ratio and format information, on DVI and HDMI.

EIA-J CPR-1204 This EIA-J recommendation specifies another widescreen signaling (WSS) standard for NTSC video signals. WSS may be present on 20 and 283.

Electric piano A piano-style keyboard which produces piano-like sounds as an electrical audio signal which is amplified and fed to a loudspeaker where it becomes an acoustic audio signal. Electric pianos differ from electronic pianos in that some physical component must actually move in order to generate the electrical audio signal. Many older electric pianos (and some new ones) don't speak MIDI which means they are unable to control (or play) any additional keyboards or MIDI sound modules available.

Electrical audio signal A stream of electrical impulses which represent sound in electric form. An electrical audio signal can be processed by many different devices to add qualities such as reverb, more bass, more treble, etc. An electrical audio signal cannot be heard until sent using electrical wire to an amplifier and speakers. At this point, it is translated into an acoustic audio signal.

Electrical signal A means of conveying information through use of electricity to carry the message. There are many types of electrical signals such as analog, digital, and visible, differing in the method used to convey the information.

Electrolytic capacitor A polarized capacitor with a negative and a positive terminal that is commonly used for DC power filtration and energy storage. As with all capacitors, the dielectic insulator separates two plates and holds a charge. In this case the dielectric is a form of chemical electrolyte that is polarized. Smaller types are mesured in microfarads while the large ones used for amplifier stabilization are measured in farads. Values in the range of .5 to 3 farads are typical for use with car audio amplifiers.

Electronic display Showing images through the computer.

Electronic funds transfer (EFT) At the point of the sale this is the system which takes money straight out of your bank account when you pay for something.

Electronic journal Similar to a traditional journal but published only in electronic form - on a CD-ROM or the World Wide Web.

Electronic mail (e-mail) Most electronic mail packages provide a method for mailing to other users' electronic mail addresses that are not on the local machine.

An e-mail address has two parts, separated by @ .The portion before the @ sign is the username, or mailbox name, of a particular user. The portion after the @ is the location adress. The suffix, in this case .gov, denotes what type of organization.

Electronic media Any of the media used to publish information electronically (as opposed to print).

Electronic publishing Composition of text (and frequently graphic images) using a computer for display in a computer presentation program or on the Web.

Electronic signature Sometimes written as e-signature or digital signature. A code that can be attached to an electronically transmitted message that uniquely identifies the sender. Like a written signature, the purpose of a digital signature is to guarantee that the individual sending the message really is who he or she claims to be.

Electrostatic driver The Electrostatic Driver generates a motive force for its diaphragm by the interaction of electric rather than magnetic fields as is the case for the dynamic driver. The electrostatic driver is basically "hung" on a frame. It does NOT have a box enclosure, so a great deal of "coloration" (frequency response fluctuations caused by the enclosure reflections) is avoided. A large diaphragm of lightweight material is placed between two perforated (acoustically transparent) electrodes. The diaphragm is electrically polarized at a few thousand volts relative to the electrodes, which maintain a large electrostatic field. The audio signal is applied to the two electrodes in a push-pull fashion. Under these conditions, the diaphragm will vibrate in step with the audio drive signal and produce sound. Because it is a true push-pull driver (i.e. its diaphragm is driven from both front and rear), it operates in a linear fashion.

In an electrostatic driver, the driving force is uniform over the entire diaphragm surface (note that for the Dynamic Driver, the diaphragm is driven over a small portion of its overall surface) as a result, Electrostatic Drivers do not suffer drastically from "breakup" effect as dynamic drivers. Gross distortion typically results only if the driving amplifier clips into the speaker, or when, in an attempt to play the driver at a higher sound level than its design permits, its step-up transformer may reach a point of saturation. Due to the diaphragm of the electrostatic driver being of low mass (lightweight), its transient response is excellent and reproduction of subtle, low-level musical details is exceptional.

Electrostatic loudspeakers A form of loudspeaker in which the driver is a panel that responds to a varying electrostatic charge. Such speakers incorporate electronics which convert the moderate voltage, moderate current output from an amplifier into the high voltage, low current signal required to drive the panels. Electrostatic speakers are noted for producing little harmonic distortion and an excellent amount of detail in the reproduction of music. However they often present a difficult load upon amplifiers, can be subject to arcing (producing electrical sparks) in high humidity situations and tend to be somewhat inefficient. Because they use a large panel, these speakers do not employ an enclosure and so are bass limited. For this reason many models are hybrid, with standard woofers in an enclosure for bass. Electrostatic speakers are by their nature dipolar in operation since each side of the panel is generating an out-of-phase sound wave to the other.

Element An element marks a document content object so that a computer program can manipulate that kind of object effectively. As almost any object in the real world that is presented in a document may be regarded as an important element that needs to be marked as such in the document, many millions of elements are possible.

To make it easier to mark these elements, in HTML there are only about 80 pre-defined elements that a web author can use. Eelements are defined in DTDs. Most elements also have their own sets of attributes that may be used to describe some of its features or characteristics.

The set of elements in HTML are obviously limited. To address this, a related but much more powerful markup language, called XML, was developed by the W3C. In XML applications there may be millions of elements defined according to specific needs. The set of possible elements can be restricted by designing a specific XML-application in which only the relevant elements are defined.

In markup languages there is a specific syntax to be used for marking element content so that computers may know how to distinguish between different kinds of objects in a document. Elements have specific names in specific applications. For example, in HTML the paragraph object's element name is p, and is written between special symbols: <p>. These markup commands do not execute like programming commands, but indicate to a user agent (such as a browser) the structure of the marked document. A parser (which is a part of a browser) investigates the elements and their relationships and determines the structure of the document. The parser then passes that information along to a rendering engine which manipulates the content, typically using associated style sheets to determine how the content is to be rendered. The most typical manipulation is to display the content graphically on a computer screen, but it could also be manipulated to be rendered on other types of devices, such as speech synthesizers or tactile devices (eg Braille devices).

ELMO Electric light machine organization, maker of visual presenters for teleconferencing and distance learning applications; the camera used to send document images over videoconferencing systems to remote sites.

Embed Placing a movie on a web page where it can be viewed without requiring a helper application.

Embed tag An HTML tag used to place a media file (such as an audio, video, or Flash file) into a web page. The embed tag defines an area on the page in which the media file will appear if it involves graphic elements, helps the browser understand what type of file it is, and specifies other information as well, such as whether the file will play automatically when the page loads.

Embedded media are contrasted to media controlled through a separate player, such as when the RealPlayer pops up over your web browser to display a video.

Embedded links A link within the content of a webpage.

Enclosure The box of a loudspeaker. In any half decent speaker, this is not merely a device to keep the drivers off the floor, but an integral part of the design of the whole loudspeaker, contributing greatly to – or, if done badly, detracting from – its performance. The most common enclosure designs are bass reflex and acoustic suspension. Good quality enclosures include strong bracing to resist sympathetic vibrations in their panels, which can lead to sound colouration.

Enclosure volume The total amount of internal airspace of an enclosure. Each woofer has an optimal airspace volume that helps it meet it's bass potential. This resonance cavity specification usually measured in cubic feet, includes the net driver and vent volumes. To find the volume of a cube multiply HxWxD in inches. divide the result be 1725 (the number of inches in a cubic foot) to get the volume in cubic feet.

Enclosure, or box A cabinet in which the various Drivers are housed. This arrangement is absolutely essential if bass response is desired from the woofer, which by itself in the open air, will produce very little low frequency response. This is so because of an effect called phase cancellation. This means that the sound wave coming from the back of the speaker at low frequencies is identical in form and intensity to the one coming from the front of the cone. When they meet, as in the open air, they are exactly 180 degrees out of phase and thus cancel each other out. An enclosure either prevents this from occurring or modifies the interaction so that the backwave actually reinforces the front wave. Tweeters and midranges are less severly effected by the phase cancellation effects, and are not in need of enclosures.

Encode In the context of Indeo video, the process of converting the color space of a video clip from RGB to YUV and then compressing it.

Encoded video The encoded video signal is formed by starting with an RGB signal from the color television camera. This RGB signal is then processed through an encoder, known as the I and Q encoder, which converts the RGB into a composite NTSC signal. The encoded signal has all of the elements of the composite video signal: sync, burst, chroma, and luminance.

Encoding The process of compressing a media file for a specific purpose, such as streaming on the Web, One can encode a file that is in analog form (such as a VHS tape) or one that is already digital (such as the signal on a Mini-DV tape).

Encryption Translating data or documents into a code that cannot be read without a "key." Encryption is the best way to ensure that e-mail is not intercepted and tampered with between the time it is sent and the time it is received, but the technology is not yet user friendly enough to warrant everyday use. Encryption also does not offer any protection once the document has been decrypted by the recipient, since it can be altered at that point. PGP is currently the most commonly-used encryption software.

End of file The last line of readable code in a file or the last record in a database.

ENG camera Electronic news gathering camera Refers to CCD cameras in the broadcast industry used for outside broadcasts when gathering news.

Enhanced definition television (EDTV) EDTV is content or a display capable of displaying a maximum of 576 progressive active scan lines. No aspect ratio is specified.

Enhancer Video signal processor that compensates for picture detail losses and distortion occuring in recording and playback.

Ensemble 1) The quality of a performance in which the whole is greater than the sum of its parts; that is, the rapport among and the combined performances of the cast have a personality and importance greater than that of the performers individually; a work benefiting from strong ensemble is often called an ensemble piece;

2). of such a quality;

3) a) The cast of a production; b) the performers in a repertory company.

Epiphany, epiphanal moment (from Gr., "showing forth") 1) In drama, especially in tragedy, the protagonist's sudden insight into his/her condition or circumstances, caused by his/her struggle with antagonistic forces, that leads him/her to take action that brings on the climax or reversal (called by Aristotle anagnorisis);

2) a literary expression introduced by James Joyce to denote a gesture or action that sums up or reveals the essence of a fictional character to an audience.

Episodic 1) adj, Containing many totally or partially self-contained episodes; 2) used pejoratively, containing too many scenes or episodes, and, hence, structurally weak or unwieldy; 3) a broadcast series of self-contained episodes, usually melodramas, featuring recurring lead characters and any number of transient secondary characters.

EPROM Erasable and programmable read only memory An electronic chip used in many different security products that stores software instructions for performing various operations.

EPS (encapsulated postscript) Graphics file format often used in desktop publishing packages, like PageMaker.

EPS File Encapsulated PostScript file which is a graphic format that can represent both vector and bitmap data.

EQ (equalizer) A class of electronic filter circuits designed to augment or adjust electronic or acoustic systems. Equalizers can be fixed or adjustable, active or passive. Most consumer audio equallizers divide the spectrum into 3 to 12 bands, allowing each section to be either increased or decreased in amplitude without changing the response of the rest.

In the early years of telephony and cinema, the first equalizers were fixed units designed to compensate for losses in the transmission and recording of audio signals. Hence, the term equalizer described electronic circuits that corrected for these losses and attempted to make the output equal to the input. Equalizers permit the modification the frequency response spectrum of the signal passing through them; that is, they modify the amplitude versus frequency characteristics.

Equalization pulses These are two groups of pulses, one that occurs before the serrated vertical sync and another group that occurs after. These pulses happen at twice the normal horizontal scan rate. They exist to ensure correct 2:1 interlacing in early televisions.

Equalizer Equipment designed to compensate for loss and delay frequency effects within a system. A component or circuit that allows for the adjustment of a signal across a given band.

Erasable optical disk A type of optical disk that can be erased and loaded with new data as opposed to a read-only (or non-erasable disk) such as a CD-ROM.

ERCIM (european research consortium for informatics and mathematics) The ERCIM is the European host of the W3C.

Ergonomics The accessibility and ease of controlling a system in normal operational mode with a minimum of motion and thought required.

Error A situation in which the computer cannot proceed through the normal course of a task. This can be for a number of reasons including a "bug" in the software or an incorrect piece of code. Often an error message is displayed to try to help you.

Error concealment The ability to hide transmission errors that corrupt the content beyond the ability of the receiver to properly display it. Techniques for video include replacing the corrupt region with either earlier video data, interpolated video data from previous and next frames, or interpolated data from neighboring areas within the current frame. Decoded MPEG video may also be processed using deblocking filters to reduce blocking artifacts. Techniques for audio include replacing the corrupt region with interpolated audio data.

Error correction Redundant data included with a signal in transmission or storage that allows the signal to be reconstructed even if some data has been damaged or lost. Error correction is used in most digital systems, from CDs through to digital television.

Error log A record of events, generally errors, that happen in code or during execution.

Error resilience The ability to handle transmission errors without corrupting the content beyond the ability of the receiver to properly display it. MPEG-4 supports error resilience through the use of resynchronization markers, extended header code, data partitioning, and reversible VLCs.

E-serial Similar to a traditional serial but published only in electronic form - on a CD-ROM or the World Wide Web.

ESP Electronic shock protection An electronic circuit that stores the audio data stream from a CD or MD in a memory buffer. If the laser pick-up mistracks, audio still flows from the buffer preventing an interruption.

Establishing shot A full shot used to open a new scene. It shows significant details and characters, so that viewers can get their bearings before the camera focuses more tightly.

Ethernet Network access system using the Carrier-Sense Multiple Access with Collision Detection (CSMA/CD) access method in which nodes may transmit a signal at any given time, and if two devices transmit at the same time both devices will wait a random period of time before attempting to resend.

ETSI EN 300 163 This specification defines NICAM 728 digital audio for PAL.

ETSI EN 300 231 This specification defines information sent during the vertical blanking interval using PAL teletext (ETSI EN 300 706) to control VCRs in Europe (PDC).

ETSI EN 300 294 Defines the widescreen signaling (WSS) information for PAL video signals. For (B, D, G, H, I) PAL systems, WSS may be present on line 23.

ETSI EN 300 421 This is the DVB-S specification.

ETSI EN 300 468 This is the DVB SI (service information) specification.

ETSI EN 300 472 This is the specification for the carriage of teletext data (ETSI EN 300 706) in DVB bitstreams.

ETSI EN 300 706 This is the enhanced PAL teletext specification.

ETSI EN 300 708 This specification defines data transmission using PAL teletext (ETSI EN 300 706).

ETSI EN 300 743 This is the DVB subtitling specification.

ETSI EN 300 744 This is the DVB-T specification.

ETSI EN 301 775 This is the specification for the carriage of Vertical Blanking Information (VBI) data in **DVB** bitstreams.

ETSI ETS 300 731 Defines the PALplus standard, allowing the transmission of 16:9 programs over normal PAL transmission systems.

ETSI ETS 300 732 Defines the ghost cancellation reference (GCR) signal for PAL.

EVD EVD (Enhanced versatile disc) is a red-laser DVD disc and player specification from China. It uses the MPEG-2 video codec (H.264 eventually) and EAC 5.1-channel audio codec. Content may be 1920x1080i, 1280x720p, 720x576 or 704x480. One DVD9 disc supports up to 105 minutes of 1280x720p content or up to 50 minutes of 1920x1080i content.

Event Any input or interaction caused by the user such as a keystroke, mouse click, etc.

Event listener A runtime routine inside of an application that waits for events to occur and then calls the appropriate handler.

Evernet Buzzword that refers to the next generation of Internet access. The Evernet concept anticipates the convergence of broadband, wireless, and current Internet technologies that will include easy, wireless and inexpensive access to the Internet.

Exabyte When written in capital letters, it is the name of a manufacturer of a tape based mass storage device. When in lower case it is 2 to the 60th power

[260 or 1,152,921,504,606,846,976] bytes. One exabyte is equal to 1,024 petabytes.

Exchange In drama, a more or less unified chunk of dialogue between two or more characters; a question or statement by one character and its response from another.

Excursion limited power handling Based on the maximum amount of power the driver can handle without appreciable distortion. All frequencies 30 Hz and above are considered in this limit.

Excursion limited SPL The maximum sound pressure level the system can produce given an input signal equal to the rated excursion limited power handling.

Excursion The degree of fore and aft movement of a mechanical component in an audio system. Loudspeakers, for example, produce sound by vibrating their drivers' cones or domes. The distance between the furthest the cone, say, protrudes forwards and the furthest it moves back into the housing is the excursion of the driver. Woofers tend to have a greater excursion than drivers for higher frequencies. The drivers in some compact subwoofers deliver an excursion of up to 50mm. This wide excursion is necessary because output level is related to the area of the cone and the excursion. A smaller driver in a subwoofer can only provide equivalent output levels by allowing a greater excursion of the cone. Another example of excursion is the stylus of a cartridge. When playing a stereo LP it moves from side to side and up and down. Each of these is referred to as the excursion (horizontal and vertical) of the stylus.

Executable (.exe) A file type (.exe) that contains a program. Double-clicking an executable file (a file that ends in .exe) will open that file. When an executable file is opened, the computer operating system will run the program. Many downloaded files are .exe files. Viruses can also come disguised as .exe files. Always verify the source of an .exe file before it is opened, especially if it arrives via e-mail.

Executable program A file that will start and run when you type in the name and press enter, click the file icon or put its name in the Run window of the Windows Program Manager.

Expander A type of dynamic range processor which reduces the gain of audio signals which are under an adjustable 'threshold' level, therefore increasing the dynamic range. Generally allows the operator control over threshold, ratio, attack, release and 'hold' times. Both analog and digital types are available.

Extended Pole Piece.

Extended pole pieces on the magnet assembly allow for more voice coil travel, and thus lower Frequency Response, and less chance of "bottoming out".

Export Sending an image out of a program in a different file format.

Exposition Presentation of information essential to the understanding of the dramatic action, especially of events that occurred prior to the opening scene or off-stage.

Exposure A measure of the amount of light in a photograph created by the cameras aperature, shutter speed and other settings.

Expressionism A stylized and highly personal form of theater in which reality is distorted by the passionate and distorted vision of the writer.

Ext script abbreviation for "exterior."

Extended play (EP) Slowest tape speed of a VHS.

Extensible markup language Asepcification developed by the W3C which applies to web pages so that developers can define their own customized elements.

External CD-ROM drive A CD-ROM drive that is installed outside the computer and connected by a cable to the computer.

External synchronization A means of ensuring that all equipment is synchronized to the one source.

Extra Accessory talent not essential to a scene.

Extreme close up (ECU) A shot that is even tighter than a close-up, such that only part of the subject can be seen (a pair of eyes).

F

F stop A series of number corresponding to the camera's iris opening.

F3 (measured in Hz) The frequency at which the acoustic power output from a system has fallen to one-half its reference value. Known as the systems 3dB down point. F3: determined by the frequency at which the output is 3dB lower than the level at 100Hz. This frequency was chosen because it is a typical crossover point. In the case of a Bandpass system, F3 is determined by the frequency at which the output is 3dB lower than the level at the middle of the pass bandGain

An increase in volume or amplitude, usually measured in dB.

Fade Fading is a method of switching from one video source to another. Next time you watch a TV program (or a movie), pay extra attention when the scene is about to end and go on to another. The scene fades to black, then a fade from black to another scene occurs. Fading between scenes without going to black is called a dissolve. One way to do a fade is to use an alpha mixer.

Fade out 1) To gradually lower volume until the sound disappears;

2) a change in volume so made.

Fade up 1) To gradually raise volume;

2) a change in volume so made.

Fader Rather like the right to left balance control, however the fader moves the sonic position between the front and back speakers.

Fair use (law) A stipulation in the Copyright act of 1976 (Section 107) under which some limited "fair use" may be made of a protected work without permission "for purposes such as criticism, comment, news reporting, teaching . . . scholarship or research." Whether fair use includes such things as excerpting sections of commercial recordings for background music in audio drama is not clear.

Farad (F) The basic unit of capacitance. A capacitor has a capacitance of 1F when a charge of 1 Volt across the capacitor produces a current of 1 Ampere through it. Named after Michael Faraday.

Farce A broad style of comedy that relies on ridiculous situations.

Fast motion A shot in which time appears to move faster than normal, usually achieved by deleting frames (called "skip frames").

Fast start An option found in some programs (QuickTime Pro) which allows for a faster delivery of the panoramic image into web browsers by starting to display the image before the whole file is downloaded. It's a good saving option to use if you are going to display a panoramic image over the Internet.

Fast-wind To spool or wind tape around a reel or hub at high speed.

Faux bold style A style applied to type that allows you to add a bold effect into a font family where a bold version of the font is not available.

Favored nations or favored nations clause A contractual stipulation guaranteeing that no other contractee is receiving more favorable conditions (although others may receive conditions equally favorable).

Favourite A computer shortcut designed to help you mark and revisit your favourite items easily. Sometimes "favourites" are called bookmarks for this reason. You can store favourite websites or bookmarks in your browser by choosing the appropriate command from the Favourites or Bookmarks menu.

Fb The tuned frequency of a Vented Enclosure, measured in Hertz. A combination of the resonance frequency of the air in a Port and the resilient pressure of the air in a Ported System. Below this point the Frequency Response of a Tuned Port system rapidly Falls Off, and the system can become unstable if asked to reproduce lower frequencies at high Amplitude.

FCC (federal communications commission) A federal bureau that regulates radio and television broadcast standards. FCC regulations carry the force of law.

FDDI Fibre distributed data interface.

FDF (Form data format) A text file format that contains data exported from a PDF document.

Feature A Feature is a distinctive characteristic of the data which signifies something to somebody.

A Feature for a given data set has a descriptor (i.e. feature representation) and an instantiation (descriptor value).

Examples Color of an image, pitch of a speech segment, rhythm of an audio segment camera style of a video, title of a movie, actors in a movie, etc.

Feed Act or result of transmitting a video signal from one point to another.

Feedback Your opinions are very important to us. We have tried to make this website as easy to use as possible and we take great care to make sure information is up to date and relevant. However, sometimes we miss things or make the odd mistake. We welcome your views, whether good or bad, so please get in touch.

FFT(fast fourier transform) A computationally efficient mathematical technique, which converts digital information from the time domain to the frequency domain for rapid spectral analysis. FFTs generally utilize a "time weighting" function to compensate for data records with a non-integer number of samples; some popular weighting functions are Hanning Window and 4-term Blackman-Harris.

Fiber-optic cable Type of cable used to connect devices on a network. Made of plastic or glass fibers covered with an opaque sheath. Digital signals are sent via code pulses of light. These cables are fast, reliable, and have extremely wide bandwidth.

Fibre optics A technology designed to transmit signals in the form of light. A Fibre Optic system uses Optical Fibres. Optical Fibre cable is noted for its properties of electrical isolation and resistance to electrostatic and electromagnetic interference.

Fidelity A term used to describe the accuracy of recording, reproduction, or general quality of audio processing. Getting it "high" is every designer's goal.

Fields The engineers who developed television had a problem: how to deliver massive amounts of video and audio over the air waves, yet have it able to be received and acted upon by affordable electronics. One of the many decisions they made was to halve the amount of data by adopting interlacing. This halved the bandwidth required for the signal. If the original picture source is a movie, it is displayed in the cinema at a rate of 24 frames per second. With PAL TV systems, the pictures are shown 50 times per second. What happens is that the movie is scanned into 576 horizontal line, but only every odd-numbered line is sent in the first 1/50th of a second. In the next 1/50th of a second, the even-numbered lines are sent. The TV shows first the odd lines, then the even lines (which are shown in between the fading remnants of the odd lines). The whole process of showing one frame takes 1/25th of a second (that is, a four per cent shorter time than the original movie's, so PAL movies have a slightly shorter run-time than when in seen in the cinema). Each half-picture shown in 1/50th of a second is called a field. Material sourced directly from video cameras is already broken up into fields before being recorded. The whole thing is far more complicated for NTSC TV. Consumer videotapes and DVDs conform to this scheme.

Field of view (FOV) 35mm cameras produce rectangular pictures (36 x 24mm negatives) and therefore the field of view is greater for the longer dimension. Generally when someone refers ambiguously to the field of view of a 35mm image they are referring to the field of view along the longer of the two dimensions, regardless of which way up the camera was (portrait or landscape).

FIF (fractal image format) FIF is a bitmap compression format for storing graphic file data. Fractals are geometrically describable units originally developed by Benoit Mandelbrot in the 1960s that reflect the patterns of nature much better than traditional Euclidean geometry.

File A file is the storage unit of a digital document. Files are typically stored with file extensions (such as *.html for HTML files, or *.JPEG for JPEG files) that are linked to the programs that can interpret the digital data of the document. A digital document typically consists of a set of files. For example, a web document typically consists of a base HTML file. Associated with this file there may be any number of graphic files (for images), style files, script files, etc. All http compliant files can be accessed from a browser as local files from a client computer.

File element A complete file contained in a resource interchange file format (RIFF) compound file.

File extensions File extensions are listed alphabetically, but there is also a single document containing all the file extensions for easy reference.

File format The specific way digital information is made and stored by the computer. Not all software applications can read and/or manipulate all file formats.

File formats for video ASF, AVI, MP3, and MPEG file formats.

File server A computer or device on a network dedicated to storing files and providing file services to users.

File transfer A means of providing access to files on a remote IT system without requiring detailed knowledge of the structure and characteristics of the remote system.

File transport Protocol (FTP) - FTP is an acronym for File Transfer Protocol and is a method for retrieving files from a remote Internet site. Many sites out there allow what is termed an 'anonymous' connection. In other words, there exists a special username called 'anonymous' so that the site can act as a library of useful public domain programs and documents.

Fill flash A flash setting that creates an extra or secondary burst of light. Helps to reduce contrast and shawdows in bright light situations.

Fill layer A lyer within images that allows you to apply a color, pattern or gradient to your image.

Fill light Soft lighting that is used to supplement the main light, called key light. Fill light is used to control unwanted dark or shadowy areas on the set or on an actor.

Film While videotape is simple in structure but requires complex machines for recording, film is complex in structure but requires simple recording machines. Film cameras are simple and elegant machines, and when you think about it, the film itself is the recorder.

Film is often used in the production of video for a variety of reasons, including the high image quality of film transferred to video and the ability to record film at any frame rate the camera allows. There are no technical requirements for a particular frame rate as there are with video, each film frame is simply exposed to light, then advanced. Many film cameras have variable frame-rate capabilities—a concept totally foreign to video.

Film chain A device used to transfer film to video. They are still used by some TV stations to broadcast programming distributed on 16 mm film.

Film grain The tiny particles of light-sensitive material on film stock that record images. Finer grains are less visible, and so offer higher image resolution and what some would consider higher picture quality. However, they are less sensitive, and so require more light and/or longer exposure time than higher speed films. The coarser grains of higher speed films allow a faster shutter speed and have a pronounced grainy look that can sometimes be a desirable stylistic choice.

Filter Any of various electric, electronic, acoustic, or optical devices used to reject signals, vibrations, or radiation of certain frequencies while passing others. Electronically, filters can be as simple as a single capacitor, or as complex as a dedicated computer circuit. For audio use the most common electronic filter is a bandpass filter, characterized by three parameters: center frequency, amplitude (or magnitude), and bandwidth. Bandpass filters form the heart of audio graphic equalizers and parametric equalizers.

Finger Finger is a method used for determining user data on a server such as which users are currently logged onto the network, or their contact details.

Firewall A security measure that prohibits users in certain local area networks (LANs), such as one belonging to a corporation, from receiving or sending certain types of digital content. Some firewalls prevent the transmission of audio and video files.

Firewire Apple computer's name of a high capacity digital connection standard, capable of delivering up to 400mb/s. Frequently used for transferring video and audio from digital video cameras to DVD recorders and computers. Also known as IEEE1394 (the formal name) and i.- (Sony's name).

First generation The first time the signal is recorded on tape, that tape is called a first generation tape. Each time the tape is dubbed, a generation is added.

First name analysis A transparency technique wherein the first frame of the video file is a dummy frame that supplies the color or range of colors to be rendered as transparent: the color of the chroma-key background, for example.

Fisheye lens A wide angle lens that captures the scene exactly as it appears, thereby incorporating curves which the human eye does not perceive because the focal length of the human eye is approximately 50mm. Fisheye lens images tend to cause all straight lines to appear curved. You can use such lenses and use a program like DeFish to make it rectilinear and therefore usable in a simple stitching program like PhotoStitch.

Fixed focal length lens A lens with a predetermined fixed focal length, a focusing control and a choice of iris functions.

FLA A Flash file extension The .fla file extension is used for the basic Flash document file, used in the development context. After its development, a Flash document needs to be "published" to the Web. It then gets a .swf extension which can be played with a Flash player.

FLAC FLAC stands for free lossless audio codec.

by encoding audio files with FLAC, the quality is exactly the same as the original audio file's quality is. This is exactly unlike the audio formats such as MP3 and WMA work – these audio formats are called "lossy" and that means that when the original audio is encoded into the lossy audio format, some of the audio data is lost forever and can't be brought back by any means.

Flare Flashes of light that are evident in an image.

Flash A product from Macromedia (as is Shockwave) that produces interactive vector-based animations called "Flash movies". Like Shockwave movies, Flash movies are intended for web-based distribution to web browsers. Netscape ships with the Flash plug-in. +/-'s of Flash

Flash animation Animation program developed by Macromedia. Quickly becoming the standard for animation on the Web.

Flash memory Nonvolatile, digital storage. Flash memory has slower access than SRAM or DRAM.

Flashback 1) To show events in retrospect; to interrupt a scene or scenes of current events with a scene, scenes, or scene fragment(s) of past events;

2), a retrospective scene.

Flat response An output signal in which fundamental frequencies and harmonics are in the same proportion as those of the input signal being amplified. A flat frequency response would exhibit relatively equal response to all fixed-point frequencies within a given spectrum.

Flatten The process of converting a Macintosh file into a self-contained, single-forked file so that it is compatible with a Windows* environment.

FLC An animation or moving picture file format originally created by Animator Pro. FLC files contain one or more frames, so you can see animated pictures from the screen when you display these files. A "FLC" file has an extension .flc.

Fletcher-munson curves Fletcher and Munson were pioneering researchers who provided the basis of High Fidelity in the '30s. They accurately measured and published a set of plots showing the human's ear's sensitivity to loudness verses frequency. They conclusively demonstrated that human hearing acuity is essentially dependent upon loudness. The curves show the ear most sensitive to sounds in the 3 kHz to 4 kHz area. This means sounds above and below 3-4 kHz must be louder in order to be heard just as loud. For this reason, the Fletcher-Munson curves are referred to as "equal loudness contours." They represent a range of sensitivity from "barely heard," (0 dB SPL) all the way to "painfully loud" (120 dB SPL), usually plotted in 10 dB increments.

FLI FLI files are also animation files. Although a FLI file's structure is very similar to that of a FLC file, they are different file formats. A "FLI" file has an extension .fli.

Flicker No, it's not the horse. It's the same phenomenon that gave the early cinema the nickname: 'the flicks'. It is the ability of the eye to see the dark interludes between each picture displayed on your TV, or at the cinema. Remember, a TV or cinema picture comprises of a series of picture frames shown in sequence, changing very rapidly. If the display flashes bright, but then fades away enough before the next frame is displayed, many people can perceive this as a slight flicker. It is more perceptible with unchanging flat colours on the screen, and with the peripheral vision. For TVs, it is more common for PAL than for NTSC because the former scans the whole screen 50 times a second while the latter scans at 60 times a second. This increase in speed reduces the ability to perceive flicker substantially. More expensive PAL TVs overcome this by doubling the scan speed to 100 times per second (displaying each frame twice).

Flies Area over the stage in a theater, where weights (typically sandbags), curtains, cycloramas, special effects, and scenery may be raised and stored out of the audience's view.

Flipper A DVD in which the movie is not entirely on one side of the DVD, so the DVD has to be turned over, or 'flipped', partway through viewing. Note, a DVD which has the movie on one side and some extras, such as a documentary or cast interviews, on the other is not a 'flipper' because the turning over doesn't interfere with enjoyment of the main feature.

Float To protect a recording or broadcast environment from outside vibration, as from passing traffic, by building it as an inner room connected to an outer room by shock absorbers, or raising a false floor over the real one.

Floppy disk A magnetic disk that can be used to store information. Floppy disks are available in two different sizes, 3½ inch or 5¼ inch. 3½ inch disk drives are more common, with the older 5¼ inch disks only being used on very old computers. Floppy disks are slower to access than CD ROMs or computer hard drives, and cannot store much information.

The floppy disk is so called because the older 5¼ inch disks were quite soft.

Floptical Disk drive technology using a combination of magnetic and optical techniques for better storage capacity.

Flub 1. An actor's mistake of delivery;

2. to make such a mistake.

Flush (mounting) Mounting a speaker in such a way that the speaker and its Grill do not protrude above the surrounding surface. Usually, this means mounting it at the back of the baffle board (the board the speaker is mounted on).

Flutter A defect affecting analogue audio signal sources that rely on rotating the medium, particularly LPs and compact cassettes. Flutter is a rapid, repetitive speed variation, typically repeating at least ten times per second. If an LP or audio cassette undergoes this, it produces rapid variations in the playback frequency. At the slower end of the scale, it can sound like an unwanted tremolo or vibrato. At higher rates it can add an unpleasant harshness to the sound. Flutter is specified in per cent and specifications of more than around 0.1% are unacceptable. Digital sources such as CDs are immune to flutter because they lock their playback speed to a solid-state timing device.

Flux The flow of magnetic energy in a circuit. Flux density is the measure of the strength of the magnetic field typicaly used in speakers, and which governs its power handling capacity.

Flyback The period where the scanning beam returns to the starting point for the next scan.

Flying/on the fly "Winging it," especially overdubbing or punching in a sound or piece of music without preparation.

FM Frequency modulation. A system of storing or transporting a signal by using it to modulate a carrier in the frequency, rather than amplitude, domain. FM radio, high-fidelity audio on VHS, and numerous other systems are based on FM. FM tends to be more resistant to interference than AM.

F-number In lenses with an adjustable iris, the maximum iris opening is expressed as a ratio (focal length of the lens)/(maximum effective diameter of aperture). This maximum iris will be marked on the front ring of the lens.

Focal length A term used in general photography for the distance between the rear principal point of the lens and the rear focal point when the lens is focused on infinity.

Focal plane In general photography the area perpendicular to the axis of the lens which intersects the rear focal point is known as the focal plane, which is the same as the film plane.

Focal point When parallel light rays enter a lens a perfect lens will cause the light rays to converge on a single point before fanning out again to reach the film. This point is the 'rear' or 'image' focal point. There is also a 'front' or 'object' focal point.

Focus The sharpness of an image, or the adjustments made on a camera necessary to achieve this. On film crews there is usually an individual who is in charge of focus, called the focus puller.

Focusing control A means of adjusting the lens to allow objects at various distances from the camera to be sharply defined.

Foil A character whose dramatic purpose is to set off another character by contrast; a side-kick.

Foldback Sound which is fed into an earphone during a recording or Adr session.

Folder Formerly called a 'directory' under the DOS/Windows operating systems. This is a logical division on storage media containing files and other folders. It is relevant for DVDs because these use standard folders and files to hold their data. The folder holding the data for DVD Video is called VIDEO_TS while that for DVD Audio is called AUDIO_TS. Audio CDs, by contrast, do not use standard computer filing systems which is why their contents generally do not show up in a sensible form when inspected by standard computer file tools.

Foley or foley effects (from Jack Foley, a film sound mixer) In broadcast drama and film, sound effects laid in live during mastering or overdubbing, and not prerecorded. A studio built for the production of such effects is a foley stage, foley room, or (rarely) adr room.

Foley walker One who specializes in foley effects, so called because making footfall sounds is a principal responsibility.

Follow focus Controlling lens focus so that an image maintains sharpness and clarity despite movement.

Font A font is the overall design for a set of written characters. It describes the size, weight (for example, bold) and spacing of a character. The choice of font is very important and often different fonts are used in printed publications and websites.

Foot-candle An illumination light unit used mostly in American CCTV terminology. It equals 10.76 times the illumination value in lux (1m2 = 10.76 sq ft).

Foreshadow, foreshadowing In a play or other literary work, it is often necessary to drop hints of a major happening or revelation, so that when it occurs it will not appear to come out of nowhere. This is called foreshadowing. It also helps build suspense and provide unity.

Form Forms are used on websites to allow you to place orders, login into secure areas, and send data, comments and information.

Formant A formant or resonance of the vocal tract above the vocal folds is a frequency region that will strongly pass energy in that frequency region if it receives energy at those frequencies from the glottal source (glottal flow). The formant frequencies depend on the size and shape of the vocal tract. An important frequency region that "rings" typically independently of the sung vowel is the "singer's formant." This may be created when the area at the top of the larynx tube is small relative to the area of the pharynx just above the larynx tube. The larynx tube then "rings" at about 28,000 - 32,000 Hz. This phenomenon is more prevalent in male singers. This technique can also be used by nonsingers to create additional loudness and carrying power to the voice.

Former The cylindrical portion of a speaker's voice coil section. A wire is wound around this cylinder to form a coil such that when current interacts with the magnetic field it produces a pumping motion that alternatively compresses and rarifies air, and creates the velocity for such air masses to reach our ears as sound.

Forum An online discussion area with messages and replies. A forum may have one or more topics. You have to login to some forums to read and put messages on the forum.

Fotovix The brand-name of a device available from Tamron which provides a relatively inexpensive way to transfer still 35mm film slides and negatives to video.

FOURCC (four character code) A code used to identify Resource Interchange File Format (RIFF) chunks. A FOURCC is a 32-bit quantity represented as a sequence of one to four ASCII alphanumeric characters, padded on the right with blank characters.

Fourier Actually, Fourier analysis. Fourier found that every repeating signal could be expressed as the sum of some particular sine wave, called the fundamental frequency, plus its harmonics at various levels. This understanding permitted the development of all forms of signal processing, whether digital or analogue.

Fourier transformation Mathematical transformation of time domain functions into frequency domain.

Four-way loudspeakers A loudspeaker which divides the incoming signal into four different frequency bands for distribution to drivers. It sends high frequencies to the tweeter, upper middle frequencies to a small midrange driver, lower middle frequencies to a larger midrange driver, and the lowest frequencies to one or more woofers.

FPI (formal public identifier) The FPI is part of the Document Type Declaration (DTDecl). This is an identifier (a statement) informing a user agent what kind of document follows. It is usually followed by a URI where the relevant DTD can be found.

Example: <!DOCTYPE HTML PUBLIC "-//W3C//DTD HTML 4.0//EN">

This FPI reads:

The type of document that follows is an HTML document. The DTD is publically available (not on a private system). The DTD is not an ISO standard (indicated by the -). The owner of the DTD is the W3C. The SGML application is HTML. The release of HTML is 4.0. The specification is in English.

Frames For movies, as seen in a cinema, this is an actual frame on the strip of film. Frames are shown in sequence, 24 times per second. On a TV or DVD, a frame consists of two fields which are interlaced together. For a PAL TV frames are shown at a rate of 25 per second (50 fields per second). For NTSC they are shown at 30 per second. If the original source of the picture is film, then the two fields constituting a frame in the PAL system consist of alternating lines from the same film frame, interlaced together. However if the material is video sourced, then the two fields will have been recorded 1/50 of a second apart. This can be seen on many DVD players by setting the still mode to Frame, rather than Field or Auto. Movies, when paused, while hold a stable picture. Video material (music clips, many TV shows and so on) will flicker, with moving objects appearing in two different places. Video material in the NTSC system appears in a similar way, but the transfer of film to NTSC uses a complicated 3:2 pulldown process.

Frame buffer A frame buffer is a memory used to hold an image for display. How much memory are we talking about? Well, let's assume a horizontal resolution of 640 pixels and 480 scan lines, and we'll use the RGB color space. This works out to be:

640 x 480 x 3 = 921,600 bytes or 900 KB

Frame grabber A device allowing the real time capture of a single frame of video in a temporary buffer for manipulation or conversion to selected computer file formats. Some frame grabbers have buffers large enough to store several complete frames, allowing rapid capture of a number of images. The distinction between a frame grabber and a digitizer is that a digitizer captures a sequence of complete frames, and therefore must employ some form of compression and/or acceleration in order to operate in real-time.

Frame integration Is mis-named. It is actually field integration and is the technique of adding sucessive fields together to enhance an image in low light conditions. Integration over more than a few fields will cause motion blur to become an issue.

Frame rate Refers to the number of frames or images that are displayed per second. Also describes the rate at which AVI and QuickTime movies play. Lower frame rates typically produce a choppy or jerky playback. Higher frame rates result in a smoother playback. Processor speed and hardware acceleration are two factors that affect frame rate.

Frame relay A data service similar to X.25, but providing higher speeds and LAN interconnection.

Frame store An electronic device that digitizes a TV frame (or TV field) of a video signal and stores it in memory. Multiplexers, fast scan transmitters, Quad displays and even some of the latest colour cameras have built-in frame stores.

Frame switcher Another name for a simple multiplexer, which can record multiple cameras on a single VCR (and play back any camera in full screen) but does not usually have a multiscreen image display. Note : all cameras must be synchronized.

Frame-interline transfer (FIT) Refers to one of the principles of charge transfer in CCD chips. It combines the principles of both frame transfer and interline transfer to give the benefits of both, without their disadvantages.

Frames per second (FPS) The number of video frames displayed each second (also called frame rate). Most people perceive continuous motion at about 17 fps. A common standard for video delivered over the web is 15 fps, which reduces file sizes substantially (since most video is shot at roughly 30 fps) but still but allows for fairly smooth motion.

Framing device A plot device to set off the dramatic action within the context of an amplifying situation, which opens and closes, or frames, the main action, as when the play unfolds in retrospect, or in a "play within a play."

Free sound field A sound field without acoustic boundaries or where the boundaries are so distant as to cause negligible reflections over the frequency range of audible sound. If the boundaries exist but completely absorb the sound then a virtual free field is created, thus anechoic chambers are used to accurately measure loudspeakers for their unique properties.

Free-air configuration This description usually indicates a speaker that, in the opinion of the manufacturer, is suitable for mounting in only a minimal enclosure, such as a baffle board that separates the back wave from the front.

Freeware The software author retains rights to the program, but allows users to copy and use the program without fee. The program thus cannot be resold or relabelled without the consent of the originator.

Freeze frame A stylistic effect in which the motion of a film sequence appears to halt—an effect created by reprinting a single frame of film repeatedly.

Frequency The rate at which a repetitive signal repeats, measured in cycles per second or hertz (or its convenient multiples). Audio frequencies are generally in the range of 20 to 20,000 hertz because those are the frequencies to which the human ear sensibly responds. Equipment measurements often extend this range to 0 to 100,000 hertz. Video frequencies typically deal with a range of 0 to 7 MHz because that is the bandwidth available for PAL and NTSC signals. The human eye responds to light in the frequency range of 385,000 GHz to 789,000 GHz. The frequency of a signal can be calculated by dividing the speed with which the signal propagates through a medium by its wavelength.

Frequency hopping system Carrier frequency shifting in discrete increments in a pattern dictated by a code sequence. The transmitter jumps from frequency-to-frequency within some predetermined set: the order of frequency hops is determined by a code sequence, which, in turn, is detected and followed by the receiver.

Frequency modulation (FM) In radio broadcasting, a method of modulation in which the frequency of the carrier voltage is varied with the frequency of the modulation voltage.

Frequency modulation (FM) synthesizer A synthesizer that creates sounds by combining the output of digital oscillators using a frequency modulation technique.

Frequency response A measure of how accurately a system reproduces different frequencies. In the case of audio in a home theatre system, it is desirable for the frequency response of a whole system, including speakers and subwoofer, to be from 10 hertz to 20,000 hertz ±3dB. This performance requires a very expensive system indeed and, in practice, very few systems will produce bass down to anything like that bottom limit. Manufacturers who claim a frequency response for speakers of, say, 20 to 20,000 hertz without specifying decibel boundaries are telling you nothing. A tinny two inch transistor radio speaker can reproduce that range, although you won't actually hear it at either extreme because its output will be so low. Even subtle variations of less than half a decibel across the audio band can be quite audible, especially if they're spread over a fairly wide band of frequencies, and can thus change the character of the sound. Indeed, with speakers the single measure most closely related to their sound is the frequency response.

Frequency shift keying A modulation scheme that shifts between two frequencies to represent a "1" or "0" state of data transmission.

Frequently asked questions (FAQs) FAQs are used to provide direct, useful answers to commonly asked questions.

Fricative A vocalization — such as the letters f, s, v, and z — produced by forcing breath through a narrow opening in the mouth. These sounds tend to pop the mike.

Front porch The blanking signal portion that lies between the end of the active line period and the leading edge of line sync (horizontal sync), 1.5μs long in a CCIR/PAL system.

FrontPage A created by Microsoft. FrontPage is one of the most popular applications used for creating Web sites.

Fs Fs or Free Air Resonance is the frequency at which a speaker naturally resonates, like a tuning fork. Sometimes known as ringing response.

F-stop A number that represent the size of the lens opening allowing a certain amount of light in. The smaller the number the larger the lens opening resulting in more light. The larger the number the smaller the lens opening resulting in less light.

FTAM File transfer, Access and Manipulation. An alternative file transfer protocol to FTP.

FTP (file transfer protocol) FTP is a protocol for transferring files between systems, i.e. different computers in a network. The function of FTP is thus very similar to copying files between different disks on a PC. The difference is that the files are transported via a network to a different computer, and not between, say, a hard drive and a stiffy.

FTP uses connection-oriented TCP, thus better than TFTP (Trivial File Transfer Protocol), which is quicker than FTP. But with TFTP you have to wait until the entire file is downloaded before you may discover that there were bad frames and have to start downloading again. FTP checks the frames while they are downloading.

The ftp service is used for transferring files between computers, regardless of where they are on The Internet. A user typically needs ftp privileges to use this service, but ISP's often allow access as a guest. Sometimes a server may allow ftp from their server, but not to it. For example, you may download files from the server, but cannot upload to it.

FTTH/FTTP (Fibre-to-the-home or fibre-to-the-premises) The fibre deployment architecture in which optical fibre is carried all the way to the customer's home or premise, allowing for a high speed broadband connection. FTTH is not yet widespread in Australia.

Fulfillment The segment of business operations dealing with fulfilling orders, as when listeners order cassettes, transcripts, or other premiums. A firm that specializes in this is called a fulfillment house.

Full duplex Sending data in both directions at the same time. Usually higher quality, but requires more bandwidth. In video conferencing, full duplex will be much more natural and useable. Cheap speakerphones are half duplex, whereas more expensive ones are full duplex.

Full logic deck A cassette mechanism where the tape operations are carried out by logic circuit operated solenoids rather than soley mechanical methods.

Full motion Refers to NTSC-quality video—a video signal that is 30 fps, and at least 640x480 pixels in size.

Full-motion video Not compressed. A standard video signal of 30 frames per second and 525 horizontal lines per frame, which is capable of complete action. Level 3 Video utilizing 2 audio channels suitable for use in Distance Education credit courses employing rapid motion (i.e. Grass Valley "E Series" codec and associated equipment).

Full shot A shot long enough to encompass the action taking place before the camera in its entirety.

Fullscreen A way of viewing images in which the content (such as a CIF video file) is accommodated to the size of the monitor you are using. This can result in noticeable distortion if the data rate of file is low, as for video's intended for delivery via standard modems.

Full-screen video Digital video filling the entire screen (use 640 x 480 pixels) for typical graphic, not just a smaller window. Typical video window sizes.

Function, dramatic The author's theatrical purpose in including a character,scene, or other element into a dramatic work.

Fundamental frequency Any musical tone primarily consists of a particular simple tone (a sine wave) and a series of higher frequency tones, where the frequencies of those higher tones are whole multiples of the first-mentioned tone. The frequency of that simple tone is called the fundamental frequency. When we say that the Middle C of a piano has a frequency of 261 hertz, we are actually talking about its fundamental frequency, not that of the harmonics without which a piano note would have no distinguishing character.

Fuse A device designed to provide protection for a given circuit or device by physically opening the circuit. Fuses are rated by their amperage and are designed to blow or open when the current being drawn through it exceeds its design rating. They can be fast or slow acting, depending on type.

Fusible link Designed to perform the same task as a fuse, but the resembles a wire. Fusible links are commonly used in power transformers, ignition switches and other high current circuits.

Future proofing Anticipating rapid advancements in ICT and aiming to accommodate these changes through structured systems. Future proofing simply refers to adapting to new generation technologies, for example, rolling out FTTH in greenfield estates instead of the standard copper DSL for broadband services.

FVD FVD (Finalized versatile disc) is an increased-capacity red-laser DVD disc and player specification from Taiwan. It uses Microsoft's Windows Media Video 9 (WMV9) and Windows Media Audio 9 (WMA9) codecs. The 5.4GB/9.8GB FVD-1 disc supports up to 135 minutes of WMV9 720p content. The 6GB/11GB FVD-2 disc will support up to 1080i content.

G

G2 RealPlayer file format.

Gaffer The person responsible for wiring and electricity on the set.

Gain Any increase or decrease in strength of an electrical signal. Gain is often measured in terms of decibels, the logarithmic ratio of input to output.

Gamma A correction of the linear response of a camera in order to compensate for the monitor phosphor screen non-linear response. It is measured with the exponential value of the curve describing the non-linearity. A typical monochrome monitor's gamma is 2.2, and a camera needs to be set to the inverse value of 2.2 (which is 0.45) for the overall system to respond linearly (i.e., unity).

Gamma correction Before being displayed, linear RGB data must be processed (gamma corrected) to compensate for the nonlinearity of the display.

Gamut The range of voltages allowed for a video signal, or a component of a video signal. Signal voltages outside of the range (exceeding the gamut) may lead to clipping, crosstalk, or other distortions.

Gas plasma Gas plasma emitters are a type of Horn Driver wherein a plasma or ionized gas field is developed and then propelled between two electrostatic grids. The onrushing gas is then compacted or dispersed in conformity to the frequency and level of the high voltage input signal. This type of driver, while very effective, is also extremely expensive, and so has not been commercially successful.

Gate or noise gate A machine that reduces tape hiss, room tone, and other unwanted noise during transmission or recording by reducing or shutting off sound below a preset floor.

Gate weave An artifact of poor registration either during the film-to-tape transfer process or the actual filming that manifests itself as a weaving back and forth of the film image.

Gatekeeper A gatekeeper controls access to an H.323 network, managing elements such as authentication, bandwidth allocation, tracking and billing.

Gateway A device interfacing networks that use different protocols. It thus translates between the different protocols. When the definition of Gateway is strict, it translates only between different high-level architectures, such as, say, between TCP/IP and IBM's SNA. When the definition is more loose, it translates between lower-level network types, say between Ethernet and Token Ring.

In a manner of speaking the function of a router and gateway is similar: they both act as interfacing translators in a network. Gateways are more general than routers as they translate between most (if not all) protocol layers of the OSI model.

Gating Employing a device that shuts off sound under a preset minimum and turns it on again when it exceeds the minimum. Used for noise reduction.

GB Short for gigabyte (1,024 megabytes). This unit is typically used to measure very large data storage or data transfer capacities, by current standards. Hard drives that can store several gigabytes have become commonplace, and technologies that can send and receive up to one gigabyte of information at a time are becoming increasingly available, though not yet widespread.

GBR The same signals as RGB. The sequence is often rearranged to indicate the mechanical sequence of the connectors in the SMPTE standard.

Gen lock The synchronization of a piece of video equipment with an external video signal - in video systems.

General MIDI A synthesizer specification created by the midi manufacturers association (MMA) defining a common configuration and set of capabilities for consumer musical instrument digital interface (MIDI) synthesizers.

Generation A recording considered in relation to its distance from the original live sound; the original recording of the live sound, the master, is the first generation; a dub of that recording, which may or may not include additional sounds, is the second generation; a dub of the dub is third generation, etc.

Generation loss With analog video formats extensive efforts are made to keep generations to a minimum since each successive generation will exhibit some loss of image quality in the form of noise and other artifacts. This characteristic varies from format to format. For example, 1-inch Type C exhibits almost imperceptible loss up to 4 generations while VHS shows considerable degradation each generation. With digital formats such as D-1 and D-2, however, this requirement is no longer necessary, since each copy can potentially be very close to perfect. This is important for applications such as compositing which require images to be dubbed several times.

Generator A machine that produces AC electricity from a rotating coil interaction within a magnetic field. In automotive applications, a rectifier is used to convert this output to DC. Also, an electronic device used for converting DC voltage into AC of a given frequency and wave shape. An amplifier is often a form of generator.

Genlock A video signal provides all of the information necessary for a video decoder to reconstruct the picture. This includes brightness, color, and timing information. To properly decode the video signal, the video decoder must lock to all the timing information embedded within the video signal, including the color burst, horizontal sync, and vertical sync. The decoder looks at the color burst of the video signal and reconstructs the original color subcarrier that was used by the encoder. This is needed to properly decode the color information. It also generates a sample clock (done by looking at the sync information within the video signal), used to clock pixel data out of the decoder into a memory or another circuit for processing. The circuitry within the decoder that does all of this work is called the genlock circuit. Although it sounds simple, the genlock circuit must be able to handle very bad video sources, such as the output of VCRs, cameras, and toys. In reality, the genlock circuit is the most complex section of a video decoder.

Genre A literary "species" or form, such as tragedy, sitcom, Western, soap, docudrama, etc.

Genre writing Writing in a genre subject to highly prescripted structure, tone, atmosphere, style, dialogue and characterization.

Get-a-date Cyberdating Leave an audio messsage for a Web Personal.

Ghost A shadowy or weak image in the received picture, offset either to the right or to the left of the primary image. It is the result of transmission conditions where secondary signals are created and received earlier or later than the primary signal caused by a reflected RF signal.

Ghost cancellation reference A reference signal on (M) NTSC scan lines 19 and 282 and (B, D, G, H, I) PAL scan line 318 that allows the removal of ghosting from TVs. Filtering is employed to process the transmitted GCR signal and determine how to filter the entire video signal to remove the ghosting. ITU-R BT.1124 and ETSI ETS 300 732 define the standard each country uses. ATSC A/49 also defines the standard for NTSC.

GHz Giga hertz One thousand million (American billion) cycles per second.

GIF (graphic interchange format) GIF is a bitmap method of compressing images, originally developed for quicker transport of images on The Internet, as file sizes of other graphic formats were too large. GIF87 is the basic compression scheme, while the later GIF89a supports transparency and animation.

Layering: GIF images that have more than 256 colors can be layered in order to display the image properly. Your graphics program must have the ability to save the file as such. Not all browsers support this feature. GIF uses the LZW (Lempel-Ziv-Welch) lossless compression scheme and supports 8-bit color (ie 256 colors).

GIFs are typically used for relatively simple images, such as company logos, stick figures, simple buttons, line images and so on. These images also have relatively few color hues. For more complex images, rather use JPEGs.

Gig Slang for job, engagement of musicians to play and perform.

Gigabit A unit of information transfer rate equal to one billion bits per second.

Gigabyte A measure of memory storage, a gigabyte equals (ie. 1,024 x 1,024 x 1,024 or 230) bytes, 1,048,576 (ie. 1,024 x 1,024 or 220) kilobytes or 1,024 megabytes. However, if used as a measure of hard disk storage, the 'giga' prefix normally means a round billion.

GIS (Geographical information system) GIS is a computerised data management system designed to capture, store, retrieve, analyse and report geographical and demographic information.

Glitch A spike caused by the skew (difference in turn-on/turn-off time) of switches or logic. Glitches are a troublesome source of error in high-speed D/A converters, and they are most prevalent at the mid-scale switching location when all digital input bits are switching. Glitch energy is specified in picovolt-seconds, which describes the area under the voltage-time curve at its worst case occurence.

Glottal stop (or click) A transient sound caused by the sudden onset or offset of phonation as in the common American pronunciation of the word "button."

GND Ground (electrical).

Gobo (studio slang) a free-standing, usually portable, sound baffle .

Gopher Gopher is an internet service — its method similar to ftp. Before more advanced and user-friendly FTP programs gopher was often used instead of FTP as it provided a graphical directory structure. File descriptions are also found on gopher sites, and links are often made to other similar sites. It is thus more useful than FTP.

Older internet users may remember using the gopher service Veronica that consists of a database of menu items that structures the information.

Gothic. As applied to drama and literature, an atmosphere of foreboding, oppressive gloom, suspense and the other-worldly.

Grams (BBC usage, short for "gramophone") 1) A script indication, usually in documentaries, that signifies the use of a prerecorded, often historical or vintage, sound byte, or bed;

2) recorded effects.

Grams operator (BBC) The studio technician in charge of laying down prerecorded music, sounds, and voices.

Grand guignol (from Fr. Theâtre du grand guignol [Theatre of the Big Puppet] in Paris, a notorious hole-in-the-wall playhouse at the turn-of-the-century where such performances originated), sometimes simply guignol (pronounced geen-yole).. A theater movement or style characterized by excessive melodrama, violence, gore, and spectacle; hence, anything graphically shocking, violent, and gory.

Granulation noise A type of audible distortion resulting from quantization error in digital transmission modes.

Graphic equalizer A multi-band variable equalizer using slide controls as the amplitude adjustable elements. Named for the positions of the sliders "graphically" illustrating the resulting frequency response of the equalizer. Only found on active (amplified)designs. Center frequency and bandwidth are fixed for each band.

Graphical user interface (GUI) A computer interface using point-and-click mouse actions (rather than the keyboard exclusively) and pictures (rather than text exclusively). Windows, Macintosh, Netscape and Mosaic are examples of GUI products.

Graphics accelerator Video adaptor that uses its own specialized processor focused solely on the display. It allows the other components of the computer to focus on other elements. Graphics accelerators often contain their own memory, which is separate from the computer. With the popularity of computer games, graphical programs and multimedia applications, a graphics accelerator is a necessity for today's computer user.

Graphics Graphics is a generic term for image-based signs and symbols. Technically text in a document is also a graphic symbol, but popularly text refers to human language characters, while graphics refer to pictures, icons and similar images.

The following terms are important for graphic images. Not all the graphic image compression techniques (GIF, JPEG, PNG) support each of these methods.

Dithering - the process by which a large number of colors are forced into a smaller color palette.

Transparency - some parts of the color palette can be set as being transparent.

Anti-aliasing - the technique used for the smooth transition of colors into one another to avoid jagged edges.

Interlacing - the method used to load an image in small parts.

Graphics, bitmap Images are laid out in pixels, much like dots of paint on a canvas. As such, bitmap objects are not independent entities, which can be singled out for manipulation, but patterned series of dots. To enlarge (or reduce) bitmap images, the number of pixels is increased (decreased), often giving the resulting image a jagged appearance. Scanners produce bitmap images (.TIF), as does Windows' PaintBrush (.BMP, .PCX): Bitmaps are one of the most commonly compatible types of image formats.

File formats include: IMB, DIB, GIF, MTX, PCX, TIF, TGA, BMP, WPG, JPG, CUR, CO. PaintShop Pro can be used to convert to/from various formats. Its help menu provides full definitions for all graphics file formats. PaintShop Pro maintains the aspect ratio of pictures when sizing, thus can reduce sizing distortion.

Graphics, vector Graphics consisting of objects, each of which can be separately manipulated - e.g. sized, moved, (un)grouped, positioned to the back/front. The graphic components are calculated, hence can be sized without distortion. File formats include: AutoCAD DXF, CBM, EPS, HGL, PIC, DRW, WMF, WPG.

Gravel box, gravel pit A Foley device for making the sound of footfalls on various surfaces, whether of gravel or another material.

Grayscale A system of displaying images in gray tones (or "levels of gray"), simulating the continuous gray tones of a photograph. To achieve grayscale, a monitor must be able to display 2 to 16 bits of information per pixel. This allows the monitor to display a black or white pixel as well as several values between black and white.

Green book Format for CD-i.

Grill A barrier meant to prevent damage to the Driver that it covers, or that creates a more attractive appearance.

Ground A term that describes anything having an electrical potential of zero relative to other points in a circuit. Most modern vehicles are designed around a negative ground system, with the metal frame being the vehicle's ground.

Ground loop (Also known as an Earth Loop) An unwanted interference in the copper electrical signal transmissions with shielded cable, which is a result of ground currents when the system has more than one ground point. For example, in CCTV, when we have a different earthing resistance at the camera end to that at the switcher or monitor end. It must NEVER be cured by removing either ground connection, it should be removed using an isolation transformer or other isolating device , eg opto-isolator.

Group delay Distortion resulting from non-uniform speed of transmission of the various frequency components of a signal through a transmission medium, specifically the propagation delay of a lower frequency is different from that of a higher frequency. This creates a time-related "delay distortion" error.

Group The major divisions for content on a DVD Audio disc. Typically the surround sound mix is in a different group to the stereo mix, while bonus video clips are in a separate group. This is the equivalent of a Title on a DVD Video. A Group is normally subdivided into Tracks.

GSM Global system for mobile communications (European standard).

H

H.221 A CCITT standard describing a method in inverse multiplexing for videoconferencing terminals, to be used to Px64 videoconferencing

H.261, H.263 The ITU-T H.261 and H.263 video compression standards were developed to implement video conferencing over ISDN, LANs, regular phone lines, etc. H.261 supports video resolutions of 352 x 288 and 176 x 144 at up to 29.97 frames per second. H.263 supports video resolutions of 1408 x 1152, 704 x 576, 352 x 288, 176 x 144, and 128 x 96 at up to 29.97 frames per second.

H.264 The "next-generation" video codec. Previously known as "H.26L", "JVT", and "AVC"it is now also a MPEG-4 Part 10 standard.

ITU-T H.264 offers bit rates up to 50% less than the MPEG-4 advanced simple profile (ASP) video codec for the same video quality. It is designed to compete with Microsoft's WMV9 video codec in bit rate and quality.

H.26L Early name for the video codec.

H.320 A standard for video conferencing via dedicated ISDN lines. H.320 is being eclipsed by H.323 (Internet-based) video conferencing because H.320 is typically more expensive.

H.323 Runs over local area networks (LAN's). H.320 and H.323 use many of the same protocols and both support H.261 and H.263 video algorithms. H.323 is the standard for visual telephone systems and equipment for local area networks (LAN's) that provide an unguaranteed quality of service (QOS).

Haas effect Also known as precedence effect, describes the human psychoacoustic phenomena of correctly identifying the direction of a sound source heard in both ears but arriving at different times. Due to the head's geometry (two ears spaced apart, sometimes separated by a barrier) the direct sound from any source first enters the ear closest to the source, then the ear farthest away. The Haas Effect describes how humans localize a sound source based upon the first arriving sound, if the subsequent arrivals are between 25-35 milliseconds. If the later arrivals are longer than this, then two distinct sounds are heard. The Haas Effect applies even when the second arrival is louder than the first (even by levels as great as 10 dB.)

Hacking Breaking into programs or codes without permission. "Crackers" are another type of hacker who specialise in doing damage to systems over the Internet.

HAD hole accumulated diode A type of CCD sensor with a layer designed to accumulate holes (in the electronic sense), thus reducing noise level.

Halftone A way of printing continuous-tone (photographic) images with various size dots. The printing is normally done through a screen.

Hard disk An internal or external device for your computer for storage of data.

Hard dome (tweeter) A characteristic of some Dome tweeters in which the dome is made of some light, hard metal such as neodymium, titanium, or some of the more rigid plastic compounds. The differences in reproduction between hard and soft dome tweeters, are distinctive, but very subtle. Pay close attention to how these sound before purchase.

Harmonic A tone the frequency of which is a whole multiple of another tone with which it is associated. Virtually all physical sound producers (including, unfortunately, loudspeakers) produce complex sounds which consist of a fundamental tone and many harmonics. Harmonics are also known (more in musical, than home entertainment, contexts) as overtones.

Harmonic distortion When a signal (usually audio) is not reproduced perfectly, it is said to be distorted. Harmonic distortion is a specific, and common, type of distortion in which a given frequency that is supposed to be in the signal has added to it overtones, or additional unwanted signals which are whole multiples of its original frequency (harmonics). Equipment suppliers often quote a measurement called THD or Total Harmonic Distortion. The lower the figure the better ... in general. But relatively high levels of evenly numbered harmonics are easier to tolerate - indeed, can often be attractive, making the sound 'warmer' - than quite low levels of odd order harmonics.

Harness The universal name for a bundle or loom of wires that compose the wiring for a system.

Hash or grotzel Unwanted random sounds, such as tape hiss, print-through, clicks from bad edits and punches, intrusive room tone, etc.

Hass effect Also known as the Precedence Effect. The human ears do not rely solely on different loudnesses to determine the direction from which a sound is coming; they also use timing. It is often the case that timing trumps loudness. If the same sound arrives from two different directions, the ear will tend to identify the direction of the source as that of the first sound to arrive, even if the other sound, arriving a few milliseconds later, is significantly louder. This is why it is important to properly adjust the time alignment of surround speaker systems. This effect is also made use of in high quality sound reinforcement systems in concert halls, since by delaying the sound coming from speakers near the back of the hall, it can be made to sound as though the high volume coming from those reinforcing speakers is actually coming from the front of the hall.

Hatchback (box or enclosure) An enclosure of such size and shape as to enable its efficient use in hatchback-style vehicles. Normally, these enclosures are somewhat deeper than standard angled enclosures and have either handles on the end panels or no handles at all.

HD High definition.

HDCD (High definition compatible digital) This is an encoding/decoding system intended to improve the resolution of CDs (and other digital audio sources) while retaining full CD compatibility. It is said to provide performance equivalent to a PCM system with a resolution of 20 bits, with retaining CD's bit depth of 16. The trick is in re-introducing the old-fashioned compander, albeit carefully implemented in a sophisticated digital fashion. This applies a 'limiter' to the peaks of the signal so that they can be reduced by 6dB, providing an effective two more bits of resolution. It also increases the level of low-level signals in the

-45dBFS to -65dBFS range by up to 4dB, giving greater clearance from the noise floor. When played back with a HDCD decoder, the peak limiting and low level boost are reversed (a HDCD switching signal is embedded in the dither noise). HDCD also incorporates a dynamic low pass filter optimised for different types of signals (its operation is also signaled by the dither noise signal) and the dither itself is noise-shaped to provide a very low floor of noise and harmonic distortion below 16,000 hertz, but it seems likely that such severe noise shaping would produce a rather high noise floor between 16,000 hertz and the 22,050 hertz cutoff. Whatever benefits HDCD CDs may deliver when decoded with a HDCD decoder, it seems that the processing of the signal would adversely impact on playback in regular CD players. Read more at the HDCD site.

HDCP(High-bandwidth digital content protection) An encryption protocol developed by Intel and accepted for DVD use by the DVD Forum. This encrypts digital video output in real-time solely for the purpose of decrypting at the other end of a DVI or HDMI cable. It provides for two DVI-equipped devices to conduct a handshake, establish an encryption key, and then feed the video signal at full resolution in uncompressed digital format. HDCP supports high definition video signals as well. This system is supposed to protect against high quality digital video copying.

HDD(Hard disk drive) A magnetic medium for storing digital information on most computers and electronic equipment that process digital data.

HDDTV(High definition digital television) The upcoming standard of broadcast television with extremely high resolution and aspect ratio of 16:9. It is an advancement from the analogue high definition, already used experimentally in Japan and Europe. The picture resolution is nearly 2000×1000 pixels, and uses the MPEG-2 standard.

HDMI(High-definition multimedia interface) A new connection standard for feeding signals from sources to output devices in digital format. This carries both uncompressed digital video (in a form compatible with DVI) and uncompressed digital audio. Suitable encryption protocols are implemented on both (that for the video is HDCP) to resist digital copying. It has a huge bandwidth (up to 5 gigabits per second) allowing it to carry even 1080i video and, at the same time, up to eight channels of 24 bit, 192kHz digital audio. Plus it handles interaction between equipment, easing the way towards true single-remote-control of all devices. From a user perspective, though, it will mean that a DVD player need be connected to a home theatre receiver with just one cable (rather than the up to twelve currently: analogue audio x 6, digital audio x 1, component video x 3, S-Video x 1, composite video x 1). The receiver will then, presumably, provide a DVI output to on-forward the video to the display device.

HD-SDTI High data-rate serial data transport interface, defined by SMPTE 348M.

HDSL high bit rate digital subscriber line A digital transmission path that can be used for the transmission of CCTV pictures (1 camera) at up to 2Mbps. Up to 5 cameras can be transmitted but the data rate is shared (i.e. 384kbps for each camera).

DTV High definition television It usually refers to the analogue version of the HDDTV.

HDTV (High definition television) Because of the larger picture size (16-by-9 display ratio for HDTV versus 4-by-3 for regular TV) and more horizontal picture lines, HDTV will have a higher quality display than conventional TV. Also, HDTV has cd-quality sound and involves digital transmission instead of analog. FAQ's on HDTV. WRAL-TV 5 in Raleigh, NC, is the first television station in the nation to apply for an HDTV license.

HDV High definition DV.

Head, sync A head that plays back previously recorded sounds in synchronization to new sounds as they are being laid down on the same tape.

Head/tape head The magnetic device on a recorder that touches the tape and either records (record head) or reproduces (playback head) sound.

Headend The electronic equipment located at the start of a cable television system, usually including antennas, earth stations, preamplifiers, frequency converters, demodulators, modulators and related cable transmission equipment.

Headroom A term related to the dynamic range of amplifiers, used to express in dB, the level between the typical operating level and the maximum output level (onset of clipping). For example, a nominal +5 dBu system that clips at +25 dBu has 20 dB of headroom. Because the term depicts a pure ratio, there are no units or reference-level associated with headroom; only relative "dB." Therefore headroom expressed in dB accurately refers to both voltage and power. Which means the example above has both 20 dB of voltage headroom, and 20 dB of power headroom.

Heat dissipation The function of transfering heat away from a component into the air to prevent damage to the output section of an amplifier or the voice coil of a speaker.

Heat sink Parts of an amplifier, typically heavy metal "fins," and a section of the frame of the speaker used to conduct and radiate heat away from the ponit of electrical consumption, or motor assembly.

Helical scan A system of recording tracks of data or signal onto magnetic tape in which the tape is wrapped partway (up to about three quarters) around the circumference of a spinning cylinder. The cylinder houses one or more reading and writing heads. The tape is also drawn linearly across this contraption. This results in the tracks being written diagonally across the face of the tape. It has the advantage of allowing an effectively higher relative speed of tape to head, allowing a much greater density of data to be held on the tape than a linear system. Used by VCRs and DAT.

Helper applications Programs to view multimedia files that your web browser cannot display/play. Files must be downloaded before it will be displayed/played.

Herringbone Patterning caused by driving a colour-modulated composite video signal (PAL or NTSC) into a monochrome monitor. It is also often a characteristic of Radio Frequency Interference (RFI) picked up along a coaxial cable length.

Hertz The measurement of frequency One hertz is equal to one cycle per second, or the complete cycle of an alternating (AC) waveform. Higher frequencies are measured in kilohertz, (thousands of cycles per second) Megahertz, (millions of cycles per second), etc.

Hertz cycles per second A measure of frequency. Young healthy humans can hear from around 20 hertz to around 20,000. Frequencies lower than that can often be detected by other parts of the body.

Heterodyne A process by which two signals are mixed for the purpose of cross-frequency translation. Integral Nonlinearity (INL) This term describes the absolute accuracy of a converter. It is the maximum deviation, at any point in the transfer function, of the converter's output from its ideal value.

HFOV Short for "Horizontal Field of View". The horizontal angle in degrees that a particular image represents of the world. The wider a lens the greater the angle of view. When using a 35mm camera the HFOV is calculable from the focal length as follows:

if camera is used portrait HFOV = 2 * tan-1(12 / focal_length).

if camera is used landscapeHFOV = 2 * tan-1(18 / focal_length)

(Don't be frightened of these calculations you won't need them to create a basic panoramic image-TM).

Hi Fi high fidelity This is a tricky set of four letters. 'Hi fi' is frequently used a generic noun for any stereo sound system. But it should more properly be regarded as an adjective, taking due note of the Latin roots of the word fidelity, which means 'truth'. Originally high fidelity described a sound reproduction system that gave a more accurate rendition of the recording than was commonly available. The greater the accuracy, the higher the fidelity. Some audiophiles mistake pleasing sound for accuracy. Note that in absolute terms, it changes over time. As audio systems improve, so do those properly described as 'high fidelity'. A very fine high fidelity system from 1970 would not qualify for the term today.

HI8 (high-band 8mm) Improved version of 8mm videotape format characterized by higher luminance resolution for a sharper picture. Compact "conceptual equivalent" of Super-VHS.

HIBIS (Higher bandwidth incentive scheme) HiBIS is an initiative of the Australian Government that provides registered Internet service providers with incentive payments to supply broadband services in regional, rural and remote areas at prices comparable to those available in metropolitan areas.

High angle shot, or down angle A shot which views the subject from above. This angle tends to diminish the relative stature or power of the subject.

High fidelity A method of sound reproduction that emphasizes the highest possible adherence to the exact character of the original sound. This is a principal that must be paramount in every stage of the recording, transportation, and re-creation of the signal to be fully operational. It is usually the listener's equipment wherein this objective is most seriously compromised.

High key lighting A style of lighting that is bright and even, with few shadows and little contrast. Used generally in comedies, musicals, and light entertainment films.

High level input An audio input configured to accept speaker level signals.

High level technical options Transmission options which operate at a higher level than low level technical options, e.g. EDIFACT, Warwick Framework, PICS, RDM, Web Crawler, Search and Retrieve. The high level technical options use one of the low level technical options as the underlying transmission medium. High pass filter An electronic filter of a type commonly incorporated in Crossover circuits that permits the passage of high frequencies while suppressing lower ones. The place in the frequency spectrum where this occurs is called the crossover point and is different for each set of Drivers being considered. The most basic form of such filter is a non-polarized capacitor. Typical values for such a unit would be in the range of 1 to 100 microfarads. High power output Speaker level outputs driven by an amplifier, typically at least 15 watts RMS per channel. High sierra ISO 9660: a format for placing files and directories on CD-ROM. High voltage switching power supply An amplifier's internal power supply that converts the vehicle's 12 volts to higher voltage for improved dynamic range and higher amp output power.

Highlight The lightest colors within an image - opposite of shadow.

Highpass filter A circuit that passes frequencies above a specific frequency (the cutoff frequency). Frequencies below the cutoff frequency are reduced in amplitude to eliminate them.

HIGs human interface guidelines A set of recommendations and procedures for software developers to follow for creating a common look and feel for a software application based on studies of human-computer interaction. A well defined set of HIGs is critical to developing software that is efficient and intuitive to use.

HIS HSI stands for Hue, Saturation and Intensity. HSI is based on polar coordinates, while the RGB color space is based on a three-dimensional Cartesian coordinate system. The intensity, analogous to luma, is the vertical axis of the polar system. The hue is the angle and the saturation is the distance out from the axis. HSI is more intuitive to manipulate colors as opposed to the RGB space. For example, in the HSI space, if you want to change red to pink, you decrease the saturation. In the HSI space, if you wanted to change the color from purple to green, you would adjust the hue. Take a guess what you would have to do in the RGB space. However, the key thing to remember, as with all color spaces, is that it's just a way to represent a color-nothing more, nothing less.

History A list of past actions performed within an application.

Hits Hits are one way of measuring how many people go to a website. Over the years, the popularity of using hits to measure website traffic has decreased as more accurate statistics like page impressions and user sessions have become available. Unlike page impressions one hit does not mean that one web page has been viewed by a user.

HMS time format A time format used by Media Control Interface (MCI) to express time in hours, minutes, and seconds. The HMS time format is used primarily by videodisc devices.

Hold book To read the script while talent performs and note errors, interpolations, transpositions that may necessitate retakes.

Home page A Home Page is the first web page that is accessed when a domain name is requested. This page contains links to other pages at the site and is technically known as the hub document. Technically there is absolutely no difference at all between a Home Page, Portal, Hub Document, Front Page, Main Page, First Page, Default Page or whatever other term you may have come across. They are just marketing names to sell the same thing.

Home theatre receiver A multichannel amplifier with a digital decoder and tuner built in. The decoder always provides at least PCM and Dolby Digital decoding, and almost always DTS as well. A few also incorporate MPEG audio decoding.

Horizontal blanking During the horizontal blanking interval, the video signal is at the blank level so as not to display the electron beam when it sweeps back from the right to the left side of the CRT screen.

Horizontal blanking interval The time between the display of the rightmost pixel on one line and the leftmost pixel on the next line.

Horizontal drive (also horizontal sync) This signal is derived by dividing sub-carrier by 227.5 and then doing some pulse shaping. The signal is used by monitors and cameras to determine the start of each horizontal line.

Horizontal resolution Chrominance and luminance resolution (detail) expressed horizontally across a picture tube, it is often given as Television lines (TVL). This is usually expressed as a number of black to white transitions or lines that can be differentiated. Limited by the bandwidth of the video signal or equipment.

Horizontal retrace At the end of each horizontal line of video, a brief period when the scanning beam returns to the other side of the screen to start a new line, sometimes called flyback.

Horizontal scan frequency The frequency at which horizontal sync pulses start the horizontal retrace for each line. A high frequency is needed for a non-interlaced scan. The horizontal sync frequency for a color Macintosh connected to the 13-inch RGB display is 35 KHz, while the NTSC frequency is 15.75 KHz. Projection of high resolution non-interlaced Macintosh color video requires projectors capable of 35 KHz horizontal sync frequency.

Horizontal scan rate This is how fast the scanning beam in a display sweeps from side to side. In the NTSC system, this rate is 63.556 ms, or 15.734 kHz. That means the scanning beam moves from side to side 15,734 times a second.

Horizontal sync A signal created and used to synchronize the horizontal scan of a video signal, often combined with vertical sync into a composite sync. This signal is derived by dividing sub-carrier by 227.5 and then doing some pulse shaping. The signal is used by monitors and cameras to determine the start of each horizontal line.

Horizontal sync pulse The synchronizing pulse at the end of each video line that determines the start of horizontal retrace.

Horn A type of speaker system now principally used for high-frequency reproduction, but which is capable of full range sound in its largest format. As with those huge alpine horns, even the smallest transducer or diaphragm can produce the lowest sound if the horn is long enough and large enough at its business end.

Horn loaded driver A loudspeaker driver in which a horn is placed over the front of the driver. The primary advantage of this is to increase the efficiency of the transfer of mechanical energy from the driver to the air. However it usually results in reduced dispersion of sound, particularly for higher frequencies which tend to be 'beamed' from the horn, and can colour the sound. Nevertheless, some speaker makers have specialised in using horns, especially Klipsch, and they are frequently used in professional sound-reinforcement installations. The increase in efficiency can be quite marked. Klipsch loudspeakers tend to offer around nine decibels higher output than equivalent non-horn loaded loudspeakers, which means they can produce the same output from just one eighth of the power required for conventional speakers. This can, in turn, mean lower harmonic distortion because driver excursion is significantly reduced.

Horn tweeter A driver consisting of a relatively small emitter surmounted by a curvilinear or exponential horn. This is an effective system for radiating high frequencies in a variety of situations. The size and shape of the horn will usually dictate the pattern and use of the driver. Long horns with narrow apertures, tend to have the narrowest radiation pattern, and are very useful in large listening rooms, especially where highly directional effects, such as surround sound requires, are mandatory. Shallower versions have more general applications, especially in car stereo applications where a wider field of coverage is desired, along with a robust driver that can withstand severe environments. In such situations, a Piezo driven emitter (driver) is highly desirable for its ability to handle high-energy inputs on a variable basis. Horns can be driven by a number of different driver types: Dynamic ,(magnet and coil) Piezo, Electrostatic, Ribbon, and even Gas Plasma have been used effectively for this purpose.

Host A computer that acts as a file server. Users at remote computers (i.e. client computers) are allowed to access information that's stored on the server, or host computer.

Hot on mike Intimate and very close to the microphone, said of delivery.

Hotlist A list of frequently-accessed Web documents. Fun spots!.

House 1) A "live" audience, that is, an audience bodily present in the performance environment. "What a great house we had today" translates as "What a receptive and responsive audience we had today;" "nice house" = "large audience;" etc.;

2) the area of a performance space reserved for the audience, as distinguished from the stage, wings, and back stage.

House sync A common sync signal generated by a sync generator and fed to all video devices in an editing facility in order to synchronize the devices.

Housings environmental Usually refers to the containment of the camera and lenses and associated accessories, such as heaters, washers and wipers, to meet specific environmental conditions.

HS Horizontal synchronization.

HSB / HSV Hue-Saturation-Brightness/Value. The HSB color model is also known as the HSV color model — brightness and value are synonyms,

The HSB color model is an additive 3-feature color mixing system, like RGB. The 3 aspects are:

Hue - the feature that makes a particular color

Saturation (or intensity; also called chroma) - how much of the same hue is present.

Brightness - this is achieved by adding white or black to the basic color hue. Adding white adds to brightness, while adding black makes it duller, thus having less brightness.

HSI An acronym for the Hue-Saturation-Intensity color representation. A mathematical conversion from RGB. Often used for machine vision analysis.

HSI conversion A mathematical conversion from the color RGB space to hue, saturation, and intensity values.

HSL This is similar to HSI, except that HSL stands for Hue, Saturation and Lightness.

HSV This is similar to HSI, except that HSV stands for Hue, Saturation and Value.

HSYNC Check out the horizontal sync definition.

HTML(Hypertext markup language) HTML is a subset of SGML and was conceptualized by Tim Berners-Lee in 1989. HTML 0.0 was released by him in 1990. The success of the World Wide Web is partially due to the simplicity of HTML, the markup language used for marking documents to be distributed through the Internet.

HTML files take the extension html, but as DOS-based computers could only take 3-character extensions, it is often written as htm.

HTML is a structural language that serves as a container for document objects. It is like a mammal skeleton. HTML itself cannot do anything — for that you need a program. And HTML should not be used for the appearance of a document (for which you should rather use a style sheet). From a purist persepctive, the only thing that HTML does is to mark items and locations in a document with markers (called tags). User agents (such as browsers) interpret these markers and deliver the structure of the document in specified ways. For example, if an item is marked as a Paragraph (in HTML <p>), a visual user agent will display its content according to the conventions of paragraph display.

You may have read that HTML is a language used for presentation. That is not theoretically correct as HTML is a child of SGML which is a structural language, not a representational language. However, when the WWW exploded, browser makers such as Netscape confused structure with style and when the W3C was established it merely declared the most commonly form of HTML at that stage to be HTML 3.1 (the most widely used level of HTML). This was a mistake, realized by the W3C, and rectified with HTML 4, which distinguishes between structure and style.

HTML is an extremely powerful tool, as testified by the billions of web pages that are marked with it.

HTTP (Hypertext transfer protocol) HTTP is based on 8-bit transmission and the RFC 822 character set. HTTP 0.9 was released in 1992, while HTTP 1.1 became a formal standard in 2001.

HTTP is the protocol used for transporting web documents over internet lines. Some of the kinds of files that are handled by this protocol are HTML files, graphic files, sound files, animation sequence files, script files.

HTTP streaming A form of streaming (popularized by QuickTime) in which media files begin to play before they are downloaded entirely. This means that they can be sent via HTTP and don't require specialized server software such as RealMedia files do. (RealMedia files use a specialized protocol called RTSP and require content providers to have a special server application installed.) Also called Progressive Download.

HTTPS(Hypertext transfer protocol secure) This protocol is the same as HTTP, except that it has security features built in, usually some kind of encryption scheme. Users need keys to start the secure level, otherwise files cannot be accessed.

Hub document This is the more technical name for Home Page.

Hubris Excessive confidence, cosmic arrogance, overweening pride, usually the mistaken overestimate of one's capacity to control one's destiny or contend with God; often the one tragic flaw in an otherwise noble character.

Hue (1) The distinction between colors. Red, blue, green, yellow, and so forth are hues. White, black, and gray are not considered hues. The dimension of color that is referred to a scale of perceptions ranging from red through yellow, green, blue back to red.

(2) The color tint of a video image. The color of an analog video signal is determined by three factors: hue, saturation and luminance. In a composite video signal, the hue is determined by the phase relationship to the color burst.

Huffman coding Huffman coding is a method of data compression. It doesn't matter what the data is – it could be image data, audio data, or whatever. It just so happens that Huffman coding is one of the techniques used in JPEG, MPEG, H.261, and H.263 to help with the compression. This is how it works. First, take a look at the data that needs to be compressed and create a table that lists how many times each piece of unique data occurs. Now assign a very small code word to the piece of data that occurs most frequently. The next largest code word is assigned to the piece of data that occurs next most frequently. This continues until all of the unique pieces of data are assigned unique code words of varying lengths. The idea is that data that occurs most frequently is assigned a small code word, and data that rarely occurs is assigned a long code word, resulting in space savings.

Hum A term used to describe an unwanted induction of mains frequency.

Hum components The residual artifact harmonics of the AC power supply. In the U.S. the use a 60-Hz system, places the most annoying 2nd and 3rd harmonics at 120 Hz and 180 Hz. For Europe, and other parts of the world using 50-Hz mains, these components fall at 100 Hz and 150Hz. To some extent, this is present with nearly all non automotive sound systems and is generally accounted as noise.

Humbug A trade name for an isolation transformer (to remove earth or ground loops).

HVD HVD (High-definition versatile disc) is a red-laser DVD disc and player specification from China. It supports up to 150 minutes of 720p MPEG-2 content. The player supports 1080i and 720p video outputs.

Hybrid CD-Rom A single disc containing files for both a Windows PC and a Macintosh.

Hybrid discs Optical discs which provide more than one format. Many SACDs are hybrid, consisting of two layers. One layer carries SACD-only audio while the other carries CD-only audio, providing considerable versatility for these discs. Most DVD Audio discs are hybrid in the sense of carrying material suitable for both DVD Audio and DVD Video players. However with most of these the capability is provided by logical organisation rather than physically separate layers or the like. Recently there have been experiments conducted with providing hybrid DVD/CDs, with the DVD material on one side and the CD material on the other.

Hybrid loudspeakers Loudspeakers in which two significantly different driver technologies are used. For example (and most commonly), loudspeakers which use electrostatic panels for midrange and treble combined with conventional bass drivers.

Hybrid wavelet transform A combination of wavelet and transform algorithms within the same compression technology.

Hydrolysis A chemical reaction activated by humidity.

Hyperbaric resonator impulse An audible event characterized by a sudden and often unexpected pressure wave emanating from a vent port with a driver whose energetic and propulsive energy transitions, are generated by a process involving the chemical modification of legumes. This phenomenon frequently produces olfactory irritation in associated groups in consequence. This event is also know as a Farsical Audio Report Transient.

Hypercardioid A narrower heart-shaped pick-up pattern than that of cardioid microphones.

Hyper-HAD An improved version of the CCD HAD technology, utilizing on-chip micro-lens technology to provide increased sensitivity without increasing the pixel size.

Hyperlink A synonym for "link". A hyperlink links a document to one another document, or a document fragment to another document fragment. A link on a document can be activated and the user is then taken to that linked document or fragment. In web pages links were originally underlined to indicate that there is a link. With style sheets a textual link can take on any design features. Images and other objects can also be used as links.

Hyperlinking is one of the technoloogies that contributed to the success of the WWW (World Wide Web).

Hypermedia "Hypertext" with links not only to text, but also to other forms of media - sounds, graphics, movies/video, animation.

Hypertext "Text" which allows users to "hyper-jump". Hypertext is basically the same as regular text, with one exception: hypertext contains connections within the text to other Web documents. The connections are denoted, generally, as underlined, colored text. The "documents" to which the hypertext connect may be local or remote, perhaps even in a different country.

I

I & Q In-phase and Quadrature - A modulation technique whereby signal information is derived from a carrier frequency at its 0^0 and 90^0 phase angles.

I.link Sony trade name for Firewire or IEEE 1394 technology.

I/O Input/output.

I/P Input A signal applied to a piece of electric apparatus or the terminals on the apparatus to which a signal or power is applied.

I^2R Formula for power in watts (W), where I is current in amperes (A), R is resistance in ohms.

IAB (internet architecture board) The IAB is a governing body for The Internet. It handles administrative aspects of the Net, and manages standards and contracts. The IAB is appointed by the ISOC, looking at the long-term strategic planing of the internet. This involves standardization of protocols, management of interoperatability with all the countries of the world, supervision of the physical network, analysis of user patterns.

IAFA Internet Anonymous FTP Archive.

IANA (Internet assigned numbers authority) IANA falls under the IAB and assigns new IP addresses, i.e. the numbers (such as 197.65.98.18). Domain names are handled by different bodies in different countries. For the USA domain names are handled by InterNIC.

IASA International association of sound and audiovisual archives

ICA International council on archives.

ICC Profile A color scheme that specifice how colors are represented and translate from color spaces in devices such as scanners, printer and monitors.

ICM Image Color Matching - Known as a technique that uses color profiles for images and devices such as scanners or printers.

ICMP(internet control message protocol) ICMP is defined by RFC792 and RFC950. This protocol is used by routers and hosts to send control information or error messages to other routers or hosts. As web author you do not need to worry about these. As internet network administrator you definitely need to understand this. ICMP is used, for example, to check whether a host is available. It thus functions like ping.

Icon A computer icon is a small image used to represent files, objects or specific sections of a website. Icons should be easily understood but there is often a certain amount of learning by repetition on the part of the user.

ICR (Intelligent character recognition) Scanning device/process for hand print recognition.

ICT (Information and communication technology) ICT is used to describe telecommunications, computing and related areas. It is used (over information technology or IT) to indicate the dynamism that can be achieved with the convergence of computing and telecommunications. ICT makes possible the fast and worldwide exchange of information, and has the capacity to revolutionise work processes, service delivery etc.

ID3 ID3 is a small piece of information stored physically inside the MP3 file (in the beginning or in the end of the file, depends on ID3's version). ID3 tags can contain various information about the MP3, like album name, song name, artist, original artist, genre, composer, releasing year, additional comment fields, etc.. Nowadays ID3s are de facto in audio world and they can be added to most of the audio formats and even to certain video formats in order to provide additional information of the file.

IDE Interface device electronics Software and hardware communication standard for interconnecting peripheral devices to a computer.

Idisk One of the Dot.Mac suite of services offered by Apple computer for their fee based internet services. With iDisk, you can use your files even when you're away from your computer. You can access your files from any computer connected to the Internet, or even share your files with your friends and coworkers.

IEC 60461 Defines the longitudinal (LTC) and vertical interval (VITC) timecode for NTSC and PAL video systems. LTC requires an entire field time to transfer timecode information, using a separate track. VITC uses one scan line each field during the vertical blanking interval.

IEC 60958 Defines a serial digital audio interface for consumer (SPDIF) and professional applications.

IEC 61834 Defines the DV (originally the "Blue Book") standard.

IEC 61880 Defines the widescreen signaling (WSS) information for NTSC video signals. WSS may be present on lines 20 and 283.

IEC 61883 Defines the methods for transferring data, audio, DV and MPEG-2 data over IEEE 1394.

IEC 62107 Defines the Super VideoCD standard.

IEEE(Institute of electrical and electronics engineers) The IEEE (eye-triple-e) is a non-profit, technical professional association for electrical and electronic engineers. The IEEE oversees technical publications and consensus-based standards activities

IEEE1394 The formal name of a high capacity digital connection standard, capable of delivering up to 400mb/s. Frequently used for transferring video and audio from digital video cameras to DVD recorders and computers. Also known as Firewire (Apple Computer's name) and i.- (Sony's name).

Sony's name for a high capacity digital connection standard, capable of delivering up to 400mb/s. Frequently used for transferring video and audio from digital video cameras to DVD recorders and computers. Also known as Firewire (Apple Computer's name) and IEEE1394 (the formal name).

IETF (internet engineering task force) The IETF falls under the IAB and looks after the technical standards of the Net. The used to specify HTML standards, which is now done by the W3C.

The IETF look after internet services, integration, routing, transport, services, applications of the internet.

IETF protocols The Cisco IP/TV solution ensures consistent and time-dependent data delivery with RTP and RTCP, and VCR-like media controls with Real Time Streaming Protocols (RTSP).

IFLA International federation of library associations and institutions.

IHF Institute of high fidelity The premier institution for high fidelity whose standards have come to be universally recognized in application to the operation and design of sound re-enforcement and reproduction equipment.

ILink Sony's name for their IEEE 1394 interface.

ILL Inter-library loan.

Illegal video Some colors that exist in the RGB color space can't be represented in the NTSC and PAL video domain. For example, 100% saturated red in the RGB space (which is the red color on full strength and the blue and green colors turned off) can't exist in the NTSC video signal, due to color bandwidth limitations. The NTSC encoder must be able to determine that an illegal color is being generated and stop that from occurring, since it may cause over-saturation and blooming.

IMA An audio codec which compresses 16-bit audio at a ratio of 4:1.

Image file formats BMP, .GIF, .JPG, .TIFF, .PICT, .CDR.

Image file size The amount of computer storage space a file requires; usually measured in kilobytes (K) or megabytes (MB).

Image map A grouped image (single object) that contains separate linkable elements or 'hot spots' within the image parameters.

Image sensor A video camera's image sensing element such as a CCD.

Image size The physical dimensions of the image as measured in the small squares (pixels) of a computer screen; an image filling a "typical" computer screen (13-inch diagonal) would be 640 x 480 pixels; compare to "Image file size" above.

Image stabilization (IS) A feature on certain cameras and lenses that will reduce camera shake and improves image focus.

Imaging device A vacuum tube or solid state-device in which the vacuum tube light sensitive face plate or solid-state light sensitive array provides an electronic signal from which an image can be created.

Imaging Imaging describes the extent to which an audio system reproduces the directional cues that enable the listener to locate the instruments and vocalists as they were positioned during recording and mixing . Good imaging creates a listening experience that seems natural and lifelike. Since directional cues in sound come mainly in the higher frequencies, the key to attaining the best possible imaging is to have equal and unobstructed path lengths between the tweeters and the listener's ears. That's one of the reasons why matched component speakers, with their versatile tweeter placement, sound as good as they do.

Impedance A property of all metallic and electrical conductors that describes the total opposition to current flow in an electrical circuit. Resistance, inductance, capacitance and conductance have various influences on the impedance, depending on frequency, dielectric material around conductors, physical relationship between conductors and external factors. Impedance is often referred to with the letter Z. It is measured in ohms, whose symbol is the Greek letter omega.

Improved definition television (IDTV) IDTV is different from HDTV. IDTV is a system that improves the display on TVs by adding processing in the TV; standard NTSC or PAL signals are transmitted.

In medias res (from Gr.: "in the middle of things") A plot device wherein the action begins close to the climax or at an exciting point, flashes back to the beginning and then proceeds to the end.

In point/out point The first and last frames of a selected portion of a large clip. Frame notation (00:00:00:00= hours:minutes:seconds:frame) is the used to designate an in point and an out point.

In post During post-production.

In repertory adv. Said of an engagement, season, or set of performances of a star performer or performance ensemble, especially a theatrical one: in a revolving repertory of performance pieces or plays; broadcasts in repertory are rare in American radio, but not unheard of.

Inamorata 1. the role of female love interest;

2. the actress playing or specializing in such roles;

3. the leading lady of a commedia dell'arte troupe.

Inboard. Built-in, as opposed to outboard, frequently used in relation to sound equipment.

Indeo A family of video compression CODECs developed by Intel. Indeo video files tend to be high in quality, but also higher in file size, than other CODECs.

Indeo video Intel's series of compressor and decompressor technologies for digital video, capable of producing software-only video playback.

Independent A station neither owned nor affiliated with a network.

Index 1. An electronic signal that can be laid on a Dat to mark the beginning of a take or passage to be played, so that in playback the Dat can be instantly cued to that point; hence

2. to mark a Dat with such a signal.

Indexing service A secondary service providing access to primary sources through the use of keywords appearing in metadata and/or full text.

Indicate To play a quality as an actor superficially and without investment or sincerity, usually obviously so; to employ indication.

Indication A conventionalized or broad physical or vocal gesture substituting for one that the audience could not perceive, such as a stage whisper; hence the affectation of emotion, display of all the outward signs of emotion with no inner truth; the going through the motions; in script writing, an instruction to the actor, director or engineer written into the script; a stage direction.

Inductive coupling Radiated noise that is transmitted through a magnetic field to surrounding lines. This frequently occurs in long runs owire where power and signal cables are in too close proximity. This is a frequent source of noise and interference.

Inductor A transformer, or an electrical component in which impedance increases as the frequency of the AC decreases. Also known as coils. In audio, these are used in passive crossovers. Inductors are rated in Henrys.

Infinite baffle An infinite baffle speaker design is defined as an enclosure that contains a greater volume of air than the Vas requirement of the driver. An infinite baffle system can easily be applied to an automobile. This is accomplished by mounting the speakers on a board and using the trunk of the vehicle as the other walls of the enclosure. It is important that the enclosure be tightly sealed such that no air moves from the front to the back of the cone. Look for speakers where the Qts is greater than .6, and a Vas figure lower than the volume available, when selecting a woofer for an infinite baffle system.

Info mobility (devices) Technologies used to provide information to and from mobile communities, using advance mobile technologies and platforms.

InFocus projectors Brand of data projector used by Multimedia Services.

Information/informations The code inscribed in a transmission substance (film emulsion, radio waves, electro-magnetic energy) captured on or flowing through a medium (film, tape, air, cable) that is made from light and sound that can be transformed back into light and sound.

Infrasonic Audio tones of frequencies lower than capable of being detected by the human ear, generally below 20 hertz.

Ingénue [on-zhah-noo] 1. The conventional role of attractive, young female lead;

2. an actress playing or specializing in such roles.

Input device Input devices are the ways in which a user can interact with the computer. Common input devices include peripherals such as keyboards, mice, joysticks and microphones.

Input overload distortion Distortion caused by too great an input signal being sent to an amplifier or preamplifier. It is not affected by volume control settings and often occurs when mics are positioned too close to the sound source. This distortion may be controllable through the use of an attenuator or pad.

Input sensitivity Is the SPL (sound pressure level) a speaker will produce given one watt of power as measured from one meter away given a typical input frequency (usually 1kHz unless otherwise noted on the speaker). Typical sensitivities for car audio speakers are around 90dB/Wm. Some subwoofers and piezo horns claim over 100dB/Wm. However, some manufacturers do not use true 1W tests, especially on low impedance subwoofers. Rather, they use a constant voltage test which produces more impressive sensitivity ratings.

Input voltage The power voltage provided to an amplifier. While most cars can be expect to reliably produce 12 volts, amplifiers are sometimes measured at higher voltages; up to 15 volts. In this way, higher power can be developed, albeit at the expense of longevity. It is a practice that allows higher power figures to be claimed.

INRIA (institut national pour la recherche en informatique et automatique) INRIA (based in France) inherited the World Wide Web project from CERN (where the WWW originated) and ran the W3C together with MIT (Michigan Institute of Technology) and Keio University (Japan).

Insert (insert shot) A shot that will be edited into the final version of the movie. Insert shots often are close-ups or extreme close-ups that serve to explain or illustrate. An example could be a close-up of a projected slide that an actor refers to.

Inserter (also alphanumeric video generator) A device for providing additional information, normally superimposed on the picture being displayed; this can range from one or two characters to full-screen alphanumeric text. Usually, such generators use the incoming video signal sync pulses as a reference point for the text insertion position, which means if the video signal is of poor quality, the text stability will also be of poor quality.

Insertion loss The loss of voltage (or power), as measured in dB, resulting from placing a resistor (or some other power absorbing network or component) between a voltage or power source (amp) and its load impedance (speaker.) It is the ratio of the voltage (or power) absorbed in the load without the resistor (or network) to that when the network is inserted. For example, if the voltage across a load is 2 volts without a network and 1 volt with the network, then the insertion loss is stated as 6 dB.

Insulation or insulator A non-conductive protective covering for electrically active parts and wire that prevents short circuits and other unwanted interference.

Int script abbreviation for "interior."

Integrated amplifier An amplifier consisting of both a preamplifier and a power amplifier.

Integrated Services Digital Network A high speed Internet connection available via digital or regular telephone lines. Integrated Services Digital Network (ISDN) offers higher than modems, but lower bandwidth than or Internet connections.

Integrity Consultants The preservation of programs and data for their intended purpose.

Intellectual property A product of imagination- such as a novel, play, recording, painting, invention — capable of some sort of physical embodiment.

Intelligent agent This is software which does not yet exist; it would create and manage class and field-of-study profiles, conduct sophisticated program searches, and make recommendations to users who request age-appropriate programs or segments. This component represents the primary value-added service of the ECB. This function cannot be done by any other existing agency.

Intensity Intensity is also known as chroma or saturation.

Interactive multimedia association (IMA) A professional trade association of companies, institutions, and individuals involved in producing and using interactive multimedia technology.

Interactivity An open-loop control where a programmed system is directed by its user through mutual and simultaneously activity where either can interrupt the other without crashing the operation, where there is limited ability to anticipate, no default path and there is the impression of an infinite database.

Interconnect The cables used to transfer an analogue line level signal from a source component in a home entertainment system to an amplifier or recording device. Thus a set of interconnects is commonly used to plug a CD player into the analogue inputs of a home theatre receiver. They are normally two sets of electrically shielded cables with RCA plugs on each end, however some systems have adopted the XLR plugs and sockets used in much professional equipment.

Intercut 1) To interrupt the recording of a scene because of a flub and then to resume recording from or just prior to the stopping point; 2) a correction thus made.

Interface There are several types of interfaces applicable to the IT world. A 'user interface' allows the user to communicate with the operating system through the keyboard, mouse or menus of a computer system. A software interface involves languages and codes that software applications use to communicate with each other and with the hardware. A hardware interface involves the wires, plugs and sockets that hardware devices use to communicate with each other. A human interface allows humans to better communicate with and within the wider IT world, by using modalities such as spoken and written language, facial and prosodic expressions, gestures and emotions, and haptics.

Interference Disturbances of an electrical or electromagnetic nature that introduce undesirable responses in other electronic equipment.

Interframe A video frame that is compressed by comparing it to adjacent frames in order to find data that remains similar over time, such as the background behind a talking head. This type of compression is also called Temporal Compression.

Related terms: Intraframe, Compression.

Interframe compression A form of compression in which the codec compresses the data within one frame relative to others. These relative frames are called delta frames.

Interior monologue A soliloquy representing the unspoken thoughts of a character in a play; in radio often electronically set-off from normal dialogue.

Interlace The two fields that constitute a TV frame each have only half the number of lines of a whole frame (576 visible lines for PAL, 480 for NTSC). One field has the odd numbered lines, the other has the evenly numbered ones. One field is first displayed, followed by the other, before the system moves onto a new frame. On the screen, though, the lines of each of these two fields alternate, or are interlaced. Because of the lingering glow of the TV's phosphors and the phenomenon of persistence of vision in our eyes, we see the two fields as one frame.

Interlaced scanning A technique of combining two television fields in order to produce a full frame. The two fields are composed of only odd and only even lines, which are displayed one after the other but with the physical position of all the lines interleaving each other, hence.

Interlacing Interlacing is method used to accommodate long waits on a busy network. This method makes it possible to load an image in spurs of small bits bits scattered from all over the image. The image starts displaying hazy or fuzzy, and as loading proceeds, it becomes clearer and clearer. It is possible to s receiving further data of the image from the server once the viewer decides he/she does not need to see the complete image.

Interline transfer This refers to one of the three principles of charge transferring in CCD chips. The other two are frame transfer and frame-interline transfer.

Interlude A conversation, skit, scene, musical number, often only tangentially related to the plot, that suspends the flow of dramatic action.

Intermodulation distortion If two tones are produced at the same time as each other, they can interact in a piece of equipment to produce other tones. Those tones are the sum and difference between the two original tones and, consequently, are generally not harmonics of either tone. As such, intermodulation distortion is generally more audible, and objectionable, than harmonic distortion. If the standard SMPTE test tones are applied (60 hertz and 7,000 hertz sine waves), then you can expect to see intermodulation distortion peaks at 6,940 and 7,060 hertz. In practice, small levels of harmonic distortion in the original signals will lead to other IM peaks, so you might see one at 6,880 hertz (ie. 7,000 - 2 x 60) and so on.

Internal CD-ROM drive A CD-ROM drive that is installed inside the computer.

International midi association (IMA) The nonprofit organization that circulates information about the Musical Instrument Digital Interface (MIDI) specification.

Internet "The network of networks" . The Internet originally developed out of the ARPAnet. The ARPAnet model specifies that communication occurs between the source and destination computer in small parcels of data known as Internet Protocol (IP) packets. Each computer transmitting a packet has the responsibility of addressing and delivering it to the destination computer. Berkeley Systems adopted the IP networking system in their version on the UNIX operating system and over the years added many extra network oriented commands to the operating system. Before long, because of the device independence of this protocol, many different vendors adopted the IP system.

In the late 80's, the National Science Foundation (NSF) created five super-computer centers. They decided to link these centers using the IP protocol as a method of sharing the expensive resources. Academic institutions soon connected their local networks to the central NSF network backbone to be able to access the supercomputer resources. The collection of inter-connected networks became known as the Internet.

Today the Internet has become a global "information highway", connecting almost every country in the world together. Anyone with a computer, modem and the money (or opportunity) to connect into an online service provider (like America Online) can tap into the "network of networks." The World Wide Web (WWW) is one of the most popular Internet services.

Internet explorer (IE) The web browser developed by Microsoft which is currently the most popular web browser on the web.

Internet information services (IIS) Microsoft's web server that runs on Windows platforms. IIS comes bundled with windows NT, 2000 Professional and XP Professional.

Internet publisher An organisation or person who publishes documents on the Internet. These will be on-line documents.

Internet service provider (ISP) To get access to the internet you will need to sign up with an ISP which will provide you with a connection to the internet. Every time you connect to the internet, your computer calls up the ISP's computer. When you want to visit a website, the ISP's computer finds the site and makes the necessary connection to send the information to your computer.

Internet studio A Web programming "language", developed by Microsoft, that uses drag-and-drop and OLE - not HTML - to publish Web pages. Internet Studio will support numerous file formats and software programs - VRML, Macromedia Shockwave, Adobe Acrobat, GIF, JPEG, Microsoft Office (Word, Excel, PowerPoint, Access), among others.

InterNIC internet network information center InterNIC is jointly owned by three companies (AT&T, Network Solutions Inc, and General Atomics) contracted to the NSF (National Science Foundation) of the USA. InterNIC handles the daily running of the internet by assigning IP addresses, managing domain name hierarchies, managing routing information for backbones, monitoring the growth of the internet, and distributing information about the internet. InterNIC assigns domain names to IP addresses on application. In countries other than the USA there are other bodies handling the domain names.

Interpolation Interpolation is a mathematical way of generating additional information. Let's say that an image needs to be scaled up by a factor of two, from 100 samples to 200 samples. The "missing" samples are generated by calculating (interpolating) new samples between two existing samples. After all of the "missing" samples have been generated – presto! – 200 samples exist where only 100 existed before, and the image is twice as big as it used to be.

Intraframe A video frame that is compressed, much like an image file, by finding blocks of similar color that can be grouped together. This type of compression is also called Spatial Compression.

Related terms: Interframe, Compression

Intraframe compression A form of compression in which the codec compresses the data within one frame relative only to itself. Key frames are compressed with intraframe compression because they must reconstruct an entire image without reference to other frames.

Inverse square law In mathematics, the law that states that in the absence of reflective surfaces, sound pressure (or light) falls off at a rate inverse to the square of the distance from its source. In other words, every time the distance from the sound source is doubled, the sound pressure level is reduced by a factor of 4, or 12 dB.

IP internet protocol IP is defined by RFC791 and RFC1349.

IP provides a datagram service between hosts on a TCP/IP network - IP thus runs "on of" TCP. It routes the packets of data that are transmitted to the correct host. IP also takes apart datagrams and puts them back together again.

The IP (i.e. IPv4) address of a device is a hierarchical and numerical 32-bit address such as 123.143.221.225 (with numbers ranging from 0-255 in each block). IPv6 is a 128-bit system, permitting many more IP addresses than IPv4.

Older server architecture allowed only one IP address per box, which meant that you needed a different server for each IP address. Soon "virtual boxes" aliasing was possible allowing more than one IP address to be on the smae box, and allowing each such IP to alias to a different domain name.

IP is connectionless (thus not guaranteed). But when used together with TCP, error control is handled, and as TCP does that, IP does not need to bother about it.

An IP address is a software address assigned by a network administrator. For the internet IP addresses are officially allocated by approved domain administrators. Commercial internet connection companies (ISPs) often handle these registration on behalf of their clients.

The IP address is typically used by machines. Domain names are human friendly addresses that map to IP addresses. When you type in a domain name a nameserver looks up the IP address and connects thus to the appropriate server.

IP address Also called Internet address. The unique address for each computer on the Internet. The IP address appears as four numbers. These sets of numbers indicate the domain, the network, the subnetwork and the actual host machine.

IP conferencing Video conferencing using IP networking.

IP Index of protection A 2, (sometimes 3) digit numbering system that describes the quality of protection of an enclosure from outside influences, such as dust and moisture (the third digit relates to impact).A

IP multicasting For schedules or live broadcasts, bandwidth-saving the Cisco IP Multicast permits single-sender and multiple-receiver program transmission. Only one real-time stream of data is sent for each program, no matter how many people tune in.

IPS Inches per second, a standard unit of analogue recording and playback speed in America. Professional recordings are made no slower than 7-1/2 ips, and may be made at 15 ips, 30 ips, or faster, to increase sound quality.

IR light Infrared light, invisible to the human eye. It usually refers to wavelengths longer than 700 nm. Monochrome (B/W) cameras have extremely high sensitivity in the near infrared region (715 to 800nm) of the light spectrum.

IRE Institute of radio engineers Units of measurement dividing the area from the bottom of sync to peak white level into 140 equal units. 140 IRE equals 1Vpp. The range of active video is 100 IRE.

IRE scale, IRE units A unit used for the measurement of video levels. The scale used for the graticule on a waveform monitor. 140 IRE represents 1.000 V, 100 IRE represents 0.714 V, while 1 IRE represents 0.007 V.

Iris A means of controlling the size of a lens aperture and therefore the amount of light passing through the lens.

Irony A literary device, and one particularly used in drama, in which what is stated contrasts or conflicts with what is wryly suggested.

ISBD International standard bibliographic description There are seven specific ISBDs as well as the general ISBD -(G): monographs

-(M), serial publications -(S), cartographic material -(CM), non-book material -(NBM), printed music -(PM), antiquarian publications -(A), computer files -(CF).

ISDN (integrated services digital network) A network/telephone connection that transfers data at rates more than 4 times faster than a 28.8Kbps modem. Ordinary modems (non-ISDN) convert computer data to audio tones/analog to transfer over the phone lines. ISDN "modems" connect digitally: Inherently faster digital signals rather than tone signals transfer over the lines. Basic Rate ISDN, often called "2B+D" or RI, arrives on 3 channels - one Delta ("D") 16 Kbps channel carrying telephone signals and two "Bearer" ("B") channels delivering data at 64 Kbps. Primary Rate ISDN, also known as T1 service, has 23 B channels and one D channel, delivering at a rate of 1.544 Mbps (T3 transmits at an extremely high rate - 44.7 Mbps).

ISIT Intensified silicon intensified target A type of detector tube for use in very low light conditions such as starlight.

ISMA Abbreviation for the Internet Streaming Media Alliance. ISMA is a group of industry leaders in content management, distribution infrastructure and media streaming working together to promote open standards for developing end-to-end media streaming solutions. The ISMA specification defines the exact features of the MPEG-4 standard that have to be implemented on the server, client and intermediate components to ensure interoperability between the entire streaming workflow. Similarly, it also defines the exact features and the selected formats of the RTP, RTSP, and SDP standards that have to be implemented.

The ISMA v1.0 specification defines two hierarchical profiles. Profile 0 is aimed to stream audio/video content on wireless and narrowband networks to low-complexity devices, such as cell phones or PDAs, that have limited viewing and audio capabilities. Profile 1 is aimed to stream content over broadband-quality networks to provide the end user with a richer viewing experience. Profile 1 is targeted to more powerful devices, such as set-top boxes and personal computers.

ISO(International standards organization) The ISO is an international body that certifies standards ranging from visual signs (such as the i-sign for information, seen at places such as airports and information kiosks) to language characters (such as proposed by ANSI and ASCII). SGML standards are also decided by the ISO since it became a standard in 1986. HTML is a subclass of SGML, and complies in that respect to ISO standards, but HTML itself is not an ISO standard.

If you are a programmer of an HTML browser you definitely need to know the ISO standards. As an HTML author following a certain release of HTML you only need to know that release as recommended by the W3C (and fortunately not SGML).

There are many ISO standards that form the basis of multimedia related products. For example, the MPEG-1 ISO standard made possible CD's .

ISO 9660 A format for placing files and directories on CD-ROM. Readable by both Macintosh and PC-compatible computers.

ISO booth (isolation booth), a small room, often adjacent to or within a larger studio, for recording a sound in isolation from other sounds.

Isobarik Sometimes spelled Isobaric, this is an enclosure design in which two or more Drivers are coupled together by a sealed air mass to operate as a single driver. With proper sealing and design, very impressive results can be obtained from an unusually small box. A popular version of this simply consists of two woofers placed over each other in a 'clamshell' design. The downside consists of the fact that it does require at least twice the amplifier power as would be needed for a conventional speaker, in order to be operated successfully.

ISOC (internet society) ISOC is a non-profit society concerned with the state of the internet. It publishes a newsletter Internet Society News and holds an annual conference, INET.

ISO-DIN mounting Refers to a receiver mounting system in which the headunit is mounted behind the dash panel with side brackets, employing factory installed trim panels.1.

Isolation Electrical or acoustical separation to prevent the spread of noise and the effect on the signal of unwanted elements produced by internal or external devices.

ISSN International standard serial number.

IT Information technology.

ITS The International teleproduction society.

ITU International telecommunications union (also UIT).

ITVA The International Television Association.

J

Jack A receptical for a plug used to interconnect electronic devices.

JAVA An object-oriented , Web programming language, similar to C++, developed by Sun MicroSystems. JAVA applications are compiled into Java bytecode, executable on any java-enabled browser, i.e. browsers which have the "Java Virtual Machine" Thus, JAVA will run the same on any operating system. JAVA applications, technically, are stand-alone programs, whereas JAVA applets are code snipets, designed to run within Webpages. JAVA is NOT Javascript. +/- of Java

JAVA Applets Small programs written in JAVA that produce various special effects, which are embedded right into the Web pages. When someone accesses a Web page with applets, the applets automatically download with the page: All that is needed to view the effect comes with the page itself, making applets independent of the eccentricities of various operating systems. This design feature makes applets particularly desirable for multimedia applications, which typically are very platform-dependent.

JAVA beans Component API's allowing Java applications to run in other frameworks, e.g., Microsoft Word.

Java runtime environment (JRE) A run time environment developed by Sun Microsystems to convert Java bytecode into machine language and execute it locally.

Java scripting Not Java, but a scripting language sort of like HTML. It can be used to enhance a web page by allowing a degree of interactivity. It can be used to integrate panoramic images into a web site.

Java virtual machine (JVM) An abstract computing machine which is a platform independent execution environment.

JavaScript JavaScript is a scripting language originally developed by Netscape in 1995 for Netscape 2.0. It was originally called LiveScript, but renamed JavaScript as it was viewed to be complementing Java. JavaScript is an interpreted scripting language that is typically executed by the browser (i.e. on the client-side). However, there is also server-side JavaScript which is executed on the server. JavaScript 1. 0 has become a standard, known as ECMAScript.

Jewel cases Plastic carrying cases for CD's.

Jitter Jitter is the phenomenon of a drift in the digital audio data delivered so that it does not precisely match the sampling frequency, causing confusion in the receiving equipment as to the appropriate value of the sample. A host of allegedly audible problems with CDs and other digital formats have been laid at the feet of jitter. Jitter was a problem in the early days of all-digital production studios because each piece of equipment would have its own circuit to generate a digital clocking signal, and these would tend to drift apart from each other. The results were sometimes subtle, as when they resulted in dropped samples (due to the receiving device reading a little more slowly than the source). But they were equally likely to be obvious as a result of the source running more slowly than the receiving device. From time to time a 'zero' sample would result, producing an audible click in the sound. Professional studios have long-since overcome these early problems by providing a standard clocking signal source which controls all equipment, ensuring that they remain fully synchronised. For consumer equipment connected using the universal S/PDIF standard, there is equally no problem. The source always runs in master mode, providing the clocking signal to the receiving device (for example, a home theatre receiver) which always runs in slave mode with its timing locked to the incoming clocking signal.

Jog Also known as a shuttle wich is a manual control on some vcr's shaped as a ring to fast forward or rewind.

Joule A unit of energy equal to one watt per second.

JPEG/JPG (joint photographic experts group) JPEG is a bitmap compression format for images. The proper abbreviation is JPEG, but DOS-based computers could only take a 3-character extension, so you will often see the shortened version: JPG. JPEG is based on a 24-bit color palette, but it is lossy, which means that it drops information that is compressed out. Compression ratios may range from 10:1 to 20:1 and most graphic application programs (such as Adobe Photoshop) allow you to choose the compression rate. Obviously, the more compressed, the more data is lost, but the less compressed the larger the files size of the image. It takes considerable experience and skill to play around with different modes and pallettes as well as compression ratios to get a good quality result with a relatively small JPEG file size. JPEG is typically used for complex images and photographs. It supports 16.7 million colors.

Jscript JScript is Microsoft's version of JavaScript, based on the published documents of Netscape. However, Netscape did not publish all the features, so Microsoft developed their own stuff, which led to discrepancies as these different versions clashed. Fortunately Microsoft has dropped JScript altogether, but, unfortunately they are still pushing their own platform-specific products to the Web, whose purpose is to be platform independent.

Judder An instability that results from conversion between frame rates. It can be accentuated when frames are repeated or deleted in order to obtain slow motion or fast motion.

Jump or jump cut A sudden transition between scenes of a radio and teleplay, indicated in scripts by the phrases jump to . . . or cut to .

Jump, jumper To provide a temporary circuit around a component or other circuit A device that anables this action

JVT Abbreviation for Joint Video Team, a group of video experts that work on new video codecs. It is a collaborative effort between the International Telecommunication Union (ITU), the International Electrotechnical Commission (IEC) and the International Organization for Standardization (ISO). "JVT" was also an early name for the H.264 video codec.

K

K codes A binary code inserted in the vertical interval of a video signal, by a multiplexer. The binary number represents the input number of the multiplexer is usually one line per binary bit.

Kangaroo lens A lens with only two fixed iris positions one fully open and the other partly closed. Designed for use with Electronic Iris (Auto Electronic Shuttering or CCD Iris) cameras as a way of controlling the output video level. It should only be used with compatible cameras.

Kapton A voice coil design in which multiple layers are used on a Kapton coated coil form to create the rotor element in the speaker driver's linear motor. This allows greater power handling, and cooler operation.

KB Short for kilobyte. This unit is typically used to measure the size of computer files (i.e. files created in Word, WordPerfect, Adobe Acrobat, and other computer applications). A kilobyte is equivalent to 1,024 bytes, and is one of the most common units currently used for measuring electronic data.

Kb/s or kbps (Kilobits per second) A measure of the data flow rate for digital audio from a DVD. Stands for thousands of bits per second. Generally, the higher the number the better the quality.

Keeper (studio) A good take.

Kell effect TVs produce their pictures by shooting electron beams across a vacuum tube to its flat, or flattish, end. This end is coated in stripes of phosphor which glow red, green or blue (thus RGB) when hit by the beams. However the relevant beam does not always hit the relevant bit of phosphor so some resolution is lost. This is termed the Kell Effect. Some books claim that this can reduce resolution by around 30%.

Kelvin One of the basic physical units of measurement for temperature. The scale is the same as the Celsius, but the 0 K starts from -273.16°C (0 K on the Kelvin scale or 0°R on the Rakine scale or –459.60°F on the Fahrenheit scale). Also the unit of measurement of the colour temperature of light is expressed in Kelvin or K. In colour recording, light temperature affects the colour values of the lights and the scene that they illuminate.

Key frame A "complete" video frame, containing all the image detail, not just the changes from the previous frame.

Key light The main light used for illumination of a subject.

Keyboard A common piece of equipment for inputting information into a computer. It can also be used to navigate programs and websites. Keyboards for different languages differ significantly, and some even exist as "virtual" devices that are displayed on a screen.

Keyframe A keyframe is a special kind of frame that contains info about changes in the properties of an object. For example, animated movement may proceed from a starting point to an end point through time. Each of these points would be a keyframe as their respective frames indicate where the animation begins and ends through time.

Keying The process of replacing part of one television image with video from another image.

Keykode A machine-readable code printed on the edge of motion picture film which allows the film edge numbers to be electronically read and inserted in to an edit list. Very useful for generating a negative cut list from a video off-line EDL.

Keypad A panel usually made of metal or plastic with numbered push-button switches (like a touch-tone telephone) designed to provide access to certain types of control functions. Security, CD changers, and cellular systems represent typical examples.

Keystoning A perspective distortion shot at a non perpendicular angle to give the nearer portion a focused view with the farther portion a feathered view.

KHz (kilohertz) A frequency of one thousand (1,000) cycles per second.

Kilobaud A unit of measurement of data transmission speed equalling 1000 baud.

Kiosk A booth or stand containing a computer that is used for a single purpose, such a video installation in a museum or an ATM machine. The presentations running on these computers are authored by multimedia developers with programs like Macromedia Director.

Kirchoff's current law (KCL) A law stating that the total current entering a point or junction in a circuit must equal the sum of the current leaving that point or junction.

Kirchoff's voltage law (KVL) A law stating stating that the voltage supplied to a DC circuit must equal the sum of the voltage drops within the circuit .

Kodak photo CD ("PCD's") Photographs/ images are "printed"/digitized on CD's. Your Photo CD comes with a contact sheet, showing small pictures of each image on the disc. You can keep adding pictures to the CD. To view the CD images, you need a viewer. Nowadays, many multimedia programs can import these already-digitizied image files into documents.

KPBS In the US recognized as kilobits per second (thousands of bits per second). Typically refers to the rate at which data can flow across a data transmission medium such as a telephone line. Kbps is a measure of bandwidth. Other measurements include Mbps (millions of bits per second) and Gbps (billions of bits per second).

Kuntskopf (Ger.: "art head") The head-shaped microphone assembly used in recording binaural audio.

L

LA, LAM, LMA These are Netscape's streaming audio formats and are automatically handled bt generation 4 browsers.

Label A PICS label, generated by a labelling service, contains a rating of Internet material.

Labelling service within the PICS environment, a labelling service generates ratings of Internet material. These ratings are contained in PICS labels.

Lambertian source or surface A surface is called a Lambert radiator or reflector (depending whether the surface is a primary or a secondary source of light) if it is aperfectly diffusing surface.

Lampoon 1) A light, good-humored satire;

2) to satirize light-heartedly.

LAN (local area network) A privately-operated communications system interconnecting computers and communications equipment over a limited geographic area, usually 5 miles or less. LAN's enable local resource - sharing (printers, files, etc.).

Laser Light amplification by stimulated emission of radiation A laser produces a very parallel and coherent light (all wave fronts in phase) of a single frequency.

Laserdisc On optical disc, 30cm in diameter, used to carry movies. The video signals are held in analogue form, while the audio signals were originally FM encoded analogue, but later were in PCM digital and later still in Dolby Digital or DTS.

Laserdisc player Like a VCR, this device plays back analog video stored on laserdiscs.

Last mile A phrase used to describe the final part of a transmission path to the ultimate user of the service,

Lavaliere A type of small, personal microphone that may be worn unobtrusively on the body.

Law of diminishing returns In all types of performance and presentation, whether theatrical, literary, musical, sports-related, journalistic, or otherwise, the effect of boredom produced by duration on an audience; the longer a performance or presentation, the more the law of diminishing returns must be counteracted by ever more impressive effects or ever more absorbing content.

Lay down To record (something).

Layer In a digital movie-making program such as MovieShop™, the term "layer" refers to a single collection of clips that can be viewed on screen at one time. Adding another layer of multiple clips to a movie project will allow you to view both layers on screen at once if desired. For example, Layer #1 consists of video clips and transitions, while Layer #2 consists of a scrolling credit clips. When both layers are viewed simultaneously, the video clips will play and the scrolling credits will show, too. The ability to create layers when producing a video project allows multiple clips to be viewed on screen at the same time. Layers can be used to create a side-by-side or picture-in-picture effect.

Lazzo, plural lazzi Recurring or running gag, skit, stage business or comic routine of the commedia dell'arte, hence any such business recurring or imbedded in various contexts and various works, such as the "Slowly I Turned" lazzo of Vaudeville.

LCD Display Short for Liquid Crystal Display, any device that projects data or video using Liquid Crystal Display technology. LCD computer monitors are usually very sharp. LCD projectors.

LCD Liquid crystal display A screen for displaying text/graphics based on a technology called liquid crystal, where minute currents change the reflectiveness or transparency of the by changing the polarization angle. The advantages of LCD screens are very small power consumption (can be easily battery driven) and low price of mass-produced units. The disadvantages are narrow viewing angle, slow response, invisibility in the dark unless the display is back lighted, and difficulties displaying true colors with colour LCD displays.

LCD panel (liquid crystal display) A device used to present computer images to a class or audience. The LCD panel, connected to the computer, sits on an overhead projector and displays the computer monitor's image onto a movie screen or wall.

LCOS Liquid crystal on silicon A form of liquid crystal display panel used in projectors. Unlike normal LCD panels, the light does not shine through these but reflects from their surface. This allows the enabling electronics for each pixel to be placed behind, rather than around, the pixel, allowing a greater pixel density for a given panel size, and reduced border widths for effective elimination of the screen door effect.

Le (Measured in millihenries, mH) The electrical inductance of a speaker's voice coil.

Leader 1) A length of non-recordable film, tape or paper that can be edited to analog recording tape or film to mark cues or protect the ends from damage;

2) to separate tracks with leader.

Leading man or leading lady An actor who usually plays only the most important roles in dramatic productions; the actor playing the most important role in a specific production.

Leak To leak from one track or microphone to another; said of sounds.

Leased line A dedicated sommunication line between two points.

LED Light emitting diode A semiconductor diode, that produces light when a certain low voltage, forward bias, is applied to it. Like a normal diode it conducts only in one direction.

Legal signal A video signal in which each component does not exceed the specified gamut for the given format. Compare valid signal.

Legibility The ease with which written words can be read. Legibility is affected by things like typeface, font size, style and colour. Legibility differs from "readability", which is the ease which content can be understood.

Lens An optical device for focussing a desired scene onto the imaging device in a CCTV camera.

Letterbox This can have two meanings. The first is a movie in widescreen format. When displayed on a standard 4:3 TV, this means it will have black bars on the screen at the top and bottom. The second is the presentation of a widescreen movie on DVD in a non-anamorphic format. This second sense is not consistently used, but should be.

Level A term used in sound recording in reference to the intensity of the signal being captured. Setting the levels too low can result in ambient noise, and setting them too high may cause distortion.

LFE Low frequency effects channel, sometimes imprecisely known as the subwoofer channel. This carries audio information covering frequencies up to 120 hertz and is designed to provide a substantial foundation to the bomb blasts, rumbling trucks and the like in movies.

Libretto The spoken portion of a musical play script; in opera, the entire text.

Light valve projector A video projector design with very high light output. An example of a projector using this technology is the Talaria from General Electric.

Limdow A process aimed at speeding the copying of information to CD-ROM.

Limiter An electronic compressor with a fixed ratio of 10:1 or greater. The dynamic action effectively prevents the audio signal from becoming any larger than the threshold setting. For example, if the threshold is set for, say, +12 dBu and the input signal increases by 10 dB to +26 dB, the output only increases by 1 dB to +13 dBu, essentially remaining constant. Used primarily for preventing equipment overloads, thus reducing clipping distortion.

Line A unit of dialogue equivalent to a phrase, sentence, or speech, depending upon the context in which the word is used.

Line flicker With the interlaced display systems most commonly in use, horizontal lines and edges shown on the screen can appear to flicker up and down rapidly. That's because every second line is only being display once in one fiftieth of a second. This problem is resolved in the PAL world by using the more expensive 100 hertz TV sets instead of the standard 50 hertz sets.

Line level An electrical signal at a voltage level suitable for transferring a signal between components of a home entertainment system (for example, CD player to amplifier, amplifier to VCR). Most modern equipment operates with a maximum of level of not much more than two volts RMS. Line level signals demand high impedance inputs. At least 10,000 ohms is suitable, although the de facto standard is 47,000 ohms.

Line store A line store is a memory used to hold one scan line of video. If the horizontal resolution of the active display is 640 samples and RGB is used as the color space, the line store would have to be 640 locations long by 3 bytes wide. This amounts to one location for each sample and each color. Line stores are typically used in filtering algorithms. For example, a comb filter is made up of one or more line stores.

Linear 1. Referring to mechanical movement, the ability of the voice coil to move in and out in the air gap without moving side-to-side. Non-linear movement can damage the voice coil.

2. Referring to woofer response, the ability to maintain power or movement without loss of drive force.

3. Referring to enclosure port operation, the relationship bewteen the amount of air moving through the port vs. the amount of air moved by the cone. Non-linear response in a port can cause audible distortion.

Linear phase response Any system which accurately preserves phase relationships between frequencies.

Linearity In any home entertainment system, at each stage the input and output signals should be precisely proportional to each other (except where specifically provided such as RIAA equalization or Dolby noise reduction). Thus if a momentary 0.5 volts is fed to the input of an amplifier and it produced a three volt output at its speaker terminals, then a momentary 1.0 volt input should produce a six volt output. Any other output means that there is a non-linearity which will manifest itself as harmonic distortion. Another example relates to digital to analogue converters. Each particular quantization level in a PCM digital signal has a precise analogue voltage level associated with it. Any variation means distortion.

Line-locked In CCTV, this usually refers to multiple cameras being powered by a common alternative current (AC) source (either 24 V AC, 110 V AC or 240 V AC) and consequently have field frequencies locked to the same AC source frequency (50 Hz in CCIR systems and 60 Hz in EIA systems).

Link A "description link" is a capital letter D inside square brackets placed next to an image on a web page. This [D] links to another web page that contains a detailed written description of the image.

A D link allows visually impaired users and users of text browsers to understand the content of an image without seeing it. D links are useful for people who use browsers that do not support the Alt tag.

Data Protection Act 1998

The Data Protection Act covers personal data in electronic and manual formats (for example paper files). The key points of the act state that any data (information) collected by an organisation must be done so fairly and legally, and that the information stored about a person must be kept accurate and up-to-date and not kept for longer than is necessary. Also, security measures must be put into place to stop unlawful or unauthorised processing of personal data and accidental loss or damage to personal data.

The Act also gives rights to the individuals as regards to the data stored about them. Amongst other things, individuals are entitled to request a copy of all personal data stored on them and can prevent their details being used for direct marketing. They can also stop their details being used in a way that is likely to cause distress or discomfort.

Linux An implementation of unix that runs on PCs and other platforms developed mainly by Linus Torvalds.

Liquid crystal display (LCD) A panel on a camera that previews photographs and acts as a viewfinder.

LIST chunk A Resource Interchange File Format (RIFF) chunk with a chunk identifier of LIST. LIST chunks contain a series of subchunks.

List type A four-character code (FOURCC) identifying the type of data contained in a Resource Interchange File Format (RIFF) chunk with a chunk identifier of LIST. For example, a LIST chunk with a list type of INFO contains a list of information about a file, such as the creation date and author.

Listening position A feature which can optimize frequency response and imaging for a particular position in a vehicle through the use of signal delay.

Listserv/mailing lists Mailing lists or list servers are a one to many electronic mail conferencing system. Once subscribed to a list, the subscriber receives electronic mail messages from all contributing members of that list. A subscriber can mail to the list e-mail address and the message will be distributed to all subscribed members.

There are a number of different types of lists. An open list is one in which any person with an e-mail address may subscribe and be a part of the conference. A closed list is one in which the list owner will approve or not approve any subscription request. For example, a list may be very specific to a certain profession or group that you must belong to before subscribing. A moderated this is one in which the entries are reviewed by the list owner before being mailed out to the subscribers. The list owner may in fact choose to make a digest out of the submissions, and then post that to the list server. An unmoderated list is one in which all mail coming to the mail server is distributed regardless of the content.

Live [pronounced with long "i"] 1. An acoustical environment possessing reverberation;

2. & adv., unrecorded, in real time, during performance, as "a live broadcast."

Live feed Real-time continuous broadcast.

Load balancing Directs user requests to the least-busy server within each server cluster, minimizing bandwidth consumption and maximizing performance and scalability.

Load The resistance or impedance to which energy is being supplied. In amplifiers, the speaker or speakers connected to the output of the amplifier.4

Local Area Network A local area network (LAN) is a network of connected computers that are all in the same location. House and Senate offices typically maintain at least two LANs, one in Washington and at least one in the district or state. When LANs are connected over distance, they are referred to as a (WAN).

Local decode A feature of Indeo video interactive allowing the playback application to tell the codec to decode only a rectangular subregion of the source video image: the viewport.

Locator The reference to an anchor. A locator is the structure (such as linked text, image or other object) that a user activates to be taken to the anchor location. In HTML the Locator is declared as a value of the href or id attributes of the Anchor (a) element. It serves as the Source of the hypertext anchored link. In HTML this value must be exactly the same as the value of the Destination anchor.

Lock It down A direction given by the assistant director for everyone on the set to be quiet.

Locked layer A layer whose content is protected from being editited or changed.

Locked When a PLL is accurately producing timing that is precisely lined up with the timing of the incoming video source, the PLL is said to be "locked". When a PLL is locked, the PLL is stable and there is minimum jitter in the generated sample clock.

Login When you login to a computer system, website or a part of a website, you usually enter your username and password, and sometimes other information that identifies you. This gives you access to areas, or allows you to carry out certain functions, that you would otherwise not be allowed unless you entered these details.

Logout The process by which you formally end your connection with a website or computer system. It is very important that you logout after visiting a restricted website, area or computer system to make sure that only you use your username and password. In some cases it is also advisable to close your browser window after logging out.

Lombard effect The adjustment of vocal loudness according to the level of auditory stimulation, particularly in noisy environments.

Long play (LP) Middle tape speed on vcr's.

Long shot A shot in which the object of principal interest is distant from the camera, often used to place a person within his or her environment.

Longitudinal time code (LTC) Longitudinal time code (LTC) is recorded as an audio signal on the address track or one of the audio tracks of a video tape. It may also be recorded on a track of audio tape. LTC can be read at high tape shuttle speeds, allowing time code readers to stay "in-sync" during rewind or fast forward. Unfortunately, LTC cannot be read at very slow shuttle speeds (such as when you are "crawling" the tape frame by frame) or in pause.

Look-up table A cross-reference table in the computer memory that will return an output value for any given input value. It can be a programmed algorithm or data entered in a table.

Loop, or tape loop A tape that has been spliced into a loop so that the sound recorded on it can be extended indefinitely, usually to provide a bed for other sounds.

Looping A term indicating that a high impedance device has been permanently connected in parallel to a video source.

Loss The difference between potential energy output and actual energy output.

Lossy compression A type of data compression which permanently discards data that humans supposedly "cannot hear" to create much smaller audio, video and image file sizes. When the file is decompressed by the recipient, this compression method replaces the data for the sections it removed with calculated values to restore the file. The decompressed file is similar but not identical to the original file.

Lossless Describes a type of compression for image files in which data is not lost. Thus, files compressed using a Lossless CODEC retain the quality of the original, uncompressed file.

Related terms: Lossy, Compression

Lossy A form of compression commonly applied to JPEG files which reconstructs the data approximately instead of exactly by attempting to eliminate redundant or unnecessary information, thereby reducing the level of detail in a file.

Loudness The Sound Pressure Level of a standard sound which appears to be as loud as the unknown. Loudness level is measured in phons and equals the equivalent SPL in dB of the standard. [For example, a sound judged as loud as a 40 dB-SPL 1 kHz tone has a loudness level of 40 phons. Also, it takes 10 phons (an increase of 10 dB-SPL) to be judged twice as loud.].

Loudness control A sad, sad circuit on a preamplifier that boosts the bass and, to a lesser extent, the treble of an audio signal. The idea was to overcome the reduced sensitivity of the ear to bass and treble at low volumes, but in fact this could only be achieved with any degree of realism by providing a complex means of calibration, which was never actually provided.

Loudspeaker A device for transforming electrical energy into acoustic energy (ie. vibrations in the air). A loudspeaker normally consists of one or more drivers, a crossover network and an enclosure.

Low angle shot (up angle) A shot in which the subject is seen from below, emphasizing or enhancing the subject's importance.

Low frequency Refers to radio frequencies within the 30-300 kHz band. In audio it usually refers to frequencies in the 20-160 Hz band.

Low key lighting A form of lighting characterized by shadows, high contrast, and mystery. Contrast with High-key Lighting.

Low level technical options Generalised IT techniques for the transmission of data, e.g. e-mail, file transfer, opto-magnetic media and World Wide Web.

Low pass filter An electrical circuit that impedes signals above a particular frequency. In other words, it lets signals below that frequency pass through. An example is the circuit in a home theatre receiver that allows bass frequencies to go to a subwoofer. Compare high pass filter and bandpass filter.

LP Long play record The vinyl record that was introduced in the early 1950s to replace the shorter-play records previously used. Rather than their 78 rpm rotational velocity, the LP rotated at 33 1/3 rpm and used narrower grooves. Accordingly, it gave a playing time of between 15 and 30 minutes per side, depending on the how heavily the signal was modulated, the amount and character of its bass content and the amount of material available.

L-pad A low resistance (commonly 8 ohms) potentiometer used primarily to control the input delivered to a speaker. A remote site volume control.

LPCM Linear pulse code modulation For all practical purposes, the same as PCM. This tends to be called LPCM when dealing with DVDs.

LSB Least significant bit The bit of the binary number that varies the value of the binary number by no more than one (which is why it is the least significant). This bit is often randomised in PCM digital audio in order to add dither to the signal.

LTC linear time code Time code recorded on a linear analog track on a video tape. Also called Longitudinal Time Code.

Luma As mentioned in the definition of chroma, the NTSC and PAL video systems use a signal that has two pieces: the black and white part, and the color part. The black and white part is the luma. It was the luma component that allowed color TV broadcasts to be received by black and white TVs and still remain viewable.

Luminance The brightness or black and white component of a TV picture. It is created from the original RGB source signal by adding the three colours together in the correct proportions (0.3, 0.59, 0.11 respectively) to produce grey shades that more or less match the level seen by the human eye. On DVDs the luminance signal is encoded separately to the colour signals and, with some TVs, can be kept separate via S-Video or component video cables all the way to the TV, avoiding cross interference between the luminance and colour signals. If a component video connection is used, the luminance connector is identified by its green colour and a marking of 'Y'.

Lux [lx] Light unit for measuring illumination. It is defined as the illumination of a surface when luminous flux of 1 lumen falls on an area of 1 m2. It is also known as lumens per square metre. One lux is equal to approximately 0.09290 foot candle.

M

M JPEG (motion-JPEG) A standard for digital video. Uses JPEG compression to store each frame of the video file.

M2P MPEG-2 program stream5.

M3U M3U is a special type of metafile playlist that is used with MP3 files that have an .mp3 file extension. The .m3u files list one MP3 or other media file on each line, normally with full path or URL to the file. If the .m3u file is loaded to an MP3 player, the player normally plays the list of media files in the order they are listed in the playlist (unless options such as "randomize" have been selected in the MP3 player).

M4A The audio file format used by Apple in their popular iTunes Music Store often appears on your system with the ".M4A" filename extension. M4A can produce better audio quality than MP3 using less physical space for the files.

M4P M4P format is "protected AAC". It is a format of purchased music that can be listened to only through the iTunes softer or an iPod.

Mac OS The Apple Macintosh operating system.

Macintosh video Typically refers to the signal produced by a Macintosh 824 display card or Quadra built-in video. Although several scan rates and resolutions are supported, when connected to the 13-inch RGB monitor the display resolution is 640 by 480 pixels with a 67.7 Hz scan rate.

Macro A lens capable of extreme closeups on smaller objects.

Macro lens A lens used for photographing extreme close ups.

Macrovision A copy protection system incorporated into most pre-recorded video tapes and DVDs. A signal is added into a part of the video signal that is not otherwise used. For video tapes this is recorded on the tape as part of the movie, for DVDs it merely consists of a single code that tells the DVD player add the macrovision signal. When this is detected by a VCR which has been set to record, the VCR interferes with the video signal by randomly varying its brightness, giving a very poor quality of transfer. DVD recorders also recognise the signal, but when they do they refuse to record and advise that the source is copyright protected.

Magnet boot A rubber or plastic cover for the magnet housing for protection or appearance, mostly the latter.

Magnet/magnet structure A combination of magnetic material and connected field concentrators that creates the magnetic field within which the voice coil interacts to produce sound. Magnetic materials have changed greatly over the years to produce much higher concentrations of magnetic fields (rated in gauss) with lighter and smaller volumes of material.

In marketing speakers, a great deal of hype is often applied to the question of magnet weight. But many of these claims should be treated with skepticism. With greater and greater concentrations of gauss fields being developed from ever lighter and smaller mass metallurgical materials, the only good measure of adequate power handling is the manufacturer's RMS Wattage rating. Hefty magnets may look impressive, but while capable,they are no longer an essential index to a speaker's power capacity.

Magnetic cartridge A turntable cartridge that produces the signal by moving a magnet within a coil (moving magnet cartridge), or vice versa (moving coil cartridge).

Magnetic flux density The measurement of magnetic flux, in units of Gauss, inside the air gap in which a voice coil of a speaker operates.

Magneto-optical (MO) drives/cartridges MO drives store data on removable, rewritable disc cartridges, each with a capacity of 640 MB (soon to be 2.6 Gb). When filled, you swap in another cartridge. Thus, instead of buying a new hard drive (at $500), you buy another cartridge ($30). Get LIM/DOW (Light Intensity Modulation/Direct Overwrite) disks/drive, which re-writes in one pass, resulting in 100% increase in write speed. Contrast with zip drives which store only 100-230 Mb.

Mail agent An electronic mail program that helps end users manage messages.

Mail exchanger A system used to relay mail into a network.

Mailto email (electronic mail) The mailto method is used to activate "send email" from a web page. This method starts the email program on the client. Originally email was handled by special programs that were totally separate from web browsers, but later versions of web browsers could handle email to such an integrated degree that users are not even aware that they are busy with a different service.

Mannerism, to be mannered An actor's often repetitious affectation of performance, used to disguise fatigue, indifference, jitters, or a lack of real technique; in art and literature, any overused and stale stylistic device.

Manual iris A lens with a manual method of varying the size of the aperture.

MARC (Machine readable cataloguing) A family of formats based on ISO 2709 for the exchange of bibliographic and other related information in machine readable form. For example, USMARC and UNIMARC.

Mark In film and television, a position on a set where an actor is to stand or is to move to, in order to be in the frame of the camera; hence, in audio, the actor's mike position as spiked on the studio floor; to hit one's mark is to arrive at the mark after a cross.

Markup languages In markup languages color can be described with values indicating more specific frequencies within these three basic ranges. In HTML there are three methods for describing a color:

reserved keywords (such as "black" and "red")

the 16-base hexadecimal notation

the 10-base RGB system.

In Graphics application programs there are typically be more methods available for describing color hues than just the RGB method, such as CMYK and HSB.

Marquee tool The selection tool in some software applications that looks like a box of dotted lines and is used to select a rectangular part of an image for scanning or manipulation.

Marquee value The ability of the publicized name of a performer, author, director, composer, et al., to attract audiences to a production.

Mash An acronym for Multi-stage noise shaping. This is the name given to the digital advances that were introduced after the CD specification had been established.

Mask or masque A character of the commedia dell'arte (e.g. Harlequin, Pierrot, Pantalone); hence any stereotyped comic character (e.g. Chaplin's Tramp, Mickey Mouse, Paul Rubens's Peewee Herman) whose name, personality, costume, and make-up recur in various otherwise disconnected theatrical works.

Master 1) The raw first generation recording from which the overdub and mix is made; also voice master, music master, etc.;

2) the final mix or completely packaged program from which all copies are to be made; also broadcast master, transmission master; 3) to record a master.

Matrix A mathematical array. A logical network configured in a rectangular array of intersections of input/output channels.

Matrix switcher A device for switching more than one camera, VCR, video printer and similar, to more than one monitor, VCR, video printer and similar. Much more complex and more powerful than simple video switchers.

MATV. Master Antenna TeleVision.

Matte A film term sometimes used in video production work to denote a keyed effect; an insert of video signal information keyed from one source into a second video signal. Also, the term is used to refer to an opaque piece of art or a model that leaves a selected area unexposed to be filled on a subsequent pass or in composite. It is also referred to as a mask.

Mavica The name-brand of a popular still video camera sold by Sony.

MB Short for megabyte (1,024 or 1,048,576 s). This unit is typically used to measure (RAM) and hard drive space in computers, though hard drives that are able to store several a much larger unit of measurement – have become commonplace.

Mb/s or Mbps Megabits per second A measure of the data flow rate for digital video from a DVD. Stands for millions of bits per second. Generally, the higher the number the better the quality.

MCA (media control architecture) A specification developed for addressing various multimedia devices from Macintosh computers.

MCI (Media control interface) Multimedia commands/calls comprising Windows API (Application Program Interface).

MDS MPEG-7 Multimedia Description Scheme sdfdsf

Measurements Transport measurements

There are different units of measurements used in computing technology. Transport size is measured in bits, and speed in bps (bits per second). As there are a many millions of bits involved in processing, larger units have been established to make it easier to talk about these units.

Here is a table with terms used for larger units. One byte = 8 bits.

Bytes

1 Kilobyte

1Kb

1'000 (= 8'000 bits)

1 Megabyte

1Mb

1'000'000

1 Gigabyte

1Gb

1'000'000'000

1 Terabyte 1Tb

1'000'000'000'000

Dimension measurements

There are various measures available for measuring the dimensions of objects. Some units are based on an absolute reference, while other units have values relative to other objects.

Media A means of communication. Media can take several forms. Video clips, sound files, and still images are media common to digital movie making.

Media cabinet A locked cabinet located in the classrooms which houses media equipment that remains permanently fixed in the classroom.

Media control interface (MCI) High-level control software that provides a device-independent interface to multimedia devices and media files. MCI includes a command-message interface and a command-string interface.

Media type Content stored in electronic format can be delivered on many different types of devices. The following media are presently recognized as valid delivery systems on an internet. This list may be expanded in future versions:

Screen used for computer screens; documents are delivbered in a non-paged format, i.e. a user needs to scroll through the document.

Tty used for media that have a fixed-pitch character grid, such as teletypes, terminals, or portable devices with limited display capabilities.

Tv used for television-type devices (which, compared to computer monitors, have low resolution, color, limited scrollability).

Projection used for projectors, such as used in boardrooms.

Handheld used for handheld devices that have small screens, typically monochrome, with bitmap graphics, and limited bandwidth.

Print used for material to be printed and for documents viewed on screen in print preview mode.

Braille used for braille tactile feedback devices.

Aural used for speech synthesizers.

All used for documents that can be delivered on all the above devices.

MediaStream Pinnacle video server product series capable of over 1,000 hours of online storage.

Medium long shot A shot that is wider than a medium shot but tighter than a long shot.

Medium shot A shot that is tighter than a long shot and wider than a close-up, including, for example, an actor from the knees or waist up. It was heavily used in the classical Hollywood style.

Megapixel One megapixel equals one million pixels.

Meiosis Rhetorical understatement.

Melodrama 1) Used pejoratively, an inflated, unctuous style of writing or performing; hammy performance;

2) a style of drama in which good and evil are personified in opposing characters, and often including sensational elements;

3) a theatrical form of the 18th Century in which spoken lines are heavily underscored by instrumental music, which evolved into a popular 19th century form, incorporating elements of definition 2 with songs or ballads, which heavily influenced grand opera and led to melodrama in the modern senses.

Memo list A Custom File feature that allows the user to toggle through the discs, selection titles, or station call letters currently loaded without interrupting playback of the existing disc or station.

Memory Active storage for information, consisting of microchips usually refered to as RAM chips, (Random Access Memory). This is distinct from the disc drives which typically can store larger amounts of information. When data is accessed from a hard drive, it typically is transferred to the RAM chips in order to provide in and out repeatable access to this data, without the user having to wait for it to be accessed from the hard disc each time it is required. Ram is typically used to hold applications while they are in use.

Memory card A removable storage device used to store digital images

Memory stick A small, removable flash memory (ie. non-volatile) cartridge developed by Sony, used in a host of digital storage situations, notably in digital cameras and digital audio players.

Menu A menu is a set of options that you can choose from that then direct you to different web pages. The menu can be a series of text links, a menu bar, a list or a pulldown or dropdown menu.

Menubar Located under the title bar and displays the names of all available menu lists.

Meridian Lossless Packing (MLP) is a lossless compression method that has an approximate 2:1 compression ratio. The use of MLP is optional, but the decoding capability is mandatory on all DVD-Audio players.

Mesecam A technique of recording secam video. Instead of dividing the FM color subcarrier by four and then multiplying back up on playback, mesecam uses the same heterodyne conversion as PAL.

Meta files Graphics that contain both vectors and bitmap data.

Meta Tag Special HTML that provide information about a given Web page. The most common meta tags are: <Title> Creates the page title that appears in the blue bar at the top of the screen

< meta name="keywords" content=""> Allows you to include a list of keywords that describe the page.

< meta name="description" content=""> Allows you to include a description of the page.

The most important reason to use these three meta tags are that most search engines use them to "find" and list your Web site. For example, most search engines list both the title and description in their search returns, and they use the keywords to help match your site against a user's search. If you do not include these meta tags, search engines will not always list your site, even if you are best source for the information a user is looking for.

Metadata A set of 'flags', or predefined digital bits, carried in a Dolby Digital bitstream that provide instructions to the decoder. They do not carry actual audio data, but guide the decoder in the interpretation of the audio data. Examples include a flag for dialog normalization and some for dynamic range control.

Metal particle tape Videotape using iron in its pure metallic form, instead of as an oxide. Offers improved frequency response and wider dynamic range than traditional oxide formulations.

Metal tape EQ An equalization circuit that compensates for the unique frequency response characteristics of metal tape.

Metalanguage A metalanguage is a formal language used to create a "lower level" language. A metalanguage consists of the rules and conventions to be used when the lower-level language is created. SGML is the metalanguage of both HTML and XML.

Metaphor The comparison of essentially unlike things, such as "the slings and arrows of outrageous fortune." (Shakespeare) When the things compared are joined by a connective, it is a simile, as in "Life is like a sewer; you get out of it exactly what you put into it." Sometimes the metaphor is submerged or implied, as in this 16th century lyric comparing love's absence to drought:

Western wind, when wilt thou blow,The small rain down can rain?Christ, if my love were in my armsAnd I in my bed again!.

Metonymy The substitution of the name for one thing for another that it closely relates to, as when speaking of someone's hand to mean someone's handwriting.

MHz Short for megahertz. This unit is typically used to measure the speeds of computers. One megahertz is one million cycles per second. Every command given to a computer (from the keyboard, mouse, software, hardware, etc.) requires a fixed number of megahertz to execute. The more megahertz available, the faster commands can be executed, and the faster a computer will perform.

Mic level The typical level of a microphone signal. Usually lower than -40 dBu.

Micro browser A browser within a handheld wireless device that displays WML pages.

Microbar 1. A unit of atmospheric pressure equal to one millionth of a bar.

2. A place to consume the product of microbreweries.

Micromoney Proposed Web-payment scheme where funds are subtracted from your bank account when you buy digital tokens. You then spend this encrypted micromoney at participating Web sites without the hassle of a credit card transaction. Ecash and CyberCash are two such digital-cash schemes.

Microphone (Mic) A device which converts sound into electrical impulses, usually for recording ɔr amplification.

Microphone level A microphone level audio signal is lower (quieter) than a typical line-level signal. It requires special pre-amplification before recording. Some equipment has special mic-in jacks that provide this pre-amplification. You can also buy a dedicated pre-amplifier or mixer to boost a microphone signal to line level for recording.

Microphone, shotgun A long thin microphone which is designed to reject all sounds except those directly in front of it.

Microprocessor A multiple semiconductor IC device that can be dedicated or programmed to perform a variety of tasks in many different systems. These exist in virtually all consumer and commercial electronic devices of more than rudimentary functionality.

Microsoft outlook express A mail client application developed by Microsoft.

Microsoft palette file A color table attached to an image file.

Microwave One definition refers to the portion of the electromagnetic spectrum that ranges between 300 MHz and 3000 GHz. The other definition is when referring to the transmission media where microwave links are used. Frequencies in microwave transmission are usually between 4 GHz and 60 GHz.

Midbass Those frequencies roughly between 100 and 300 Hertz. (CPS).

MIDI An acronym for musical instrument digital interface. MIDI was designed for the purpose of getting one MIDI device (a MIDI-capable music keyboard) to play music when played from a 2nd MIDI keyboard connected to it with a MIDI cable. The 2nd MIDI keyboard (a music synthesizer, as well) can not only operate its own music-making abilities, but also those of the MIDI keyboard attached to it in a 2-for-1 deal. A daisy-chain approach even allows several MIDI devices to be strung together, all operated by the first MIDI device in the chain. You can even choose how you play them: all together, like one giant instrument, or separately, where you decide how each device in the chain is to respond to the MIDI data. Analogy of MIDI.

MIDI data can be recorded and played back so that any button-pushing, slider-sliding, or music-note-playing needed can be performed automatically by a MIDI sequencer or recorder. This is how one person, having one or more MIDI synthesizer modules, can create flawless musical performances of anything imaginable.

Up to 16 MIDI devices can share a single MIDI cable, typically with one MIDI device being a conductor/performer of nearly all of the parts of the performance. The performance is typically a song, but can now include other performance and non-performance related functions.

MIDI is a language, not a thing. If a device can speak (transmit) MIDI, it is considered to be a MIDI Controller. If a device can respond to MIDI, but has no actual performance keys available to it, then it is often considered to be a MIDI Module or sometimes, a Synth Module. It's quite common to have a MIDI device which both speaks and listens to MIDI, in which case you are most likely talking about a MIDI music keyboard, or sometimes, incorrectly, an electric piano.

MIDI controller A transmitter (or speaker) of MIDI data. MIDI Controllers include, but are not limited to:

MIDI Sequencer (a sort of "word processor" for music)

MIDI Keyboard (piano-style device which speaks its keyboard's performance in MIDI)

MIDI Wind Controller (an oboe, flute, or saxophone-like device modified to speak MIDI)

MIDI Proximity Controller (a device which speaks MIDI in response to hand gestures)

MIDI Slider Controller (a device which resembles an audio mixer but produces MIDI data)

All MIDI controllers have a MIDI output jack to "speak" with. By connecting this jack with a MIDI cable to a product with a MIDI input jack, the first MIDI device can operate the second. This is the basic principal of MIDI.

MIDI controllers differ from MIDI Modules in that MIDI controllers do not typically produce any sound or other directly noticeable output.

MIDI files A computer file format containing musical information and performance data capable of being used in MIDI capable devices.

MIDI mapper Windows systems software that modifies musical instrument digital interface (MIDI) output messages and redirects them to a MIDI output device using values stored in a MIDI setup map. The MIDI Mapper can change the destination channel and output device for a message, as well as modify program-change messages, volume values, and key values.

MIDI program-change message A musical instrument digital interface (MIDI) message sent to a synthesizer to change the patch on a specific MIDI channel.

MIDI sequencer A program that creates or plays songs stored as Musical Instrument Digital Interface (MIDI) files. When a sequencer plays MIDI files, it sends MIDI data from the file to a MIDI synthesizer, which produces the sounds. Windows provides a MIDI sequencer, accessible through media control interface (MCI), that plays MIDI files.

MIDI setup map A complete set of data for the Musical instrument digital interface (MIDI) Mapper to use when redirecting MIDI messages. Only one setup map can be in effect at a given time, but the user can have several setup maps available and can choose between them by using the MIDI Mapper Control Panel option.

MIDI time code A time code system allowing timed device control through MIDI protocols. It has become more important in video post production as more and more people are working with personal computer based systems. Compare SMPTE time code.

Midrange A Driver that is usually much smaller than a woofer, but with a surface area greater than the typical tweeter. It reproduces the mid frequency range from approximately 300 to 5000 Hertz. This optimum range can vary considerably from one driver to the next, thus giving the system designer more flexibility in choosing Crossover points for the other drivers.

Mike 1) microphone;

2) to use a microphone.

Mike technique the skill and methodology by which talent uses a microphone to advantage.

Milliamps A unit of measurement of electric current equal to 1/1000th of an ampere. The milliampere is the most common unit used when measuring quiescent current drain in consumer audio electronics.

MIME(Multipurpose internet mail extensions) MIME Type (also known as Content Type) was first proposed in 1992 to specify more complex data than plain text. In essence MIME is used to specify the datatype for HTTP. Its purpose is to include textual and non-textual objects in the same message. The HTTP 'Content-Type' value is thus stating the type of content of the document, and by implication the application program through which it would be rendered. Today MIME types include sound, video, graphics, HTML, PostScript, and others.

The Mime type is specified to inform user agents about the type of content a document contains.

By following RFC2045 and RFC2046 the phrase Content type is used rather than MIME type. So whenever you need to specify a MIME type, remember to use Content type.

MINI DV MiniDV is the most popular digital camcorder format at the moment.

miniDV is a video cassette designed for use in miniDV digital camcorders. The picture quality of digital video (DV) recorded on a miniDV cassette is basically identical or better to the quality of DV recorded on a Hi8 or 8mm cassette by a Digital8 camcorder. miniDV can have up to 530 lines of video resolution for some camcorder models. However, miniDV tapes are smaller which allows for smaller camcorders. miniDV tapes are available in lengths of 30 and 60 minutes (plus, recording in LP mode lets you extend total recording time with a 60-minute tape to 90 minutes).

Minidisc A digital audio music delivery system using a disc mounted inside a small, robust plastic cartridge. The audio is encoded using ATRAC. Interestingly, the audio may be carried on the disc in two different ways. Sony designed it both for acting as a recorder, and playing back commercially-produced Minidiscs. So in the former role it acts as a magneto-optical recorder. For the latter, it uses discs which have been pressed in a similar manner to commercial CDs.

Mis en scène (Fr. literally "placement/setting in the theater."). 1. the staging or production design of a dramatic work, considering such factors as blocking, scenery, props, lighting, costuming, sound plot and direction of the actors as they form an artistic physical, optisonic, or sonic interpretation of the work; hence,

2. in cinema (and by extension in any form of theater), a director's, especially an auteur's, style, as manifested in a particular work, or in the director's collective ouvre.

Mixer/Mixing In live recording, refers to combining sound from different microphones, such as narration and ambient sound. The sound technician responsible for balacing audio uses a device called a mixer, which allows him or her adjust the balance and levels of sound from these different sources. In editing, this also refers to combining more than one recorded soundtrack in the finished product.

MLP meridian lossless packing A digital audio standard used for DVD Audio. Also known as Packed PCM or PPCM. This provides superb sound, from mono through to multichannel, with a number of technical advantages over Dolby Digital and DTS. The middle word, 'Lossless', is important. It is not a perceptual encoding system that abandons some of the original source material to achieve space savings. It preserves the original signal perfectly, even through multiple encoding/decoding cycles.

MMC (Multimedia card) A small, removable flash memory (ie. non-volatile) cartridge, used in a host of digital storage situations, notably in MP3 players. This seems to be going out of favour.

MMX (Multimedia extension) A multimedia accelerator in Intel's Pentium processors that speed media and communications processing 40 to 60%. Standard Pentiums move 1 byte of data at a time into the CPU for processing. In contrast MMX Pentiums move 8 bytes, all processed simultaneously. The catch? Not all application programs, as yet, have been written to take advantage of the specialized instruction set for the MMX's, hence you see no performance improvement for most programs currently on the market.

MOD (Minimum object distance) Feature of a fixed or a zoom lens that indicates the closest distance an object can be from the lens's image plane, expressed in meters. Zoom lenses have MOD of around 1 m, while fixed lenses usually much less, depending on the focal length.

Model release A written document signed by everyone appearing in the video allowing the producer protection from privacy laws.

Moderator The moderators control what messages appear on the forum and help to make sure that all posts comply with our terms and conditions. A moderator can edit or delete offensive posts and can warn users against further similar conduct.

Modulate To modify or alter a signal so as to transmit information. For example, conventional broadcast television transmits the video image by modulating the amplitude and frequency of a carrier signal. Compare demodulate.

Modulator A modulator is basically a circuit that combines two different signals in such a way that they can be pulled apart later. What does this have to do with video? Let's take the NTSC system as an example, although the example applies equally as well to PAL. The NTSC system may use the Y'IQ or Y'UV color space, with the I and Q or U and V signals containing all of the color information for the picture. Two 3.58-MHz color subcarriers (90 degrees out of phase) are modulated by the I and Q or U and V components and added together to create the chroma part of the NTSC video.

Moire Optical disturbance caused by interference of similar frequencies. The wavy effect produced by the convergence of lines. It usually appears as a curving of the lines in the horizontal wedges of a test pattern. It is a natural optical effect when converging lines in a television picture are nearly parallel to the scanning lines. Compare aliasing.

Moiré pattern An unwanted effect that appears in the video picture when a high-frequency (lines close together) pattern is looked at with a CCD camera that has a pixel pattern close to (but lower) the object pattern.

Monitor A particular type of television that receives a composite and/or component video signal (as opposed to an RF signal) directly from a VCR, camera, or separate TV tuner for high quality picture reproduction. Does not contain a channel selector. Compare television receiver.

Mono (monaural) The operation of an amplifier in one channel for both input and output.

Can refer to an amplifier with only one channel of amplification or operating in bridged mode. For low frequency amplification applications, it provides better phase coherence and less distortion than stereo operation.

Monochrome A monochrome signal is a video source having only one component. Although usually meant to be the luma (or black-and-white) video signal, the red video signal coming into the back of a computer display is monochrome because it only has one component.

Monochrome signal A single color video signal; usually a black and white signal or, sometimes, the luminance portion of a composite or component color signal.

Monograph A publication either complete in one part or complete, or intended to be completed, in a finite number of separate parts. A non-serial publication.

Monopod A one legged camera support.

Monotonic This is a term that is used to describe ADCs and DACs. An ADC or DAC is said to be monotonic if for every increase in input signal, the output increases. Any ADC or DAC that is nonmonotonic – meaning that the output decreases for an increase in input – is bad! Nobody wants a nonmonotonic ADC or DAC.

Montage This French term for "editing" refers to a series of brief scenes used to quickly establish a mood or a dramatic setting.

Morpheme In grammar, the smallest unit of meaning; any word or part of a word that conveys meaning and cannot be further divided into smaller meaningful elements.

MOS Man-on-the-street; when MOS occurs as a script indication, it means that the dialogue that follows comes from an interview with an ordinary citizen recorded in the field.

Mosaic Mosaic was the first popular browser that supported images and was developed by Marc Andreessen at NCSA.

MOSFET (Metal oxide semiconductor field effect transistor) A type of large output transistor used in the final stages of many power amplifiers, and commonly found in most car and home amplifiers today.

These field-effect transistors are controlled by voltage rather than current, like a bipolar transistor. MOSFETs have a significantly higher switching speed than bipolar transistors. They generate almost no loss (little heat generation), which lends the power supply fast response, excellent linearity, and high efficiency.

Mosfet transistors are most often discrete devices, used with smaller driver transistors and other devices, to convert a small signal to a large one. They are highly stable and efficient, compared to the bipolar types that preceded them.

MOSFET power supply A power supply that employs MOSFET transistors to convert DC to AC. Offers superior thermal stability and more accurate switching.

Motion capture An animation technique based on the motion of a real actor or object.

Motion control A camera setup which records the motion of a camera during a shot so that visual effects can be easily synchronized with the photographed scene.

Motion control photography A system for using computers to precisely control camera movements so that different elements of a shot can later be composited in a natural and believable way.

Motion estimation Motion estimation is trying to figure out where an object has moved to from one video frame to the other. Let's take an example of a video source showing a ball flying through the air. The background is a solid color that is different from the color of the ball. In one video frame the ball is at one location and in the next video frame the ball has moved up and to the right by some amount. Now let's assume that the video camera has just sent the first video frame of the series. Now, instead of sending the second frame, wouldn't it be more efficient to send only the position of the ball? Nothing else moves, so only two little numbers would have to be sent. This is the essence of motion estimation. By the way, motion estimation is an integral part of MPEG, H.261, and H.263.

Motion JPEG A digital movie compression format that consists of a sequence of still frames, each of which has been compressed using the JPEG algorithms.

Motor impairments A disability affecting the ability to control muscle movement, often limiting mobility. Examples include cerebral palsy, arthritis, paralysis or limb loss. Assistive technologies, such as alternative keyboards and speech input equipment, can help people with motor impairments.

Motor structure In speakers, the complete sound generator or transducer that converts incoming electrical signals to mechanical/ acoustic energy or sound. In a dynamic Driver, this includes the magnet, its directive field concentrators or Pole Pieces, and the voice coil that interacts with them.

Mount To produce or direct something, as "to mount a production."

Mounting depth The amount of physical space required to mount a Driver without having any of its parts touch objects below. This is particularly relevant to car speakers where such mounting spaces may be sharply limited as to their ability to accommodate deep speakers with large magnets. Door panels with movable windows are a typical example of where care must be taken in selecting speakers to be mounted.

Mounting ring Often used to describe the circular gasket seal incorporated into the edge of a speaker, traditionally the term "mounting ring" refers to a separate device placed between a Driver and the surface on which it is mounted, for the effect of raising the speaker so that larger and deeper speakers can be accommodated in limited spaces.

Mouse An input device used to control the position of a pointer on the screen by detecting the relative position of the mouse.

Mouse event A general term referring to actions generated by the computers mouse device.

Mouseover A Web site feature that causes an element of the page to change when a user passes the mouse cursor over it. More sophisticated mouseovers can be created using Java and a variety of other programming languages

MOV MOV is a file extension used by the QuickTime-wrapped files.

QuickTime Content (.mov, .qt), developed by Apple Computer, is a file format for storing and playing back movies with sound. This flexible format isn't limited to Macintosh operating systems. It's also commonly used in Windows systems, and other types of computing platforms.

Movie When the film industry began images could "move" and the term moving pictures, shortened to movies, began to be used.

In Macromedia Flash and Director a movie is a multimedia application for the Web that may contain graphics, text, sound and video. A Flash movie also contains some level of user interactivity. The basis of a Flash movie is vector graphics, but it can contain bitmaps and other media such as sound and video.

Moving coil cartridge A magnetic cartridge in which the stylus moves a coil via the cantilever, while the magnet is fixed in position. Moving coil cartridges tend to have lower moving mass than moving magnet cartridges, but also tend to be lower in output by an order of magnitude. There are, however, high output MC cartridges available that produce comparable levels to MM cartridges. Because the coil must be wired to the outputs, they also tend to be somewhat lower in compliance than MM cartridges, so are not normally amenable to very low tracking weights (they typically operate best at around two grams).

Moving shot (truck shot) A shot taken from a camera mounted on something that is moving.

Mozilla Mozilla is an open source web browser. This means that the code and programming that make the browser work can be viewed by anybody and you can get involved in improving the program.

Mp2 (mpeg layer 2), A commonly used digital picture compression format used for moving and still images. It is the format used for the visual elements on DVD disks.

MP3 MP3 stands for MPEG1 (or MPEG2) Audio Layer III. Too often people refer MP3 as MPEG3, which is incorrect, because such format doesn't even exist.

MP3 is a popular compression format used for audio files on computers and portable devices. It is a method to store good quality audio into small files by using psychoacoustics in order to get rid of the data from the audio that most of the humans can't hear.

MP3's bitrates vary from 8kbps to 320kbps. A typical MP3 file encoded at 128kbps is near CD quality. MP3 audio is increasingly being used in video production coupled with various MPEG4 video codecs like divx.

Mp4 (mpeg layer 4), A more recent audio compression format that is similar to mp3 in use, except that it is often used for more than two channels of audio. It is the format used for Dolby Digital surround sound on DVD disks.

MPA MPEG audio stream.

MPC/MPC2/MPC3 (Multimedia PC) Industry standard for a "minimal" multimedia computer system. (Now outdated; of historical interest).

On June 12, 1995, the Multimedia PC Working Group, an independent special interest group of the Software & Information Industry Association, released the latest standards for multimedia equipment. The MPC3 "does not replace MCP2. It takes multimedia a step further, opening the door for new applications and a vastly improved multimedia experience." Software titles that run under MPC and MPC2-compliant hardware will also run on MPC3-compliant hardware.

MPEG (moving picture experts group) MPEG is a series of International Organization for Standardization (ISO) standards for digital video and audio, designed for different uses and data rates.

MPEG-1: a standard designed to allow for playback of video on CD. VCDs are encoded with MPEG-1. This format has dimensions of 352x240 pixels, and is sometimes considered comparable to VHS in quality. The bit rate of a standard MPEG1 is 1.5Mbps. Included in MPEG-1 is a popular standard for audio called MP3 (MP3 is technically MPEG-1 layer 3)

MPEG-2: the standard for DVD video. Supports higher data rates than MPEG-1. MPEG-7: an emerging standard for describing multimedia objects so that they can be accessed in a database. MPEG-7 will allow users to access video based on elements such as instances of a particular color or shape.

MPEG-1 A standard designed to allow for playback of video on CD. VCDs are encoded with MPEG-1. This format has dimensions of 352x240 pixels, and is sometimes considered comparable to VHS in quality. The bit rate of a standard MPEG1 is 1.5Mbps. Included in MPEG-1 is a popular standard for audio called MP3 (MP3 is technically MPEG-1 layer 3).

MPEG-2 Offers resolutions of 720x480 and 1280x720 at 60 fps, with full CD-quality audio. This is sufficient for all the major TV standards, including NTSC, and even HDTV.

MPEG-2 is used by DVD-ROMs. MPEG-2 can compress a 2 hour video into a few gigabytes. While decompressing an MPEG-2 data stream requires only modest computing power, encoding video in MPEG-2 format requires significantly more processing power.

MPEG layer 2 audio Generally used for high bandwidth MPEG audio at near CD quality. Used for audio with both MPEG-1 and MPEG-2.

MPEG layer 3 audio (MP3) MPEG audio format which is very popular on the Internet. Generally used in audio-only files (.mp3 files), this is a lower-bandwidth format than MPEG Layer-2 audio, but still not ideal for modem streaming.

MPEG-4 MPEG-4 (ISO/IEC 14496) supports an object-based approach, where scenes are modeled as compositions of objects, both natural and synthetic, with which the user may interact. Visual objects in a scene can be described mathematically and given a position in a two- or three-dimensional space. Similarly, audio objects can be placed in a sound space. Thus, the video or audio object need only be defined once; the viewer can change his viewing position, and the calculations to update the audio and video are done locally. Classical "rectangular" video, as from a camera, is one of the visual objects supported. In addition, there is the ability to map images onto computer-generated shapes, and a text-to-speech interface.

H.264, a "next-generation" video codec, has been included in the MPEG-4 standard as Part 10.

MPEG7 MPEG7 doesn't itself offer any new encoding features and it is not meant for representing audio/video content, unlike its siblings MPEG1, MPEG2 and MPEG4. Instead, it offers metadata information for audio and video files, allowing searching and indexing of audio/video data based on the information about the content instead of searching the actual content bitstream.

MPEG7 is based on XML and therefor is universal and all the existing tools that support XML parsing should be able to read the data as well, provided that they can ignore binary parts of the file.

MPEG7 is not used at the moment, but it is under serious development and standardization process at the moment and hopefully we see first fully featured MPEG-7 tools within few years.

Ms pattern A stereophonic recording technique which uses two microphones. Unlike x-y, the microphones are not identical and they must be physically as close to each other as possible.

MSF time format A time format used by Media Control Interface (MCI) to express time in minutes, seconds, and frames. The number of frames in a second depends on the type of device being used; compact disc audio devices use 75 frames per second. The MSF time format is used primarily by compact disc audio devices.

MSN Microsoft network.

Mulitpoint videoconferencing Video-conference allowing three or more participants to sit in a virtual conference room and communicate as if they were sitting right next to each other.

Multi session A CD-ROM drive that can read CD's that have been updated/changed. As CD's are updated, new directories are written, with the newer directories written further and further out to the edge. Multi-session CD-ROM drives begin searhcing for directories by reading out to in, thus can find the furthermost directory. Single-session CD-ROM drives begin searching for directories from the inside out, thus only the first directory nearest the hub would be encountered.

Multi thread describes a program that is designed to have parts of its code execute concurrently.

Multicast In streaming media, it is the method of carrying a compressed video signal across multiple routers to various clients.

Multichannel sound Often called surround sound. Any system designed to deliver more than two channels (stereo) of sound to the consumer. The most common forms these days deliver 5.1 channels of audio. Some systems can process two channels, or even one channel, of sound to produce the effect of multichannel sound.

Multimedia kit A combined package of software and hardware that provides multimedia capabilities to computers.

Multimedia Strictly speaking multimedia refers to the use of more than one medium at a time. The most common media that get used together are text, graphics, video, audio and animation. Websites, CD ROMs and DVD ROMs increasingly include multimedia content.

Multimedia website content often combines text, graphics, video, animation and sound to create a rich experience for the user. To view multimedia content you will often have to download small programs known as "plug-ins". These plug-ins are normally free but can take a long time to download and install. One of the most common ones used for multimedia content is the Macromedia Flash Player.

Multimedia tutorial A presentation of information about a specific subject using a combination of text, graphics, sound and video. A how-to article on the Web that uses animation and sound to present important information about a specific software program is an example of a multimedia tutorial.

Multimedia victoria (MMV) MMV is the agency responsible for implementing the Victorian Government's information and communication technology policy, Connecting Victoria.

Multipass encoding True multipass encoding is currently available only for WM8 and MPEG-2. An encoder supporting multipass will, in a first pass, analyze the video stream to be encoded and write down a log about everything it encounters. Let's assume we have a short clip that starts out in a dialog scene where we have few cuts and the camera remains static. Then it leads over to a karate fight with lots of fast cuts and a lot of action (people flying through the air, kicking, punching, etc.). In regular CBR, encoding every second gets more or less bitrate (it's hard to stay 100% CBR but that's a detail) whereas in multipass VBR mode the encoder will use the bitrate according to his knowledge about the video stream, i.e. the dialog part gets the available bitrate and the fighting scene gets allotted more bitrate. The more passes, the more refined the bitrate distribution will be. In single pass VBR, the encoder has to base his decisions on where to use how much bitrate solely on the knowledge of the stuff it previously has encoded.

Multipath propagation A transmission path anomaly that acts as a time-varying source of signal non-linearity. Multipath can distort or reduce a received signal to the point of unreliable reception. In television, multipath is manifested as image "ghosting".

Multiplexing In CCTV it is correctly named Time Division Multiplexing and is the technique used to enable a number of video inputs (up to 34) to be recorded onto a single tape. Frequency Division Multiplexing is a technique used to allocate individual frequencies within a band of frequencies. In fibre Optic systems there is also Wavelength Division Multiplexing WDM, and Dense Wavelength Division Multiplexing DWDM where a number of wavelengths of light can share the same fibre, to enable more information to be communicated.

Multiplexor (MUX) A device used for division of a transmission facility into two or more subchannels , either by splitting the frequency band into a narrower bands or by allotting a common channel to several rent transmitting devices one at a time.

Multipoint conferencing server (MCS), Multipoint conferencing unit (MCU) A hardware or software H.323 device that allows multiple video, audio, and/or data conferencing users to connect together. Without an MCS typically only point to point conferences can take place. Commonly supports voice activated switching, where whomever is talking is broadcast to all users, but new systems support "Hollywood squares", where multiple windows show each participant. ITU-T standard H.231 describes the standard way of doing this. Many current systems only support H.320 (ISDN) but many vendors are working to upgrade their products to support H.323 (LAN, Internet) as well. In the H.320 space, this functionality is referred to as a multipoint control unit (MCU). Sometimes these terms are used interchangeably, although they refer to somewhat different implementations.

Multipurpose internet mail extension A specification for formatting non-ASCII messages so that graphics, audioand video can be sent over the internet.

Multiread An OSTA approved specification for CD-ROM and compact disc players enabling them to read discs generated by CD-RW drives.

Multiscan A term taken by a particular manufacturer often used to refer to any multisync device.

Multi-session A CD-ROM drive that can read CD's that have been updated/changed. As CD's are updated, new directories are written, with the newer directories written further and further out to the edge. Multi-session CD-ROM drives begin searhcing for directories by reading out to in, thus can find the furthermost directory. Single-session CD-ROM drives begin searching for directories from the inside out, thus only the first directory nearest the hub would be encountered.

Multisync monitors (and projectors) Video displays which accept a wide variety of horizontal and vertical timings, from NTSC to computer video signals. Multisync monitors and projectors often automatically adjust to the appropriate timing. Since the horizontal frequency range varies among different models, product specifications should be checked to assure a monitor or projector will support the Macintosh connected to it. Multisync monitors manufactured by Apple are called multiple scan displays.

Multi-tracking The process of recording a multi-part performance on separate tracks at different times which allows the engineer to subsequently combine, balance and process those tracks during mixdown.

Music, background Music that the characters supposedly do not hear and that the audience pretends not to hear, that seems to arise from ethereal musicians, and that reinforces the mood or atmosphere of a scene.

Music, source As distinguished from background music, music that supposedly originates in the environment of a scene and that the characters hear, as the band in a night club.

Music, stock Generic prerecorded music.

Music, title The theme music or leitmotif for a program or series. Main title The theme music that opens a program, hence, the entire program opening; the billboard. Closing or end title: The theme music that closes the program, hence, the entire program closing, outro.

Musical instrument digital interface (MIDI) A standard adopted by the electronic music industry for controlling devices such as synthesizers and sound cards which emit music.

Mute A control found on receivers, some mixers, and certain signal processing units that silences (mutes) a signal path, or output.

2. Someone with much to say but lacking the hardware or software to do so.

MUX Multiplexing protocol, MUX is an asynchronous messaging support at a layer below HTTP

MySQL A popular SQL database server which is a free open source software and available on all major platforms.

N

NAB The National association of broadcasters. An important professional trade organization, primarily serving commercial broadcasting industry.

NABTS North American Broadcast Teletext Specification (EIA-516). This is also ITU-R BT.653 525-line system C teletext. However, the NABTS specification goes into much more detail.

Name A star; a well-known or prestigious performer, director, or producer whose participation will lend prestige, credibility, legitimacy, or audience appeal to a production.

Nano A one thousand millionth 10^{-9}.

Nanosecond One billionth of a second. It is commonly used to measure the speed of memory chips.

Narrate To describe or tell at length, in drama especially of off-stage action.

Narration Descriptive speeches, especially of off-stage action; any speech of a Chorus or narrator.

Narrative A story, tale.

Narrative hook A plot device or any other stratagem that grabs the audience's attention at the beginning of a dramatic program.

Narrowband A low-capacity communications circuit/path. It usually implies a speed of 56Kbps or less. (Contrast with wideband and broadband).

Narrowcasting As compared to "broadcasting" - television and radio designed to reach small, targeted audiences with an audio or video signal that is transmitted from a central point and can be received by persons around the transmitter using special radio and television equipment. ITFS, cable television, fiber optics and satellite are examples of narrowcast technologies.

National bibliography A listing of all national publications. May include all publications produced in that country, or in the language of that country, or sometimes about that country.

National character set All of the numbers, letters and symbols associated with a given language.

Native resolution The resolution at which the video file was captured.

Naturalism A style of writing and performance in which the situations are presented with convincing but selective verisimilitude.

NBA National bibliographic agency.

ND filter A filter that attenuates all colours of light in the visible spectrum, equally.

ND Spot A graduated "spot" filter in a lens that restricts the amount of light passing through the lens at small apertures.

Needle drop A fee paid to the copyright owner or publisher every time a stock effect or piece of music is used in an audio production.

Netscape browser (NS) The web browser developed by Netscape Communications.

Network Computers and software connected for the purpose of exchanging information.

Network computer An inexpensive PC "box" ($500), used with your television monitor, which is dedicated for use with the Internet.

Neutral colors The range of gray levels, from black to white, but without color. For neutral areas in the image, the RGB signals will all be equal. In color difference formats, the color difference signals will be zero.

Newsgroups A newsgroup is like a bulletin board: any subscriber can post a message to the newsgroup, and each subscriber can read any or all of the messages. Newsgroups can be useful for gathering information on subjects that are popular among other Internet users. The most active newsgroups are usually those focused on high-tech topics, topics of concern to academics or students. However, newsgroups devoted to entertainment and non-technical professional topics often have a significant number of regular participants. You can read news using the Netscape browser, or through a variety of news reading programs.

NexTView An electronic program guide (EPG) based on ETSI ETS 300 707.

NFS network file system NFS is a distributed file system (a protocol suite) that allows a user to access a remote file as if it is in the local hard drive. NFS provides an upper layer file system service. On the lower level it uses TCP/Ip for transport. NFS was originally developed by Sun Microsystems and consists of three protocols:

NFS: Network File System.

XDR: eXternal Data Representation.

RPC: Remote Procedure Call.

NIC network interface card Network cards are plugged into computers and allow them to be connected to networks. Each manufactured card gets a globally unique number that allows computers to communicate with it. A software address can also be assigned to the card. This software address would typically be an IP address.

NICAM 728 A technique of implementing digital stereo audio for PAL video using another audio subcarrier. The bit rate is 728 kbps. It is discussed in BS.707 and ETSI EN 300 163. NICAM 728 is also used to transmit non-audio digital data in China.

Nickel cadmium (NiCad) Popularized by SAFT America for lightweight camcorder bettery type designed to maintainpower longer than traditional acid batteries.

NIS (network information system) An organization responsible for administering the Internet, TCP/IP addresses and domain names.

Nit A measurement of luminance = 1 candela/ m^2.

NNTP (network news transport protocol) The protocol used for the service originally called Usenet, but nowadays commonly referred to as Newsgroups. Usenet was developed in 1979 and standardized in 1983. Messages are stored in a database which holds them in groups of interest to which users can subscribe. The naming scheme is hierarchical. Pointing to a newsgroup from an HTML web page would look like this: news:za.travel.cape Today there are tens of thousands of newsgroups to which a user can belong. ics range from the sublime to the esoteric, from the useful to the useless, virtually anything under the sun that somebody thinks is worthwhile to discuss.

Nodal point In virtual reality, the optical center of a camera lens where all light rays converge. For making panoramic images the nodal point or exact center of the camera lens ideally should be directly above the axis of rotation.

Noise Any unwanted signal produced by all electrical circuits working above the absolute zero. Noise cannot be eliminated but only minimized.

Noise shaping A system of adding dither noise to a digital audio signal so that it is biased towards high frequency noise. This permits the noise floor to be lower in the range of frequencies to which the ear is most sensitive, at the cost of poorer noise performance in the higher frequencies where the ear is less sensitive. Read more.

Noise, pink A defined spectrum of noise which, when its frequncy contents are divided into musical octaves, contains equal energy in each octave. It is used to align electronic and acoustic playback devices. It sounds like a somewhat muffled white noise.

Nominal impedance A specification of the load a loudspeaker places on an amplifier, measured in ohms. It tends to oversimplify the actual situation because the impedance of a loudspeaker varies according to frequency. So a speaker with a nominal impedance of eight ohms may actually present a load of six ohms at some frequencies and thirty ohms at others. Common loudspeaker impedances are four, six and eight ohms. Back in the 1960s, higher impedance speakers – 16 and 32 ohms – were fairly common.

Noninterlaced This is a method of scanning out a video display that is the total opposite of interlaced. All of the lines in the frame are scanned out sequentially, one right after the other. The term "field" does not apply in a noninterlaced system. Another term for a noninterlaced system is progressive scan.

Non linear editing The computer-assisted editing of video without the need to assemble it in linear sequence. The visual equivalent of word processing.

Non-repudiation A security service which prevents the receiver of a message from denying that the message had been received.

NPR National public radio, the radio equivalent of PBS, with which it is often confused by civilians.

NTSC(National television system committee) The television system used in several countries, most notably the United States and Japan. It is substantially different from Australia's PAL system. Rather than 25 frames, or 50 fields, per second, it uses 30 frames or 60 fields. Instead of 576 visible lines, it produces 480 (on a timing signal equivalent to 525 lines). It also uses a different colour coding system. While the PAL colour system automatically compensates for drift in the colour information, NTSC doesn't. That's why NTSC TV sets have a 'Hue' or 'Tint' setting in addition to the familiar 'Colour' one. That's also why NTSC is sometimes waggishly known as Never Twice the Same Colour. For films on DVD, there are issues with NTSC relating to the requirement for 3:2 pulldown.

NTSC composite A video signal standard proposed by the National Television Standards Committee of the Electronics Industries Association and adopted by the FCC for broadcast television in the United States. The signal is a composite video signal of 525 lines, interlaced, 60 fields per second (30 frames per second) with a bandwidth limited to 4 MHz so that it will fit into a 6 MHz broadcast television channel without interfering with adjacent channels. NTSC is also the standard system for Japan.

The standard was created to allow color television signals to be compatible with existing monochrome (black and white) television. The restriction of compatibility with the earlier technology results in compromises in color image quality. The

NTSC composite signal format is required for video recording except with devices which support component video.

Though there are 525 scan lines, more than 40 lines are blanked during vertical retrace periods. Overscanning and poorly adjusted televisions reduce the number of visible lines further, leaving viewers around 360 lines of video information in a normal television picture.

Macintosh video can be converted to NTSC composite using an encoder or scan converter. When using an encoder with a Macintosh video card there is an unavoidable reduction in image quality and single pixel lines, for instance, will flicker (unless the video card supports convolution) due to the interlaced nature of the NTSC signal. Images intended for NTSC use should be designed according to the limitations of the format, unless a more expensive scan converter is being used.

NTSC PAL, SECAM NTSC is the standard for video signals in the US, Japan and Canada. NTSC uses 30 fps. PAL and SECAM are international/European standards, using 25 fps.

NTSC RGB Interlaced red, green, and blue video signals timed to NTSC standards. Refers to three monochrome signals representing the primary colors of the image. This is a superior signal format to composite video which is one signal encoded from the three signals. An NTSC RGB signal differs from a component video signal which consists of Y, R-Y, and B-Y signals.

Numerical aperture A number that defines the light gathering ability of a specific optical fibre. The numerical aperture is equal to the sine of the maximum acceptance angle.

NVOD Abbreviation for near-video-on-demand.

Nyquist theorum This theorum says that if a continuous bandwidth-limited signal contains no frequency components higher than fC then the original signal can be recovered without distortion if it is sampled at a rate of at least 2 fC. This theorum applies to A/D converter applications as well as data transmission density over limited-bandwidth channels.

O

O and O or O & O A station owned and operated by a national network.

O/p Output.

Object Any item that can be individually selected and manipulated - including shapes and pictures appearing on a display screen and less tangible software.

Object linking and embedding (OLE) A technique used in Microsoft Windows in which copying of one object to another occurs.

Object movie An object movie allows the user to rotate and/or tilt a virtual object. It is created by capturing a series of images taken from different angles around the object. For example taking pictures of a statue as you walk around it.

Object oriented A programming technique that focuses design on the data (=objects) and on the user interfaces to it.

To make an analogy with carpentry, an "object-oriented" carpenter would be mostly concerned with the chair he was building, and secondarily with the tools used to make it; a "non-object-oriented" carpenter would think primarily of his tools. Object-oriented design is also the mechanism for defining how modules "plug and play." (from Sun MicroSystems).

Objective The (often covert) aim of a character in a scene, the theory being that every character in every scene has some sort of objective that performers must recognize to make the scene work dramatically.

Object-oriented A programming technique that focuses design on the data (=objects) and on the user interfaces to it.

To make an analogy with carpentry, an "object-oriented" carpenter would be mostly concerned with the chair he was building, and secondarily with the tools used to make it; a "non-object-oriented" carpenter would think primarily of his tools. Object-oriented design is also the mechanism for defining how modules "plug and play." (from Sun MicroSystems).

OC 3 Network transport capability equivalent to approximately 155Mbps.

OCR (Optical character recognition) Scanning/process for machine print recognition. Compare to ICR.

Octave In audio, the interval between any two frequencies having a ratio of 2 to 1. One octave up from 100 Hz is 200 Hz, where one octave down from 100 Hz is 50 Hz. A harmonic is a doubling (2nd harmonic), tripling (3rd harmonic), quadrupling (4th Harmonic... etc) of a fundamental frequency.

Musical instruments (with the exception of electronic synthesizers) do not create pure tones. The fundamental (main frequency) is combined with its harmonics at various levels to create the sonic signature, or timbre of that instrument.

Ocular The very last optical element at the back of a lens (the one closest to the detector).

Off-line publication An off-line publication is an electronic document which is bibliographically identifiable, which is stored in machine readable form on an electronic storage medium. For example, a CD-ROM.

Ogg Ogg is the umbrella for a group of several related multimedia and signal processing projects that are open source and royalty free. Development of these projects is controlled by Xiph.org.

First and best-known project of these is called Ogg Vorbis, a royalty-free audio compression technology.

Ogg vorbis Ogg Vorbis is an "open-source" digital audio compression format. like MP3, It is a "lossy" compression system, removing frequencies deemed inaudible. Both formats offer variable-bitrate encoding options, for better efficiency. But the algorithms Ogg Vorbis uses to decide which information to discard differ from those used by MP3. Proponents claim that the Ogg Vorbis format outperforms MP3, producing files that are significantly smaller than MP3s of similar sound quality (or files that sound better than similarly sized MP3s).

OHCI compliant IEEE 1394 OHCI (open host controller interface) Was created by several hardware and software industry leaders to ensure that software (applications, drivers and operating systems) work properly with compliant hardware. IEEE 1394 (a high performance serial bus) is the industry standard for connecting devices (such as digital cameras, digital camcorders, etc.) to a computer. Two popular implementations of IEEE 1394 are FireWire and i.LINK.

Ohm The measurement of electrical resistance and system impedance. It is a measure of the degree to which electrons are limited in both velocity and quantity in passing through a circuit. In Impedance measurements, this takes into account, the mechanical resistance inherent in the motion of transducers. The standard is usually 4 ohms for car audio and 8 ohms for home and commercial audio. Some specialty woofers may be rated at 16 ohms.

Ohm's law The mathematical relationship between voltage, current, and resistance. It is named after George Ohm, it's discoverer. Ohm's law states that current volume in a conductor is directly proportional to the voltage flow across it and inversely proportional to its resistance. In general, this means that more voltage will produce more current, if resistance stays the same, but higher resistance will cause current to decrease if voltage stays the same. In mathmatical terms, $V = I \times R$, where V is voltage, I is current, and R is resistance. Ohm's law is a description of electron behavior upon which virtually all understanding of electronics is based.

OIRT Organisation Internationale de Radiodiffision-Television.

OLE (object linking and embedding) Windows' "magic" to transfer objects from one program "document" to another. The process involves copying the selected object to the clipboard, then switching over to the receiving document and pasting. Paste Linking (available as a Paste Special option), plants a trail back to the original/source document so that when the original changes, you see the changes in the receiver. Paste Embedding, the default paste mode, places a copy of the original into the receiver. Because the two programs are not linked, any changes to the original are not reflected in the receiver.

Omnidirectional Literally, from all directions. In audio, microphones are said to be omnidirectional if they can detect sound with equal sensitivity from all directions. Speakers are omnidirectional if they produce sound pressure level that is the same without regard to the position of the listener vis a vis the axis of the driver or port; this tends to be the case with subwoofers and low frequency drivers. Low frequencies, in general, tend to be omni-directional, unlike high frequencies, where directionality increases with frequency.

On axis A listening experience which takes place with the ear precisely lined up with the central pressure axis of the emitter. Headphones are a normative example of this effect. Sitting directly in front of a speaker is another.

On demand feed Playback of a previously recorded session during which the viewer/listener can fast-forward, back up, or pause.

Online The most common use of the word online means "connected to the internet", but it can refer to any active connection that someone makes from their computer over a telephone or cable link to another computer. Often people will say they are online if they have access to the internet and an email address, but they may not necessarily be connected to the internet at that time.

Online editing The final edit of a video using original master tapes to produce the finished piece. An on-line edit suite usually has a full range of high-end video devices (switcher, TBCs, DVE, character generator, and so forth) which would normally be too expensive to use during an off-line edit session.

The on-line session is where the actual editing and effects take place. It occurs in an edit suite with a professional editor (known as the on-line editor). Again, the more prepared you are, the better since "things happen." It is very easy to go way over your budget estimate for an off-line edit if your EDL contains little surprises like a mislabeled in-point. Computer based editing systems like the Digital F/X and Avid Media Composer automatically generate EDLs which are very accurate, reducing on-line time considerably.

Online resource An on-line resource is an electronic document which is bibliographically identifiable, which is stored in machine readable form on an electronic storage medium and which is available on-line. For example - a Web page.

Onomatopoeia A word or expression that sounds like the thing it describes, such as slush, pow, sizzle, thud.

Op amp (operational amplifier) An analog integrated circuit device having two opposite polarity inputs and one output; frequently used as a basic processing unit in the design of analog signal circuits.

Opacity The condition of lacking transparency or translucence. We cannot see through objects which are 100%% opaque. Adjusting opacity determines to what degree information is hidden or revealed below. For example, an opacity of 100%% hides all information below. An opacity of 10%% would appear almost transparent, allowing you to see through to objects below.

Opaque Opposite of transparent meaning that you cannot see through an opaque object.

Open (or open-frame) composition A style in which the frame seems not to include everything. Other elements enter and exit, implying that there is a larger world outside.

Open architecture A standard, or system that is public, encouraging third-party manufacturers to develop add-ons. A good example of open architecture is the PC.

Open database connectivity (ODBC) A standard database access method developed by Microsoft.

OpenGL 3D graphic programming API written by Silicon Graphics. Allows programs to interface and use built in high speed 3D graphic routines on graphic cards. The standard for high end 3D modeling and recently adopted by Apple Computers as their standard 3D interface.

Opera A popular web browser from Opera Software.

Operating system (OS) The software that allows the operation of a computer. e.g. DOS, UNIX, Linux, Mac OS, Microsoft Windows, to name a few.

Opex Also referred to as operating expense, Opex is the essential items a business must purchase in order to maintain itself.

Optical digital A method of communicating digital audio between components using light carried on optical fibre. The data format accords with the S/PDIF specification.

Optical disk A medium for writing, storing and reading data using lasers. Optical disks can store up to 6 gigabytes (6 billion bytes) - than most portable. There are three basic types: CD-ROM; WORM (write-once, read-many); EO (erasable optical) disks.

Optical soundtrack The traditional medium for carrying a film's soundtrack. The sound was converted to markings which were developed onto the edge of the film. The majority of optical soundtracks were analogue (in the form of squiggly lines, like the track on an LP). However Dolby Digital is also carried on the film in optical form. Rather than replacing the analogue soundtrack (which is left on for broad compatibility), the Dolby Digital data is optically recorded between the sprocket holes on the edge of the film.

Optical storage unit CD-ROM drive.

Opticals Visual effects produced optically using an optical printer that contains one camera head and several projectors. The projectors are precisely aligned in order to produce multiple exposures in exact registration on the film in the camera head. Rapidly being replaced with special high-resolution video devices for all but feature applications.

Optimize Honing a Web site to ensure that it downloads and performs as quickly as possible. For most Web sites, optimizing requires minimizing the size, number, and quality of the graphics on the page and ensuring that special features, such as Java, load quickly using a 56kbps modem.

Optisonic. Pertaining to remote dramatic forms combining light and sound, such as film, video tape, optical disk and other technologies; multimedia. (my coinage).

Opto-magnetic media Various media used for the physical exchange of electronic information between IT systems, using postal or courier services.

Orange book Standard for WORM (Write Once Read Many) CD's. Used for archiving/ backing up catalogs, directories and other computerized paperwork.

Organic In playwrighting, arising intrinsically, as from the natural consequences of the characters, their situations and interactions, as opposed to a contrivance such as a deus ex machina; in acting, employing one's own emotional equipment appropriately and spontaneously in performance, as opposed to "indication".

Orphan page Strictly speaking, an orphan page is a web page with no outgoing links. From a practical point of view, however, an orphan page is any page where it is not obvious to users where they should go next, so they abandon that website. Ideally, web pages should be designed so that they end with a suggestion of where the reader might go next.

Orthogonal Term used to signify that two signals (or signal attributes) are mutually transparent and non-interfering with each other. Frequency and amplitude modulation are orthogonal signal attributes.

Oscillator A device which produces an alternating current or pulsating current or voltage at varying frequencies, electronically.

Oscilloscope (also CRO, from cathode ray oscilloscope) An electronic device that can display changes of voltage on the vertical scale against time horizontally. The single most important piece of test equipment in CCTV.

OSD On screen display The menus and information screens shown by TVs, DVD players, VCRs and some home theatre receivers on the TV screen. These make setting up these devices somewhat easier than those devices that lack them.

OSI Open systems interconnection model, Work began in 1977 by the ISO to simplify communication between different computer systems. This work resulted in the OSI which is a model specifying functions on a network. OSI does not specify how the functions are to be performed.

The OSI model consists of seven layers:

1. Physical layer the cables: physical network connections such as voltage levels, pin assignments

2. Data Link layer chunks (packages) date into frames (packets)

3. Network layer routes data through network

4. Transport layer sequencing and acknowledgement of transmission

5. Session layer synchronizes dialogue between network applications

6. Presentation layer converts data for universal exchange

7. Application layer access from application to other OSI services

OSTA Optical storage technology association.

Out or sound out A script indication for an abrupt drop to zero volume.

Outboard. In electronics, external; as a device that can be wired to a tape recorder or console that enhances its performance.

Output (audio) The high level (speaker) or line level (RCA) signals sent from one system component to another, or the high level signal from an amplifier to the system speakers.

Output impedance The impedance a device presents to its load. The impedance measured at the output terminals of a transducer with the load disconnected and all impressed driving forces taken as zero.

Output resolution The detail and clarity (achieved by tightness of dots) with which the image will be displayed or printed (depending on the capability of the display or printing device).

Outtake Source footage that has been removed and is not included in the final production.

Over the shoulder shot This type of shot looks over the character's shoulder to see what he sees, though not exactly as he sees it. (The shoulder may still be visible in the edge of the frame, to remind the viewer of being outside the character and somewhat detached.)

Overcranking In early days film was fed through the camera by a manual cranking process. When the camera operator turned the crank too quickly, the frame rate was increased, which caused the action to seem sped up. Contrast with Undercranking.

Overdub 1) In multitracking, to record sounds, music or voices on empty tracks of an already recorded tape in preparation for mixing;

2) the stage of the production process in which this is done.

Overexposure An image that appears too birght because it has received too much light through the lens

Overhead projector Sometimes referred to as a transparency projector, it contains a glass plate with a light from below that when powered on reflects an image through the lens on an arm to magnify transparent film onto a screen.

Overmodulation Sound distortion and/or signal break-up in a recording, playback or broadcast resulting from two much gain.

Oversampling A technique where each sample from a data converter is sampled more than once, i.e., oversampled. This multiplication of samples permits digital filtering of the signal, thus reducing the need for sharp analog filters to control unwanted frequencies created when sampling a signal of a frequency higher than half the sampling rate.

Overscan In order to make sure the sides of the picture form nice vertical lines, and to use the whole screen, TV makers tune their sets so that a little bit of the picture flows off the visible screen on all four side. If this overflow is too much you might be missing something important. The overflow is called 'overscan'.

Overtone Similar in concept to a harmonic. Overtones are sounds produced by an instrument (or sound source) that are higher in frequency than the fundamental frequency. They may or may not coincide with the frequencies of a harmonic series (harmonics), although they usually do. Harmonics are always musically related to a fundamental in that they are integer multiples of it. Overtones of a sound are often identical to its harmonics except the first overtone is considered the second harmonic because the first harmonic is the fundamental. Overtones are also sometimes called partials.

Oxidation Traditionally defined as a chemical reaction in which oxygen combines with another element to form an oxide. Today it is defined as a chemical reaction in which one or more free electron are released.

Oxymoron An expression combining contradictions, as "thunderous silence" or "honest politician."

P

P.O.V. Point of view, the desired illusion of physical audience orientation towards a scene or scene fragment, as when all sounds are heard from a specific character's POV.

PA or production assistant The producer's and/or director's assistant in the studio; the radio equivalent to the stage manager.

Pacifica A small but influential public radio network and program syndicator, generally considered far less politically neutral than PRI or NPR.

Package 1) To add the wrap-arounds, credits, break announcements and previews to a final mix so that the program is ready to air;

2) a bundle of programs, or a bundle of services accompanying a program, offered to stations by a distributor, or to the distributor by a producer.

Packaging level option A high level technical option which structures the data according to content.

Packet A digital communications technique involving the transmission of short bursts of data in a protocol format that contain addressing, control, and error-checking information, along with the field information, in each transmission burst.

Pad An electrical circuit used to attenuate or reduce the amplitude of an audio signal by a fixed amount, e.g a -15dB pad reduces the signal by a fixed 15 decibels.

Page impression/view A page impression, or page view, is what is counted for every page on a website that a user visits. This gives website owners a method for monitoring how busy their websites are. Page impressions are often wrongly called "hits".

Pageant An elaborate celebratory or "occasional" (i.e., celebrating or marking a special event) kind of loosely constructed theatrical work, often essentially dramatic, emphasizing sentiment and spectacle, built around a central theme of great significance to the community at large.

Paintbox Paintbox is the trade name for a device made by Quantel, however, it is geneneally used to describe a digital video paint program capable of drawing and shading images from scratch or from digitized video frames. The Paintbox creates only still images, but sequences of animated images can be made from the still images by loading frame by frame onto a Harry or equivalent.

PAL (Phase alternating line) The television system used in Australia, most of Europe and

India. This runs at 25 frames or 50 fields per second and produces 576 visible scan lines. It is often referred to as having 625 lines, but some of these are merely timing lines at the start of each field. Some of these lines can also carry Teletext information and switching signals. Technically, PAL refers to the colour system used rather than the field rate and resolution of the system, but given the ubiquity of PAL across parts of the world, even a monochrome TV based on this rate and resolution tends to be called PAL.

PAL60 PAL60 is a television format that is sort of a hybrid of NTSC and PAL. It is used in many VCRs and DVD players to convert NTSC signals to PAL, sort of. Basically it leaves the signal in standard NTSC format (that is, 60 fields per second and 480 visible lines) but converts the colour signal into the format that PAL TVs can handle. Many older TVs that could not display NTSC signals could handle PAL60 (a standard NTSC colour picture shows on these TVs in black and white). Some of these need to have their vertical hold control adjusted to stop the picture from rolling. Some TVs can't handle either NTSC or PAL60. Why not convert the picture to PAL completely? Converting the colour standard is a relatively trivial exercise. Converting the number of lines and scan frequency is a much harder undertaking. The professional equipment used to convert US TV shows to PAL for Europe and Australia costs tens of thousands of dollars. In recent years an increasing number of DVD players will do full NTSC to PAL conversion, sometimes with excellent performance, sometimes rather poorly. The poor ones typically produce a very jerky result.

PAL format A color television format having 625 scan lines (rows) of resolution at 25 frames per second (25 Hz).

Palette (color palette) The set of colors used to display a digital image.

Palette flash A phenomenon caused by simultaneously displaying more than one bitmap or video that do not share the same palette.

PALplus PALplus is 16:9 aspect ratio version of PAL, designed to be transmitted using normal PAL systems. 16:9 TVs without the PALplus decoder, and standard TVs, show a standard picture. It is defined by BT.1197 and ETSI ETS 300 731.

Pan A shot taken, by a camera moving horizontally.

Pan and scan This is the technique used to crop a widescreen movie so it fits onto a standard TV with a 4:3 aspect ratio. Since the early 1950s most movies released to the cinema have been presented with a 1.66:1 to 2.35:1 aspect ratio. If these were presented on a standard TV in this way, there would be black bands at the top and bottom of the screen. So the edges of the picture are cut off. In some movies, though, the action might be over near, say, the left edge of the screen. In such cases the left part of the picture is presented and the right cut off. As the action moves towards the centre, the cut picture usually follows it. With DVDs most movies are presented in their original widescreen format. However the DVD specification permits widescreen movies to be encoded with invisible crop marks which can be interpreted by the DVD player and thus performs the cropping itself. Very few DVDs are so encoded.

Pan and tilt head (P/T head) A motorized unit permitting vertical and horizontal positioning of a camera and lens combination. Usually AC motors (24 VAC, 110 VAC, & 240 VAC) of fixed speed, are used in such P/T heads, but increasingly DC variable speed motors are being installed.

Pan pot Short for panoramic potentiometer, this is a knob controlling a voltage divider that can send a signal to a combination of two busses, such as left and right. Always found on mixing consoles to set up (pan) a signal within the stereo field, it is also called a 'balance' control on domestic stereo amplifiers.

Pan unit A motorized unit permitting horizontal positioning of a camera.

Pander to an audience To subvert artistic integrity by creating or altering a literary work or performance opportunistically, thus lessening its artistic merit, to gain the approbation of an audience.

Panorama A.k.a. Immersive Image, VR - an image or series of images "stitched" together to produce a virtual-world within which the user can navigate a full 360 degrees in a horizontal plane. (Additional features such as sound, video, Flash files etc. can be integrated into the panorama for a fuller sense of interactivity).

Panoramic head or Panoramic rig Short for "panoramic head". An additional piece of equipment to put on top of a tripod which can be small or very large. Allows the camera to be positioned so that one of the nodal points of the lens is perfectly above the point of rotation. By using a pano-head the camera can be rotated to take a set of pictures for making a panorama without suffering from "parallax". There are various manufacturers.

Paper the house To stack an audience of a live performance with friends, family, supporters, and others to make the house appear full or to ensure a warm audience reaction, or both.

Paradox A statement or situation that seems, but need not be, self-contradictory.

Parallax If you shoot a sequence of images for creating a panorama without using a pano-head and tripod you will suffer from parallax. It may be barely noticeable, or it may completely ruin the panorama. The most important factors are: how far off-centre the camera lens's nodal point is when turning, the angle of view of the lens (wider is worse), and how short a distance there is from the camera to the nearest object (shorter is worse).

Parallel ports Also called "printer ports", parallel ports transfer several bits simultaneously. Thus, they are faster than serial ports. However, they can only send, not receive, information; whereas serial posts can handle 2-way transmission.

Parallel wiring A circuit in which two or more devices are connected to the same source of voltage, sharing a common positive and negative point, so that each device receives the full applied voltage.

Parametric equalizer A multi-band equalizer enabeling control of at least three essential "parameters" of the internal bandpass filter sections. These parameters being: amplitude, center frequency and bandwidth. This allows the user to not only control the amplitude of each band, but also to shift the center frequency and to widen or narrow the width or coverage of the affected section of the aural spectrum. Regulation is done by either rotary and slide controls. Other types of parametric equalizers exist which allow control of center frequency, but not bandwidth. For rotary control units, the most common term is quasi-parametric. For units with slide controls the popular term is paragraphic. The frequency control may be continuously variable or switch selectable in steps. Cut-only parametric equalizers (with adjustable bandwidth or not) are called notch equalizers, or band-reject equalizers.

Parody 1. a literary or artistic work that imitates the characteristic style of an author or a work for comic effect or ridicule; a travesty;

2. To make a parody of.

Partial panorama Like a panorama but with a range of motion that is limited to less than 360 degrees. It's created in a way similar to a full 360 degree panorama but restrictions are put on the manipulation of the image.

Parts per quarter note (PPQN) A time format used for Musical instrument digital interface (MIDI) sequences. PPQN is the most common time format used with standard MIDI files.

Pass n, One continuous pass of the recording tape over the record head of the tape recorder, during a session; a take.

Passive component In a crossover system, a non-powered component used to separate an audio signal into a specified frequency band before it goes to a particular amplifier or driver. A passive device usually incurs some loss (expressed in decibels) to a system. Typical such components include capacitors, coils, and resistors.

Passive loudspeaker A loudspeaker without built-in amplification for all the drivers. Most loudspeakers are passive, not active.

Passive radiator Sometimes known as a "drone cone," these passive devices respond to internal pressure within the speaker and react to it to produce reinforcing emissions to extend the output of the lower frequencies below the resonance point of the active woofer. They may look like Drivers but they lack an active motor assembly.

Passive subwoofer A subwoofer without built-in amplification. Most subwoofers are active, not passive.

Password field A text entry field for entering passwords. As you type in your password, asterisks are usually displayed in the password field instead of the actual letters or numbers, which helps to keep your password secret.

Patch A particular setup of a Musical Instrument Digital Interface (MIDI) synthesizer that results in a particular sound, usually a sound simulating a specific musical instrument. Patches are also called programs. A MIDI program-change message changes the patch setting in a synthesizer. Patch also refers to the connection or connections between MIDI devices.

Patch bay A bank of receptors, usually on the console and resembling an old fashioned telephone switchboard, for patching.

Patch caching A technique that enables some internal Musical instrument digital interface (MIDI) synthesizer device drivers to preload their patch data, reducing the delay between the moment the synthesizer receives a MIDI program-change message and the moment it plays a note using the new patch. Patch caching also ensures that required patches are available (the synthesizer might load only a subset of its patches).

Patch, phone A hook-up between a telephone line and a recording or broadcasting device so that sound information may be captured or broadcast directly from the line.

Pathos That which evokes sympathy, sorrow, or pity.

Pattern A fill or paint effect that can be applied to a image to create a predefined design or texture such as brick or concrete.

PC Personal computer (IBM standard).

PCI Peripheral component interconnection, bus architecture. The bus analogy refers to channels that are used to send data to different computer components and back. Bus architecture is a simple reference to the type of bus that your system uses.

PCM pulse code modulation This is standard, uncompressed digital audio of the kind that is on compact discs. However while normal CDs are always encoded with 16 bits and 44,100 hertz sampling rate, on DVD bit depths of up to 24 and sampling rates of up to 96,000 are permitted.

PCMCIA Personal computer memory card international association.

PDF (portable document format) A proprietary document format from Adobe that preserves formatting such as specific fonts and graphics by embedding them into the file. PDF files are created with Adobe Acrobat.

Peak power handling (MAX) Peak power handling refers to the amount of power a speaker is estimated to handle during a brief high-intensity musical burst. Since this can vary with both frequency and amplitude, it is a much less accurate way to judge speaker durability and performance than RMS.

Peak white inverter An electronic circuit that turns white parts (highlights) of a picture, above a set threshold, to black or a shade of grey.

Peak to peak (pp) The amplitude (voltage) difference between the most positive and the most negative excursions (peaks) of an electrical signal.

Pedestal Pedestal is an offset used to separate the black level from the blanking level by a small amount. When a video system doesn't use a pedestal, the black and blanking levels are the same. (M) NTSC uses a pedestal, (B, D, G, H, I) PAL does not. (M) NTSC-J used in Japan also does not use a pedestal.

PEP protocol extension protocol An extension mechanism for HTTP.

Perceptual encoding A compression technique for digitally recorded sound. Digital audio does not compress at all well using conventional 'non-lossy' schemes because there is very little redundancy in the data stream. Perceptual encoding techniques rely on extensive psycho-acoustic analyses of how the human ear and brain detect and interpret sound. In essence they manage to achieve high levels of compression by discarding elements of the sound that such analyses suggest cannot be heard. In this way they can reduce the data volume of the sound by a factor of 10 or more without obviously degrading the sound quality. Examples of perceptual encoding compression systems are Dolby Digital, DTS (although DTS claims that it first uses non-lossy compression techniques to reduce or eliminate the need for perceptual encoding), MP3, SDDS, Windows Media, RealAudio and ATRAC.

Period In relation to a repeating wave form, the reciprocal of the frequency (ie. 1/f).

Peripheral A piece of computer equipment, such as a disk drive, printer, modem, mouse or joystick, that is connected to the computer.

Periphrasis The substitution of a descriptive phrase for the name of something, either because it expresses more than the name alone, or because expressive precision is for some reason impossible; as "wet roads" for sea, "tawny majesty" for lion, or "whatshisname, that writer with the beard who blew his brains out" for Hemingway.

Perlscript The script engine from Active Perl to allow Perl language to be used int Active Server Page (ASP).

Permalloy tape head A cassette tape head constructed of permalloy, an alloy made primarily of nickel and iron, used for its superior high wear resistance and permeability, offering superior frequency response at a low cost.

Permanent paper Paper manufactured to high standard for long-term survival good condition under reasonable storage conditions. It must have good resistance to internal and external chemical reactions, good mechanical strength and be composed of only virgin, or un-recycled fibres containing no lignin.

Persistence of vision A very short lingering of an image in the eyes and brain of a person. It is this which allows the continuous stuttering of still images at the cinema to look like smooth motion.

Personal data assistant (PDA) A handheld device that combines computing, telephone and networking features.

Personification The giving of human attributes to non-human things, as in expressions like "cruel sea," "howling gale," "blushing rose," "rosy-fingered dawn," etc.

Phase The alignment or otherwise of two signals in time. 'In phase' means that they are aligned. 'Out of phase' means that one or the other is shifted in time by one half the period (inverse of frequency) of the tone in question. If an out of phase pair are played together, they will cancel each other out.

Phase is usually measured in degrees. A zero degree shift is in phase, while a 180 degree shift is out of phase. Causes of phase shift include filters (especially those in loudspeaker crossover networks) and the (lack of) time alignment of drivers in a loudspeaker.

Phase adjust This is a term used to describe a method of adjusting the hue in a NTSC video signal. The phase of the color subcarrier is moved, or adjusted, relative to the color burst. PAL and SECAM systems do not usually have a phase (or hue) adjust control.

Phase cancellation Audio signals are complex phenomena expressed mathematically as phasors, or vectors. When two signals have the same exact time relationship to each other, they are said to be "in-phase;" if they do not, they are said to be "out-of-phase." If the energy of two out-of-phase signals are combined, they will, in fact, subtract from one another. This is called phase cancellation. Another type of phase cancellation can be seen when water waves interact. One wave's energy becomes stronger when two waves collide in-phase (summing) and becomes weaker when they collide out-of-phase. Air (barometric) fronts act in the same way.

Phase delay A phase-shifted sine wave appears displaced in time from the input waveform. This displacement is called phase delay.

Phase laternate line (PAL 625 line 50 field per second tevlevision standards used in Europe and South America.

Phase linear Any audio system which accurately preserves phase relationships between frequencies, i.e., that exhibits pure delay.

Phase locked loop (PLL) A circuit containing an oscillator whose output phase or frequency locks onto and tracks the phase or frequency of a reference input signal. To produce the locked condition, the circuit then detects any phase difference between the two signals and generates an error voltage which can be used independently or to correct its own oscillator phase or frequency.

Phase noise The amount of phase noise energy contained in a frequency carrier. Specified in dB/Hz, phase noise amplitude is usually characterized and plotted in 1 Hz increments, offset from the carrier.

Phase shift keying (PSK) A digital modulation technique whereby the phase of a carrier frequency is shifted to represent a digital "1" or "0" state. In "Quadri-phase-shift keying" systems, the phase angle locations of 0^0, 90^0, and 180^0 are used as reference points to represent sixteen possible digital states (2^4).

Phase shift The fraction of a complete cycle elapsed as measured from a specified reference point and expressed as an angle; out of phase; in an un-synchronized or un-correlated way.

Phon A unit of apparent loudness, equal in quantum to the intensity in decibels of a 1,000 Hz tone estimated to be as loud as the sound being measured.

Phonation The production of sound by means of vocal cord vibration.

Phoneme An individual sound unit of a spoken language, whose combination with other phonemes, in a particular order, produces morphemes.

Phono From phonogram. An adjective relating to systems for playing vinyl recordings, such as LPs. Thus the phono input of an amplifier is the input into which a turntable is plugged. This is usually equipped with an RIAA equalization circuit.

Phot A photometric light unit for very strong illumination levels. One phot is equal to 10,000 lux.

Photo multiplier A highly light-sensitive device. Advantages are its fast response, good signal-to-noise ratio and wide dynamic range. Disadvantages are fragility (vacuum tube), high voltage and sensitivity to interference.

Photodiode A type of semiconductor device in which a PN junction diode acts as a photosensor.

Photo-effect Also known as photoelectric-effect. This refers to a phenomenon of ejection of electrons from a metal whose surface is exposed to light.

Photography Any method of producing an image by using the action of light to change a chemical layer.

Photon A representative of the quantum nature of light. It is considered as the smallest unit of light.

Photopic vision The range of light intensities, from 105 lux down to nearly 10-2 lux, detectable by the human eye.

Photostitch A Canon company image stitching software application. It allows for creation of panoramic movies as well as mosaics.

Physicality In audio drama, an element of palpable reality, such as touching, movement, gesture, etc. used by talent as a performance aid; the physical relationship with other characters, gesture, environment and movement that the talent can convey vocally, though standing still at the mike.

Pick up 1) a wild line or intercut;

2) a line or sequence of lines recorded wild;

3) directorial note given to actors between takes, run-throughs or performances.

PICS (platform independent content selection) PICS is an infrastructure for associating labels (metadata) with Internet content. These labels are used for code signing, privacy, and intellectual property rights management.

PICS was originally designed to assist in the control of internet content – to prevent children and sensitive users from stumbling upon unwanted sites.

PICT An Apple Macintosh file format for saving raster (pixel based) images. The file format is uncompressed and therefore loss-less. The file format typically cannot be opened natively on Windows Operating System, however some cross platform applications such as Adobe Photoshop can read the file format on both the Macintosh and Windows Operating Systems.

Picture element The smallest discrete part of a video image, the size of which is controlled by an analog-to-digital conversion sampling process and subsequent other compression processes. The more picture elements per line, the higher the resolution of the image. To convert H Pixels to a close approximation of TV lines of resolution for the NTSC system, simply multiply the number of H pixels by 0.78.

Picture in picture(PIP) Image from a second video source contained within a screen's main picture.

Picture resolution How much detail appears in the picture. This is a function of how many pixels are devoted to the picture. The more dots, the finer the detail. As computer and television technology draw closer together, there's a problem with defining resolution. Traditionally the vertical resolution of TV has been expressed in terms of lines. PAL has 576 visible horizontal lines (NTSC has 480). This is easy to understand because these are the scan lines built into the signal. Traditionally TVs don't produce all of these lines because of overscan and because of the Kell Effect. For TV, the horizontal resolution has also traditionally been expressed in terms of lines, in this case vertical ones. This is a fairly subjective judgment based on density of closely spaced lines that can be perceived on a screen. DVDs, deriving from computer technology, are instead expressed in terms of pixels. PAL ones have a vertical resolution of 576 pixels (subject to letter boxing, and 480 for NTSC). They also have a theoretical horizontal resolution of 720 pixels. At least, that is the resolution at which the pictures are encoded on the DVD (both for PAL and NTSC). However the great majority of DVD players do not have digital video outputs. So this horizontal resolution has to be down-converted to a resolution that a TV is capable of handling, typically between 500 and 540. DVD players which incorporate DVI or HDMI outputs are now appearing. These can deliver the full 720 pixels of horizontal resolution.

Piezo (tweeter) A tweeter whose motor is simply a crystal of Piezo material through which the signal current flows. The crystal lattice responds to this by bending in proportion to the Amplitude and frequency of the incoming signal. Because it is a high impedance device, it does not need a Crossover in line with the source. Piezo tweeters are very efficient Drivers and are relatively inexpensive. They come in a large variety of designs and radiators.

Piezoelectric driver This is among the most robust and least expensive alternative drivers for the high frequency reproduction. The material used in the Piezoelectric Driver is a piezoelectric polymer first developed in the early 1960's. This piezoelectric polymer is a plastic-like material that, unlike a crystal, can be made into thin sheets and fashioned into a great variety of shapes. Its transient and high frequency response is very good because the moving mass is negligible. The driver operates by bending the lattices in the crystalline structure of the piezoelectric polymer film. The Piezoelectric Driver is inappropriate for low frequency applications, as it is incapable of large air displacements. This high frequency transducer is very uniform in response from approximately 2 kHz to 20 kHz. It typically is used in many car stereo enclosures and other compact space environments.

Pigtail A length of optical fibre with one "bare end" and the other end terminated in a connector.

Ping A utility that sends a packet to an Internet server and wait for a response. It is used to check if a host (i.e. a server) is running.

Pinhole lens A fixed focal length lens, for viewing through a very small aperture, used in discrete surveillance situations. The lens normally has no focusing control but may offer a choice of iris functions.

Pink noise Pink noise is a random noise source characterized by a flat amplitude response per octave band of frequency, i.e., it has equal energy, or constant power, per octave. Pink noise is created by passing white noise through a filter having a 3 dB/octave roll-off rate. Due to this roll-off, pink noise sounds less bright and richer in low frequencies than white noise. Since pink noise has the same energy in each 1/3-octave band, it is the preferred sound source for many acoustical measurements in respect to the critical band concept of human hearing. The name comes from the filtering of white noise. White noise is analogous to white light in that it contains all audible frequencies distributed uniformly throughout the spectrum. Passing white light through a prism (a form of filter) breaks it down into a range of colors. Examination shows that red light is characterized by the longer wavelengths of light, i.e., light in the lower frequency region. Similarly, pink noise has higher energy in the low frequencies, hence the term, pink.

Pipeline burst cache Designed to take advantage of the PCI architecture. The term pipeline comes from the fact that the cache is connected directly to the PCI slot in the CPU. The term burst comes from the process of information and the retrieval of data is faster due to this improved cache system.

Pitch scale factor In waveform audio, the amount by which a waveform audio driver scales the pitch. A scale factor of two results in a one-octave increase in pitch. Pitch scaling requires specialized hardware. The playback rate and sample rate are not changed.

Pitch The pitch of the voice corresponds perceptually to the number of times per second the vocal folds come together during phonation. For example, a pitch corresponding to 250 Hz (near middle C on the piano) means that the vocal folds vibrate away from and then back toward each other 250 times per second (250 cycles per second).

Pixel A pixel, which is short for picture element, is the smallest sample that makes up a scan line. For example, when the horizontal resolution is defined as 640 pixels, that means that there are 640 individual locations, or samples, that make up the visible portion of each horizontal scan line. Pixels may be square or rectangular.

Pixel clock The pixel clock is used to divide the horizontal line of video into samples. The pixel clock has to be stable (a very small amount of jitter) relative to the video or the image will not be stored correctly. The higher the frequency of the pixel clock, the more samples per line there are.

Pixel data Data that describes information about the pixels in an image such as color values and specific locations.

Pixel depth The number of bits of color information per pixel. A system using eight bits per pixel can display 256(28) colors. A system using 16 bits per pixel can display 65,536(216) colors. A system using 24 bits per pixel can display over 16.7 million colors. Twenty-four bit color is often called true color because the human eye can distinguish among approximately six million different colors, or fewer than are available in a 24-bit color system.

Pixel drop out This can be a real troublemaker, since it can cause artifacts. In some instances, a pixel drop out looks like black spots on the screen, either stationary or moving around. Several things can cause pixel drop out, such as the ADC not digitizing the video correctly. Also, the timing between the ADC and the frame buffer might not be correct, causing the wrong number to be stored in memory. For that matter, the timing anywhere in the video stream might cause a pixel drop out.

Pixelization Pixels that make up an image get exaggerated or enlarged. This makes the image look jagged and is often the result of compression artifacts.

Plain English campaign The Plain English Campaign is an independent organisation that campaigns for the use of clear language without jargon, gobbledygook and other confusing language. Using plain English doesn't mean changing the meaning of a sentence or being over simple. It is about making English fast to write and easy to read, which then gets your message across quickly.

Plain text file A human-readable file of data. The data may be structured in some pre-defined format.

Plasma display A flat panel display technology which consists of three tiny cells for each pixel. Each cell contains a gas which, when electrically stimulated, emits ultraviolet light which, in turn, activates a phosphor coating on the edge of the cell facing the viewers. The phosphors for the three cells are selected for red, green and blue light. Plasma displays have the advantage of being relatively modest in thickness (typically around 75 to 100mm including casing). Some models require internal fans for cooling, but for home theatre use those without are preferable to eliminate this source of noise. Older panels may suffer 'burn-in' in which a ghost of the image is retained if left displayed for too long. But this can be easily avoided simply by not leaving menus and the like displayed too long. Some models also incorporate TV tuners and speakers and are thus called plasma TVs.

Platform Refers to the hardware and software that makes a computer function. The most common platform for desktop computers on Capitol Hill, for example, is PC computers running Windows 95, 98, 2000, or NT. This term is also often used to refer only to the operating system of a computer — the software that "drives" it — which is usually Windows, Macintosh, or Unix.

Playback rate scale factor In waveform audio, the amount by which the waveform audio driver scales the playback rate. Playback scaling is accomplished through software; the sample rate is not changed, but the driver interpolates by skipping or synthesizing samples. For example, if the playback rate is changed by a factor of two, the driver skips every other sample.

Player, supporting An actor playing a secondary of tertiary role in a production.

Plosive A vocalization produced by the total stoppage and sudden release of breath, such as the initial sounds in the words Pet, kite and tar. Such sounds tend to "pop" the mike.

Plot 1. As opposed to story, the events of a fictional work arranged in order of presentation;

2. to arrange a story into a plot.

Plot point A bit of information that must register with the audience before it can understand why the dramatic action is moving in certain directions.

Plug-in A module that can be added to a larger computer application to give it greater capabilities. For example, there are many plug-ins available for Microsoft Internet Explorer and Netscape Navigator that enable these two browsers to access and use different kinds of files. Napster and Adobe Acrobat Reader are two examples of plug-ins.

PMPO (Peak music power output) This is a measure of power output, sometimes quoted for home stereo systems.

PNG Standing for "portable network graphics" and pronounced "ping", is a proposed replacement/improvement for the GIF format. It allows for both up to 8-bit and 8x8x8 palettes, variable transparency, gamma correction, better interlacing and better compression than GIF. It does not, however, allow for animation. PNG has only recently seen support from Netscape and IE, neither one supports the PNG standard fully, though plug-ins are available for most platforms to allow both browsers to be more PNG compliant. Macromedia's Fireworks uses PNG as its native format.

Poetic justice The doctrine that fictional characters should receive their just deserts in a fitting way, that by the end of the work, evil should be punished and virtue rewarded.

Point of attack The point in a story at which the playwright begins the action. The point of attack does not necessarily coincide with the beginning of the story. Easy changes of scene permit a playwright to present most of the story directly; in Macbeth, for example, the point of attack is near the beginning of the story, but in such modern plays, such as Ibsen's Ghosts, ... the point of attack (is) almost immediately before the catastrophe and (tells) most of his story through exposition.

Point of view (POV, POV Shot, First-person camera, subjective camera) A camera angle which represents the view of a character in the film: what that character sees.

Pointer A pointer is a small image on the computer screen that indicates where the user is pointing. The pointer is moved by a device such as a mouse and changes shape according to the type of item it is above: it often looks like an arrowhead or crosshair.

Pointers are often mistakenly called "cursors", but a cursor marks the place where text will be added if you type a letter on your keyboard, for example. If you use a mouse you can set the position of the cursor by moving the pointer and clicking your mouse button once.

Pointing device A piece of equipment that is used to move the pointer and so indicate a position on a screen. The most common pointing device is the mouse, but others include lightpens, trackballs and touchscreens.

Polar response A plot of the Amplitude measurement of a speaker's output at a given frequency relative to an off-axis angle. In other words, the difference that exists between how a speaker sounds when being heard directly in front, compared to how it sounds while standing off to one side.

Polarizing filter An optical filter that transmits light in only one direction (perpendicular to the light path), out of 360° possible. The effect is such that it can eliminate some unwanted bright areas or reflections, such as when looking through a glass window or the surface of water. In photography, polarizing filters are used very often to darken a blue sky.

Pole piece The ends or "Poles" of a magnet from which the magnetic lines of force, measured in Gauss, are at the greatest strength. In a typical speaker, this will be at the gap within which the voice coil is located.

Polorizing An effect that makes whites whiter and darks darker

Polycarbonate A polymer based plastic material offering superior resistance against resonance.

Polyphony The total number of sounds a sound card can reproduce at the same time. A 32-note card can play 32 notes at a time.

Polypropylene A plastic based material used primarily for speaker cones due to its rigidity, damping and resistance against harsh environmental conditions.

Pop 1. To make a popping sound by pronouncing a plosive or fricative too directly into a microphone;

2. a sound so made.

Pop filter/wind screen A device fitting over the microphone to reduce unwanted sounds from pops, exhalations, and the flow of air in a recording environment.

POP2 POP mail server which requires SMTP to send messages.

POP3 POP mail server which can be used with or without SMTP for sending messages.

Port diameter The measurement across the port opening. Measured as internal diameter (not outer diameter .

Port length The measurement of the length of the port tube.

Portable document format (PDF) The PDF file format was created by the Adobe company to provide a standard way of editing and storing documents. A file saved in PDF format is often referred to simply as a PDF.

PDFs can be made from files that were originally created in a variety of programs, but they can easily be viewed and printed by users on a variety of computer and platform types. They are often found on websites because, unlike an HTML web page, a PDF document will always look the same.

To view a PDF you will need to download a free piece of software called Adobe Acrobat Reader

Ported (enclosure) Any enclosure design with ports. In such designs the internal pressure wave is processed to be used either solely, or in conjunction with the woofer front wave in order to produce sound. A port can be a simple opening, a tube or a Passive Radiator.

Portmanteau word A word derived from fragments of other words to express a combined meaning; for instance, "grumble," to complain under one's breath, combines "gripe" and "mumble."

Post office protocol A standard protocol that enables a user to retrieve e-mail from a server. The Post Office Protocol (POP) is not the only way to retrieve e-mail, but it is the most common.

Posters A single frame of a QuickTime movie that is designated as a static substitute for the movie's video data. The poster is typically the frame that would be printed if a movie was pasted into a document.

Post-production (Post) Work performed on a movie after the end of principal photography, such as editing and digital compositing.

Postscript A programming language developed by Adobe which allows the programmer to describe text, graphic, shapes and other image data on printed or displayed pages.

Pot, pan A rotary device on a mixing console for adjusting stereo, which can by rotated to "pan" a sound right and left.

Potentiometer A three-terminal variable resistor. Two terminals connect to the ends of a flat resistor, while the third terminal is attached to a moveable contact that interfaces with the resistive element. The moveable terminal, or slider, is capable of being positioned from one end of the element to the other. There are many physical types, with the rotary design being the most common, followed by linear slider used in graphic equalizers, for example. Often used as voltage dividers in electronic circuits, the input voltage is applied to the top of the resistive element, while the other end is tied to ground or a common reference and the output is taken from the slider. When the slider is positioned to the top extreme, the output equals the input less of course, the effect of the resistor, moving it to the bottom extreme gives an output of zero volts; and every possible level between is available as the slider is moved from one end to the other. The most commonly encountered application of this arrangement to control the volume of an audio device. In this way the electrical potential is varied, hence, a potentionmeter. The rate at which the voltage changes as the slider is moved is controlled by the taper of the pot. The taper defines the amount of resistive change as a function of travel. Several popular examples are listed below:

Audio taper (aka A-taper): Usually 15% resistance at the 50% rotation point .

Linear taper (aka B-taper): Always 50% resistance at the 50% travel point

Log taper: Often used an an audio taper since its 50% rotation point has 10% resistance

MN taper (" balance control") Special taper developed for home stereo. Consists of two sections (one for each channel) operating opposite each other. Exactly one-half of each section is a zero resistance surface (i.e., solid-copper or equivalent), the next 50% of travel is linear taper. Therefore for one channel rotating the slider through the first 50% of travel does not change the level at all, while the other channel is reduced from full to zero, and vice-versa, with the middle position (usually featuring a center-detent) always passing full signal to each channel.

POTS plain old telephone service The only name recognized around the world for basic analogue telephone service. Telephone System takes the lowest 4kHz of bandwidth on twisted pair wiring. Any service sharing a line with Telephone System must either use frequencies above Telephone System or convert Telephone System to digital and interleave with other data signals.

Power a. The product of applied voltage (potential difference) and current in a direct-current circuit (or the voltage squared divided by the resistance, or the current squared times the resistance). b. The product of the effective values of the voltage and current with the cosine of the phase angle (between current and voltage) in an alternating-current circuit. c.Power The amount of energy (in joules) that a device delivers or consumes divided by the time (in seconds) that the device is operating.

Power amplifier A device that increases a line level signal (typically around two volts into a high impedance) and boosts it in voltage, while allowing sufficient current to be supplied to drive low impedance loudspeakers (that is, impedances nominally in the four to eight ohm range). Most power amplifiers are analogue in design and most use transistors, although some analogue amplifiers use valves. New digital amplifiers are appearing which effectively use a form of pulse width modulation, low pass filtered to reduce the ultrasonic noise, to drive the loudspeakers.

Power factor The ratio of the total power in watts (resistive load) to the total apparent power in voltamperes (VA) (reactive load). The difference between watts and VA is due to reactive load impedance. Apparent power equals watts only for a purely resistive load (i.e., zero degrees phase shift between the applied voltage and the resultant current). Power factor is best thought of intuitively as the multiplier (ranging between 0 and 1) that you must use to obtain the real power from the apparent power. For example if the rms voltage and current of a circuit is measured and multiplied together, the apparent power is obtained, but this value must be multiplied by the power factor to obtain the real power. If the load is purely resistive then the phase difference between the voltage and current will be zero and the power factor will be one, and the apparent power will equal the true power — but only for a resistive load. For a reactive load (any load with inductive and/or capacitive reactance, i.e., any real world load) there will be a phase difference between the voltage and the current due to the phase delay introduced by the reactive elements. Simply put, since the maximum voltage and current do not occur at the same instant of time the amount of power developed is less than the measured rms voltage and current multiplied together.

Power handling (continuous or RMS) A rating of a Driver's ability in optimum conditions to handle a specified amount of audio power (electrical current power) on a constant basis, without damage. This is generally considered to be a conservative and reliable figure to use in judging what types of amplifier power will be most successful with a particular speaker design.

Power supply Within a home entertainment device, the section that provides a suitable voltage and current for the operation of the device. This typically consists of a transformer, rectifier (to turn AC into DC) and regulator (to smooth out fluctuations in the voltage). Power amplifiers in particular are heavily dependent upon the quality of their power supplies, which contribute a significant proportion of their cost and weight.

Powerpoint Microsoft presentation graphics program used frequently at NCAR.

PPCM(Packed pulse code modulation) Another term for MLP. Frequently displayed on the OSD of DVD Audio players as the audio type for MLP material.

PPD(Postscript printer description) A text file that defines the specific characteristics of a postscript printer. The PPD file contains various printer specific options such as margin sizes, page sizes, or custom printing options that a specific model of printer supports. Each printer manufacturer has a PPD file for their various models of printers which work in conjunction with an Operating Systems printer utlities to communicate and generate accurate printed output.

P picture (or P frame). Prediction-coded picture. An MPEG term to describe a picture that is coded using motion-compensated prediction from the past reference picture.

PPP point to point protocol A driver used for accessing a network communications protocol over a phone line. PPP allows connection to the TCP/IP protocol which is the basic internet protocol. A dial-up user gets connected to The Internet via PPP.

Pracical extraction and report language (PERL) Peril is the programming language developed by Larry Wall and known for its strong processing capabilities.

Pre production (pre) Scouting locations, constructing sets, arranging for lighting, planning special effects, editing the script—all the arrangements that precede filming a production.

Pre roll Almost all videotape decks need a running start to get up to speed. This is called pre-roll, and varies between machines from about 3 to 10 seconds. This means that for every edit, source and record decks must first stop, count backward the exact number of frames required for pre-roll, begin playing simultaneously, then at the precise edit point begin recording. It is a mechanical and electronic marvel that video editing can be frame-accurate at all.

Pre-amp A circuit unit which takes a small signal and amplifies it sufficiently to be fed into the power amplifier for further amplification. A pre-amp includes all of the controls for regulating tone, volume, and channel balance.2.

Preamp output Typically found on headunits, a preamp output provides low level, high quality audio signal for use with external amplifiers.

Preamplifier Sometimes called 'Control Amplifier'. Nominally this boosts a low level signal to a level suitable for delivering to a power amplifier, but in these days of fairly high output source components (such as CD players), their main function is to provide a volume control and switch between different sources. Some preamplifiers may incorporate such things as loudness and tone controls and mute buttons. Many preamplifiers also incorporate a phono preamplifier which boosts the low level signal (say 5 to 100 millivolts) of a phono cartridge's output and applies RIAA equalization.

Precedence effect Also known as the Haas effect, this phenomenon identifies the tendency for the ear to attribute all perceived sound to the nearest emitter, even if a more distant speaker is actually louder. Thus, drums that yield 90 percent or more of their energy in the non-directional lower frequencies are perceived as located in the space created by the tiny amount of higher frequency overtones. It is also for this reason that sounds from the rear speakers of a surround system are delayed by 10 to 30 milliseconds, so that they can be experienced as coming from the rear direction.

Preimaging The process of building a movie frame in a memory buffer before it is displayed.

Premastering The process of creating an exact image of what will be placed on a finished CD, including the data, filenames and directories, error detection and correction routines, indexes, and programs.

Pre-mix 1. To mix part of the sounds of a scene or production before mixing all of them or before the voice session;

2. a partial sound mix.

Preparation Information that has to be planted in advance of an action in order to make it believable. Also called priming or the set-up.

Pre-production The first or planning stage in the process of creating a video project

Presence 1. Stage or mike presence, the quality in a performer of looking or sounding as if he or she belongs on a stage, or sounds as if he or she belongs in front of a mike ; presence comes from confidence, technique and indefinable intuitive factors; (studio) overtones on sounds,

2. the audible flow of air and ambient noise picked up by a mike or mics and peculiar to the sonic environment; also called room tone.

Presentation graphics program Allow end-users to put together multimedia shows for presentations, meetings, lectures, and special events.

Presentation software Packages, such as Microsoft Powerpoint, which allow users to create "electronic overhead transparencies". Typically easy to use, presentation software does have all the full multimedia capabilities that you will find in authoring software.

Typical presentation systems:

Gold Disk's Astound (Mac & Windows)

Microsoft's PowerPoint (Mac & Windows)

Kai's Power Show (Mac & Windows)

Harvard Graphics (Windows)

Lotus Freelance Graphics (Windows)

Presenter A person, often well-known, who introduces a production on screen or via voice-over.

Preservation The overall package of administrative and/or practical measures, such as boxing, good housekeeping, careful handling and environmental control, which ensure the survival of documents without specialist intervention. Conservation and restoration procedures are part of a preservation policy.

Preset A collection of system settings stored in a memory that is virtually instantly recallable, typically at the touch of a button.

Preset positioning A function of a pan and tilt unit, including the zoom lens, where a number of certain viewing positions can be stored in the system's memory (usually this is in the telemetry receiver) and can be recalled when required, either upon an alarm trigger, programmed or manual recall.

Pretty good privacy A process for encrypting electronic messages and documents. Pretty Good Privacy (PGP) is the most common form of encryption because it is public, free, and comparatively user-friendly. PGP requires the sender to have special software, available free, to encrypt messages. Once a message is encrypted, it requires an electronic "key" to decrypt. The decryption key can be distributed by the sender or accessed at a public Web site. Because the decryption key is publicly available, PGP does not offer protection from e-mail tampering by recipients. PGP only really protects electronic documents from being intercepted and altered en route.

Primary colors A set of colors that can be combined to produce any desired set of intermediate colors, within a limitation call the "gamut". The primary colors for color television are red, green, and blue. The exact red, green, and blue colors used are dependent on the television standard.

Prime To prepare an audience for an action or an effect, by planting information or employing other preparatory stylistic elements in advance of the action or effect.

Principal One of the lead actors or roles in a dramatic production.

Principal photography (principal filming, principal, shoot) The shooting of the components of a film that involve the lead actors.

Principal point One of the two points that each lens has along the optical axis. The principal point closer to the imaging device is used as a reference point when measuring the focal length of a lens.

Print A positive image on an opaque support. The image may be a photographic still or produced from an engraved plate or similar master.

Print-through An unwanted echo of sound recorded on a reel of analogue tape, caused by saturated layers printing through to adjacent layers wound above and below it.

Privacy As applied to the Internet, this term refers to the desire to prevent personal information from being collected about a Web user without that person's express knowledge and consent. The Internet, which is essentially a worldwide network of connected computers, provides opportunities for computers to collect various types of information from the computers that access them. The information can range from special cookies that enable e-commerce to run more smoothly to a list of recently visited Web sites to personal information stored in files on a computer's hard drive. The degree of access to your computer via the Web depends on the security measures you take to protect your privacy. One of the best ways to protect your privacy is to upgrade your Web browser when a new product becomes available and to use to privacy tools available in the software. Reputable Web sites will post privacy statements that explain what information they collect and why. The privacy of House and Senate information is protected from access via the Web with very strong firewalls.

Privacy statement A statement posted on reputable Web sites that explain the kind of personal information being collected without a visitor's express consent, the reasons it is being collected, and how personal information collected via Web forms or e-mail will be used.

Private data networks Data networks owned by an organisation. The lines are rented from carriers but switching equipment belongs to the organisation.

Problem play A play written to examine a moral, societal, or political problem.

Processor Short for microprocessor, the central processing unit in a computer. The processor is the logic of a computer and functions comparably to a human central nervous system, directing signals from one component to another and enabling everything to happen.

Producer A job title with many definitions, from a kind of glorified flunky to the big boss or creative agent employed on a program or production. In theater outside the United States, the producer is what we call the director. In audio drama, the executive who oversees all production activity and personnel, and who has the creative and managerial responsibility for the final production.

Producer, executive The executive who supervises the producer and who has all administrative and fiscal (sometimes also marketing, promotion and distribution) responsibility for a production.

Production, aphonic Aphonic vocal production means that there is no phonation (no vibration of the vocal folds), as in voiceless whisper or severe laryngitis that prevents vocal fold vibration.

Production assistant (set production assistant, PA, gopher, personal assistant, assistant to, assistant to producer) A person responsible for odd jobs on the set, either for the production as a whole or for individual actors or film makers.

Production breakdown An outline of work to be done on a production meant to increase efficiency.

Production designer An artist responsible for designing the overall visual appearance of a movie.

Production illustrator A person responsible for drawing the storyboards and anything else that needs to be drawn during the production of the movie.

Related terms: Storyboard Artist, Illustrator

Productivity The output of any production process, per unit of input. To increase productivity means to produce more with less.

Program bank A Custom File feature that allows the user to flag the tracks on a disc, indicating whether they should be played or skipped.

Program delivery control Information sent during the vertical blanking interval using teletext to control VCRs in Europe. The specification is ETSI ETS 300 231.

Program play A Custom File feature that allows the user to define a sequence of 12 tracks, in a specific order, for customized playback. Up to two banks of 12 track sequences can be recalled, for up to 24 tracks total.

Programmable gain (PGA) An amplifier with an analog- or digitally-controlled gain amplifier function. A PGA can be used in front of an A/D converter to effectively increase its dynamic range.

Progressive download A component of multimedia architectures such as QuickTime that allows users to watch a video as the file is downloading.

Progressive scan Most video formats are interlaced, which means that to create a single frame the first line is scanned, then the third, then the fifth. When the bottom of the screen is reached the signal returns to the top and scans the second, fourth and so on lines. Progressive scan is a system of writing the whole picture in one sweep, first line, second, third, etc all the way to the bottom. Progressive scan is said to provide a noticeably cleaner, sharper and more stable picture than interlaced. While progressive scan appears to offer significant technical advantages for NTSC DVDs, its advantages for PAL DVDs appear to have been significantly overstated.

PROM(Programmable read only memory) A ROM that can be programmed by the equipment manufacturer (rather than the PROM manufacturer).

Promo A spot announcement advertising the program.

Prompter A person who supplies actors with the their lines if they forget.

Prop Any noise maker (excluding body parts and shoes) during Foley recording.

Property 1. A script, or literary work used as the basis for a script, considered as a production commodity; 2. in theater, any object picked up and handled by actors on stage during a performance, often abbreviated to "prop."

Prosumer A term that combines both Professional and Consumer. Commonly seen as Professional quality with Consumer or lower prices.

Protagonist The main character of a play; the hero.

Protocol A protocol is a standard of technical conventions allowing communication between different electronic devices. It consists of a set of rules for the communication between devices. From a human perspective, different customs of greeting would constitute human greeting protocols. Some cultures raise their right hands; some shake hands, some kiss on the cheeks, some breathe the same air, and so on.

Proximity effect An increase in the bass response of some microphones as the distance between the mike and its sound source is decreased.

Proximity management Allows configuration of servers into logical groupings or clusters, enabling VOD requests to be directed to the nearest server cluster.

Ps (postscript) A standard format for exchange of printable files.

PSA Public service announcement; a commercial for a non-profit organization or a charitable cause.

PSD The suffix or extension used to by Adobe for files created using Adobe Photoshop software. Applications other than Photoshop may also be able to save or open files in this file format.

Pseudo color Pseudo color is a term used to describe a technique that applies color, or shows color, where it does not really exist. We are all familiar with the satellite photos that show temperature differences across a continent or the multicolored cloud motion sequences on the nightly weather report. These are real-world examples of pseudo color. The color does not really exist. A computer uses a lookup table memory to add the color so information, such as temperature or cloud height, is viewable.

Pseudo-noise Any group of code sequences that exhibit a noise-like characteristic.

PSTN Public switched telephone network.

PSU Power supply unit.

Psychoacoustics The scientific study of the relationship between human hearing and its stimulus; in other words, how we hear.

PTZ camera Pan, Tilt and Zoom camera.

PTZ site driver (or telemetry receiver or decoder) An electronic device, usually located with the camera equipment, which receives telemetry control signals in order to operate pan, tilt, zoom and focus functions.

Public domain A concept in copyright law concerning the expiration of copyright and other intellectual property protections (e.g. patents, trade marks). A work is protected only for a limited time, after which it "falls into the public domain," or becomes the common property of the human race.

Public e-mail This is the term we use to differentiate unformatted Internet e-mail from the formatted Internet e-mail sent via a Web form. This is the e-mail that people are most used to. It is sent to an e-mail box using any e-mail editor (netscape communicator, eudora, microsoft outlook, etc.) a person has on his or her computer. The person will type a message and send it directly to an e-mail address, such as contact@domain.com.

Public key The digital key mode available to the public in a public key cryptographic structure.

Publications Documents containing either text or sound or images, or combinations of these, packaged for wider distribution, whether off-line (e.g. printed book, CD-ROM) or on-line (e.g. Web, database for information retrieval).

Pulldown menu A pulldown menu is similar to a dropdown menu but you need to hold the button down to keep the menu open.

Pulse A current or voltage that changes abruptly from one value to another and back to the original value in a finite length of time. Used to describe one particular variation in a series of wave motions.

Pulse code modulation A method of quantizing audio-range analog signals into a digital form for transmission in digital communications systems or for processing in DSP. Effectively the same as Analog-to-Digital conversion.

Pulse distribution amplifier An amplifier designed to boost the strength of the sync as well as other control signals to the proper level for distribution to a number of cameras, special effects generators, or other equipment.

Pumping An undesirable distortion of sound caused by too much compression.

Punch 1. To make an edit or to overdub a sound by turning on the record button as the moving tape passes the record head (also punch in);

2. an edit so made; in theater:

3. to emphasize a word, line or sound;

4. emphasis of a word, line or sound.

Push model When applied to a transfer of metadata between a Publisher and an NBA, the push model describes the scenario whereby the Publisher initiates the transfer by providing or "pushing" data to the NBA.

Push web technology Also referred to as "Web-casting" or "channel-casting", this technology publishes/broadcasts personalized information to subscribers. Then, instead of using bookmarks and search engines to pull down information, users would run a client application that gets updated with data that is "pushed" down by a server.

PVR personal video recorder A device which can record broadcast TV, whether digital or analogue, onto a built in hard disk drive for later replay.

PX64 Common reference to the CCITT standards (H.261 et. al) which describe methods to allow for video system interoperability .

Q

QAM (Quadrature amplitude modulation) Method for modulating two carriers. The carriers can be analogue or digital.

QCIF (Quarter common intermediate format) A videoconferencing format that specifies data rates of 30 frames per second (fps), with each frame containing 144 lines and 176 pixels per line. This is one fourth the resolution of Full CIF. QCIF support is required by the ITU H.261 videoconferencing standard.

Qes The Q of a speaker driver at its free air resonance considering only its electrical losses.

QSIF (quarter standard interface format) The computer industry, which uses square pixels, has defined QSIF to be 160 x 120 active pixels, with a refresh rate of whatever the computer is capable of supporting.

QTC The total Q or resistance of a woofer and sealed enclosure at the system's resonance frequency, considering all resistive losses. A Qtc of .7 has smoothest response and the lowest resonant frequency response. A Qtc of above 1.1 should only be used by those who prefer a "boomy" response.

QTS The total resistance in a series or parallel circuit. This takes into account all Driver resistances, both electrical and mechanical.

Quad Short for quadraphonic; four-channel stereo requiring two front and two back speakers.

Quad chroma Quad chroma refers to a technique where the sample clock is four times the frequency of the color burst. For NTSC this means that the sample clock is about 14.32 MHz (4 x 3.579545 MHz), while for PAL the sample clock is about 17.73 MHz (4 x 4.43361875 MHz). The reason these are popular sample clock frequencies is that, depending on the method chosen, they make the chrominance (color) decoding and encoding easier.

Quad display Equipment that simultaneously displays four images from four separate sources on a single monitor each occupying a quadrant of the screen.

Quad, matrixed Three-channel stereo, required when broadcasting quad under certain conditions, using two front channels and one rear channels matrixed to give a quadraphonic impression.

Quadrature amplitude (QAM) This communication scheme involves the modulation of a carrier by two different signals. One signal modulates the carrier (I) and the other signal modulates the carrier shifted by 90^{0} (Q). The two modulated carriers are then summed and transmitted as a single I&Q modulated carrier. The receiver decodes the I&Q channels and demodulates them 90^0 apart. QAM lends itself to the transmission of data in a digital format by assigning discrete levels to the two signal inputs which creates a "constellation" of possible digital word combinations on the I&Q graph. The following illustrates a 16-QAM constellation (4 levels of input on the I channel/4 levels of input on the Q channel).

Quadrature modulation The modulation of two carrier components, which are 90 degrees apart in phase.

Quality or voice quality The quality of the sounds we hear is determined by the sound made at the larynx, the filtering of the sound by the vocal tract (the airway above the larynx), and the reception and processing of the sound by the ear and brain. Breathy voice quality suggests that a relatively large amount of air is used during phonation . Some of the air is not modulated by the vibrating vocal folds, but comes through the glottis as turbulent flow converted to noise. Usually when there is breathy phonation, the glottis does not fully close during vocal fold vibration.radio, commercial. The system of stations financed primarily by the sale of advertising time.

Quantization The process of converting, or digitizing, the almost infinitely variable amplitude of an analog waveform to one of a finite series of discrete levels. Performed by the A/D converter.

Quantization error Error resulting from quantizing an analog waveform to a discrete level. In general the longer the word length, the less the error.

Quantization noise or 'quantisation noise' in Australian A form of harmonic distortion produced in all digital systems. Low level signals do not use all the bits available in the digital system (that's why they are low level signals!) Consequently they operate as though the digital system has a low bit depth (say, an eight bit system or even four). This increases their harmonic distortion. By its nature, harmonic distortion generated by digital systems tends to give relatively high levels of odd-order harmonics, which are far more irritating than the even order harmonics to which analogue systems tend. This is routinely addressed by adding dither to digital signals.

Quasi-parametric A type of equalizer. A quasi-parametric (also known as "semi-parametric") EQ will allow control over the frequency and gain of each band of equalization, but not the number of frequencies controlled (bandwidth). The midrange EQs on mixing consoles are often quasi-parametric. More flexible in some ways than a graphic EQ, a quasi-parametric EQ does not offer the full range of adjustment found in a fully parametric design.

Quick compressor A compressor compatible with Indeo video interactive that handles data more quickly than the offline compressor. Videos that compress in hours can take minutes using the quick compressor.

Quick release (terminal) A means for securing a wire conductor to a terminal connector that permits easy attachment and removal. In the usual form, this will involve a spring-loaded clip, which needs only to be pressed to either secure or detach a cable end.

QuickTime QuickTime is a file format for storing and playing back movies with sound. Though developed and supported primarily by Apple Computer, this flexible format isn't limited to Macintosh operating systems. it's also commonly used in Windows systems, and other types of computing platforms. In Windows, QuickTime files usually appear with the ".MOV" filename extension.

Since 2002, Apple has started using MPEG4 video encoding on its QT streams, producing much better, if not excellent, video quality.

Quicktime for windows Apple's multimedia playback environment for Microsoft's Windows operating system.

Quicktime streaming Apple's streaming media addition to the QuickTime architecture.

Quicktime virtual reality An application from Apple that offers tools create panorama, objects, and scenes.

Quicktime VR (QTVR) A part of the QuickTime architecture that allows 360-degree interactive panoramas to be developed and viewed.

Quiescent current The term given to describe the amount of current consumed by a circuit when it is not performing any work (sometimes referred to as standby current).

R

R′-Y′ In video, the red-minus-luma signal, also called a color difference signal. When added to the luma (Y′) signal, it produces the red video signal.

RA RA stands for real audio.

RA is a Real Media audio file extension, indicating a file readable by the RealOne Media Player.

Rack focusing Abruptly shifting the focus during a stationary shot from one plane of depth to another, often from one character to another, so that the viewer's attention will shift to the sharper image..

Radio button When you have a list of items in a website form, for example, and you can only choose one, then they are usually presented with small, round "buttons" next to them. One of these is always preselected by default, but this is cleared if you select a different option. For example, if there are two radio buttons labelled "yes" and "no", and "yes" has been preselected, then clicking the "no" button will deselect the "yes" button.

Radio data system (RDS) RDS stands for radio data system. RDS tuners can automatically tune in stations according to the types of music (or talk) they broadcast. RDS also enables a receiver to display text messages and even graphics (usually call letters and format information) that many FM stations include on a subcarrier signal within their normal broadcast signal. Some RDS equipped tuners can even override with traffic alerts or emergency broadcasts, during playback of other media CD MD, or cassette. There are other useful features too, many of which are offered by the growing number of RDS stations.

Radio, community The system of non-commercial broadcasters, many of them public radio stations, emphasizing volunteer, inclusive, community participation in station operations.

Radio, public The system of non-commercial stations operating nominally in the community interest, under qualifications set by the Corporation for Public Broadcasting.

Radio, university The system of non-commercial stations, usually not CPB qualified, operated at low power by universities primarily to serve the university community and to train or provide recreation for student volunteers. Many American colleges have their own 50-watt stations.

RAID (Redundant array of inexpensive disks) This a technology of connecting a number of hard drives into one mass storage device, which can be used, among other things, for digital recording of video images.

Rainbow effect A sometimes irritating optical illusion produces by many DLP projectors. These are flashes of short tri-colour RGB stripes that tend to appear away from the centre of vision while watching a movie. They are more apparent during monochrome, or near-monochrome scenes. They appear to be an artifact of the spinning colour wheel used in most DLP projectors. When three-panel DLP projectors become feasible in the home, it is likely that this effect will no longer be a problem because these do not use a colour wheel. Manufacturers have attempted to eliminate this effect by increasing the number of colour filter windows in the wheel and spinning it faster. Recent high quality DLP projectors have certainly reduced the effect until it rarely appears. Apparently not everyone notices the effect.

Random access memory The short term memory of a computer. The random access memory (RAM) stores recent and frequently used information and commands, which enables programs to operate more efficiently. If programs require more RAM than you have available, then information and commands must be stored on the computer's hard drive – the computer's long term memory. It is more difficult for a computer to access information from the hard drive, so it takes longer. Programs operate sluggishly or crash frequently when there is not enough RAM. The more RAM your computer has, the faster programs can function. The primary limitation on the performance gains you can realize by adding RAM to your computers is the speed of their processors.

Random code encryption (or varicode2 transmitting system) In auto security systems, these terms describe anti-code grabbing technology, a feature which prevents malicious persons who use a special receiver to intercept remote control codes, from using it to defeat the alarm.

Random interlace In a camera that has a free-running horizontal sync as opposed to a 2:1 interlace type.

Random play Also known as shuffle play. In CD players and changers, this function randomizes the order of selections during playback. Some CD players offer a "Random Play with Delete" feature that prevents a piece from being repeated once it has been played.

Range (audio) Usually described as frequency range, this is a system's frequency transmission limits, beyond which the frequency is attenuated below a specified tolerance. Also, the frequency band or bands within which a receiver or component is designed to operate.

Rank The brand-name of a device used for film-to-video transfer.

Rarefaction In sound waves, the opposite of compression. An area of decreased air pressure caused by a sound wave. In a graphical depiction of a cyclical waveform rarefaction occurs when the wave is in the bottom segment. Sound is simply the alternating compression and rarefaction of air at varying and often overlapping frequencies, within a range to which humans are sensitive.

RARP (Reverse address resolution protocol) This protocol makes life easier to change IP addresses on machines. For all the machines on a network to see one another, they must know the others' IP addresses. If the IP address of one machine changes, the change must be done on each of the other machines. This would take a million years, so enters RARP which makes it possible to manage changes centrally and broadcast them to the other machines. RARP looks for an IP address when given a hardware address (the opposite of ARP).

Raster and raster graphics On CRT (cathode ray tube) and LCD (liquid crystal display) monitors images are displayed on a raster along X- and Y-axes. A raster graphic is an image displayed on this raster grid. When reference is made to the image file that is displayed on the raster, it is called a bitmap file as the image information bits are mapped onto the raster.

Ratio One of the parameters which can be varied on dynamic range processors such as compressors and expanders. It represents the compression or expansion ratio between input and output levels. A compressor with a 2:1 ratio would reduce the output gain to half of the input value above the threshold. An expander with a 1:80 ratio would reduce the output gain to 1/80th of the input value below the threshold.

Raw A bitstream format in which the video data is uncompressed.

Raw footage Pre-Edited recordings usually taken directly from the source recorder.

Raw VBI data A technique where VBI data (such as teletext and captioning data) is sampled by a fast sample clock (i.e. 27 MHz), and output. This technique allows software decoding of the VBI data to be done.

RC Time code Rewritable time code, used in consumer video products.

RCA Also called "phono plug" or "RCA phono," popular cable connector for home audio as well as video components. Standard connection for direct audio/video inputs/outputs. Not to be confused with phone plug.

RCA connector A connector typically used for audio and video signals, with some professional equipment and most consumer equipment. Compare BNC connector, XLR connector.

RCA plug/socket The most common audio and video connection standard. They are used for composite video (usually with a yellow colour code), component video (three of them in this case, inappropriately but traditionally marked with red, green and blue colour codes), digital coaxial and standard audio connections. Sometimes called a 'cinch' plug/socket.

RD (Resource description) Consists of a URL and a number of value-attribute pairs.

RDM (Resource description messages) A technique for encoding and transmitting metadata relating to an Internet resource accessible via a URL.

RDM agent Generates Resource Descriptions (RD) based on the content of Internet material.

RDM server Stores a collection of RDMs, to be accessed across the WWW.

RE The inherent Direct Current resistance of a speaker's voice coil.

Reactance In Ac circuits, whether passive or active, a form of frequency dependent resistance produced by inductors. Such an inductive loading will allow all dc current to pass without change, but will attenuate various, mostly higher frequencies, depending on the nature of the coil.

Reaction shot A shot (usually a close-up) that shows a character's response to what we have just seen in the previous shot..

Read only Read Only applies to file permissions and specifies that the file can be opened but not altered and saved as the same file.

Read To copy data to a place where it can be used by a program. The term is commonly used to describe copying data from a storage medium, such as a disk, to main memory.

Readability This is the ease with which content can be read and understood. Readability is affected by the complexity and length of sentences, and the difficulty of the language that is used.

Read-through 1. A run-through in which the cast reads a play aloud without movement or interruption from the director; table work;

2. to hold or participate in a read-through.

Real media A real networks, Inc file format for encoding digital audio and video files. Can be of any size compressed to match many different connection speeds, or bandwidth.

Real time compression Compression of movies as soon as they come into the computer - also known as one-step capture.

Real time Sending and receiving of messages occurs simultaneously without delay, "live". A transaction which occurs without significant delay from start to finish, i.e., taking a class from a "live" instructor and getting immediate feedback as opposed to watching a videotape of the class sometime after the actual event.

Realism A type of political expressionism originating in Germany after World War I; the theatrical and literary equivalent to the editorial cartoon.

RealMedia One of the first CODECs for delivering streaming video over the Internet. Like other CODECs, RealMedia (comprised of RealVideo, RealAudio, and other file formats created by Real) use compression algorithms for eliminating data that can be considered as extraneous or not as important as other information. RealMedia and Windows Media are the two most widely used technologies for streaming video today.

Realplayer Formerly known as RealAudio which is a browser plugin and independent media player which allows you listen and view audio and video files.

Real-time compression Compression of movies as soon as they come into the computer - also known as one-step capture.

RealVideo RealVideo is a streaming video format developed by RealNetworks. RealVideo is probably the most popular streaming video format in the world, although its quality is horrible if you compare it to MPEG4-based formats like DivX or WMV.

Recap 1. (recapitulation) a summary of the action that has transpired thus far in the dramatic work, as at the beginning of serial episodes or as appears when necessary to reinforce plot points;

2. to make such a summary, to recapitulate.

Receive only codec A video codec configured so as to be able only to receive communications signals and process them for local output, for use at receive locations in point-to-multipoint or for broadcast applications where two-way codec communication with the sending location is not required.

Receiver authentication A security service which guarantees that the recipient of a message is the person to whom the message was addressed.

Receiver In the stereo world, an amplifier with a tuner built in. Often used as short hand for home theatre receiver.

Record creation The generation of bibliographic records by, for example, a bibliographic agency.

Record supply The transmission of previously generated bibliographic records.

Recordist The recording engineer; the engineer operating the console during mastering.

Rectangular pixels Pixels that are not "square pixels" are "rectangular pixels".

Rectilinear lens A lens which produces an image in which lines that appear straight to the human eye appear straight in the image. Most lenses fall into this category and all that are 35mm and above will simply because they are within the range of our own eyes. However wide angle lenses capture more than our eyes can see and inherently produce large amounts of distortion. Because of the complex optics of wide angle rectilinear lenses it is not possible to buy a 180 degree rectilinear lens. Generally rectilinear lenses are available down to a focal length of around 14mm (approx. 114 degree VFOV, portrait).

Red book A music CD.

Red, green and blue (RGB) RGB is the colour system used on electronic devices that emit light, such as televisions, computer monitors and colour handheld devices like personal digital assistants (PDAs). Websites are displayed in the RGB system. Printed matter (which reflects light) uses the cyan, magenta, yellow and black (CMYK) system.

Red eye An effect caused by light from a camera's flash bouncing off a subjects eye back into the camera's lens.

Redundant Video data information that does not change over time (temporarily redundant) or video data information where a given pixel is surrounded with similar pixels (spatially redundant).

Reflectors A surface used to reflect light toward something that needs to be illuminated, such as when photographing a person's face. Reflectors can be purchased or constructed cheaply with aluminum foil and a backing material such as cardboard.

Refraction The deflection away from or towards the normal, of a beam of light as it passes between two media of differing densities.

Region codes Region codes in this instance mean flags implemented in DVD-Video discs that determine the geographic area where the DVD-Video disc is being sold and where it can be watched. These codes ensure that one country doesn't get a DVD movie before the same movie is out in that country's theatres. In their corporate omniscience, movie studios have carved the planet into regions with each region having a specific code.

All DVD players and discs have region codes. A DVD player and disc must be of the same region or the disc will not play. If you want to watch movies from other countries, you need a multiregion DVD player. This will allow you to play any disc from any region.

The region controls are also implemented in PC's DVD-ROM drivers, normally in three levels. First of all, if the DVD-ROM driver is manufactured after 1st of January, 2000, the driver itself has physical locks implemented in it to permit playback of only specific region code. Secondly, all newer operating systems, including Windows 2000 and Windows XP, have region control measurements built-in. And finally, the DVD player software, such as WinDVD or PowerDVD, have region control measurements built-in.

Register Perceptually distinct region of vocal quality as pitch or loudness is changed; speaking registers are commonly differentiated as (from low to high) pulse, modal and falsetto.

Registration 1. An adjustment associated with color monitors and projectors to ensure that the three electron beams (the three primary colors) are hitting the proper color dots/stripes on the phosphor screen, A similar adjustment exists on color tube cameras.

2. The alignment of film frame-by-frame in a camera, projector or telecine. Good registration is critical in order to eliminate gate weave.

Rehabilitation act A law first passed in 1973 and amended in 1993 and 1998 whose primary goal is to foster economic independence for people with disabilities in part by providing funding and enabling greater access to government information and services for people with disabilities. Section 508 of the Rehabilitation Act requires that federal electronic information, including Web sites, be accessible to people with disabilities

Rem or remote wire The cable connected between the amplifier and the receiver that turns on the amplifier whenever the receiver is on. The receiver's connection supplies a 12 volt signal only, that may be used simultaneously to turn on such devices as an equalizer, amplifier, and to raise the antenna.

Remote a television or radio session held "in the field," that is, outside of the studio; a production or part of a production so made;pertaining to field production;

Remote control A transmitting and receiving of signals for controlling remote devices such as pan and tilt units, lens functions, wash and wipe control and similar. It may also refer to the hand held controls for some VCRs and other CCTV equipment.

Remote location Videomaking performed at a certain location other than the producer's studio.

Removable media drive A computer file storage device with media (tapes, optical discs, magnetic cartridges, and so on.) that can be inserted and removed.

Rendering The final step in creating a 3-D animation that involves giving objects attributes such as colors, surface textures, and degrees of transparency; the process of creating individual frames of a transition in a digital movie

Repertory company or repertory ensemble A theater troupe consisting of actors engaged for the season, presenting works in repertory; used somewhat improperly, a theater troupe presenting regular seasons of works, whether sequentially or alternating, whether with an ensemble engaged for the season or performers engaged per production.

Representationalism Playwrighting and theatrical presentation in which action is presented on a bare or austere stage and in which much of the action and locale are suggested by the lines are said to be "representational." Examples include Greek tragedy and Elizabethan plays.

Residual subcarrier This is the amount of color subcarrier information present in white, gray, or black areas of a composite color video signal (ideally, there is none present). The number usually appears as -n dB. The larger "n" is, the better.

Resistance Most all conductors of electrons exhibit a property called resistance. Resistance impedes the flow of current. It is measured in units called Ohms. With a water hose, resistance could be regarded as friction between the water and the hose. A larger hose would create less friction and have a lower resistance than a smaller hose. In electrical circuits, small round cylinders with wires on either end are called resistors. These typically reduce the flow of electrons to serve the specific requirements of the circuit elements, such as amplification or switching functions.

Resize To change the size of an image by reducing or increasing the resolution and/ or the square measurement of the file.

Resolution This is the basic measurement of how much information is visible for an image. It is usually described as "h" x "v". The "h" is the horizontal resolution (across the display) and the "v" is the vertical resolution (down the display). The higher the numbers, the better, since that means there is more detail to see. If only one number is specified, it is the horizontal resolution.

Displays specify the maximum resolution they can handle, determined by the display technology and the electronics used. The actual resolution will be the resolution of either the source or the display, whichever is lower.

Vertical resolution is the number of white-to-black and black-to-white transitions that can be seen from the top to the bottom of the picture. The maximum number is the number of active scan lines used by the image. The actual vertical resolution may be less due to processing, interlacing, overscanning, or limited by the source.

Horizontal resolution is the number of white-to-black and black-to-white transitions that can be seen from the left to the right of the picture. For digital displays, the maximum number is the number of active pixels used by a scan line. For both analog and digital displays, the actual horizontal resolution may be less due to processing, overscanning, or limited by the source.

Resolution independent A term to describe equipment that can work in more than resolution. For example, most equipment can do film resolution or video resolution, but not both. Resolution independent equipment can work in both.

Resolution, graphic considerations for the web RGB Red-green-blue, the primary colors composing light. Applied to color monitors, for example.

Resonance The tendency for a mechanical or electrical systems to vibrate or resonate sympathetically at a certain frequency when stimulated by external energy. Every element and material has a particular natural resonance point. The job of the speaker designer is to minimize these output peaks whenever they appear so that a smooth response is created.

Resonant frequency The frequency at which a system offers the lowest impedance, allowing the highest power transfer. In the case of physical systems, it is the frequency at which the vibration is greatest for a given input. For loudspeaker drivers, the resonant frequencies of the drivers are very important characteristics to take into account in the design process, avoiding placing them in the range of operation for higher frequency drivers, and carefully designing the enclosure to make best use of the resonant frequency of the woofer.

Resource interchange file format (RIFF) A tagged-file specification used to define standard formats for multimedia files. Tagged-file structure helps prevent compatibility problems that often occur when file-format definitions change over time. Because each piece of data in the file is identified by a standard header, an application that does not recognize a given data element can skip over the unknown information.

Restoration The process of restoring an object to a condition as close as possible to that when it was first made.

Retake The re-shooting of a scene.

RETMA Former name of the EIA association Some older video test charts carry the name.

Retrace Retrace is what the electron beam does when it gets to the right-hand edge of the CRT display to get back to the left-hand edge. Retrace happens during the horizontal blanking time.

Reverb Abbreviation for reverberation, a complex blend of multiple interacting reflections within an enclosed space which combines with the direct sound from a source and defines the character of the sound in a room or hall. It is also used for a signal processor which can generate an approximation of natural reverb.

Reverberant sound field A speaker system in which a significant amount, perhaps most, of the sound that you hear is coming from reflections from surfaces within the listening space rather that directly from the loudspeakers. Reverberant sound field speakers tend to have a larger sweet spot, and produce a more rounded stereo image with greater depth than direct sound field speakers. Reverberant sound field sound can be achieved by choosing speakers with a very wide dispersion, such as bipole speakers, or by purpose designed speakers from companies such as Bose.

Reverse angle A shot of the action from the opposite perspective.

Revert Similar to undo in which the application will change your document back to a previous state.

RF interference Noise in a video signal caused by unwanted broadcast signals (often from AM radio signals)

RF Modulator A device that converts a signal (typically audio and/or video) into a radio frequency. This can be received by a tuner and converted to perceptible information

RF radio frequency Refers to a composite video signal superimposed on a very high (radio) frequency capable of being broadcast through the atmosphere. Standard television sets receive these signals, separate the composite signal from the RF, and then decode and display the composite signal.

Until recently, television sets were designed to receive only RF signals, which were applied to their antenna terminals. VCRs, videodisc players and some computers provide RF signals for use with televisions. The process of mixing composite video with RF, only to have it removed again by the television, further degrades the image quality.

RF signal Radio frequency signal that belongs to the region up to 300 GHz.

RFC request for comment An RFC is a documents that states protocol standards, proposed changes, information bulletins about the internet. The name is somewhat of a misnomer in some cases as an RFC document often serves as the standard which is already being accepted as valid from a certain date until it is officially changed. An RFC may also be an explanation of an existing practice.

RG-58 A coaxial cable designed with 50 Ohm characteristic impedance; therefore, not suitable for CCTV.

RG-59 A video coaxial cable with 75 Ohm characteristic impedance. A type of coaxial cable that is most common in use in small to medium-size CCTV systems. It has an outer diameter of approx. 6 mm and it is a good compromise between maximum distances achievable (up to 266m) and good transmission.

RGB (Red green blue) The most widely-used color model for images displayed on electronic screens. It is based on the color subtraction that results from shining white light through a colored medium such as a slide. Contrast with CMYK.

.rtf File extension that is associated with digital documents created in a text based editor but saved as Rich Text Format (RTF), an open source document formatting scheme that allows files to be saved with formatting intact where it would otherwise be lost if simply saved as a text file.

RGB monitor A type of color monitor that receives separate signals for each color (red, green, and blue).

Rhetoric 1. The art or study of using language effectively and persuasively; a treatise or book discussing this art;

2. Skill in using language effectively and persuasively;

3. a style of speaking or writing, especially the language of a particular subject;

4. Language that is elaborate, pretentious, insincere, or intellectually vacuous.

RIAA equalization (record industry association of America equalization) When converting an electrical signal to mechanical motion, there is an inconvenient fact: the lower the frequency, the higher the excursion of the moving part for a given signal level. This is important in several fields, particularly with LPs. The grooves of an LP would wobble very widely if the bass frequencies were cut in direct proportion to the signal. The playing time would, consequently, be very short and turntables would have a great deal of difficulty in holding their styli in place within the groove. So before LPs are cut, the signal is subjected to RIAA equalization. This reduces the bass by an enormous amount (-17dB at 50 hertz), and increases the treble equally hugely (+13dB at 10,000 hertz). A circuit built into the phono preamplifier of the playback equipment reverses this EQ, boosting the bass back to its proper level and handily cutting the treble. This last has the welcome effect of substantially reducing the hiss produced by the scraping of the stylus within the groove. Note: old-style ceramic cartridges did not require this second step of reversing the EQ because their frequency response characteristics roughly approximated this anyway.

Ribbon driver The ribbon tweeter driver is a very thin corrugated aluminum "voice coil" hanging freely like a streamer in a side-by-side magnetic field. A ribbon is actually a type of dynamic driver, in which the voice coil is in the form of a flat, ribbon-shaped conductor which, positioned between opposite magnetic fields, actually becomes the diaphragm itself. The ribbon is free of the stretched film resonance's and obstructing magnets of the planar-magnetic, so it offers outstanding pulse response, uniform drive, and a good approximation of a line source, but the efficiency and impedance are both phenomenally low and the base technology is not usable as a woofer due to the small area. Most practical ribbons either use a step-down transformer or ask the amplifier to drive a ½ ohm load (not a practical solution for most).

The ribbon cannot be used to produce low frequencies. To create a moving element large enough to generate frequencies lower than a few hundred Hertz would mean moving opposing magnetic poles so far apart that they no longer exert a sufficient magnetic field over the entire area of the ribbon. But, a ribbon offers very precise treble around, superior to dynamics or electrostatics.

In many ways, a ribbon driver can be an excellent performer: the moving element (the ribbon itself) is extremely light, allowing good speed and transient performance as well as freedom from coloration. They are however, expensive, and hard to find.

Ride gain To manually control the volume during recording or mixing.

RIFF (resource interchange file format) File format for storing sound and graphics so they can be played by different types of computers.

RIFF chunk A chunk with chunk identifier Resource interchange file format (RIFF) that includes an identifying code and zero or more subchunks, the contents of which depend on the form type.

RIFF file A file whose format complies with one of the published Resource interchange file format (RIFF) forms. Examples of RIFF files include WAVE files for waveform audio data, RMID files for Musical Instrument Digital Interface (MIDI) sequences, and RDIB files for device-independent bitmaps.

RIFF form A file-format specification based on the Resource interchange file format (RIFF) standard.

Rim light The dimmer portion of light at the outer edges of a video light's light pattern.

Ringing The tendency for any vibrating surface to continue to produce the same frequency. This is limited by the decay time over which the inertia of other forces act to repress the motion. In acoustics, this tendency is known as reverberance. In human physiology, a condition called tinitus causes the sensation of ringing, which is actually a nerve disorder rather than a problem with the ear's mechanism.

Ripple (speaker) The maximum deviation from flat response, measured in decibels-it indicates the port's effect on woofer output.

Rise time The time taken for a signal to make a transition from one state to another; usually measured between the 10% and 90% completion points of the transition. Shorter, or faster rise times require more bandwidth in a transmission channel.

RLE (run length encoding) Microsoft's CODEC used for no more than 256 colors.

RM RM stands for real media.

Real Media is one of the most popular formats for streaming content on the Internet, RealMedia includes the RealAudio codec for sound clips and RealVideo codec for movies.

RealAudio and RealVideo files are often given the common RealMedia ".RM" file extension. RealMedia files are often heavily compressed so they can stream over dial-up Internet connections.

RMS (Root mean square) This is a measure of voltage or (incorrectly) power output. The latter is often quoted in the specifications for an amplifier or home theatre receiver. Measuring voltage is simple with direct current, even if it varies in level. You can simply average the values over time. But alternating current, when arithmetically averaged, gives you a value of zero or close to zero. If you square each value (multiply it by itself) before taking the average, and then take the square root of that average, you not only get a reasonable representation of the voltage, but a value that provides effectively the same amount of power as a similar DC voltage into a resistive load. What is called 'RMS power output' for amplifiers is calculated using the RMS voltage delivered by the amplifier to test loads, so in that sense the term is not entirely misleading (however something like 'average sine wave power output' is far less irritating). Such figures should include a measure for the amount of distortion generated at that power. This should be well under 0.5%. If the figure is 10% (often used with home entertainment systems) the figure should be discounted substantially.

RMVB RMVB stands for Real Media Variable Bitrate.

RMVB is commonly used to contain Real Video 9 and RA (Real Audio).

Robot A robot is a piece of software that browses the web, retrieving and analysing web documents. This data can be used to index documents for search engines.

Role, supporting A secondary character in a dramatic work.

Roll off A graduated reduction in the strength of audio output above and below certain specified frequencies.

Rollover image A rollover image is used in the context of navigation where an image button, that serves as a link elsewhere, changes into a different image because of some or other associated pointer behaviour (e.g. mouse down).

Romance A literary work or play appealing to a sense of adventure, often episodic and melodramatic, taking place on a vast terrain and emphasizing thrilling incidents and romantic love; a literary work or play, about the love lives of appealing principal characters, and celebrating the importance of romantic love.

Roof-mount antenna A permanently-installed antenna located in the center of a vehicle's roof.

Room response The effectiveness of any speaker system is a function of the room or environment in which it is played. The coupling of the speaker to the room or listening space is a function that is as critical as that between the woofer and the enclosure. When in doubt, experiment! This is the only practical method of achieving the optimal response form speakers in nearly any situation. Of course, computer modeling based on real time measurements could be substituted, albeit quite expensively.

Room tone The audio characteristics of a space in which recording takes place. A sound recordist will typically make a recording of the natural ambient "silence" in a set/ location for when silence is required. Inserting this recorded "silence" will sound more natural in the finished production than complete absence of audio.

Room-size video This system is also based on a microcomputer, with the video display projected through one or two large (27" or larger) monitors, or through a digital video projector for screen or wall display. These systems are designed for visibility and interaction of larger groups of people, such as a classroom of 30 students or a meeting of

12 people. Often, such a system includes microphones set in the middle of a table designed to pick up voices from anywhere around the table. In a classroom setting, demonstration and presentation tools, such as overhead projectors and electronic blackboards are used to support typical instructional settings, and may include a microphone for each participating student.

Roswell Odetics Facility Management System - Software that automates the acquisition, preparation, media management, and on-air presentation of video and audio material.

Rotary volume An analog or linear volume control operated with a knob to raise and lower the volume, as opposed to separate digital "up and down" pushbuttons or pushbar.

Rotoscoping A rotoscope is an animation stand used to project a sequence of action frames against a surface. An artist could then trace a set of animation frames. For example, the background of the scene would be projected, and the actor is drawn, or edited onto this background – i.e. compositing. This process can now be done with computers and a rotoscope is no longer used. The term rotoscoping is now used for the doctoring film or animation sequences frame-by-frame.

Rough cut A "draft" of a film that follows assembly but precedes final cut.

Router A router functions like a traffic officer, directing the flow of data to targets. It receives a packet of data, reads the address, and passes it on to the next machine in the line.

In the beginning of the internet routers were typically in a separate box so as to reduce the load on the web (i.e. HTTP) server. However, router software may reside on the HTTP server.

A router operates at the network level of the OSI model. For each protocol there would be a different router as they are protocol dependent. However, routers do not bother about different network ologies and can therefore be used to pass data along different networks such as Ethernet and Token Ring.

A router relates to a bridge and a gateway. A bridge allows any frame that is allowed to be passed on to a segment, while a router only allows addressed frames. A router is thus more intelligent than a bridge. However, routers work much harder than bridges, and therefore their throughput is much lower.

Routing switcher An electronic device that routes a user-supplied signal (audio, video, etc.) from any input to any user-selected output. This is a broadcast term for matrix switchers, as we know them in CCTV.

Routing system A system that allows the video and/or audio signal to be channeled or directed.

RPTV (Rear projection television) A large screen TV which does not use a direct view CRT, but three single-coloured CRTs, the light from which bounces off a mirror within the TV and illuminates a flat translucent screen from behind. Some newer models use LCD or DLP projectors rather than the CRTs.

RS (Recognised standard) A set of specifications for data transmission written by the electronics industries association (EIA).

RS 170 The EIA (Electronics Industries Association) standard that defines the timing of broadcast video in the United States, Japan, and several other markets. It specifies a 15.75 KHz horizontal and a 60 Hz vertical interlaced scan frequency as well as other aspects of the composite signal such as voltage, sync levels and timing of blanking.

Interlacing is the process by which two fields, called scan lines, are interleaved on the screen. Due to the limitations of video devices at the time the standard was being set in 1957, the speed of broadcast signals and picture tubes required the image to be displayed in parts.

The solution allowed the partial update of video pictures to remain unnoticed to the viewer. An RS-170 video frame contains 525 lines and is displayed 60 times per second for a total of 15 750 lines, or 15.75 KHz. Of these lines, only the odd or even lines are displayed with each frame. A total of 60 frames per second allows 30 frames per second, or a 30 Hz update of each line.

Like the RS-343 standard, RS-170 is strictly a timing specification for monochrome video signals. By combining three such signals to control individual red, green, and blue sweep circuits, you can create a full-color system. The RS-170 mode is available with the Macintosh video card as a way for VCRs and large screen projectors, not capable of high-frequency scans, to interface with the Macintosh. Compare RS-343, RS-170A, RS-170 RGB.

RS 343 An EIA (Electronics Industries Association) standard for non-broadcast high resolution monochrome video, specifying a 60 Hz non-interlaced scan with a composite sync signal with timings that produce a non-interlace (progressive) scan at 675 to 1023 lines.

While the Macintosh version of the RS-343 signal varies somewhat, it essentially follows the guidelines necessary for connection to RS-343 display devices. Therefore, with a display adapter (available from Covid , Extron, or Inline) the Mac can drive a RS-343 device (i.e. video projector or large monitor).

The major differences between Macintosh video and the RS-343 standard are: a separate TTL level composite sync signal on pin 3, the separate video lines used to produce RGB color, a vertical scan rate of 66.67 Hz to reduce screen flicker, and a voltage white level of 1 volt for its red and blue signals and 1.3 volts on its green signal. RS-343 provides for a 60-Hz signal but has been changed to 66.67 Hz on the Macintosh video card to prevent the screen flicker which is visible at 60 Hz. The inclusion of the analog composite sync found on pin 5 of the video card connector, called the green signal, allows for monochrome composite video.

RS 125 A SMPTE parallel component digital video standard.

RS 232 A format of digital communication using a three wire unbalanced presentation. The RS-232 standard defines the presentation and voltages for asynchronous communications, but it does not define how the data should be represented by the bits, i.e., it does not define the overall message format and protocol. It is very often used in computers, CCTV and communications between keyboards and matrix switchers.

RS 422 This is an advanced format of digital communication when compared to RS-232. A major difference is that the presentation is balanced line and the signalling is differential. In simple terms, the signal transmitted is read at the receiving end as the difference between the two wires without a reference to earth. So if there is common mode noise induced along the line, it will be cancelled out. RS-422 can drive lines of up to 1200m and distribute data on to up to 10 receivers.

RS 485 This is an advanced format of digital communications compared to RS-232. It is a balanced line transmission system. The major improvement over RS422 is in the number of receivers that can be driven with this format, up to 32. It is classically a half duplex 2 wire presentation.

RSDL RSDL stands for Reverse Spiral Dual Layer. It is a storage method that uses two layers of information on one side of a DVD. For movies that are longer than can be recorded on one layer, the disc stops spinning, reverses direction, and begins playing from the next layer.

RSS Is short for Rich Site Summary. RSS is an XML-based language which represents information on the World Wide Web in a form which may be syndicated (subscribed to) in special news reader applications. RSS allows your news reader program to bring a websites news feed directly to your computer.

RSVP RSVP (resource reservation protocol) Is a control protocol that allows a receiver to request a specific quality of service level over an IP network. Real-time applications, such as streaming video, use RSVP to reserve necessary resources at routers along the transmission paths so that the requested bandwidth can be available when the transmission actually occurs.

RTP RTP (real time transport protocol) Is a packet format and protocol for the transport of real-time audio and video data over an IP network. The data may be any file format, including MPEG-2, MPEG-4, ASF, QuickTime, etc. Implementing time reconstruction, loss detection, security and content identification, it also supports multicasting (one source to many receivers) and unicasting (one source to one receiver) of real-time audio and video. One-way transport (such as video-on-demand) as well as interactive services (such as Internet telephony) are supported. RTP is designed to work in conjunction with RTCP.

RTT real time technology Which allows a user to receive data in real time (measured in milliseconds or microseconds).

RTV real time video A form of interframe compression that allows for compression rates of up to 150 to 1.

Rule of thirds A composition theory based on a screen being divided into three parts or segments andplacing the subjects along the resulting lines.

Rules Instructions that describe how information should be processed. Many computer programs rely on rules to function. The rules that we refer to most often are the instructions you would use in conjunction with filters in your e-mail management software or CMS to automate e-mail processing. You could, for example, set up rules that tell your e-mail management software to place messages that do not contain a zip code in your state in a different folder from the ones that do.

Rumble Low frequency noise, usually from a turntable. Given that RIAA equalization boosts the bass signal from a cartridge by an enormous amount (17dB at 50 hertz), the highest quality bearings and excellent isolation from the turntable's motor are required to control rumble.

Run length coding Run length coding is a type of data compression. Let's say that this page is wide enough to hold a line of 80 characters. Now, imagine a line that is almost blank except for a few words. It's 80 characters long, but it's just about all blanks — let's say 50 blanks between the words "coding" and "medium". These 50 blanks could be stored as 50 individual codes, but that would take up 50 bytes of storage. An alternative would be to define a special code that said a string of blanks is coming and the next number is the amount of blanks in the string. So, using our example, we would need only 2 bytes to store the string of 50 blanks, the first special code byte followed by the number 50. We compressed the data; 50 bytes down to 2. This is a compression ration of 25:1. Not bad, except that we only compressed one line out of the entire document, so we should expect that the total compression ratio would be much less.

Run length coding all by itself as applied to images is not as efficient as using a DCT for compression, since long runs of the same "number" rarely exist in real-world images. The only advantage of run length coding over the DCT is that it is easier to implement. Even though run length coding by itself is not efficient for compressing images, it is still used as part of the JPEG, MPEG, H.261, and H.263 compression schemes.

Running in A frequently recommended process for the installation of new equipment. Essentially, running in is operating the new equipment for some hours, or tens of hours, to bring it up to peak performance. As with many such areas of performance, there is both validity and silliness in this. Loudspeakers are physical systems with suspensions and surrounds that do benefit from being run in. But running in speaker cables achieves precisely nothing. Those who claim that their speaker cables sounded better after being run in are imagining the improvements.

Run-through or run through 1) The uninterrupted rehearsal of an extended portion of a script or the entire script; 2) to rehearse an extended portion of or the entire script without interruption.

S

S VHS Video format of superior quality to standard VHS.

S video A type of video signal that transfers light and color separately, using multiple wires. S-video delivers a higher quality picture than formats such as NTSC which encodes the data. A consumer form of component video (Y/C) used primarily with Hi8 and S-VHS equipment.

S/PDIF Sony/philips digital interface format A widely used digital audio protocol. It is used as the protocol for all consumer home entertainment equipment. It is distinguished from the professional AES/EBU protocol by incorporating the clock timing information in the main signal. Originally designed for 44.1 and 48 kHz and 16 bits, it now carries up to 96kHz and 24 bits, plus the bitstreams for the various compressed digital audio standards. The connections used are generally coaxial or optical.

SABC South Africa broadcasting corporation.

SACD (Super audio compact disc) SACD is one of two main emerging new standards for high-resolution audio on compact discs. The other is DVD-Audio. It was developed by Sony and is based on a licensed technology called Direct Stream Digital, which was developed by Sony and Phillips and is theoretically capable of sample rates up to 2.8 MHz. The SACD format allows for playback of multi-channel audio and a bandwidth of 100 kHz at over 120 dB dynamic range while retaining compatibility with existing compact disc technology. There are several subformats in the works (single layer, dual layer, etc.) that are optimized for different tasks, but Sony claims that all SACD discs have fully uncompromised audio quality. That is, no data compression, and no computer generated surround mixes from stereo data or vice versa. The potential success of this format in the mainstream is currently under scrutiny amidst other developments such as DVD Audio, but there are a number of titles available on the Sony label with promised support from other record labels.

Safari A web browser developed by Apple computers.

Safe area Areas outside what will appear in the final product but still visible through the camera's viewfinder. Film crew members such as sound technicians operating boom microphones who are entering this space can be warned that going further will ruin the scene.

Safe title area 80 Percent of the TV screen, from the center of the screen; that area of the display screen (and therefore of the camera scanning area) which will reproduce legible title credits no matter how poorly adjusted the monitor or receiver may be.

Safety copy or safety A good quality copy of the final mix or packaged program kept in case something happens to the master.

Sample One from a series of digital measurements taken of an analogue signal at regular intervals. The timing of the intervals is determined by the sampling frequency. The accuracy of the sample is determined by the sample's bit depth and the quality of the ADC.

Sample and hold A circuit that samples a signal and holds the value until the next sample is taken.

Sample rate Sample rate is how often a sample of a signal is taken. The sample rate is determined by the sample clock.

Sampling When coverting video or audio waves to digital format, digitizing software picks out points along the wave and records or "snapshots" these points. These "snapshots" can then be replayed in much the same way that motion pictures are recreated from the individual frames. The higher the sampling rate, i.e. the more snapshots/points, per unit time, the more accurate the computer's representation of the wave.

Sampling frequency The number of digital samples taken each second of an analogue audio signal. For the compact disc, this is always 44,100 samples per second (usually expressed as hertz). For DVD it is typically 48,000 hertz, but may be 96,000. The higher the figure, the more accurately the analogue source is recorded, giving an extended high frequency response, and the more space the signal requires.

Sampling rate Sound files are created by taking "samples" or snapshots of sound waves. As the sampling rate increases, more samples are taken in a given time interval. The higher the "sampling rate", the better the quality of the sound.

Satellite A vehicle put into orbit and used as a platform for data collection and transmission.

Satellite radio Digital radio transmission system that utilizes satellites in space to broadcast directly to ground based and mobile receivers. Two existing networks, Sirius and XM offer hundreds of channels of diverse offerings for a subscription fee. Separate standards govern the reception of each, so a choice must be made prior to aquiring the system.

Satellite speakers Small loudspeakers designed to deliver only midrange and high frequency audio. They are intended to operate in conjunction with a subwoofer which delivers the bass.

Satire A type of comedy, low or high, that ridicules aspects of human behavior, the purpose of which is to arouse contempt for the object.

Saturate To raise the sound levels during recording above the highest point that the recording medium can tolerate, incurring resultant distortion and possibly print through.

Saturation (in colour) The intensity of the colours in the active picture. The degree by which the eye perceives a colour as departing from a grey or white scale of the same brightness. A 100% saturated colour does not contain any white; adding white reduces saturation. In NTSC and PAL video signals, the colour saturation at any particular instant in the picture is conveyed by the corresponding instantaneous amplitude of the active video sub-carrier.

SBM (Super bit mapped) An analogue to digital conversion system developed by Sony that incorporates a form of noise shaping, designed to deliver very good performance results in the middle frequencies, at the cost of a poor signal to noise ratio in the high frequencies.

SC phase The phase of the color subcarrier.

Scalability A feature of the Indeo video codec with which quality can be optimized during playback depending on the system resources being used to play the video.

Scaling Scaling is the act of changing the resolution of an image. For example, scaling a 640 x 480 image by one-half results in a 320 x 240 image. Scaling by 2x results in an image that is 1280 x 960. There are many different methods for image scaling, and some "look" better than others. In general, though, the better the algorithm "looks", the more expensive it is to implement.

Scan converter A device that changes the scan rate of a video signal and may also convert it from non-interlaced to interlaced mode. A scan converter allows computer graphics to be recorded on videotape or displayed on a standard video monitor.

Scan lines A TV works by sweeping its electron beams from one side of the screen to the other, then repeating this just below the line it has just drawn, and so on from the top to the bottom of the screen. With PAL systems, this creates 576 visible lines (480 for NTSC). These are called scan lines. If your screen is big and you are sitting too close to it, you can sometimes actually see the scan lines. This is rarely a problem on standard CRT TV sets, but often a problem with rear projection TVs. The solution is to sit further away or get a smaller, or better designed, viewing device.

Scan rate The scan rate is the time it takes the electron gun to move across one line of the screen or repeat one entire screen. These values are known as the horizontal and vertical scan rates, respectively. The number of times a screen is redrawn each second. Computer display scan rates differ from standard video scan rates.

Scan tuning In FM receivers, Preset Scan automatically plays a brief sample of what's on each of the preset stations. Station Scan samples each strong station regardless of whether it has been preset. Seek tuning moves to the next strong station and stops there – the "Seek" button must be manually initiated again to repeat the process.

Scanconverter An adapter card used to convert a computer's digital signal to the analog signal needed as input in a TV. Used to display the computer's image on a standard television set.

Scanner Computer device which "reads" text or graphics and converts them into digitized documents/files. Most scanners work by lighting an image and measuring the light reflected through it. The scanner them converts the reflections into distinct voltages which are, in turn, transformed into patterns of dots. The resolution or clarity of the image is measured in dots per inch.

SCART(Syndicat francais des constructeurs d'appareils radio et television) A large connector, carrying 21 pins, designed to connect VCRs and DVDs to TVs. The cable has the convenience of carrying both audio and video. Most modern SCART-fitted equipment can use the cable for composite, S-Video and RGB video signals, switching between the latter two within some kind of setup menu. Some recent models also support component video on the same cable, once again after setup switching. SCART connections are mostly found on higher-end European TVs, matching DVD players, and a few Japanese DVD players aimed at the European market.

Scenario A narrative outline of a plot.

Scene A segment of the entire movie

In Flash a scene consists of a number events that the developer regards as constituting a sub-theme of the entire Flash movie. A Flash movie should be divided into scenes to facilitate the management of the project.

Scenes thus segment the production into smaller more manageable parts.

Scene illumination The average light level incident upon a monitored area. Normally measured for the visible spectrum with a light meter having a spectral response corresponding closely to that of the human eye and is quoted in lux.

Scene, French A unit of continuous dramatic action delimited by the entrance or exit of one or more characters; for logistical reasons, the director sometimes divides a play into French scenes for rehearsal or taping purposes.

Scene, obligatory The climactic scene in a well-made play in which all the threads of the plot are unsnarled; a scene necessitated by audience expectations, balance, completeness, poetic justice, etc. though not essential to the plot, as when the fate of a character the audience has taken an interest in is shown after the character has stopped playing an important role in the action.

Schema W3C XML Schema recommendations are still in Working Draft status.

A Schema is a mechanism similar to a DTD for defining data types. Schema are closer to the notions of programming objects and database data types than DTD element definitions. The concept of Schema was introduced to the XML-family in order to overcome some of the limitations of DTD, and also to be somewhat simpler. However, the enterprise proved to be much more difficult than first envisaged, and the W3C Recommendation is now more than a year late as the proposed documents were referred back to the work groups.

Schmaltz (Yiddish: "chicken fat") Lugubrious and insincere sentimentality; `laying it on thick.'

Scitex file A very high quality and high resolution file for use with Scitex systems. Many applications can open these files after a resampling of the data.

Score In music the score contains the notes of a composition. It is a synonym for sheet music.

In Macromedia Director the term score means timeline and used to indicate the position of objects within a time-based production.

Scotopic vision Illumination levels below 10-2 lux, thus invisible to the human eye.

Screen door effect The visual effect of a projector (typically LCD) showing the video with a thin black border around each individual pixel.

Screen reader A program that reads out a computer display for visually impaired people or those who do not have access to a monitor.

A screen reader can be used with other equipment to produce a Braille or voice output. Some screen readers can be customised by the user to help with the navigation of a website. For example, the screen reader might be set to read out only the links on a page.

Screen saver A visual program using moving graphics to prevent monitor burn-in.

Screenshot A screenshot is a picture of the screen that captures the appearance of the user interface at the time it is created. It is also called a screendump, screen snapshot or screen capture.

Screw type (terminal) The most secure method of interconnecting the wire from the amplifier to a speaker. In its best realization, the terminal has a post with a hole drilled through it at the base, through which the incoming conductor is placed. A cap is then screwed down from the top of the terminal, compressing the wire below.

Scrim Wire mesh used to reduce the intensity of a light without diffusing it.

Script Similar to a macro or a batch file in that it is a list of commands or procedures that will be executed at some point in the future.

Scripting language The programming language you can use tho write scripts. Example languages are APS, VBScript, PHP, Perl and others.

Scroll arrow A small arrow at either the top or bottom of the scroll bar that, when clicked, will move the area of a document that you can see.

Scroll bar Scroll bars are normally found to the right and beneath a document or browser window. The scroll bar allows you to move the viewing area if a document or web page is too large to be displayed at one time on the screen.

The vertical scrollbar to the side of the screen moves the view up and down, and the horizontal scrollbar moves the view to the left or right. You can either use the scroll arrows to move the view one step at a time or "drag" the scrollbox along the scroll bar with your pointing device to navigate quickly to a specific area.

Scrub In conventional audio editing, the tape is sometimes rocked back and forth over the playback head to find the exact editing point; scrubbing is the digital equivalent.

SCSI(small computer systems interface) A very fast, versatile parallel port allowing a computer to connect (or "daisychain") up to 7 peripheral devices, like laser printers, CD-ROM drives.

SD (Secure digital) A small, removable flash memory (ie. non-volatile) cartridge, used in a host of digital storage situations, notably in digital cameras and digital audio players. Physically it is very similar to the MMC, but incorporates support for digital rights management. Major non-Sony Japanese consumer electronics companies tend to support this format.

SDDS(Sony dynamic digital sound) A discrete channel surround sound system developed by Sony, based on its ATRAC sound compression technology for the Minidisc. It provides eight channels of sound and is optically printed on the film, using the space outside the sprocket holes. The eight channels are allocated as LFE, surround left, surround right, and five front channels. This adds a centre left and centre right channel to the three front channels provided by other systems. SDDS is used only in cinemas, not home theatre. It uses perceptual encoding compression techniques to reduce the amount of data space required to carry the signal. The home page for SDDS is here.

SDI Serial Digital I/O. Another name for the 270 Mbps or 360 Mbps serial interface defined by BT.656. It is used primarily on professional and studio video equipment.

SDTV (Standard definition television) A TV transmission standard that uses digital technology to supply a picture of similar picture resolution to Australia's existing PAL system.

Sealed (enclosure) Sometimes known as an Acoustic suspension type, the sealed enclosure is a simple design in which each woofer is mounted in a sealed, airtight box or compartment with a specific internal volume for precisely the woofer being used. The air contained within the box or compartment then acts as a spring that allows more control over the speaker's behavior. Great care must be taken in design, as too small a box will sound "boomy," while too large a box may have hardly any bass at all. This should be remembered when replacing a woofer in such an enclosure. Best results can be expected when using woofers with a QTS between .30 to .90. These speakers offer good control, low Distortion and high power handling.

Seamless layer change With dual layer DVDs there is normally a pause partway through the movie as the laser reaches the end of one layer and has to refocus on the other layer and find the correct starting point. However some DVD players eliminate this pause by reading ahead somewhat and providing a buffer memory that fills in the pause.

Search engine A program that searches documents for specified keywords and returns a list of the documents where the keyword was found.

Search service An Internet service providing the means to search for electronic resources by means of keywords.

SECAM (Sequentiel couleur a memoire) The television system used in France. It is very similar to PAL (the same frame rate and resolution) but uses a different colour encoding technique in transmission (the colour is FM modulated). This is said to have some technical advantages over PAL, but some think it was imposed in France primarily to ensure that French TV was incompatible with the rest of Europe, ensuring a good market for French-made TV sets. Since most good quality TVs are these days multi-standard, this is no longer a consideration. The colour encoding differences only apply to broadcast signals, so the video on DVDs made in France for French TVs is identical to that on the DVDs made for PAL TVs.

Second An apprentice or assistant engineer in a commercial sound studio; often merely a gofer.

Second unit A small, subordinate crew responsible for filming shots of less importance, such as inserts, crowds, scenery, etc.

Secondary audio program (SAP) Generally used to transmit audio in a second language.

Second-order The frequency attenuation that occurs at a rate of 12 dB per octave.

Section 508 The section of the Rehabilitation Act that requires any electronic information developed, procured, maintained, or used by the federal government be accessible to people with disabilities. As a result of new requirements added to the Rehabilitation Act in 1998, guidelines for electronic information – including Web sites – have been developed and were adopted on December 21, 2000. All electronic information created or acquired by any federal agency or department or, or after June 21, 2001 must comply with these accessibility standards. Congress is not yet subject to these standards.

Secure sockets layer (SSL) A protocol developed by Netscape to set up a public key connection over the internet.

Segue 1. A smooth or gradual transition from one sound to another or one scene to another without pause;

2. to make such a transition.

Selection tool A tool in some software programs that allows you to target a specific area of an image for some type of manipulation; this can be displayed as a pointer arrow, crosshairs, a lasso, or a box surrounded by dotted lines.

Selectivity Tuner specification which defines the tuner's ability to reject adjacent station interference.

Self contained A MOV file that contains all of its video and audio data, instead of including references to data in other files.

Self paced The student can start and finish the program at any time, at his/her convenience. It typically involves no moderation/ interaction with an expert/instructor. Examples include most cd-roms, video-tapes, cassettes, etc.

Semantics The relationship between words or symbols and their intended meanings. Semantic rules apply to spoken and written languages as well as programming languages.

Send only codec A video codec configuration so as to be able only to originate and transmit communications signals, for use at the sending location in point-to-multipoint or for broadcast applications where 2-way codec communication with the receiving location(s) is not required.

Sender authentication A security service which guarantees to a recipient of data that the sender of the data is who he claims to be.

Sensitivity A measure of the efficiency with which loudspeakers turn the electrical energy provided by a power amplifier into acoustic energy. The more sensitive, the greater the volume for a given amount of power. This is normally measured as the sound pressure level in decibels (dBSPL) achieved by the loudspeaker in an anechoic chamber at a distance of one metre with a 2.83 volt 1kHz signal applied. (2.83 volts is the voltage required to deliver one watt to an eight ohm load.). Each 3dB increase in sensitivity is equivalent to doubling the amount of power, so for a loud system it is far better to choose sensitive loudspeakers rather than pay for a higher-powered amplifier.

Separates or matched components A typical separates system includes a separate woofer, tweeter, and external Crossover, all of which are designed to work smoothly with one another. Generally, these components are made of better materials than two-and three-way Drivers. Separate woofers may be easier to mount in tight places because tweeter protrusion is not a factor. Separate tweeters allow positioning for optimum imaging. Given adequate power, separates can deliver excellent dynamics and detail. Separates are often a superior speaker design choice for many installations.

Separation A measure of the degree to which leakage from one channel of sound to another channel (crosstalk) is limited. This is typically measured in decibels (eg. -90dB at 1kHz). While great emphasis is placed on this figure, the reality is that very modest figures like -20 or -30dB (typical of LP records) provide excellent stereo separation and imaging. More important is that the separation should not vary widely between different frequencies, since this could lead to a positioning mismatch between the fundamental and harmonic frequencies for particular instruments.

Sepia Brassy anique effect applied to give a old photograph or video feel.

Sequence As opposed to a scene, a montage consisting of narration, snatches of dialogue, sound bytes, etc. that summarizes events or presents them in quick succession.

Serial A publication in any medium issued in successive parts bearing numeric or chronological designations and intended to be continued indefinitely. Serials include periodicals; newspapers; annuals (reports, yearbooks, etc.); the journals, memoirs, proceedings, transactions, etc. of societies; and numbered monographic series.

Serial contents database A database of the contents of journals, issue by issue.

Serial data Time-sequential transmission of data along a single wire. In CCTV, it is known as telemetry and is the mostcommon method of communicating between keyboards, matrix and PTZ cameras. It may be synchronous or asynchronous.

Serial device control Most professional video equipment can be controlled via an RS-232 serial port. The protocols used for controlling these devices varies from vendor to vendor, however, Sony's protocol is supported by most editing systems.

Serial interface A digital communications interface in which data are transmitted and received sequentially along a single wire or pair of wires. Common serialinterface standards are RS-232 and RS-422.

Serial port A computer I/O (input/output) port through which the computer communicates with the external world. The standard serial port is RS-232 based and allows bi-directional communication on a 3 wire connection, as a serial data stream.

Series A regularly scheduled program, the episodes of which share a unifying element, such as continuing characters, theme, format, setting, continuing plot line, etc.

Serif and sans serif There are two general categories of typefaces: serif and sans serif. Serif typefaces are often used in printed publications. They use small decorative marks to make characters easier to read. Times New Roman is one of the most common serif typefaces.

Sans serif typefaces are usually used on websites, as the lower resolution of websites makes serif fonts harder to read on a monitor.

Serration pulses These are pulses that occur during the vertical sync interval of NTSC, PAL, and SECAM, at twice the normal horizontal scan rate. The reason these exist was to ensure correct 2:1 interlacing in early televisions and eliminate DC offset buildup.

Server A computer on a network that is dedicated to a particular purpose and which stores all information and performs the critical functions for that purpose. For example, a Web server would store all files related to a Web site and perform all work necessary for hosting the Web site. Most congressional offices have at least one server that is dedicated as both a network server and a file server. This means that, in its network server role, the computer is responsible for holding the files and managing the processes that enable everyone in the office to access and use the network. In its file server role, it holds the central computer files and the CMS database.

Server script Scripts to be run by a server.

Server side markup (SSM) A "tag" embedded in the Webpage that gets interpreted "on the fly"/processed by the server each time the page is requested. For example, a "last modified" time/date stamp, e.g. producing Monday, 12-Apr-1999 08:00:16 EDT, is done with the tag <! – #flastmod file="name_of_file.htm" – > (an in-depth look). Related: Active Server Pages, Cold Fusion.

Session A continuous period of work on one project in a sound studio.

Set An environment used for filming. When used in contrast to location, it refers to one artificially constructed. A set is constructed to make filming easier but still appear natural.

Set decorator The person responsible for furnishings, drapery, interior plants, and anything seen on indoor or outdoor sets.

Set designer A person under the art director responsible creating the movie's physical environments.

Setup Setup is the same thing as pedestal.

Sfx or fx Sound effects.

SGI(Silicon graphics indigeo) An uncompressed, high quality, raster (pixel based) file format common in Silicon Graphics platform.

SGML standard generalized markup language ISO 8879 of 1986.

SGML is an international standard for the transport of documents in a format independent of the device, system or application.

The technical detail need not bother you as HTML author. But note that this standard is also constantly in the process of being revised. In 1993, for example, Korean Hangul characters have been added to the standard. Also, there is presently a restriction on the total of codepoints allowed in the document character set. This is also in the process of being revised.

SGML is the granddaddy of HTML and XML. HTML is an application of SGML, while XML is a metalanguage based on SGML, used for creating XML applications.

Shade The term shade refers to a color which consists of the basic color (or hue) with black added to it. The color thus consists only of a shade of its possible hue, so to speak.

Shadow mask A part of a CRT TV tube. This is a barrier within the tube, placed between the electron guns at the narrow end and the phosphor screen at the wide end. It consists of plate with thousands of perforations. The geometric arrangement permits the electrons emitted for each colour gun to activate only its matching colour phosphors. This is an alternative to the aperture grille.

Shadow The darkest colors within an image - opposite of highlight.

Shareware "try before you buy" Software. The author retains full rights to the package. It may be copied at will, but shareware cannot be used at will. There is generally a limited period of use granted without fee, commonly 30 or 60 days. After that period, the user pays a licensing fee to continue using the software.

Sheet, call A rehearsal schedule.

Sheet, contact A list of key personnel with their contact information, distributed to the cast and crew at the beginning of production work.

Sheet, cue A fact sheet or tape box label showing the cues in and out, the duration, playback speed, and other essential playback information.

Sheet, track A list in order of the takes on a recording, also showing the tracks of multi-track tape that sounds have been recorded to, often with other notes useful in post-production.

Shielding A finely woven mesh of thin wires, or a conductive foil wrapping, around a signal cable under the outer layer of insulation. The shielding is earthed and acts to protect the signal-carrying wires within from electrical fields which could introduce noise into the signal.

Shock mount 1. A device fitted between a mike and its stand to prevent unwanted sound produced by vibrations from the studio floor;

2. to rig a microphone in such a way.

Shockwave Add-in to Macromedia director that lets you create highly-compressed interactive animations and movies for Web pages. Director supports Java applets. (in-depth look) An easier-to-use, vector-based Web-animation program is Flash, also from Macromedia. +/-'s of Shockwave

"Sneaker" net when all electronic file transfers fail, files are saved to floppies, zip disks or some other removable storage medium and walked or mailed to the destination.

Shoot The actual production work of a video project.

Shopping cart/basket Taking its name from a physical shopping cart or basket that you might use when you are shopping, the shopping cart or basket on a website stores a list of products that you have selected and wish to buy. When you have finished shopping, the full list of items in your shopping cart or basket is shown on the screen so you can check it before completing your order. It is sometimes called a shoppng trolley.

Short A film of less than 60 minutes, sometimes as short as a few minutes. Contrast with Feature Film.

Short circuit The condition that occurs when a circuit path is created between the positive and negative poles of a battery, power supply, or circuit. A short circuit will bypass any resistance such as working componenets in a circuit, and cause it not to operate.

Short side The part of the face that should be pointed toward the key light.

Shortcuts A shortcut provides a faster way of completing a task. Common shortcuts can include a favourites list for websites, desktop icons for opening programs or folders, and using different keys on a keyboard to perform predefined tasks, for example using "Ctrl" plus "C" to "copy" an object.

Shot (take) Frames recorded in a single continuous run of the camera. In filming, this includes everything from when the camera starts to when it stops. After editing, a shot refers to the footage left in that strip of film, which is then put together with other shots to make a scene..

Shtick Excessive, hammy, stereotyped mannerism, or an actor's overused bag of tricks, especially when used for low humor or to pander to an audience; not always a pejorative term.

Shuffle play A feature which employs random selection from available tracks.

Shutter speed The length of time for which a single frame is exposed. Slower shutter speeds allow more light to enter the camera, but allow more motion blur.

Sibilance High frequency complex sounds in speech, such as "S", "F" & "T".

Sidebands The frequency bands on both sides of a carrier within which the energy produced by the process of modulation is carried.

Sides (always plural) A special script containing only one character's lines with cues in and out; hence, any script fragment prepared for use by talent during auditions or production.

SIF Standard (or Source) Input Format. This video format was developed to allow the storage and transmission of digital video. The 625/50 SIF format has a resolution of 352 x 288 active pixels and a refresh rate of 25 frames per second. The 525/60 SIF format has a resolution of 352 x 240 active pixels and a refresh rate of 30 frames per second. Note that MPEG-1 allows resolutions up to 4095 x 4095 active pixels; however, there is a "constrained subset" of parameters defined as SIF. The computer industry, which uses square pixels, has defined SIF to be 320 x 240 active pixels, with a refresh rate of whatever the computer is capable of supporting.

SIG A Special Interest Group devoted to discussion and information sharing about specialized areas of interest.

Sight lines Theater parlance for the lines of unobstructed view between the audience and the objects or persons on stage. Even audio drama must pay attention to good sight lines when being performed before a studio audience.

Signal processors Electronic devices which alter sound either to achieve a particular effect or to solve a problem with that sound (e.g. delays, compressors, reverbs, noise gates, equalizers).

Signal The sound source; wanted sound, as in the expression "signal to noise ratio," the ratio between wanted and unwanted noise being tracked.

Signal to noise ratio A measurement of noise level in a device compared to the level of the signal. Higher numbers signify a greater difference, which is better. In technical terms, it is the ratio, expressed in dB, of signal power at a reference point in a circuit, to the noise information that would exist if the signal were removed (the noise floor). The maximum signal to noise ratio (equivalent to dynamic range) of a given piece of equipment can be seen as a measure of functional fidelity. This ratio is how much absolute noise it produces, compared to the highest signal voltage it can pass without distortion.

Signature A musical theme used to identify a series or production entity.

Silent radio Silent Radio is a service that feeds data that is often seen in hotels and nightclubs. It's usually a large red sign that shows current news, events, scores, etc. It is present on NTSC lines 10- 11 and 273-274, and uses encoding similar to EIA-608.

Silk dome (tweeters) Dome tweeters in which the dome is composed of a treated soft silk like material. This is a design that is much less susceptible to mechanical deformation, and yet yields a fairly smooth response over the extent of its range.

SIMMs Single inline memory modules are a type of memory that is commonly used today. SIMMs are actually small printed circuit boards on which RAM chips are placed.

Simple device A media control interface (MCI) device that does not require a device element (data file) for playback. The MCI compact disc audio driver is an example of a simple device.

Simple mail transfer protocol (SMTP) A protocol for sending email messages between servers.

Simplex In general, it refers to a communications system that can transmit information in one direction only. In CCTV, simplex is used to describe a method ofmultiplexer operation where only one function can be performed at a time, e.g., either recording or playback individually.

Sin(X)/X The output of a D/A converter is a series of quantized levels that represent an analog signal whose amplitude is determined by the sin (X)/X response. At higher output frequencies, a D/A converter application may require a sin(X)/X compensation filter to normalize its output amplitude.

Sine wave An electrical signal or tone that follows a sinusoidal shape. The shape is ubiquitous in nature. All repeating waves can be generated by a combination of a sine wave with various harmonics of that wave .

Single forked A MOV file whose resources have been moved into the data fork, creating a file that can be played on a PC.

Single lens reflex (SLR) A camera that transmits the same image through a series of mirrors to the viewfinder that the lens currently is viewing.

Single speed A CD-ROM drive that accesses data at a speed of 150KB/sec. This is the speed at which standard audio CDs can be read. Single speed is the standard speed for CD-ROM drives.

Single-mode fibre An optical glass fibre that comprises a core of very small diameter. A typical single-mode fibre used in CCTV has a 9 μm core and a 125 μmouter diameter. Single-mode fibre has less attenuation and therefore transmits signals atlonger distances (easily up to 40km unrepeated). Such fibres are normally used only with laser sources because of their very small acceptance cone. SIT. Silicon Intensified Target. A high sensitivity monochrome camera usable in bright starlight.

Sitcom A type of broadcast comedy series employing farcical situations and recurring lead characters in self-contained episodes.

Site index A listing of all the pages in a website. You can use the site index to find pages on a site and to help you understand the site structure. Usually each entry is a link that will take you to that page if you click on it.

Site search A search tool for finding content on a website. Site search lets you search for content by entering keywords and looking in either the whole of the website or only the section you are currently in.

Skate The rather unintuitive tendency of the stylus of a turntable cartridge to seek to slide towards the centre. This is due to the geometry of the tonearm and results in a greater force being applied to the inner side of a groove than the outer side. Decent tonearms have an anti-skating device.

Skin effect The tendency of high frequency alternating current to travel only on the surface of a conductor. The higher the frequency the greater the effect. At high frequency, high current the effect is overcome using bunched conductors or Litz wire (many small conductors).

Skip link If you click on a skip link it will take you to a specific point further down the same webpage. A skip link allows you to skip information that may not be important to you.

Slap Sound reverberating from the walls, floor, and ceiling of a studio.

Slapstick A stick used on stage to inflict harmless blows that make loud noise, hence a type of broad comedy relying upon exaggerated physical assault for its humor.

Slate To record an announcement of the take information, such as the take number, in front of the take as a kind of audio label; the audio label so recorded.

Slew rate Slew rate measures the ability of a piece of audio equipment to accurately reproduce fast changes in amplitude. Measured in volts per microsecond, this spec is most commonly associated with amplifiers, but can bet applied to most types of equipment. In amplifiers, a low slew rate softens the definition of a signal, blurring transients and sounding "mushy." Slew rate is most critical in high frequencies reproduction where rapid changes in amplitude are most pronounced. An amplifier with a higher slew rate is often subjectively rated as tighter and more dynamic.

Sliced VBI data A technique where a VBI decoder samples the VBI data (such as teletext and captioning data), locks to the timing information, and converts it to binary 0's and 1's. DC offsets, amplitude variations, and ghosting must be compensated for by the VBI decoder to accurately recover the data.

SLIP (Serial line internet protocol) A protocol allowing connection to The Internet via a phone line.

Slope The rate of change that a frequency response curve displays, normally stated in dB per Octave. Among other things, Slope can relate to Roll Off rates in Crossover action, low-end roll off and roll on rates and other forms of increasing or decreasing response.

Slow scan The transmission of a series of frozen images by means of analogue or digital signals over limited bandwidth media, usually telephone.

Slow-wind To wind or spool analog tape at playback speed for storage to prevent print-through, stretching and other damage. Slow-winding is a very even unstressful wind, which places a thin air cushion between layers of wound tape. The most common and practical method is simply to store tape tails out after play, without rewinding it.

Smart media A small, removable flash memory (ie. non-volatile) cartridge, used in a host of digital storage situations, notably in digital cameras and digital audio players. It should be noted that many MP3 players reformat Smart Media cards in a way that will not permit them to be compatible with digital cameras.

SMDI SCSI musical data interchange.

Smear (or transfer smear) An unwanted side effect of vertical charge transfer in a CCD chip. It shows as vertical white (or sometimes red) stripes in parts of the image where there are very bright highlights. In some modern chip sets smear is minimized to almost undetectable levels.

SMPTE [Society of motion picture and television engineers] code An electronic code that can be laid on digital or analog tape for the purpose of synchronizing two sound recordings, or more commonly, synchronizing audio to video.

SMPTE 12M Defines the longitudinal (LTC) and vertical interval (VITC) timecode for NTSC and PAL video systems. LTC requires an entire field time to store timecode information, using a separate track. VITC uses one scan line each field during the vertical blanking interval.

SMPTE 170M NTSC video specification for the United States.

SMPTE 240M 1920 x 1035 pro-video interlaced standard (29.97 or 30 Hz). Covers the analog RGB and YPbPr representation. The digital parallel interface is defined by SMPTE 260M. The digital serial interface is defined by SMPTE 292M.

SMPTE 244M 768 x 486 pro-video interlaced standard (29.97 Hz). Covers the digital representation (composite NTSC video sampled at 4x Fsc) and the digital parallel interface. The digital serial interface is defined by SMPTE 259M.

SMPTE 253M Analog RGB video interface specification for pro-video SDTV systems.

SMPTE 259M Pro-video serial digital interface for SMPTE 244M.

SMPTE 260M Digital representation and parallel interface for SMPTE 240M video.

SMPTE 266M Defines the digital vertical interval timecode (DVITC).

SMPTE 267M 960 x 480 pro-video interlaced standard (29.97 Hz). Covers the digital representation and the digital parallel interface.

SMPTE 272M Formatting AES/EBU digital audio and auxiliary data into the digital blanking intervals.

SMPTE 274M 1920 x 1080 pro-video interlaced and progressive standards. Covers the digital representation, the analog RGB and YPbPr interfaces, and the digital parallel interface. The digital serial interface is defined by SMPTE 292M.

SMPTE 276M Transmission of AES/EBU digital audio and auxiliary data over coaxial cable.

SMPTE 291M Ancillary data packet and space formatting for pro-video digital interfaces.

SMPTE 292M 1.485 Gbps pro-video HDTV serial interfaces.

SMPTE 293M 720 x 480 pro-video progressive standards (59.94 Hz). Covers the digital representation, the analog RGB and YPbPr interfaces, and the digital parallel interface. The digital serial interface is defined by SMPTE 294M.

SMPTE 294M Pro-video serial digital interface for SMPTE 293M.

SMPTE 296M 1280 x 720 pro-video progressive standards. Covers the digital representation and the analog RGB and YPbPr interfaces. The digital parallel interface uses SMPTE 274M. The digital serial interface is defined by SMPTE 292M.

SMPTE 299M 24-bit digital audio format for pro-video HDTV serial interfaces.

SMPTE 305M Serial data transport interface (SDTI). This is a 270 or 360 Mbps serial interface based on BT.656 that can be used to transfer almost any type of digital data, including MPEG-2 program streams, MPEG-2 transport streams, DV bit streams, etc. You cannot exchange material between devices that use different data types. Material that is created in one data type can only be transported to other devices that support the same data type. There are separate map documents that format each data type into the 305M transport.

SMPTE 308M MPEG-2 4:2:2 profile at high level.

SMPTE 314M Data structure for DV-based audio, data and compressed video at 25 and 50 Mbps.

SMPTE 322M Data stream format for the exchange of DV-based audio, data and compressed video over a Serial Data Transport Interface (SDTI or SMPTE 305M).

SMPTE 344M Defines a 540 Mbps serial digital interface for pro-video applications.

SMPTE 348M High data-rate serial data transport interface (HD-SDTI). This is a 1.485 Gbps serial interface based on SMPTE 292M that can be used to transfer almost any type of digital data, including MPEG-2 program streams, MPEG-2 transport streams, DV bit streams, etc. You cannot exchange material between devices that use different data types. Material that is created in one data type can only be transported to other devices that support the same data type. There are separate map documents that format each data type into the 348M transport.

SMPTE 370M This SMPTE standard specifies a data structure for DV-based audio, data and compressed video at data rates of 100 Mbps.

SMPTE division type One of four SMPTE timing formats. SMPTE time is expressed in hours, minutes, seconds, and frames. The SMPTE division type specifies the frames-per-second value corresponding to a given SMPTE time. For example, a SMPTE time of one hour, 30 minutes, 24 seconds, and 15 frames is useful only if the frames-per-second value, or SMPTE division type, is known.

SMPTE format, smpte standard In component video these terms refer to the SMPTE standards for parallel analog component video interconnection. The SMPTE has standardized both RGB and Y, Pr, Pb color difference systems (a version of Y, B-Y, R-Y).

SMPTE offset A Musical Instrument Digital Interface (MIDI) event that designates the SMPTE time at which playback of a MIDI file is to start. SMPTE offsets are used only with MIDI files using SMPTE division type.

SMPTE RP160 Analog RGB and YPbPr video interface specification for pro-video HDTV systems.

SMPTE time A standard representation of time developed for the video and film industries. SMPTE time is used with Musical Instrument Digital Interface (MIDI) audio because many people use MIDI to score films and video. SMPTE time is an absolute time format expressed in hours, minutes, seconds, and frames. Standard SMPTE division types are 24, 25, and 30 frames per second.

SMPTE timecode A coding scheme standardized by the Society of Motion Picture and Television Engineers (SMPTE). Frame accuracy is achieved through timecode, a method of coding a unique "stamp" on each frame. Timecode consists of four numbers representing hours, minutes, seconds, and frames, for example, 23:59:59:29.

Since color video actually runs at 29.97 fps rather than 30 fps, two kinds of timecode have evolved: drop fame and non-drop frame. Drop-frame timecode literally drops certain agreed-upon numbers to compensate for the 0.03 fps discrepancy. Drop-frame timecode allows a 30:00:00:00 tape to really be 30 minutes long, which is critical in broadcast applications. For non-broadcast applications it tends to do nothing but create problems, and non-drop-frame timecode is usually preferred.

Most of the low-end videotape formats, like VHS and Video 8 do not have timecode. They can count frame pulses on the tape, but are not frame-accurate. Sony has introduced "8 mm timecode" in order to support more accurate editing applications with Hi8.

There are two basic techniques used to record SMPTE time code on videotape.

Sneak To fade a sound up or down so slowly that its appearance or disappearance is barely noticeable.

SNMP(Simple network management protocol) A communications protocol used for managing and controlling monitor devices on a network.

SNMP is defined by RFC1157. The SNMP client side is used a management console, while the server side is called an agent, which can reside on any TCP/IP device, such as a router, hub or host. Novell LAN is a DOS-based SNMP.

Snoot An open ended cylindrical funnel mounted on a light source to project a narrow concentrated circle of illumination.

Snow 1. Random noise on the display screen, often resulting from dirty videotape heads.

2. TV signal breakup caused by weak or no video reception.

Soap or soap opera A broadcast serial, presenting by and large domestic situations in melodramatic terms, so called because at one time such programs were sponsored by soap companies; any dramatic work resembling a soap opera in tone.

Socket In the TCP/IP network it is an addressable point that consists of an IP address and a TCP or UDP port number which provides applications with access to TCP/IP.

Solarization Electronic special effect distoring a video image's original colors which emphasize and de-emphasize for a paint brush feel.

Soliloquy A speech, usually extended, representing the inner thoughts of a character, spoken while the character is alone or believes him/herself to be alone in the scene.

Solo To turn off all but one track while recording or playing back a multi-track sound production.

Some terminology used in video multimedia Data provided by Jim Mckeown

Sony dynamic digital sound (SDDS) A noise reduction and sound enhancement process. Competes with Dolby Digital and DTS.

Sound A type of physical kinetic energy called acoustical energy that falls within the portion of the spectrum to which humans are sensitive.

Sound blaster-compatible Works with software written for the Sound Blaster video card, the sound standard.

Sound card An add-in circuit board that once installed, enables the computer to accept audio input from a microphone, edit/trim/mix recordings, play sound files stored on disks or CD-ROM's, and produce audio output through speakers or earphones. For output, sound cards can 1. create or synthesize sounds, like a keyboard/synthesizer, and

2. play previously-recorded sounds, like a tape recorder/player.

Sound designer The conceptual chief of a movie's soundtrack, responsible for designing and creating the audio component of a movie.

Sound digitizer A device for recording natural sounds and voices and storing them as computer files. Once digitized, the audio can be easily edited or used to create various effects. On the low-end there are products like the Farallon MacRecorder or Apple's built-in capability on some Macintosh models. With the AudioMedia card or Pro Tools interface from DigiDesign, CD-quality sound digitizing is possible with the Macintosh.

Sound discriminator A device designed to evaluate, and discriminate between the sounds that may be heard within the interior of a vehicle, and then trigger the security system should the sound fit within the parameters of what the sensor is designed to react.

Sound editor A member of the sound crew who performs editing on the soundtrack.

Sound effects Auditory effects created in the studio and added to a production later.

Sound field The totality of the sound presented by the audio system. This includes the sound as it was recorded, mixed, transported, reproduced, and finally heard by the listener.

Sound mix The process of combining individual audio tracks into the final soundtrack for the production.

Sound power The total amount of acoustical energy produced by a sound source and measured in Joules per second. The degree to which this measurement is constant(or linear)with respect to frequency, is an index of the overall fidelity of the system.

Sound pressure level (SPL) An acoustic measurement of sound energy. 1 dB SPL is the smallest increment in sound level to which the average human is sensitive. Theoretically, 0 dB SPL is the threshold of human hearing while approximately 120 dB is the threshold of pain.

Sound shaping A sophisticated cicuit that defines the parameters of the sonic experience with a blending of directional and tonal adjustments to acheive both realistic and synthetic effects.

Soundstage The position (front/back and high/low) that music or sound appears to be originating from, as well as the apparent depth of the stage. A car with speakers only in the front will likely have a forward soundstage, but may not have enough rear fill to make the music seem live. A car with both front and rear speakers may have anything from a forward to a rear soundstage, with an accompanying fill from the softer drivers depending on the relative power levels and the frequencies reproduced. The high/low position of the soundstage is generally only obvious in a car with a distinctly forward soundstage. The music may seem to be originating in the footwells, the dash, or out on the hood, depending on the car's design.

Sound waves Fluctuating waves of barometric pressure that travel through a physical medium such as air. An acoustic wave consists of a traveling vibration of alternate compressions and rarefactions, whereby sound is transmitted through air or other media.

Soundscape The environment for dramatic action created on the audio stage by descriptive dialogue and sonic effects; the audio equivalent to effects produced in the theater by sets, props and lighting; (audio art) a work for listening that manipulates and orders sound to create a mood or conjure the impression of an environment; the audio equivalent of landscape painting.

Soundtrack The audio portion of a video recording with voiceover, sound effects, background music, etc.

Source impedance A parameter of an audio component referring to the output impedance. A low output impedence .5 to 4 ohms, is preferred for automotive applications.

Spam Electronic junk mail.

Spatial compression An intra-frame method for compressing video that generalizes an image and removes redundant data.

SPDIF Short for sony/philips digital interface. This is a consumer interface used to transfer digital audio. A serial, self-clocking scheme is used, based on a coax or fiber interconnect. The audio samples may be 16-24 bits each. 16 different sampling rates are supported, with 32, 44.1, and 48 kHz being the most common. IEC 60958 now fully defines this interface for consumer and professional applications.

Speaker Short for loudspeaker.

Spec (industry slang) speculation. To work "on spec" is to perform a job on the promise that it may provide a financial reward if certain conditions are met, but that the reward is by no means certain. A "spec script" is one that the writer composes without pay on the hope that someone will buy it.

Special effects (SFX) Artificial effects created on the set, as opposed to those created in post-production.

Spectrum In electromagnetics, the spectrum of a signal refers to the description of a signal's amplitudeversus its frequency components. In optics, spectrum refers to the various light frequencies composing the white light which can be seen as rainbow colours, when separated.

Speech to text system A type of voice recognition software that changes spoken language into text. It is especially useful for people with motor impairments.

Speed of propagation Physical waves, whether sound or electromagnetic, have a typical speed of propagation through various media. This varies depending on the medium. Light travels through a vacuum at 3x108 metres per second. Sound travels through room-temperature air (20C) at 343.5 metres per second. The speed varies slightly according to temperature, increasing to 349.3m/s at 30C, falling to 337.6m/s at 10C.

Spider The rear suspension element on the cone of a loudspeaker. All the moving parts of the speaker are suspended by the spider in the rear and the Surround in the front. The spider is so named because of its resemblance to an arachnid, especially in the way in which flexion is obtained in the design of the concentric pleats that allow back and forth motion.

Spike 1. To fix a position on stage or before the mike exactly by marking the floor with tape, chalk, etc.;

2. (electronics) an unwanted sudden surge of power through the circuitry of electronic equipment that can sometimes cause technical aberrations and system crashes.

Spine In drama, the essential unifying element or conjoined elements of a character, a scene or an entire play.

Splice 1. To edit tape by physically cutting and joining;

2. the juncture of two pieces of tape edited together.

Split screen A special effect utilizing two or more video sources so that two or more scenes are visible simultaneously on each part of the screen. It is often used to make window-dubs of multi-camera shoots. This is a useful means for comparing two sources simultaneously. It permits a fast visual check of the phase and sync timing between two inputs.

Split sync scrambling Split sync is a video scrambling technique, usually used with either horizontal blanking inversion, active video inversion, or both. In split sync, the horizontal sync pulse is "split", with the second half of the pulse at +100 IRE instead of the standard -40 IRE. Depending on the scrambling mode, either the entire horizontal blanking interval is inverted about the +30 IRE axis, the active video is inverted about the +30 IRE axis, both are inverted, or neither is inverted. By splitting the horizontal sync pulse, a reference of both -40 IRE and +100 IRE is available to the descrambler.

Since a portion of the horizontal sync is still at -40 IRE, some sync separators may still lock on the shortened horizontal sync pulses. However, the timing circuits that look for color burst a fixed interval after the end of horizontal sync may be confused. In addition, if the active video is inverted, some video information may fall below 0 IRE, possibly confusing sync detector circuits.

The burst is always present at the correct frequency and timing; however, the phase is shifted 180 degrees when the horizontal blanking interval is inverted.

Split-screen unit Equipment that simultaneously displays parts or more than one image on a single monitor. It usually refers to two images displayed on a single screen.

Spot 1. To locate and mark the most desirable position for performing, so as to be in the optimal view of the camera or range of the microphone;

2. short for spot announcement.

Spot announcement A broadcast advertising or public service message between 10 to 120 seconds long; a commercial.

Spot check A check of the exposed recording tape for flaws made by playing only brief passages at various points on the tape.

Spotlight A directional, often adjustable, type of artificial light source for video

Spread spectrum This communications technique has been used in secure military systems for a number of years and is now becoming popular in commercial systems. This format involves transmitting information, which has been multiplied by a pseudo-random noise (PN) sequence which essentially "spreads" it over a relatively wide frequency bandwidth. The receiver detects and uses the same PN sequence to "despread" the frequency bandwidth and decode the transmitted information. This communications technique allows greater signal density within a given transmission bandwidth and provides a high degree of signal encrytion and security in the process.

Sprite In Macromedia Director the term Sprite is used for a special design tool that controls when, where, and how cast members (i.e. the objects in the production) appear in a movie (i.e. the multimedia production). Sprites are associated with cast members. More than one sprite can be associated with a particular cast members. A cast member is an autonomous object and changes to its attributes will change the sprite. However, changes to a sprite will not change the attributes of the object itself, only its behavior.

Spurious free dynamic (SFDR) This refers to the range between the highest level of the fundamental Range frequency and the highest level of any spurious, or harmonically- related, signal. SFDR is expressed in dB.

SQL Database The database system that uses the SQL language.

Square pixels When the ratio of active pixels per line to active lines per frame is the same as the display aspect ratio. This is the same as the sampling lattice having equal spatial horizontal and vertical spacing of the sampling points.

Square wave A signal, the shape of which when displayed is, well, square. In other words, it holds to a negative value for a time equal to half the wave's period, then switches abruptly to a positive value which it holds for the same length of time, then switches back negative again, and so on. How quickly it switches between these states is determined by how far into the higher frequencies the equipment in use can extend. Square waves rarely form part of music, and are primarily used as diagnostic tools, since inspection of how well equipment handles a square wave can reveal a lot about its high frequency handling and whether it shifts phase across its frequency handling range. For those who are mathematically inclined, a square wave can be defined by the formula, where f is the fundamental frequency and n is an odd natural number: sin(f) + 1/3 sin(3f) + 1/5 sin(5f) + ... 1/n sin(nf).

Square wave synthesizer A synthesizer that produces sound by adding square waves of various frequencies. A square wave is a rectangular waveform.

Stabilizer Video signal processor used primarily for tape dubbing to eliminate picture jump and jitter to maintain stability.

Stage 1. Literally or figurateively, the "place" of theatrical action; in a playhouse the stage is a physical space in an auditorium in view of the audience, shared by the sets, props, and actors; in radio it is the space between the speakers in the audience's listening environment;

2. to turn a literary property into a performance piece;

3. to produce and/or direct something; to mount a theatrical production.

Stage wait A pause intended to heighten suspense.

Stage whisper A method by which an actor gives the impression of whispering while speaking loudly enough to be heard throughout the house .

Stage, give In acting, to yield the spotlight, to help focus the audience's attention away from oneself to another actor, as by pointing one's body toward the actor, facing away from the audience or moving out of the light, etc.

Stage, take In acting, to command the spotlight, to draw the audience's attention to oneself, as by standing at the most prominent stage position, by raising one's voice, by moving when other performers are still, etc.

Staircase pattern The monochrome equivalent of colour bars. A patterngenerated by the TV generator, consisting of equal width luminance steps of 0, +20, +40, +60, +80, and +100 IRE units and a constant amplitude chroma signal at colour burst phase. Chroma amplitude is selectable at 20 IRE units (low stairs) or 40 IRE units (high stairs). The staircase pattern is useful for checking linearity of luminance and chroma gain, differential gain and differential phase and correctly setting up monitors.

Stamped (basket) The frame of a loudspeaker which has been stamp pressed to achieve its shape. It is used as a base to mount all the other elements of the driver. With a frame of adequate thickness and strength, this arrangement should perform well for the life of the speaker.

Standard 1. a set of guidelines, usually drafted by experts in a particular field of technology, that are issued for general use by national and international standards organisations.

2. the format used to distribute a television signal. Examples include NTSC, PAL, SECAM

Standard compression algorithm An algorithm convention for compression of a video signal. Adherence to standards allows communication among a wide variety of videoconferencing systems, though not with the same clarity as two similar systems using a proprietary algorithm. H.320 is the most widely accepted standard in use today.

Standard, interconnect standard The specific signal configuration, reference pulses, voltage levels, and so on which describe the input/output requirements for a particular type of equipment. Some standards have been established by professional groups or government bodies (such as SMPTE or EBU). Others are determined by equipment vendors.

Standards conversion The transfer of one video standards format to another. For example, European tapes are made in the PAL format and need to be converted to NTSC format to be viewed in North American countries.

Standing wave A phenomenon where a sound is reflected between two parallel surfaces, such that certain sounds are made more intense and others diminished in given parts of a listening environment. Technically they are created by room modes, which are modes of vibration of air in the room. The sound waves interfere with one another to produce a series of places where the sound pressure level (SPL) at some frequencies is high, and another series of places where they are low. The places are sometimes called peaks and nodes. A standing wave exists in a room where a frequency is such that the distance between any two surfaces is equal to one half of its wavelength. For a given distance there will be many frequencies that will generate standing waves, each a multiple of the fundamental frequency whose wavelength is related to the dimension in question. Standing waves are always detrimental to the acoustics of a room, but can be avoided by careful room design, or minimized by absorbing certain frequencies where they build up, which is usually along walls or in corners.

Stand-up A shot in which a standing reporter introduces or sometimes wraps up a story.

Start bit A bit preceding the group of bits representing a character used to signal the arrival of the character in an asynchronous transmission.

Station break A pause in a syndicated or network broadcast program that allows local stations to identify themselves and deliver promotional and other messages.

Step on a line or laugh In acting, to begin a line too quickly, so as to spoil the previous line.

Stereo or stereophonic In the home, an audio system which delivers two channels of music, left and right, to create the illusion of a plane of sound facing the listener. Some carefully produced recordings can use these two channels to also give a sense of fore-aft depth in that space between the speakers, occasionally generating an illusion of sound even behind the listener. Confusingly, in the professional cinema context, stereo means surround sound. Contrast with mono and surround sound.

Still video cameras Still video cameras are cameras that look like something in-between a still and a video camera. The Sony Mavica records on a two-inch disk that holds 25 frames or 50 fields on flexible disks which are erasable and reusable. The encoding is analog component, but with less bandwidth (and therefore a noticeably lower quality image).

Electronic still photography has been used for "electronic journalism," where images are shot in the field and sent by modem from any available phone. These cameras have already begun to replace still picture film cameras for many applications which do not require the high resolution and image quality of 35 mm still picture film.

Sting A short, sharp musical chord or chord series used for dramatic punctuation.

Stitching A term used to describe the process of blending or integrating a series of images into one

Stock footage For reasons of simplicity, time, or budget, some shots in a film may duplicated from other films or a film library. Such shots are called stock footage.

Stop motion A form of animation in which objects are filmed frame-by-frame and altered slightly in between each frame.

Story As opposed to plot, the chronological sequence of events in a literary work.

Storyboard The storyboard is the place within a digital movie-making program such as MovieShop™ where movie projects can be arranged and created. A storyboard will display—in a linear fashion—each video clip, still image and transition used to create the movie. A storyboard shows the sequence of media used for the movie.

STP Shielded twisted pair.

Streaming A way of transferring data so it can be processed as a continuous stream. Streaming technologies are increasingly important as the internet grows. Speed of transfer is key. With streaming, the client browser or plug-in can start displaying the data before the entire file has been transmitted. For streaming to work, the client side receiving the data must be able to collect the data and send it as a steady stream to the application that is processing the data and converting it to sound or pictures - if the streaming client receives the data too fast it needs to save the excess data in a buffer. If the data doesn't come fast enough the presentation of the data will be patchy. Real Player (from RealNetworks) is perhaps the best know software allowing the streaming of audio, video and rich media files.

Streaming audio/video Real-time and continuous delivery of video to the desktop. It sends data to the desktop continuously, but does not download the entire file. Some streaming video servers maintain a constant conversation with the client in order to determine how much bandwidth the user can support. Based on this information, the server adjusts the data-stream accordingly and sends just enough video to the client.

StreamWatch Cisco software that tracks viewer demographics and help manage, monitor and account for video programs.

Stroke The distance that the speaker cone or voice coil can travel in both directions.

Structure query language (SQL) A standardized query language for requesting information from a database.

Structure, comic A plot structure in which everything tends to go badly for the protagonist until the climax, after which his or her fortunes improve.

Studio The place where programs are recorded or performed for broadcast; more specifically the room in a production facility containing the talent, musicians and/or Foley operators, as opposed to the booth or control room.

Studio manager (BBC usage) the chief engineer on a session who coordinates the efforts of the GRAMS and foley operators, and who operates the console; the recordist.

Studio monitors Speakers used in recording studios for playback and mixing of source recordings. While these are commonly thought of as extremely highly developed speakers, it is often true that some home oriented speakers may offer better performance. The term 'monitor' has become not so much a technical description, as an advertising ploy to sell expensive speakers. Favor a more analytical approach to an individual speaker's performance.

Style The sum of elements – diction, vocal and physical gesture, tempo, ornamentation, etc. – appropriate for the writing, performance or production of a performance work; the characteristic techniques, themes and artistry of a particular author, performer, director or producer of an artistic work; panache, flair, the pleasing and distinctive affect of personality, charm, and audacity.

Stylesheets Also known as cascading stylesheets (CSS), stylesheets originate from the world of print. They allow you to separate the content of a document (for example copy and images) from the presentation (such as fonts and layouts). The main benefit is that you can change a single stylesheet and all the pages that use the stylesheet will automatically be updated.

If a website has been created using proper CSS, it is possible to apply your own stylesheet to a website, which lets you display it according to your own preferences.

Stylus A small diamond on the end of a cartridge's cantilever. This sits within the groove of an LP and picks up the vibrations recorded therein. The stylus is generally spherical or elliptical in shape, although some variations have been developed, all with a view to more accurately tracking the groove while reducing damage to it. Elliptical styli are only suitable for tracking weights of less than around two grams because their low contact area with the groove can cause damage.

Subcarrier (SC, 3.58, 3.58CW) This is the basic signal in all NTSC sync signals. It is a continuous sine wave, usually generated and distributed at 2 volts in amplitude, and having a frequency of 3.58 MHz. Subcarrier is usually divided down from a primary crystal running at 14.32 MHz, and that divided by 4 is 3.58. All other synchronizing signals are directly divided down from the subcarrier.

Subcarrier phase shifter Special circuitry designed to control the phase relationships of the two portions of the encoded color signal so that they maintain their correct relationship during recording transmission and reproduction.

Subject gateway An Internet service listing (usually) on-line resources for a particular subject area. The resources included will have been reviewed by subject specialists before inclusion.

Subjective reviewing Subjective assessment is a vital component in judging any piece of audio equipment. We have not established a set of tests which fully and accurately describe the perceived performance of audio or video components. Particularly with things like loudspeakers, an experienced listener can come to a valuable view of the performance just from a brief listen. That said, subjectivism does not negate the equal value of objective tests and has far too often been taken to ridiculous extremes. One giveaway is when the reviewer starts talking about his or her feelings. If a system is claimed to be more able generate an emotion in the listener than another system (except, perhaps, for anger and irritation when it fails to work properly), then it is time to stop reading. Emotions are primarily generated by the interactions between the music, the listener's tastes and the listener's mood. These things will swamp any due to the subtle differences between two CD players or amplifiers.

Submit To send information. "Submit" or "go" buttons can be found on a number of webpages that act as forms and let you enter information to send. Submiting the form sends it to a person or to another web page that will check or validate that the information is appropriate and correct.

A "go" button is also used to start searching for content on site after you enter keywords in the site search.

Subnet A portion of a network that shares a common address component. On TCP/IP networks, subnets are defined as all devices whose IP addresses have the same prefix. For example, all devices with IP addresses that start with 100.100.100. would be part of the same subnet. Dividing a network into subnets is useful for both security and performance reasons.

Subplot A subsidiary plot woven into the fabric of, subsidiary to, and often amplifying the main plot.

Subsampled Subsampled means that a signal has been sampled at a lower rate than some other signal in the system. A prime example of this is the 4:2:2 Y'CbCr color space used in ITU-R BT.601. For every two luma (Y') samples, only one Cb and Cr sample is present. This means that the Cb and Cr signals are subsampled.

Subscription agent A supplier of journals to libraries and other information agencies.

Substractive color Naturally perceived color

In the substractive color scheme a color is specified by the amount of it removed (substracted) from white light. This is how the human eye sees color. A substractive color absorbs, reflects and transmits light, which our eyes see as color.

Primary substractive colors are: red, yellow, blue. When they are mixed in some proportions, secondary colors are derived. Tertiary (or intermediate) colors result when two primary colors are mixed in the ratio 2:1.

Even though colors are added when mixed together, the perception is substractive — we perceive the colors absorption of light.

Subtext The covert, implicit or psychological meaning of an utterance, which may be more than, or the opposite of, the overt or apparent meaning.

Subtitles Text that is added below or over a picture that usually reflects what is being said, possibly in another language. Open subtitles are transmitted as video that already has the subtitles present. Closed subtitles are transmitted during the VBI, and relies on the TV to decode it and position it below or over the picture. Closed captioning is a form of subtitling. Subtitling for DVB is specified in ETSI EN 300 743.

Subwoofer A speaker designed to produce only deep bass frequencies. Most subwoofers are 'active' models, which means that they have an amplifier built in. 'Passive' subwoofers require an external amplifier. Active subwoofers also have a level control and, usually, an upper frequency control, although an increasing number are appearing without features not required when connected to a home theatre receiver's Dolby Digital (or whatever) LFE output, which covers a frequency band from 3 to 120 hertz. But to achieve useful output from a subwoofer below around 20 hertz, expect to pay big dollars.

Super black A keying signal that is embedded within the composite video signal as a level between black and sync. It is usually used to improve luma self-keying because the video signal contains black, making a good luma self-key hard to implement. When a downstream keyer detects the super black level, it inserts the second composite video signal.

Super tweeter A Driver constructed to reproduce the highest possible frequencies from roughly 13 kHz to 25 kHz. While most standard Tweeters can do an excellent job right up to 16 or 20 kHz, these units deliver the most extreme parts of the upper range for those fortunate (or not) few who can actually hear them.

Super videocd (super VCD, SVCD) Defined by the China National Technical Committee of Standards on Recording, this CD standard holds 35-70 minutes of digital audio and video information. MPEG-2 video is used, with a resolution of 480 x 480 (29.97 Hz frame rate) or 480 x 576 (25 Hz frame rate). Audio uses MPEG-1 layer 2 or MPEG-2 at a bit rate of 32-384 kbps, and supports four mono, two stereo, or 5.1 channels. Subtitles use overlays rather than subpictures (DVD-Video) or being encoded as video (VideoCD). Variable bit-rate encoding is used, with a maximum bit rate of 2.6 Mbps. IEC 62107 defines the Super VideoCD standard.

XSVCD, although not an industry standard, increases the video resolution and bit rate to improve the video quality over SVCD. MPEG-2 video is still used, with a resolution of 720 x 480 (29.97 Hz frame rate) or 720 x 576 (25 Hz frame rate). Variable bit-rate encoding is still used, with a maximum bit rate of 9.8 Mbps.

Support A supporting player .

Supraaural Term used in reference to headphones. Supraaural phones rest on the ear, rather than enclosing the ear. Supraaural phones typically are lightweight, and because they do not seal around the ear, tend to not provide good isolation, but permit the listener a higher degree of awareness of external sounds.

Surestream A technology developed by RealNetworks through which a video or audio file can be encoded simultaneously for multiple bandwidth settings.

Surface (mounting) A method of mounting speakers in which the external parts of the upper speaker protrude above the surface on which it is mounted.

Surrealism A style of writing and performance depicting unconscious and subjective realities.

Surround The surround is the flexible ring around the edge of the speaker cone. In conjunction with the inner suspension element called a Spider, it determines the overall impedance of the speaker. Pleated, treated cloth surrounds are usually stiffer and less compliant than their foam and rubber rolled edge cousins. A flexible suspension system in the speaker usually indicates greater efficiency. For some units, it is desirable to have suspensions that are pliable enough to let the woofer cone travel freely in and out. A technical specification for this characteristic in more expensive speakers, is XMS. The further the cone can travel and the more compliant it is, the stronger the bass can be in enclosures that take advantage of it. However, certain types of very good enclosures require a more limited, stiffer cone movement to develop their more controlled and High Fidelity response. Surrounds are usually made of cloth, foam or rubber. Rubber tends to last longest.

Surround sound An audio system which delivers sound from behind, as well as in front of, the listener. This can be artificially generated by 'virtual surround' systems which process a stereo signal to produce the effect of sounds from the rear, even with just two speakers. More commonly, though, it refers to systems such as Dolby Pro Logic, Dolby Digital and DTS which were designed to deliver specific channels of surround sound from speakers placed slightly behind and to the sides of the listener. These typically also use a centre front channel and, in some newer versions, an additional centre rear channel. In the professional cinema context, surround sound is often called stereo. Contrast with mono and stereo.

Suspense Uncertainty coupled with anxiety; apprehension causing a tense expectancy in the audience.

SVCD SVCD stands for Super Video Compact Disc (called also SuperVCD or Chaoji VCD).

SVCD is a new CD standard developed in 1998 by Chinese consumer electronics manufacturers, Chinese government and VCD consortium (Sony, Philips, Matsushita and JVC) that allows regular CD to contain 35-60 minutes of video and audio. A SVCD is very similiar to a VCD, although SVCD's video bitrate is normally higher than VCD's. SVCD contains very good quality full-motion MPEG2 video along with up to 2 stereo audio tracks (MPEG1 stereo audio layer II, MPEG2 stereo audio layer II or MPEG2 Multi-Channel 5.1 surround audio) and also 4 selectable subtitles. A SVCD can be played on many standalone DVD Players and of course on all computers with a DVD-ROM or CD-ROM driver with the help of a software based decoder/player.

Just like VCDs (and audio CDs), SVCDs require a specific way how they are burned on the CD — just sticking all the required files into CD structure doesn't make disc a SVCD compatible. Most of the new CD burning applications support SVCD already, so authoring your own SVCDs should be relatively easy.

SVD SVCD compliant video data generally in the form of MPEG2.

S-VHS super VHS This is a higher standard of video tape recorder, which approximately doubles the amount of horizontal resolution able to be recorded on video tape (from around 250 lines for VHS to around 400 lines). It also uses the S-Video system of keeping the colour and luminance parts of the video signal separate, allowing better picture quality. It typically requires an S-VHS tape, which is identical to a standard VHS tape but with better quality magnetic formulation. These tapes sell at quite a premium over regular tapes. The term is sometimes erroneously used (even by equipment makers, who should know better!) for S-Video.

S-video Separate video, also called Y/C video. Separate luma (Y') and chroma (C) video signals are used, rather than a single composite video signal. By simply adding together the Y' and C signals, you generate a composite video signal.

A DC offset of +2.3v may be present on the C signal when a letterbox picture format is present. A DC offset of +5v may be present to indicate when a 16:9 anamorphic picture format is present. A standard 4:3 receiver ignores all DC offsets, thus displaying a typical letterboxed picture.

Sweet spot The listening space between two speakers where the stereo can best be distinguished — the audio equivalent to the theatrical "Duke's chair," the most advantageous seat in the playhouse to view and hear the action on stage.

Sweeten To add sound elements for listening enhancement/story clarification.

SWF A Flash file extension.

- The .swf file extension is used for a Flash document that can be played with a Flash player. Before it is published, a Flash document, while it is being developed, has the extension .fla.

Swing gang A group within the art department that construct and take down a set. The head of the swing gang is a leadman. Contrast with grips.

Related terms: Carpenter

Switcher, video switcher The switcher is the central router and mixer of video source material in an on-line suite. Switchers are generally analog devices, and are capable of performing analog effects as well as switching incoming channels. These effects include fades and dissolves, wipes and borders, and keys (opaque overlays based on replacing black or a particular color). In earlier days this was called the "special effects generator" or SEG.

Symbol The word has many different meanings in many different contexts.

In Semiotics....

In typography a symbol is a non-alphabet character (such as the copyright symbol ©) in alphabet-based languages.

In Macromedia Flash symbol is used for a graphical object that can be animated. In terms of function Flash symbol is similar to the Director cast. A Flash symbol is any image object that is made a symbol by adding it to a library. Symbols can be reused. Animations can only be applied to symbols. A symbol put on the developer's stage is called an instance of the symbol.

Sync Sync is a fundamental, you gotta have it, piece of information for displaying any type of video. Essentially, the sync signal tells the display where to put the picture. The horizontal sync, or HSYNC for short, tells the display where to put the picture in the left-to-right dimension. The vertical sync, or VSYNC for short tells the display where to put the picture from top-to-bottom.

Analog SDTV and EDTV signals use a bi-level sync, where the sync level is a known value below the blanking level. Analog HDTV signals use a tri-level sync, where the sync levels are known values above and below the blanking level.

The reason analog HDTV signals use a tri-level sync signal is timing accuracy. The horizontal timing reference point for a bi-level sync signal is defined as the 50% point of the leading edge of the horizontal sync pulse. In order to ascertain this point precisely, it is necessary to determine both the blanking level and sync-tip level and determine the mid-point value. If the signal is in any way distorted, this will reduce the timing accuracy.

With a tri-level sync signal, the timing reference point is the rising edge of the sync signal as it passes through the blacking level. This point is much easier to accurately determine, and can be implemented relatively easily. It is also more immune to signal distortion.

Sync generator A sync generator is a circuit that provides sync signals. A sync generator may have genlock capability.

Sync noise gate A sync noise gate is used to define an area within the video waveform where the video decoder is to look for the sync pulse. Anything outside of this defined window will be rejected. The main purpose of the sync noise gate is to make sure that the output of the video decoder is nice, clean, and correct.

Sync stripper A video signal contains video information, which is the picture to be displayed, and timing (sync) information that tells the receiver where to put this video information on the display. A sync stripper pulls out the sync information from the video signal and throws the rest away.

Synchronization of video tape recorders In order for any mixing or editing of video signals to occur, all source and record decks must be in sync with each other, running at exactly the same speed and in identical phase. You can picture the process as being similar to transferring goods between high-speed trains running alongside each other. In editing facilities, all decks are fed a common sync signal, called "house sync."

Without synchronization, each individual transport would all run at slightly different rates. Analog tape transports, being mechanical, have small fluctuations in tape speed called "wow and flutter". The capstans on tape machines can slip over time as well, also generating changes in tape speed.

With disk-based systems there is no mechanical transport and no tape. Instead, the playback and record speeds are controlled by quartz crystal oscillators. However, no two oscillators are exactly the same, and an oscillator's frequency can vary with time and temperature. What all this means is that any two transports, even when started at exactly the same time, will begin to drift apart over time and the audio on the different systems will eventually drift out of sync.

Synchronization is achieved in these systems by constantly checking to see the current SMPTE frame, and adjusting the playback speed to keep all devices locked. In analog systems, this is achieved by automated motor speed control. In digital systems it is achieved by adjusting the playback sample rate.

Synchronous Communication/interaction in real time, i.e. at the same time, thus lending itself to the kind of immediacy of communication experienced in a classroom. This may be done using the telephone, chat rooms, whiteboards, etc.

Synchronous transmission A transmission process that uses a clocking signal to ensure an integral number of unit (time) intervals between any two characters. Compare asynchronous transmission.

Syndication A method of delivering programs through a syndicator, or independent distributor.

Synecdoche In discourse, the substitution of a part of something for the whole and vice versa; as when "stage" is used to mean "theater.".

Syntax In the study of grammar, the structural or grammatical rules that define how symbols in a language are to be combined to form words, phrases, expressions, and other allowable constructs.

Synthesized audio Audio output from a synthesizer.

Synthesized Sounds created by computer circuitry.

System exclusive commands or sysex commands Specially made up MIDI commands used to talk exclusively to one MIDI device using a sort of slang that only this MIDI device understands. Manufacturers make up the words for their respective MIDI devices so no two are alike. System Exclusive commands give MIDI devices the best of two worlds. MIDI defines two styles of commands: one which is understood by all MIDI devices and the other which is only understood by specific MIDI devices.

System exclusive data In Musical Instrument Digital Interface (MIDI), messages understood only by MIDI devices from a specific manufacturer. MIDI device manufacturers can use system-exclusive data to define custom messages that can be exchanged between their MIDI devices. (The standard MIDI specification defines only a framework for system-exclusive messages.)

T

T 1 Telephone term given to a digital transmission circuit whose bandwidth is equal to 24 DS-0 voice channels or 1536 Kbs (actually, 1544 Kbs with 8 Kbs bits used for overhead).

T.120 T.120 is an ITU-T standard (International Telecommunications Union) for document conferencing. Document conferencing allows two or more people to concurrently view and edit a document across a network. T.120 is the commonly used name to refer to a family of distinct standards. Many video conferencing companies were developing their own implementations of this until Microsoft released its free NetMeeting software. Now, many companies are using NetMeeting, while perhaps enhancing it in some way.

T.V Safe area 80% of the viewable screen which is considered to be readable on almost any t.v.

T1 (also T-1) A digital transmission link that can pass data at a rate of 1.544 megabits per second over normal twisted-pair wiring. It can handle 24 voice channels at 64 kilobytes per second and is a North American telecommunications standard.

T1 Line A type of high speed Internet connection that provides a great deal of bandwidth. Many businesses lease T1 lines to connect to the Internet, but because they are expensive and offer more bandwidth than most small businesses and homes need, they are not realistic solutions for small and low-demand Internet users.

Tab traversal order The tab traversal order is the order in which you would move through a webpage, or a part of a webpage, by pressing the Tab key on your keyboard. This can be used on web form pages, for example. To move the opposite way hold down the Shift key when you press the Tab key. On website you can "tab" between objects instead of using a pointing device such as a mouse.

Table work Rehearsals in which the play is read without movement, often with the actors sitting around a table, in which the focus is on characterization and interpretation; hence in radio, rehearsals held away from the mics or outside the studio, for the same purpose.

Taft-hartley (labor law) As used in talent-producer relations, The Taft-Hartley or Labor-Management Relations act of 1947, as amended in 1951, contract provisions allowed or mandated by The Taft-Hartley Act regarding non-union talent working under AFTRA auspices. Non-union talent may be hired on a union job provided the talent agrees to join AFTRA within 30 days of the job. Talent that becomes subject to this provision is said to be taft-hartleyed, that is, to be forbidden to work in a union shop after the 30-day period unless s/he has joined AFTRA.

Tagged file format A file format in which data is tagged using standard headers that identify information type and length.

Tail out or tails out adv. [Said of exposed analogue recording tape] Spooled or wound on a core or reel so that the beginning of the program is closest to the core or reel.

Take 1. One of possibly several versions recorded of the same fragment of a work, from which the most satisfactory will be chosen for the final program;

2. to record a take;

3. a physical or vocal reaction usually broad and registering surprise, as in the phrase "to do a take.".

Talent A generic term for the people or subjects assuming the majority of on screen roles.

Talkback Also called "squawk" or squawkbox," the device in a sound studio that enables the control room to communicate with recording area.

Talking head A shot of a person speaking, usually a static head and shoulder or head-only shot.

Tape equalization In tape decks, the best equalization response must be selected according to the type of tape – normal, chrome, or high-bias. In many decks, automatic sensors perform this function, in others, a switch must be set.

Tape hiss A kind of unwanted noise heard to a greater or lesser degree on all magnetic analog recording tape.

Tape recorder operator A member of the sound crew responsible for operating the audio recording equipment on a set.

TBC (time base corrector) A device used in conjunction with a playback from a VCR to provide a sufficient timing stability to permit successful encoding of the video signal by the codec. Some codecs include a built-in TBC.

TCP (transmission control protocol) TCP is defined by RFC793. It is connection-oriented with a guaranteed delivery protocol.

TCP connects different services to their apprropriate ports on a server. For example, TCP would deliver Telnet requests to port 23. The web's datagram protocol (IP) runs "on of" TCP.

TCP protocol (as well as the UDP) ensures the safe transmission of data between two hosts. Information is transmitted in packets. There are two kinds of TCP connections:

Connectionless: delivery is not guaranteed. This is like a CB radio call. When you make such a call you hope somebody hears you, but you cannot be sure that anybody is listening. Similarly, when your computer makes a connectionless TCP call there is no guarantee there will be an answer.

Connection-oriented: delivery is guaranteed. This kind of TCP first makes a connection contact, and when that is established, it sends the message. The connection is thus verified before it is sent, and connection is only shut off once the addressee responds back that it has received the data.

In other words, a message is sent to the addressee (the client), telling it how many packets of data it must receive. This addressee lets the sender (the server) know whether it has received all the information. After each packet is received it lets the server know "OK, I've received this" or "Wait! I have not received packet number 3, please resubmit". Because of this verification procedure, connection-oriented data transmission takes much longer to transmit data. But there is a major advantage. You do not have to wait for the entire file to load before you realize that the connection has been broken.

TCP/IP (Transmission control protocol/ internet protocol) TCP is the most common suite of internetwork protocols.

TDF Telediffusion de France.

TDG Time and date generator.

TDM (Time division multiplexing) Time-sharing of a transmission channel by assigning each user a dedicated segment of each transmission cycle. Video Multiplexers in CCTV use TDM techniques to record many signals onto a single tape.

Tearing A lateral displacement of the video lines due to sync instability. It appears as though parts of the images have been torn away.

Teaser An element at the beginning of a program enticing the listener to stay tuned, usually a preview or excerpt; a narrative hook.

Telecine 1. A device which consists of a projector without the lens and a video camera aimed directly at the illuminated film to record it. A telecine projector incorporates a five-bladed shutter splitting the film into 1/120 second flashes and resulting in two exposures of film for each video field. Since these would not necessarily be of the same film frame, the video fields would often have two different images superimposed. This can cause problems with videodisc still framing.

2. A Rank or Bosch. These are the highest-quality devices for film-to-video transfer. Unlike a telecine projector, they do not use a lens. Instead, a dot of light on one side of the film and a light sensor on the other side is used to scan the film. The Rank uses a small picture tube as the source of the dot of light. This is called a flying-spot scanner. The Bosch uses a one-dimensional CCD array. Both the Rank and the Bosch produce excellent results. The Rank has the advantage of changing the scanning size electronically, allowing control over the size and position of the film area being scanned. Both of these machines have highly developed methods of color correction, allowing very selective work. For example, a single shade of color in a particular area of the picture can be changed without affecting anything else.

Telecine television/cinema A device to capture film frames and convert them to a suitable video format. These days the capture is normally performed digitally.

Telecommuting Working from home using a computer that is connected the employer's network.

Teleconference A phone meeting where callers can both see and hear each other.

Telehealth Telehealth describes the application of ICT to deliver health care services from a distance.

Telemetry Serial data used for the remote control (or monitoring) of a system. Usually comprises a digital encoded data, which is represented by voltages on the line. Sometimes the signal can be audio tones, such as Frequency Shift Keying (FSK) or Dual Tone Multi Frequency (DTMF). It is intended to control pan, tilt, zoom, focus, preset positions, wash, wipe and similar. Being digital, it is usually sent via twisted pair cable but it can also be transmitted over the video coaxial cable, in the opposite direction to the video.

Telephony The science of translating sound into electrical signals, transmitting them, and then converting them back to sound; that is, the science of telephones. The term is used frequently to refer to computer hardware and software that performs functions traditionally performed by telephone equipment.

Telephoto A lens where the focal length is longer than the physical length of the lens, not to be confused with a zoom lens.

Teleprompter Mechanical device which display cues and lines for the actors to read.

Teletext A method of transmitting data with a video signal. ITU-R BT.653 lists the major teletext systems used around the world, while ETSI EN 300 706 defines in detail the teletext standard for PAL. North American Broadcast Teletext Specification (NABTS) is 525-line system C.

For digital transmissions such as HDTV and SDTV, the teletext characters are multiplexed as a separate stream along with the video and audio data. It is common practice to actually embed this stream in the MPEG video bitstream itself, rather than at the transport layer. Unfortunately there is no wide-spread standard for this teletext stream – each system (DSS, DVB, ATSC, DVD) has its own solution.

The practical place in MPEG to stick teletext data is in the user_data field, which can be placed at various frequencies within the video stream. For DVD, it is the group_of_pictures header, which usually proceed intra pictures (this happens about 2 times a second). For ATSC broadcasts the data is inserted in the user_data field of individual picture headers (up to 60 times/ sec).

Television receiver A device capable of accepting video signals broadcast as RF. Also capable of producing a demodulated video signal output from a off-air input signal. Compare monitor.

Television set A display device capable of receiving broadcast video signals (such as commercial television broadcasts) by means of an antenna. Compare RGB monitor.

Telnet This method is used for accessing a remote computer and use it as if it is the one right in front of you. The interface is text-based (on the command line), so you do not see the windows of the remote system.

Tempo The speed at which a Musical Instrument Digital Interface (MIDI) file is played. Tempo is measured in beats per minute (BPM); typical MIDI tempo is 120 BPM.

Temporal compression Adjacent frames are compared to each other in order to find data that remains similar over time (such as the background behind a talking head). The similar data is then eliminated to reduce file size and speed delivery over networks.

Related terms: Interframe, Intraframe, Compression

Tension The basic element of most music, literature, and drama in the Western World; the introduction, intensification, suspension, and relief of which provides structure and is often essential to keep a work of any length interesting and meaningful.

Terabyte (TB) A unit of measure equal to 1,000 gigabytes.

Terminal cup A plastic cabinet part that contains the terminal connectors that permits the wire from the amplifier to be connected to the speaker. Sometimes these parts contain the Crossover and protection circuitry as well.

Termination 1. The connection of a discreet impedance at the end of a transmission line. When the characteristic impedance of the cable (75 Ohms in CCTV) is the value used (as should always be the case) the maximum power is transferred with no reflections.

2. It can refer to the physical act of terminating a cable with a special connector, which for coaxial cable is usually BNC. For optical fibre cable, the most common Termination in CCTV is the ST connector.

Tessellated sync This is what the Europeans call serrated sync.

Test pattern An optical guide for television camera reference alignment.

Text browser A text browser displays webpages as text only. Lynx is the most common text browser and can be accessed by using a keyboard or a mouse. Lynx users will only be able see text descriptions for multimedia elements and images and so may not see your webpage as you intended it to look.

Text browsers are commonly used by visually impaired people, those with slower connections to the internet or if those who do not want graphics and images displayed.

Text editor Web page editing software that requires the user to view and write HTML code as a series of tags, rather than viewing and editing a screen that looks exactly like the Web page will look, which is what WYSIWYG editors can do. Text editors can be more difficult to work with than WYSIWYG editors because they require knowledge of HTML code, but they tend to offer greater flexibility and functionality.

Text files Files that contains no special codes or commands - such as bold, italics or graphics - only text. Text files, unlike binary files, can be read without any special software.

Text layer A layer in which only type elements are allowed.

Text to speech Voice synthesizers that "read" computer text. First used to read screens for blind computer users, text-to-speech is becoming increasingly popular for children's games.

TFT(Thin-film-transistor) This technology is used mainly for manufacturing flat computer and video screens that are superior to the classic LCD screens. Colour quality, fast response time and resolution are excellent for video.

THD Total harmonic distortion is a measure of the how much a given audio device may distort a signal through the introduction of added harmonics or overtones. These figures are usually given as percentages. THD figures below approximately 1% are inaudible to most people. However, distortion is a cumulative phenomenon, so that if a receiver, equalizer, signal processor, crossover, and amplifier are all rated at "no greater than 1%THD", together, they could produce 5%THD, which may well be noticeable in the perceived sound.

Theater As opposed to drama, broadly speaking, the field of performance art concerned with acting out a story through dance, mime, speech, oral narrative, song, or a mixture of these things, coupled with special effects, costume, scenery, lighting, etc.; and thus encompassing the genres of drama, ballet, opera, pantomime, masque, performance art, story telling, etc.; (also theatricality) the non-literary aspects of performance, especially those contributing to sensation and spectacle; a building dedicated to performance, or figuratively in audio drama, the mind of the listener; a company or ensemble specializing in theatrical performance, as the Dance Theater of Harlem, Molière's Comedie française, or Welles' Mercury Theater of the Air.

Theater of the absurd A misnomer (appropriately enough, perpetrated by Martin Esslin, former head of BBC radio drama) for various forms of symbolic, emblematic, expressionistic drama usually on existential themes that had a vogue after World War II, typified by the early works of Edward Albee, Samuel Becket, and Eugene Ionesco.

Theile and small parameters Back in the 1960s the Australian engineer Neville Theile and American engineer Richard Small developed a method of modelling loudspeakers. This was groundbreaking work, allowing the bass performance of loudspeakers to be explicitly designed, rather than developed through trial and error. Forty years later, their work remains the basis of loudspeaker design. To use their design techniques a number of characteristics of the woofer to be used must be known. These include such things as the driver's resonant frequency, its compliance, its 'equivalent volume' and so forth. These are collectively known as the Theile and Small parameters and are stated by all reputable driver makers for those drivers they sell (although not necessarily for drivers that are only sold installed in loudspeakers).

Three-point lighting Standard lighting setup used in most video productions, which consists of a key light, backlight and fill light. The key light is your main light sources in front of the talent; the backlight illuminates the hair and outline of your subject; and the fill light softens the shadows on the face created by the key light.

Three-way (car speaker) Three-way or triaxial speakers take the separate woofer and tweeter from a two-way design and add a dedicated midrange Driver for enhanced warmth and texture. The extra high-frequency energy also boosts overall Sensitivity.

Threshold For the joystick interface, the amount, in device units, that the stick coordinates must change before the application is notified of the movement. A high threshold reduces the number of joystick messages sent to an application, but it also reduces the sensitivity of the joystick.

Through-line The unifying element — thematic, motivational, or otherwise — of a scene, sequence, act or entire play; often used synonymously with spine.

THX A certification standard controlled and operated by LucasFilm. It covers certification of both cinemas and home entertainment equipment to meet given minimum standards. Originally, on the home entertainment front, there was just one standard 'THX Certified'. But in recent years this has been replaced by two standards: 'THX Ultra' certification, which is the highest level and is similar to the old standard, and 'THX Select' which is a lesser standard. Note that many brands and products which could easily achieve THX certification decline to seek it for reasons of brand self-respect, or to avoid the cost involved, so THX certification does not necessarily mean that a piece of equipment is superior.

TIFF (Tagged image file format) An image file output format. TIFF files are lossless, meaning the compression they apply to an image doesn't create artifacts that can degrade the appearance of the image. TIFF files are often used for archiving high quality versions of an images, such as images intended to be reproduced in print or studied digitally in minute detail.

Tighten cues To reduce the gap between the end of one sound, musical passage, or line and the beginning of a following sound, musical passage, or line.

Tilt Moving the camera on a vertical plane. Contrast with Pan.

Timbre The combination of harmonic frequencies in voices or instruments which give them their characteristic quality. Synonyms: 'Quality', 'Sonority', 'Tone Colour'.

Time alignment Systems for ensuring that audio signals from various loudspeakers or drivers arrive at the listener at the correct time. For example, with surround sound it is important that the sound from the surround speakers not arrive early, even though these speakers are often situated closer to the listener than the main speakers. So home theatre receivers incorporate a system to allow the sound to these speakers to be (adjustably) delayed by some milliseconds. Likewise, some high end loudspeaker makers will recess the tweeter further into the enclosure to ensure that the high frequencies arrive at the listener at the same time as lower frequencies, with a view to delivering a more coherent sound.

Time base corrector (TBC) A time base corrector, or TBC, is a device which corrects the timing irregularities that occur during VTR playback.

Since synchronization between videotape decks is so important, it is imperative that all decks perform at precisely the same speed. Speeds always vary, at least slightly, due to VCR velocity errors and tape stretch. TBCs are essential for any kind of multiple mixing of input from videotape source decks, including wipes, dissolves, and overlays. Each source deck must have its own TBC, and each must be synchronized to "house sync."

TBCs are also used simply to "clean up" the timing of a recorded video signal. These TBCs act like black boxes, taking in unstable video and putting out stable video. Because they work alone, without house sync, they are often called standalone TBCs.

Time base stability The maintenance of the scanning process to very close tolerances.

Time code A time reference recorded on tape to identify each frame.

Time code editing By recording a sequential time code along with the video and audio material, you can obtain a precise reference for editing. Each frame has its own number or code which tells the time in hours, minutes, and seconds, and includes a frame number. The industry standard code is called SMPTE time-code . Time code permit very fast and accurate editing. Automatic editing is possible using an edit controller.

Time lapse photography A form of animation in which numerous single frames are filmed spaced at a given interval to show a process that would take a very long time to occur (i.e., a flower blooming or the motion of the stars).

Time lapse VCR (TL VCR) A video recorder, most often in VHS format, that can prolong the video recording on a single tape up to 960 hours (this refers to a 180 min tape). This type of VCR is often used in CCTV systems. The principle of operation is very simple - instead of having the video tape travel at a constant speed of just under 24mm/s (which is the case with the domestic models of VHS VCRs), it moves with discrete steps that can be controlled. TL VCRs can have a number of other special functions for use in CCTV systems. Time lapse video recording. The intermittent recording of video signals at intervals to extend the recording time of the recording medium. It is usually measured when using a 3-hr (180-min) tape.

Time stamp A tag that enables a Musical Instrument Digital Interface (MIDI) sequencer to replay recorded MIDI data at the proper moment.

Timebase corrector Certain video sources have their sync signals screwed up. The most common of these sources is the VCR. A timebase corrector "fixes" a video signal that has bad sync timing.

Time-based program An authoring tool that uses a movie metaphor in which the multimedia title is played frame-by-frame and the screen is a stage where objects are displayed

Timecode, 8 mm 8 mm timecode is a proprietary form of timecode used by Sony with some of their Hi8 products. Compatibility problems in time-code editing environments is solved by using a third-party device made by Horita that converts the timecode from the Sony EVO-9850 and EVO-9800 editing decks to standard SMPTE time code.

Timeline Timebased media progress along as time passes. During the production of such media it is important for an editor to know where in this laps of time a particular instance of an object (visual or audio) is located. Production material is therefore mapped to some or other timeframe, which is visually presented as a line. The basis of the timeframe is usually real time in hours, minutes, seconds, milliseconds.

Macromedia Flash uses the term timeline in the above sense, while Macromedia Director uses the term score, which is quite misleading.

Timeline editing A method in editing suites to edit video in which the clips are represented as bars according to appropriate length.

Tint The tint of a color refers to the result of adding white to a pure color hue. The primary color is thus tinted.

Title Any written material which appears on a film and is not a part of an original scene, including:

Credits: Titles that designate the actors in a film and the technicians who made it.

Crawls or creepers: A title, often carrying the names of the cast of a film, which creeps slowly round on a large unseen drum in front of the camera. Sometimes called roll-ups, credit rolls, or scrolls. Called crawls or pan titles if they move horizontally past the camera lens.

End or tail credits: The title(s) which bring the film to an end.

Head titles or credits: The titles at the beginning of a film, which usually include the main title; the title carrying the name of the film itself.

Subtitles: Titles appearing in the main body of a film, generally superimposed over the image near the bottom of the frame, to make a comment, explain or summarize, present the dialogue or commentary in a silent film, or most commonly to translate dialogue from a foreign language into the language of the audience. They are sometimes printed in a bold color or placed inside black boxes to facilitate easy reading.

Superimposed titles: Titles which are superimposed over a moving shot, and not on an artificial background.

Title generator A black-and-white camera that is used to shoot titles which are electronically superimposed on the video picture while shooting or during editing. Title color can be selected and changed independently. A more sophisticated device known as a character generator (CG) can generate titles directly.

TLD Level Domain Level Domains are domain names that serve as the first level for resolving the names of IP addresses. For years the TLDs have been the following:

com: commercial

edu: education (colleges and universities)

gov: government

mil: military

net: networks

org: nonprofit organizations

From 2001 the following TLDs have been added to the above:

biz: business

info: information

pro

name

aero

coop

museum.

TMSF time format A time format used by Media Control Interface (MCI) to express time in tracks, minutes, seconds, and frames. The number of frames in a second depends on the type of device being used; compact disc audio devices use 75 frames per second. The TMSF time format is used primarily by compact disc audio devices.

Toaster Describes outdated or slow hardware. More recently, the term has been used to describe a product that packages various components or functions together as in kitchen appliances that have multiple functions.

TOC (Table of contents) The digital subcode information that identifies a disc, indicates the number of tracks, the starting and ending points of these tracks, and the total running time of the disc. When included, CD Text information is stored in the TOC.

Tone 1. The playwright's attitude, as the audience infers it, in his work;

2. timbre .

Tone controls Labelled 'bass' and 'treble', fitted to a preamplifier these provided a means of boosting or cutting the bass or treble of the signal. They typically provide up to ten decibels of boost or cut at 50 hertz for bass and 10,000 hertz for treble. Best avoided.

Tone, slate A low pitched tone recorded as a bed under the slate, which, when the tape is fast wound over the playback head, is heard as a beep; used to facilitate the editing of analogue tape.

Tonearm The long thing on a turntable which is pivoted at the back and at its end has provision for a cartridge to be attached. These normally provide for an adjustable tracking weight by the use of a spring-loaded or weight-loaded mechanism at the back, and usually have a damped cueing lever to allow the stylus to be gently lowered to the surface of the record. Over the years some makers have provided parallel tonearms which do not use a pivot, but a motor-driven rack at the back which gradually moves the rear of the tonearm as the width of the LP is traversed.

Tones, calibration White noise that tests and allows for adjustments to a recording or playback device's calibrations.

Tones, test Tones recorded at the beginning of a tape before the program, by which the playback engineer sets the playback level, and checks phasing and alignment.

Tool Program, following defined protocols, that provides a service.

Top 1. In acting, to begin a line before the previous speaker has finished and at a louder volume; to clip;

2. to produce something in time more interesting or impressive than that which came before.

Toroidal coil An inductor or transformer whose core consists of a concentrically wound ribbon of magnetic material. Also used to filter noise on a DC supply line.

TOS DVD players can be connected to digital audio decoders by means of a digital signal cable. One kind uses wires and sends an electrical signal. TOS- cables use optical fibre and send an optical (or light) signal. More correctly, TOS- refers to the kind of plug on the end of such cables. This is roughly square shaped with a small ridge to allow it to click into, and be firmly held by, a socket. Some portable Minidisc recorders and CD players can receive or generate an optical digital signal but these generally require a cable with a different plug, shaped somewhat like a standard 3.5mm stereo headphone plug.

Total harmonic distortion All the harmonic distortion components added together to give a useful, if imperfect, summary measure. The imperfection resides in the fact that, audibly, some of the harmonic components are worse than others. In particular, odd-ordered harmonics from the fifth and up are particularly poor. Solid state amplifiers and the like typically offer THD ratings of less than 0.1% at rated power output, although many all-in-one systems cheat by quoting their power outputs at a ludicrous 10% THD. This much distortion suggests that the system has been pushed well into clipping.

Touch screen Monitor input where you can use your finger to draw on a screen or select an on-screen object. Touch screen technology is often used in ATM machines or in malls, for example, in electronic information kiosks/ directories.

T-pulse to bar A term relating to frequency response of video equipment. A video signal containing equal amplitude T-pulse and bar portions is passed through the equipment and the relative amplitudes of the T-pulse and bar are measured at the output. A loss of response is indicated when any portion of the signal is lower in amplitude than the other. The test signal is called a Pulse and Bar signal and often includes a 2T a 10T a bar and a ramp signal, which contains low medium and high frequencies.

Trace The path of conductive material, usually copper, that conveys voltage or current from one point to another on a printed circuit board. Traces add a slight resistance to the circuit.

Traceroute Traceroute is a utility enabling one to trace the route that packets of data take from one server to another and eventually the client. Each time the packet is routed, the address is noted. Traceroute thus registers each hop that data takes along the internet path from the origin server to the client.

Track A sequence of sound on a compact disc - digital audio (CD-DA) disc. With a Musical Instrument Digital Interface (MIDI) file, information can be separated into tracks, defined by the creator of the file. MIDI file tracks can correspond to MIDI channels, or they can correspond to parts of a song (such as melody or chorus); a CD-DA track usually corresponds to a song.

Trackball Operating like a mouse, a trackball remains stationary while a ball on its top is rolled with the fingers. Because you don't move it around the desk/mouse pad like a mouse, it takes up less space.

Tracking The speed and angle at which the videotape passes the video heads, often adjustable during playback to maximize picture quality

Tracking shot A shot in which the camera follows the action along special tracks set up for that function.

Related terms: Dolly Shot

Trade bibliographic agency An agency providing bibliographic information to, and based on input from, the book trade.

Traffic Traffic refers to the number of visitors a website receives. There are a number of different measures for website traffic with hits, page impressions and user sessions being among the most common.

Tragedy (Gr., "goat song") The ancient quasi-religious, highly conventionalized drama of ancient Greece; the Western verse drama arising from Greek and medieval scholastic drama, written partially or completely in verse and predominantly serious in tone, in which the protagonist suffers a grave material loss or death at the end, hence; in contemporary terms, a dramatic form in which antagonistic forces compel a protagonist to confront his/her moral worth, and in choosing the moral over the materially advantageous choice is enlightened and ennobled, though outwardly suffering a grievous loss; or any play dealing with profound themes and employing tragic structure.

Tragic flaw (also hamartia) A shortcoming or weakness in an otherwise admirable character that contributes to his or her ruin; in Greek tragedy, this was often hubris .

Tragicomedy A play with many humorous moments, but tragic overall.

Trailer An advertisement for a movie which contains scenes from the film. Historically, these advertisements were attached to the end of a newsreel or supporting-feature, hence the name. Doing this reduced the number of reel changes that a projectionist would have to make.

Transcoder A device used to convert from one video component set to another. For example, to dub a Hi8 tape to Betacam SP with the highest possible results, you would need to use a transcoding TBC which includes a transcoder capable of converting the Hi8 (Y/C) signal to the Betacam SP component (Y, R-Y, B-Y) signal.

Transducer Synonym for Driver, speaker, or any electrical device that converts one type of energy into another. A microphone is a transducer that converts sound to electrical signals. A speaker reverses the process.

Transfer rate The time required for data to be transferred from the hard disk (or CD-ROM drive) to the computer's CPU.

Transformer A device used to alter the voltage of AC electricity. This typically consists of an iron ring of some kind with two coils of wire wound around it. The input current is fed to one of the coils, which generates a magnetic field in the iron ring and which, in turn, generates a voltage in the other coil. The proportion of input voltage to output voltage is the same as the proportion of the number of coil windings on the input (called the 'primary') and output ('secondary'). Most transformers use a square-shaped ring with the primary and secondary windings on opposing sides. Some transformers, which tend to appear in high quality audio equipment, are toroidal, which means that the ring is shaped like a donut and the primary and secondary windings cover the entire surface, overlapping each other. Transformers do not work with DC electricity because while DC can generate magnetism in the iron core, a magnetic field cannot in turn induce electricity in a wire unless it is changing (or the wire is moving with respect to it).

Transients A non-repeating sound (such as percussion in music) or an abrupt change of voltage. How a speaker handles transients is a good indicator of its performance.

Transistor An active (commonly three terminal) solid-state device in which a larger output current is obtained by small changes in the input current. Transistors comprise the greater number of active elements within ic's and microprocessors.

Transition In a digital movie-making program such as MovieShop™, a transition separates one video clip or still image from the media that follows. The duration and type of transition can be changed depending on the video-editing software in use. For example, a transition between the first video clip and the clip that follows can be two seconds and can show the first clip dissolving as the second video clip appears. A different transition may show a swirl or a fade into a clip.

Transition shot A shot used to combine two video segments that otherwise might not smoothly connect.

Translator A device used to convert one component set to another, e.g., to convert Y, R-Y, B-Y signals to RGB signals.

Transmission control protocol (TCP) One of the main protocols in the TCP/IP networks which enables two hosts to establish a connection and exhange data.

Transmission line A system of tuning the bass response of a loudspeaker enclosure that involves a labyrinthine internal structure, with a long internal passage between the rear of the woofer and the outside air. This can enhance bass, although it tends to result in significant phase delays in the deep bass.

Transparency Images in the computer environment are always square or rectangular. The illusion that an image is not rectangular can be created by making some areas of the image transparent. Transparency is a feature of graphic images where some parts of the color palette can be set as being transparent. As no color is then present, the transparent part of the images let the background on which the image is placed, to "shine" through.

Transparency frame In the transparency technique first-frame analysis, the first frame of the video file. It contains no video data, but merely supplies the color or range of colors to be rendered as transparent.

Transparency projector Txt File extension that is associated with digital documents created as "text only". Text only documents have no formatting saved with them (i.e., no tabs, centering, etc.), but preserve all ASCII-based characters.

Transponder The electronics of a satellite that receives an uplinked signal from the earth, amplifies it, converts it to a different frequency and returns it to the earth.

Travel presets or tuning memory With this feature the receiver automatically loads it's presets with the strongest available signals. It makes finding stations easier when driving through unfamiliar territory. It also makes loading presets easier when the receiver is first installed, or any time the battery is discharged, or gets disconnected, which often cancels the tuner's preset memory.

Travelling matte shot A shot in which foreground action is superimposed on the background.

Related terms: Bluescreen, Blue Screen

Treatment A preliminary synopsis or storyline which describes plot, characters, setting, etc., for a forthcoming script

Treble The audible frequencies typically constituted by frequencies above about 5,000 hertz, although the dividing line between midrange and treble is one of opinion. The human ear is less sensitive to treble than to midrange frequencies.

Tremolo 1. A fluctuation of amplitude applied to a sound of constant frequency. Often incorrectly used, as in 'tremolo arm' on a guitar which actually produces vibrato.

2. For stringed instruments such as a mandolin, fast up and down strokes of equal strength of the plectrum or index finger on the strings.

Tri-level sync A sync signal that has three levels, and is commonly used for analog HDTV signals.

Trim Similar to cropping in which you remove unwanted pixels from your image.

Triple speed A CD-ROM drive that accesses data at 450KB/sec. This is three times as fast as a standard audio CD player or single speed CD-ROM drive.

Tripod A device using three legs to balance a lens or camera.

Trod the boards To act professionally; to be a professional actor.

Trope Any figure of speech.

TRS (Tip ring sleeve) Another name for a 6.25mm (or 1/4") stereo jack. This terminology tends to be used in professional audio and these plugs tend to be wired for balanced mono operation.

Truck shot, trucking shot (moving shot) A shot taken from a camera mounted on something that is moving.

True color True color means that each sample of an image is individually represented using three color components, such as RGB or Y'CbCr.

True streaming Refers to technologies which match the bandwidth of the media signal to the viewer's connection, so that the media is always seen in realtime. The word "true" is added to differentiate this type of streaming from "http streaming." Specialized media servers and streaming protocols such as RTSP are required to enable true streaming.

True type Window's built-in "outline" font technology. It works by taking a mathematical description of a font's outline and using it to "paint in" on-the-fly screen and printer representations. The printed appearance is true to the displayed appearance, hence "true-type". True-type fonts are stored in two files, with the extensions .TTF and .FOT. To install a TTfont, copy the .TTF file into the directory where the font files are stored (C:\WINDOWS\SYSTEM). Then use Control Panel to ADD the font: Control Panel creates the .FOT file and adds a line to WIN.INI that enables Windows to initialize the font at start-up. A typical font-entry looks like:

Arial (TrueType)=ARIAL.FOT.

Trueview 3D rendering The process of adding light and shadows to a model created in 3D Home Architect Professional 5. The result is a photo-realistic image of the interior and exterior of the model. TrueView 3D Rendering is available only in 3D Home Architect Professional 5 .

TTL 1. **(Transistor-transistor logic)** A term used in digital electronics mainly to describe the ability of a device or circuit to be connected directly to the input or output of digital equipment. Such compatibility eliminates the need for interfacing circuitry. TTL signals are usually limited to binary i.e.. two states, low and high, and are thus much more limited than analogue signals.

2. Thru-The-Lens viewing, metering or colour measuring.

TTL RGB A type of video monitor that can accept only a limited number of digital values and display only a correspondingly limited number of colors. Compare analog RGB.

Tube (enclosure) A type of woofer enclosure consisting of a long tube with a woofer at one end, and a port or Passive Radiator at the other. A good low-end reproducer, this design is very compact and generally used in car stereo.

Tuned (port) A port opening, radiator, or tube whose size is precisely specified by the overall design of the enclosure and woofer.

Tuner A component (or module within a component) that can receive an AM or FM radio signal, demodulate it and deliver an analogue audio signal to an amplifier.

Turn 1. A variety act (e.g. knife throwing, magic act, comedy team), specialty, skit, routine or lazzo. A well-known skit or skit worthy of a great performer is a star turn, hence,

2. a term used sarcastically for a temper tantrum and over-acting.

Turning point (also reversal, peripety) The point in the dramatic action on or near the climax in which the fortunes of the protagonist turn from bad to good or good to bad.

Turnkey Refers to a complete system designed, integrated, installed and tested, so that all the user has to do is "turn the key" to start it.

Turntable A device used in a home entertainment system to rotate at the correct speed a vinyl recording, such as an LP. More generally, the word can refer to the turntable itself along with an installed tonearm and cartridge. The platter on the turntable (the rotating part) is powered by a small electric motor. Different types of turntables are defined by the drive mechanism used to connect motor to platter. The three most common types are idler-wheel, belt drive and direct drive. An idler wheel is a rubber-like wheel, perhaps two or three centimetres in diameter, that presses against the shaft of the motor and a rim on the underside of the platter. These are never used in high quality equipment because of speed variations and noise problems. Belt drive turntables use a rubber-like belt or band running around a pulley on the motor shaft and a rim on the underside of the platter. These appear in a wide range of turntables, from inexpensive ones through to some of the most prestigious models available. In direct drive turntables the motor runs slowly and the spindle at the centre of the platter is connected to the shaft. These appear in some very high quality turntables and offer particular advantages of high acceleration to speed, plus electronic speed control, prized by DJs.

TVL (Television lines) The measure of resolution of either a camera output or a monitor display. It is limited by the frequency response of the system or the Chroma sub carrier.

Tweak A subtle change to a home entertainment system intended to improve the sound. This could range from merely adjusting the system's controls, through replacing cables and experimenting with speaker positions, to all kinds of weird mystical stuff.

Tweening In the early days of animation the senior animation designer would draw the major frames where changes would take place. Assistant animators would then draw details of each of the frames in between these main changes.

Macromedia Flash mimics this by allowing the animator to draw the first and last frame of a sequence (called the keyframes), while Flash would complete all the intermediate frames.

Tweeter Tweeter Highs are reproduced by the tweeter, a small speaker mounted inside the woofer cones of multidriver 2 and 3 way car speakers and separately in other systems. Cone tweeters are efficient and the most economical. Dome tweeters the type found in most home speakers have a wider angle of dispersion and more accurate. Some domes are made of metals like neodymium or titanium that yield extended high frequency response. Others are made of Mylar, or a fine cloth like silk and produce a smoother if not as extended response. Some are made from a combination of materials.

Twisted-pair A cable composed of two small insulated conductors twisted together. Since both wires have nearly equal exposure to any interference, common mode noise is high, but the differential noise is slight thus common mode noise is rejected in a twisted pair line. Twisted pair cable is used for balanced line transmission.

Two ohm stable An X-ohm stable amplifier is an amp which is able to continuously power a load of X ohms per channel without encountering difficulties such as overheating or distrotion. Almost all car amplifiers are at least four ohm stable. Some are two ohm stable, which means that you could run a pair of four ohm speakers in parallel, or a single 2 ohm driver on each channel of the amplifier, and each channel of the amp would "see" two ohms. Some amps are referred to as high-current, which is a buzzword which indicates that the amp is able to deliver very large (relatively) amounts of current, which usually means that it is stable at very low load impedances, such as 1/4 or 1/2 of an ohm. Note that the minimum load rating (such as "two ohm stable") is a stereo (per channel) rating. In bridged mode, the total stability is the sum of the individual channels' stability.

Two shot A shot that includes two characters.

Two-way loudspeakers A loudspeaker which divides the incoming signal into two different frequency bands for distribution to drivers. It sends high frequencies to the tweeter and low frequencies to one or more woofers.

U

UCS(Universal character set) Computers originated in the USA where English is the dominant language. Computers thus basically use a character set that is biased toward English (the ASCII character set). As computers became used in other cultures where other characters (such as ö, ë, ù, é in some European languages) are used, the basic set was extended to include these characters. This extended character set is known as ISO 8895. However, even this extended ASCII character set is not enough to cope with all the variety of characters found in the many different languages of the world. The UCS was formalized and contains thousands of characters used by communities all over the world .

UDP(User datagram protocol) UDP is defined by RFC768 and is another protocol besides TCP that ensures safe transmission of data. UDP is a connectionless protocol (like CB radio) and each packet of information must contain its address. These kind of packets are called diagrams. UDP is much faster than TCP, but not reliable as it does no checking or error correction. It merely forwards data between upper-layer protocols.

UHF signal(Ultra high frequency signal) In television it is defined to belong in the radio spectrum between 470 MHz and 850 MHz.

Ultrasonic Having frequencies above the range of human hearing, commonly considered to be 20 kHz. Not to be confused with "supersonic," which means faster than the speed of sound. Ultrasonic frequencies in the signal path can sometimes cause harmonic distortion in audio components that are in the human hearing range and quite audible.

Umbrella A lighting accessory available inv arious sizes usually made of textured gold or silver fabric.

Unbalanced signal In CCTV, this refers to a type of video signal transmission through a coaxial cable. It is called unbalanced because the signal travels through the centre core and returns via an earthed condutor. One conductor is a fixed voltage ie earth and only the other moves. In a balanced line system neither conductor is referenced to earth.

Undercranking In early days film was fed through the camera by a manual cranking process. When the camera operator turned the crank too slowly, the frame rate was decreased, which caused the action to appear to happen more slowly than normal. Contrast with Overcranking.

Underexposure An attribute that occurs when an image does not receive enough light.

Underscan A mode available on professional video monitors which decreases the raster size H and V so that all four edges of the picture are visible on the monitor. Allows viewing of skew and tracking which would not be visible in normal (overscanned) mode. Also helpful when aligning test charts to be certain they touch all four corners of the raster.

Undirectional predication A form of compression in which the codec uses information only from frames that have already been decompressed.

Unfused wire Any section of wire between the power supply and a load that does not include the protection of a fuse or circuit breaker.

Unicast Sending each user their own copy of a video (or other data) stream. As opposed to Multicast, where one copy is sent and whomever wants it listens to that copy. It is the most commonly used method for video conferencing and video on demand today. Multicast, which is much more efficient, is slowly gaining ground, but requires Internet Service Providers to support it.

Unicode There are many languages in the world with many more characters than provided for in the ASCII set. The Unicode Standard is a subset of the International Standard ISO/IEC 10646-1:1993. Unicode 2.1 lists almost 40'000 characters, which are grouped into sets. Each set has a unique name. Unicode lists the characters, while the UTF-8 and UTF-16 systems map the characters for computer systems.

Uniform resource locator (URL) The global address of documents and other resources on the web.

Unions or guilds Professional American audio drama often, but not always, falls within the jurisdictions of AFTRA, AFM, the Writers Guild, and sometimes nabet or other technicians' union.

Unison In music, unison is used to describe an identity of pitch. When two or more tones are sounding at the same frequency or pitch, they are said to be in unison with one another.

Unity gain A device or setting which does not change signal level, neither amplifying nor attenuating the signal, is said to be at "unity gain." Many processors are set up for unity gain; that is, they can be plugged into a system without changing its overall levels. In practice, unity gain is often a desired setting for maintaining gain staging, and for optimizing operating levels and signal to noise ratios.

Universal resource locator The "address" of a Web site.

Universal serial bus (USB) A hardware technology that allows such things as keyboards, cameras, hard drives and other pieces of hardware external to the computer to be easily plugged in so information can be shared. It's a primary way for digital cameras to transfer digital data to a computer.

Unix An operating system written by Ken Thompson and used fro mainframes.

Unloading The tendency of an enclosure to produce no spring or pressure on the woofer. Unloading produces an uncontrollable over-excursion of the woofer cone (it vibrates out of control); the speaker will exhibit inadequate power handling at lower frequencies.

Unwired network An independent program service, or syndicator, and the stations carrying its program(s).

UOP (User operation prohibition) A control put into a DVD's control program that prohibits the user from performing certain actions at certain points on the DVD. Frequently there are UOPs against jumping back to the DVD's main menu while copyright notices are being displayed. Some particularly irritating DVDs will not allow the audio track to be changes using the 'Audio' key on the remote control. Instead they demand you go back to the main menu. Some DVD players can be modified to escape the limitation of UOPs.

Up full To fade a sound up quickly to the maximum desired level.

Uplink The carrier used by Earth stations to transmit information to a satellite.

Upload To transmit data from a computer to a bulletin board service, mainframe computer, or network. For example, if you use a personal computer to log on to a network and you want to send files across the network, you must upload the files from your PC to the network.

UPS(Uninterruptible power supply) These are power supplies used in the majority of high security systems, whose purpose is to back-up the system when the mains power fails. The duration of this depends on the size of the UPS, usually expressed in output VA (or kVA), and the hold up time expected from fully charged batteries. There are two common types, "off line" and "on line". Off line uses a switch to change from mains to battery operation, thus there can be a short break in the output. On Line UPSs are a type where the convertor is always working, hence there is no switch over break at the ouput.

Upstage 1. Away from the audience, towards the back of the stage, the opposite of downstage;

2. to displace action; to draw inappropriate attention to oneself at the expense of another performer or of the focus of the scene, originally by standing upstage of other players so that they have to turn their backs to the audience to maintain eye contact.

URC(Uniform resource characteristic) URC is a subclass of URI and used for the classification of web documents, much like the Dewey system in book libraries.

URL (Uniform resource locator) The addressing scheme used to link resources on the Web. Like the post office, which must have addresses to deliver mail, Internet users - and their computers - must have addresses in order to send and receive messages. A URL has two parts, separated by ://. Example:

http://www.google.com (Clicking here actually jumps you to the google for a cyber-visit.).

The portion before the "://" is the web protocol, which could be http://, gopher:/.

The after portion is the name of the computer the person is using - the host.

The name of this host computer may consist of several parts, each separated by a period. The last part tells you what kind of organization owns the computer. For example, gov stands for government, com for commercial organizations, edu for educational institutions, mil for the military, and so forth. Occasionally you see names which end with country codes. The India designation is in.

Usability Usability is a generic term that refers to design features that enable something to be user-friendly. The term, and the concepts it encompasses, can be applied to anything from a paring knife to a space station, but here we use it to refer to features that make a Web site user-friendly.

USB (universal serial bus) Serial interface that allows connection of up to 127 devices at speeds of either 1.5 or 12Mbits/s. It supplies power for those devices and allows the devices to be hotswaped (added and removed without rebooting). Currently used to connect keyboards, mice, printers and scanners.

Used equipment Purchasing used equipment must be done with great care, especially in the case of speakers. An inspection of a speaker's voice coil would certainly reveal if it had been severly burned by exposure to clipping distortion. Unfortunately this could only be done by effectively destroying the speaker; obviously, not very practical. Observe if you can, what music the owner prefers, and how it is listened to. If speakers are consistently played with the amplifier volume set at more than half its range, on loud, bass-heavy passages, it might be wise to consider the destructive cumulative effects of clipping distortion and other such stress.

The same caution applies little less rigorously to amplifiers, but not at all to signal source equipment (CD's, receivers, and Cassettes, etc.) and preamps, processors, etc. which are relatively impervious to high amplitude signals.

Usenet A world-wide network of systems with thousands of newsgroups.

User A User is a person who uses the internet, and typically requests an HTML document from a user agent (i.e. typically a browser). The most common user is presently a person who browses through the Web by means of a web browser. However, HTML documents can be rendered in different ways such as in the audio medium. The user then does not browse the Web, but listens to the document.

User agent A User Agent is any device that interprets HTML (or other web-) documents. The most commonly used User Agents are presently Web browsers on computer screens. However, apart from other types of visual user agents (such as PDA screens, projectors and more) there are also non-visual User Agents, such as search robots, speech synthesizer and Braille readers. To indicate this wide variety of media that HTML caters for, it is thus more appropriate to talk of a User Agent than of a browser.

User datagram protocol (UDP) A connectionless protocol for the exchange of data.

User friendly A popular term for describing something, like a user interface, that is easy to use.

User interface The user interface (UI) is the point where a user communicates with a computer. One of the most common user interfaces is a website browser. A website itself can also be described as a user interface as you interact with an organisation or company through its website.

A well-designed UI lets the user find the information they want quickly and helps them carry out their task. A poorly designed UI can often hamper a user and leave them feeling confused as they don't know where to click or where to go next.

User sessions Another measurement for website traffic. A single user session runs from when a user first goes to a website until they leave. Although still not completely accurate, user sessions are more accurate than page impressions for judging the number of visitors to a website.

Username A name used to gain access to a computer system or restricted area of a website. Your username should be unique to you for the particular website or system you are using: some websites ask you to use your email address as your username to make sure it is unique.

USO (universal service obligation) The USO is a regulatory safety net that makes a standard telephone service and payphones reasonably accessible to all people in Australia on an equitable basis, wherever they live or carry on business. The Obligation includes the provision of a suitable handset where requested by the customer. Comparable services must also be provided for people with disabilities. The USO is set out in the Telecommunications (Consumer Protection and Service Standards) Act 1999. (Cth). Telstra is currently the universal service provider for all of Australia. The USO is a legal obligation and exists irrespective of who owns Telstra.

UTC (coordinated universal time) Globally accepted time standard. Combines Greenwich Mean Time (GMT), based on the earth's rotation and set at 0 longitude, with atomic clocks.

UTP (Unshielded twisted pair) A cable medium with one or more pairs of twisted insulated copper conductors bound in a single sheath, with no overall or individual screen. Now the most common method of bringing telephone signals and data to the desktop.

UXGA A computer-oriented display resolution with 1,600 pixels horizontally and 1,200 pixels vertically.

UTF 8 UTF-8 is an 8-bit character set specified by Unicode Technical Committee. UTF-8 includes the first 128 characters of ASCII.

UTF 16 UTF-16 is a 16-bit (two bytes/two octets) character encoding system. It allows the definition of 65'536 characters. UTF-16 characters begin with a BOM (Byte Order Mark) to avoid possible confusion with UTF-8.

V

Valid signal A video signal which will remain legal when transcoded to any other format. Signals which are not valid will be processed without problems in their current format, but problems may be encountered if the signal is transcoded to a different format. For example, the Macintosh will let you generate highly saturated colors which may be legal in the RGB domain, however, when converted to composite video will exceed the NTSC specifications. A valid signal is always legal, but a legal signal is not necessarily valid.

Validation Validation has many meanings, but one of the most common is the checking of information entered into an online form. All the forms on website use some validation to make sure that you have entered enough information and that it looks correct. Any errors will be shown and you will have a chance to correct them.

Form validation helps us to provide the best possible service to you and to respond to any enquiries as quickly and as accurately as possible.

Value The lightness or darkness of a gray or of a color. The darkest level or value of gray is black and the lightest level of gray is white.

Vanity URL A vanity URL is short version of a website address that is easy to remember and quicker to type.

VANS Value added network services.

Vaporware Software or hardware that is talked about, but may never actually appear.

Variable bit rate Variable bit rate (VBR) means that a bitstream (compressed or uncompressed) has a changing number of bits each second. Simple scenes can be assigned a low bit rate, with complex scenes using a higher bit rate. This enables maintaining the audio and video quality at a more consistent level.

Variable LP/HP filter Crossover components which provide adjustable cut-off frequencies, and levels.

Varifocal A lens type that the focal length can be infinitely varied to give the exact image desired. It is similar to a manual zoom lens, except that a varifocal lens cannot be zoom tracked.

Varispeed Short for variable speed; 1. An analogue mechanism on a recorder that alters the speed of tape in order to alter the sound recorded on it;

2. to alter a sound using such a device.

VAS(Volume acoustic suspension) A volume of air in an enclosure that has the same resistance characteristic in acoustic terms as the speaker's suspension in mechanical terms. This is a factor taken into account when designing enclosures. It specifies the optimum internal volume of the enclosure.

Vas-compliance A measurement in liters or cubic feet of the volume of air that is equal to the compliance of the speaker's total suspension.

Vbox The Vbox is a an interface device which can be connected to a personal computer via an RS-232 serial interface. Through the Vbox the computer can control LANC (also called Control-L) compatible video devices. The Vbox translates the VISCA commands from the computer into Sony's LANC protocol. Up to 7 Vboxes can be daisy-chained from one serial port.

VBR (Variable bit rate) As opposed to CBR or constant bit rate. The flow of digital data increases or slows over time, according to the complexity of the encoded signal. Has the advantage of allocating more of the scarce data space to those moments of video or audio that most need it, while economising on sections that can get by with less data.

VBScript A scripting language developed by Microsoft.

VCA (Voltage controlled amplifier) An amplifier whose output is controlled by varying its voltage rather than by direct resistance (as with a potentiometer).

VCD VCD stands for Video Compact Disc.

VCD is a standard developed in early 1990's that allows regular CD to contain 74 minutes of video and audio. Both, video and audio, are encoded in MPEG1 format and stored on the CD in specific format. A VCD can be played on almost all standalone DVD Players and of course on all computers with a DVD-ROM or CD-ROM driver with the help of a software based decoder/player.

VCD is a very popular method for movie distribution in China , Singapore , Malaysia, etc.. Some studios release some of their movies officially for VCD format in Asia . It has almost completely replaced regular VHS format in Asia , because cheap VCD recorders are widely available there. VCD's successor is called SVCD.

VCF (Voltage controlled filter) An audio filter whose effective frequency band is controlled by varying its voltage rather than with a potentiometer.

VCO (Voltage controlled oscillator) An oscillator whose frequency output is controlled by varying its voltage rather than with a potentiometer.

VCR (Video cassette recorder) An analogue video recording system using tapes in a robust plastic housing. The two principal kinds were VHS and Beta although the latter is now obsolete and no Beta video recorders are made any more. There is also a higher quality version of VHS, called S-VHS.

Vector In multimedia, vector refers to formats which store graphical information in terms of mathematical algorithms, instead of as pixels. Because these images don't have any pixels, but are rather equations describing the objects portrayed, vector images scale perfectly to larger and smaller sizes. Illustrator files, Flash, and QuickTime curve media are vector formats.

Vector data Consists of mathmatical computations to create image information. Commonly used for type, fill and shape layers because file size does not increase whne enlarged due to it being a computation.

Vector graphics Images decribed by vector graphics do not contain data for each pixel (as is the case for bitmap graphics), but data about certain standard image forms (such as lines, curves, gradients, animation, and filter effects). A straight line, for example, would be described by its start and end points, and the fact that it is a line. It should be evident that this line object contains much less data than a bitmap line (which needs to describe each pixel). Vector graphics are easily scaleable without losing any quality.

SVG is a relatively new XML-based vector graphic format developed for the Web.

Vectorscope An instrument similar to an oscilloscope, that is used to check and/or align amplitude and phase of the three colour signals (RGB). It has a circular, rather than rectangular screen, to show the phase angles of the component colours.

Velocity of propagation Speed of signal transmission. In free space, electromagnetic waves travel at the speed of light (C). In coaxial cables, this speed is reduced by the dielectric material. Commonly expressed as percentage of the speed in free space i.e. 0.8C which is 0.8 x 3x108.

Velocity scan modulation Commonly used in TVs to increase the apparent sharpness of a picture. At horizontal dark-to-light transitions, the beam scanning speed is momentarily increased approaching the transition, making the display relatively darker just before the transition. Upon passing into the lighter area, the beam speed is momentarily decreased, making the display relatively brighter just after the transition. The reverse occurs in passing from light to dark.

Vented (enclosure) A type of speaker system also known as Tuned, Tuned Port, Ported, or Bass Reflex. They are basically Acoustic Suspension enclosures with the addition of a port or opening with a specific length. This allows a portion of the lower range to be coupled to the front wave produced by the woofer, in order to enhance the low frequency response. The portion of the range below the tuned point (Fb) is essentially a Free Air Driver that subjects the unloaded woofer to the possibility of severe, even catastrophic damage if the energy below this point is highly amplified. The best results for a vented speaker come when using woofers with a QTS in the range of .10 to .40.

Verification The process of checking that information or a design is consistent.

Verismo (cinema) A style of drama or literature characterized by gritty, earthy fidelity to real life; verism.

Vertical blanking interval During the vertical blanking interval, the video signal is at the blanking level so as not to display the electron beam when it sweeps back from the bottom to the top side of the CRT screen.

Vertical interval The portion of the video signal that occurs between the end of one field and the beginning of the next. During this time, the electron beams in the monitors are turned off (invisible) so that they can return from the bottom of the screen to the top to begin another scan. It is a time period where information can be inserted such as teletext, K codes and telemetry.

Vertical interval switcher A sequential or matrix switcher that switches from one camera to another exactly in the vertical interval, thus producing roll-free switching. This is possible only if the various camera sources are synchronized.

Vertical interval time code (VITC) VITC is recorded within the video signal, each timecode stamp is recorded between the video frames, during the vertical blanking interval. VITC cannot be recorded on audio tracks. With VITC, video devices can capture the timecode from the video deck when it's paused or in "crawl" mode, however, most synchronizers cannot read VITC at speeds exceeding about ten times playback speed, preventing slaved machines from maintaining synchronization during rewind and fast forward.

Vertical resolution Chrominance and luminance detail expressed vertically in the picture tube. Limited by the number of scan lines and the Kell factor (a probability factor). The limit in a 625 line, 2:1 interlace system is 409.5 lines. In a non or random interlace system the resolution will be worse.

Vertical retrace The return of the electron beam to the top of a television picture tube screen or a camera pickup device target at the completion of the field scan.

Vertical scan frequency The frequency of the vertical sync pulses, or the frequency of the vertical scan. NTSC vertical scan frequency is 59.9 Hz. The Macintosh video vertical scan frequency is 67.7 Hz.

Vertical scan rate For noninterlaced video, this is the same as the frame rate. For interlaced video, it is usually one-half the field rate.

Vertical shift register The mechanism in CCD technology whereby charge is read out from the photosensors of an interline transfer or frame interline transfer sensor.

Vertical sync A pulse used to trigger the vertical retrace of a scanning electron gun from the bottom of a frame back to the top.

Vertical sync pulse A portion of the vertical blanking interval which is made up of blanking level and six pulses (92% duty cycle at -40 IRE units) at twice the horizontal sync pulse repetition rate. Synchronizes vertical scan of television receiver to composite video signal. Starts each frame at same vertical position (sequential fields are offset 1/2 line to achieve interlaced scan.

Vestigial sideband A method of encoding digital data onto a carrier for RF transmission. 8-VSB is used for over-the-air broadcasting of ATSC HDTV in the USA.

VFOV Short for "Vertical Field of View". The visible angle of the area a camera allows you to see. Or if you like, the vertical angle in degrees that a particular image represents of the world. The shorter the lens (i.e. 15mm, 20mm) the greater the angle of view. The longer a lens (i.e. 45mm or 50 mm) the narrower the angle of view.

VFW (video for windows) An AVI-based application for playing video files on Windows machines.

VGA (video graphics array) An analog standard for video output developed by IBM. Displays text mode in 720 x 400 resolution. In graphics mode, displays 640 x 480 resolution and 16 colors, or 320 x 200 resolution and 256 colors. Also refers to the type of cable used to connect many video adaptors to their monitors. Slowly being replaced by DVI in this capacity.

VHF(Very high frequency) A signal encompassing frequencies between 30 and 300 MHz. In television, VHF band I uses frequencies between 45 MHz and 67 MHz, and between 180 MHz and 215 MHz for Band III. Band II is reserved for FM radio from 88 MHz to 108 MHz.

VHS(Video home system) A consumer-level video recording system developed by JVC in the late 1970s. Despite urban legends to the contrary, it was not noticably inferior to Sony's Beta system (although the latter offered a slightly higher horizontal resolution of around 300 lines, compared to VHS' 250 lines), which had beaten it to market. Eventually VHS prevailed through having longer record-playback times. There was also an electrically similar, but physically smaller, compact version of VHS called VHS-C for use in digital video cameras.

VHSRip In the Internet piracy scene, this term means a release of a movie, or some form of video, that has been taken from a VHS source. It has been captured and then re-encoded to a digital format. Some groups are dedicated to releasing VCD copies of movies that haven't been released on DVD as of yet.

Vibrato Expressive effect which producers a fluctuation of pitch. A rapid, slight variation in pitch in singing or playing some musical instruments, producing a stronger or richer tone. It is often used as an expressive device.

Video There are three different video formats for video files that are transported through The Internet: AVI, MOV and MPEG.

Video is technically speaking a series of frames that pass by so quickly that our eyes are fooled into viewing content as smoothly moving images. For smooth observed movement we need about 25 frames to pass by our eyes every second. That means 25 bitmap images every second. The web is far too slow for that to be of any practical use. One way of reducing the number of frames is to take out some frames. Another way to reduce file size is to display the video in a small screen window.

Video, analog True full-motion video from laser discs, videotapes. Formats: Hi8, 8mm, S-VHS, VHS

Video adaptor (aka: display adapter) A card (or board) that plugs into the computer and converts data to be displayed on the monitor. Video adaptors generally conform to video standards, such as VGA, DVI, XGA and others.

Video archive management/automation software providers Odetics, Louth, Excalibur, Virage.

Video bandwidth The difference between the lowest and the highest signal frequency that a specific video signal can reach. The greater the video bandwidth, the better the quality of the picture. A video recorder that can reproduce a very broad video bandwidth generates a very detailed, high quality picture on the screen. The accepted bandwidth in CCTV is 5.5MHz for a colour signal.

Video capture card Adapter card which allows recording and digitalization of pictures for use with a computer. The pictures may be still-images or movies. Once captured, the picture data is compressed using a CODEC, with playback requiring CODEC-decompression.

Video, component Used in Hi8 and SuperVHS cameras, component video splits the single composite video signal into colors (RGB) and improves the quality by adding a luminance or brightness (Y) channel and a color/chroma intensity (C) channel. Superior to composite video.

Video, composite Single-signal video, used in VHS. Inferior to component video.

Video cassette A self-contained video module played on a specially designed video tape recorder; similar in design to an audio cassette; houses two reels (supply and take-up) with the tape running between them but connected to both.

Video carrier A specific frequency that is modulated with video data before being mixed with the audio data and transmitted.

VideoCD Compact discs that hold up to about an hour of digital audio and video information. MPEG-1 video is used, with a resolution of 352 x 240 (29.97 Hz frame rate) or 352 x 288 (25 Hz frame rate). Audio uses MPEG-1 layer 2 at a fixed bit rate of 224 kbps, and supports two mono or one stereo channels (with optional Dolby pro-logic). Fixed bit-rate encoding is used, with a bit rate of 1.15 Mbps. The next generation, defined for the Chinese market, is Super VideoCD.

XVCD, although not an industry standard, increases the video resolution and bit rate to improve the video quality over VCD. MPEG-1 video is still used, with a resolution of up to 720 x 480 (29.97 Hz frame rate) or 720 x 576 (25 Hz frame rate). Fixed bit-rate encoding is still used, with a bit rate of 3.5 Mbps.

Video clip or clip A segment of a larger video. A clip is typically that portion of the full video or movie that will be used to create another digital project. A professionally produced full-length movie can consist of hundreds or thousands of clips.

Video disc A double-sided optical disc capable of storing and playing back full-motion video. Videodisc has come to refer to all video media that are disc-shaped, regardless of whether they are optical or magnetic, digital or analog.

Video, digital Digitized video, i.e. video converted/compressed to file format. Formats: .AVI (Video for Windows) and .MOV (QuickTime - cross-platform for both Macintosh and Windows).

Video distribution amplifier (VDA) A special amplifier for buffering the video signal so that it can be supplied to a number of items of equipment at the same time. Each output will need to be individually terminated at 75 Ohms.

Video editing Editing is the process of selecting the frames and arranging them on the edit master videotape. In professional applications usually edits must be frame accurate. For example. When mastering a laserdisc frame accuracy absolutely essential, especially when single frame elements are involved.

Video encoder providers Lucent, Vela, Barco

Video equalization corrector (video equalizer) A device that corrects for the high frequency losses and/or phase errors in the transmission of a video signal along long lengths of cable.

Video for windows A codec developed by Microsoft for video and audio files. Media created in this format are saved as AVI files.

Video format A standard determining how a video signal is recorded onto videotape. These include 1-inch Type C, 3/4-inch U-Matic, 3/4-inch U-Matic SP, Betacam, Betacam SP, M-II, D-1, D-2, D-3, VHS, Hi8, Video 8, Beta, and S-VHS.

Video framestore A device that enables digital storage of one or more images for a "frozen" display on a video monitor.

Video gain The amplification factor through any piece of equipment. Many loopthrough items are passive, i.e.. no gain.

Video home system (VHS) Half inch videotape format developed by Matsushita and licensed by JVC.

Video in-line amplifier A device providing amplification of a video signal.

Video interface port A digital video interface designed to simplify interfacing video ICs together. One portion is a digital video interface (based on BT.656) designed to simplify interfacing video ICs together. A second portion is a host processor interface. VIP is a VESA specification.

Video matrix switcher (VMS) A device for switching more than one camera, VCR, video printer and similar to more than one monitor, VCR, video printer and similar. Much more complex and more powerful than simple sequential video switchers.

Video mixing Video mixing is taking two independent video sources (they must be genlocked) and merging them together.

Video modulation Converting a baseband video signal to an RF signal.

Video module interface A digital video interface designed to simplify interfacing video ICs together. It is being replaced by VIP.

Video monitor A display device that can receive video signals by direct connection only and cannot receive broadcast signals such as commercial television; it can be connected directly to the computer. Compare television set.

Video-on-demand Video-on-demand, or VOD, allows a user to select which program to view at their convenience and playing starts almost immediately. When used over the Internet or other network, it is commonly called "streaming video". For broadcast, satellite and cable networks, it is commonly called "pay-per-view" and is usually confined to specific start times. For this reason, it may also be referred to as "near video-on-demand" or nVOD.

Video overlay Placing or nesting a full-motion video window on the display screen.

Video phone A videophone allows you to see someone, and talk or sign to them at the same time. Picture quality is good enough for sign language communication, although you may need to sign a little more slowly than usual.

Video printer A device to produce a hard copy printout from a video signal. It may be either a monochrome (B/W) or colour printer. They come in different format sizes and often special paper and inks are needed. Many computers now can be fitted with a video capture card, which means the print can be produced using a normal computer printer.

Video program system VPS is used in some countries instead of PDC to control VCRs. The data format is the same as for PDC, except that it is transmitted on a dedicated line during the vertical blanking interval, usually line 16.

Video RAM Special memory chips residing fast video cards. The more memory, the higher the resolution. For example, to put out 256 colors you need 512K of video RAM; for 16.7 million colors, you need 2 Mb.

Video recording Any image, still or moving, can be converted into a video signal, most often through a video camera. Then the video signal can be recorded. By far the most common method of recording video is on videotape.

Video scan converters Convert computer RGB signals to NTSC, PAL or SECAM video signals. Once converted, these signals may be videotaped or shown on a television monitor.

Video server A computer server that has been designed to store large amounts of video and stream it to users as required. Usually a video server has large amounts of high speed disks and a large amount of network bandwidth to allow for many users to simultaneously view videos.

Video signal A dynamic signal which represents the varying levels of a video image but does not contain the sync pulses for its display. The video signal can be combined with sync pulses into a composite signal.

Video switcher A device for switching more than one camera to one or more monitors manually, automatically or upon receipt of an alarm condition.

Video tape A magnetic medium capable of storing an electronic signal and consisting of backing, binder, and coating. The coating usually consists of iron oxide; however, metal particle or metal evaporated coatings are also used.

Video teleconferencing Ttransporting real-time voice and video over telecommunications services.

Video wall A video wall is a large screen made up of several monitors placed close to one another, so when viewed from a distance, they form a single large video screen or wall.

Video waveform The pictorial display on a waveform monitor (a special oscilloscope) of the various components of the video signal, used to check the integrity of the signal and signal components.

Viewport A rectangular subregion of the video image that is displayed using local decode.

Vignette A visual effect in which viewers see an image through a perceived keyhole, diamond or other shapped frame.

Virtual reality The experience the user has (the effect) where they feel like they are manipulating an object or in the case of panoramic images where the user feels a sense of immersion in a place.

Virus A computer program that enters a system by a legitimate program, reproduces itself and then performs an action, harmless or otherwise.

VISCA Acronym for video system control architecture. VISCA is a device control language designed for synchronized control of multiple video devices. The protocol is device and platform independent.

Visible signal An indicator which conveys information in a way that can be seen by the naked eye. It differs from electrical signals in that electrical signals generally are not intended for direct human use. Visible signals, or indicators are often used to convey the status of operation of a piece of electronic equipment.

Visitor Every time you come to a website you are classed as a 'visitor'.

Visual effects Modifications to a film during post-production. Contrast with Special Effects.

Visual impairment A general term for disabilities affecting sight, including blindness, colour blindness and low vision.

VITC(Vertical interval time code) Timecode stored in the vertical interval of the video signal. Has the advantage of being readable by a VTR in still or jog. Multiple lines of VITC can be added to the signal allowing the encoding of more information than can be stored in normal LTC.

VITS (Vertical interval test signals) Specially shaped electronic signals inserted in the invisible lines (in the case of PAL, usually between lines 6 & 18) that can be used for the measurement of many quality factors of a system.

VLF(Very low frequency) Refers to the frequencies in the band between 10 and 30 kHz.

VMD(Video motion detector) A detection device generating an alarm condition in response to a change in the video signal, usually motion, but it can also be change in light. Very difficult to set up for use externally but can be useful in carefully controlled situations. Modern VMD systems can learn the scene and ignore such things as tree and foliage movement.

VOB VOB stands for DVD Video object.

The VOB file is one of the core files found on DVD-Video discs and contains multiplexed Dolby Digital audio (normally AC3 format) and MPEG-2 video. VOB files on a DVD are numbered as follows: vts_XX_y.vob where XX represents the title and Y the part of the title. There can be 99 titles and 10 parts, although vts_XX_0.vob does not contain any video, usually just menu or navigational information. You can find them on a DVD video disc in a subdirectory labelled VIDEO_TS.

Vocal folds (vocal chords) A paired system of tissue layers in the larynx that can vibrate to produce sound.

Vocal fry Phonationat very low frequencies. Generally vocal fry sounds like a rapid series of taps. Overuse of loud vocal fry may be related to vocal problems.

VOD(Video on demand) A service that allows users to view whatever program they want whenever they want it with VCR-like control capability such as pause, fast forward and rewind.

Voice activated switching Automatically switching the video feed to whomever is speaking in a multipoint video conference. Usually a function of the Multipoint Conferencing Unit.

Voice coil The voice coil is the coil of wire fixed to a cylinder at the apex of the loudspeaker cone that interacts with a magnetic field. With the help of other speaker components, the voice coil is the active transducer that converts electrical signals from the amplifier or receiver into mechanical energy, which we hear as sound. The voice coil cylinder is the part of the speaker around which the voice coil is wound. More advanced speakers offer a heat-resistant voice coil to prolong speaker life.

Voice over Indicates that dialog will be heard on a movie's soundtrack, but the speaker will not be shown. The abbreviation is often used as an annotation in a script

Related terms: Voice Over, VO

Voice recognition Software which recognizes spoken commands. Most software has to be individually trained for each voice, making its general usage limited. For a good example of voice-recognized commands, dial 1-800-ATT-COLLECT.

VoIP (Voice over internet protocol) A technology used for transmitting standard telephone calls over the Internet using packet-linked routes.

Volt The standard unit for electrical potential.

Voltage Voltage is an electrical charge, or potential difference, between two points, one being of higher relative voltage than the other is. A 1.5-volt 'C' battery has 1.5 volts of difference between the positive and negative terminals, for example. The unit of voltage is called the "volt," named after Allesandro Volta. Voltage can be thought of metaphorically as a pressure, such as water pressure in plumbing, that is available to initiate action or work. It, however, cannot do any work until a circuit is complete so that current (measured in amperes) can fiow.

Voltage drop The amount of energy consumed when a device offers resistance in its circuit. The voltage (E) set up across a resistance (R) carrying a current (I). E=IR

Volume Loudness. In the actors' vocal production, loudness of the voice depends on how close the vocal folds are to each other, how much air pressure there is below the larynx, the fundamental frequency of the voice, and the resonance structure of the vocal tract. Loudness of the voice will generally increase when the air pressure in the lungs increases.

Volume scalar A component of a Musical instrument digital interface (MIDI) Mapper patch map that adjusts the volume of a patch on a synthesizer. For example, if the bass patch on a synthesizer is too loud relative to the piano patch, the volume scalar can reduce the volume for the bass or increase the volume for the piano. (Applications playing waveform audio can also adjust the output volume.)

VOM(Volt-ohm-meter) Sometimes called a Volt-Ohm-Milliammeter. A multimeter that measures voltage, ohms, and milliamperes.

VQF VQF is one of the "alternative" audio compression formats back in 1990s that was aimed to take over MP3 by providing better audio quality than MP3 with lower bitrate. Failed miserabely due various ieasons, most notably because of restrictive licensing. Nowadays the only serious alternatives to MP3 are probably Ogg Vorbis and Microsoft's WMA.

VR(Virtual reality) Computer-generated images and audio that are experienced through high-tech display and sensor systems and whose imagery is under the control of a viewer.

VRAM Memory chips designed specifically for use with computer video displays. Increasing VRAM in a computer system or graphics card increases the color depth viewable as well as increases the number of pixels that can be displayed.

VRML Virtual reality modeling language or virtual reality markup language (VRML) A programming language that allows for the creation of 3D-virtual worlds. Environments and objects within that virtual world can be viewed and explored. For the Professional version of 3D Home Architect 5.0, a file created in the program and exported in the VRML file format can be loaded and viewed in a CAD program. This allows a prospective architect, for example, to take a virtual tour of the plan.

VS 3 Model number of the Grass Valley equipment that can be used to distribute/ switch video signals between the fiber backbone links.

VSYNC Check out the vertical sync definition.

VTR(Video tape recorder) An electro-mechanical device capable of recording, storing, and reproducing an electronic signal which contains audio, video, and control information. The term VTR includes reel-to-reel and cassette type (VCR) recorders.

VU Short for volume unit, a sound measurement unit used in recording studios.

W

W3C (World wide web consortium) The W3C is an organization that releases "standards" (called "Recommendations") for the Web. The HTML 4 Recommendations, among others, was released by the W3C.

The World Wide Web Consortium is headed by the inventor of the Web, Tim Berners-Lee. Based at MIT the W3C is a joint effort of the MIT Laboratory for Computer Science, originally INRIA (France, Europe), but now ERCIM, and Keio University (Japan) to set standards for the Web.

Strictly speaking the W3C cannot write standards. Their "standards" are recommendations. Some of their recommendations have become standards, ratified by the ISO. In 1995 the IETF submitted HTML 2.0 as an Internet Draft.

WAF(Wireless application forum) WAF was founded in 1995 by Unwired Planet and joined by Nokia, Ericsson, and Motorola to enable a pseudo web-experience for cell phones.

The main components of its technology are WAP and WML.

WAIS(Wide area information services) This method is used for searching databases of documents and allows retrieving and viewing of documents from the databases.

Walla 1. Crowd noise;

2. talent specializing in crowd noise.

WAN (Wide area network) As distinct from a LAN (Local Area Network) this is a network of computers and devices connected via a server, or many servers over a wide geographical network, connected together using a combination of private and public telecom connections. Corporate banks, large retail establishments make wide use of this type of network allowing their operations in many different locations to be linked together in a common Mis environment

WAP (Wireless application protocol) WAP is an effort of WAF that mimics the web protocols TCP/IP and HTTP. WAP cannot operate directly on those protocols but linked with a gateway.

Watts A measurement of power. In speakers, wattage is a term that indicates power-handling characteristics in dealing with electrical voltage inputs from the amplifier. RMS or continuous power handling is the only accurate basis for comparing the capabilities of Drivers. In determining the proper power input for a speaker, use this measure only. So-called Peak Power handling is often only the manufacturers best guess at the power dissipation point, beyond which the unit will fail.

WAV WAV is a standard audio format for Windows operating systems, often used for storing high-quality, uncompressed sound. WAV files can contain CD-quality audio signals. However, CD-quality WAV files require relatively large amounts of memory.

WAV files are probably the simplest of the common formats for storing audio samples. Unlike MPEG audio and other compressed formats, WAVs store samples "in the raw" where no pre-processing is required other that formatting of the data.

The WAV file consists of three "chunks" of information: The RIFF chunk which identifies the file as a WAV file, The FORMAT chunk which identifies parameters such as sample rate and the DATA chunk which contains the actual data (samples).

Wave A single oscillation in matter (i.e., a sound wave). Waves move outward from a point of disturbance, propagate through a medium, and grow weaker as they travel farther. Wave motion is associated with mechanical vibration, sound, heat, light, etc

WAVE file A standard file format for storing waveform audio data. WAVE files have a .WAV filename extension.

Wave table synthesis A technique for generating sounds from digital signals. Wave table synthesis stores digital samples of sound from various instruments, which can then be combined, edited, and enhanced to reproduce sound defined by a digital input signal. Wave table synthesis reproduces the sound of musical instruments better than Frequency Modulation (FM) synthesis.

Waveform The waveform of a signal is a depiction of its instantaneous voltages versus time. In audio, for example, we are always dealing with periodic waveforms that make up what we hear. These periodic waveforms can be plotted on a graph and will show up as some type of squiggly line. The graph chart rom left to right represents time and from top to bottom is the amplitude of the sound or voltage at those points in time. The familiar sine wave is an example of this.

Waveform audio A technique of recreating an audio waveform from digital samples of the waveform.

Waveform monitor An oscilloscope used to display the video waveform.

Wavelength The end-to-end physical measurement of a cycle in a repetitive signal, measured in metres (or convenient multiples). Audio wavelengths are generally in the range of 17mm to 17 metres (at air temperature 20C). The human eye responds to light in the wavelength range of 380 to 780 nanometres. The wavelength of a signal can be calculated by dividing the speed with which the signal propagates through a medium by its frequency.

Wavelet A compression algorithm that samples the video image based on frequency to encode the information. This creates a series of bands representing the data at various levels of visual detail. The image is resorted by combining bands sampled at low, medium, and high frequencies.

WD MPEG-7 Working Draft asdasd.

Weave One of several strategies used in deinterlacing video. Weaving is where the two interlaced fields constituting the full video frame are simply 'woven' together without any other adjustment. This is suitable for film sourced video material, since both fields consist of parts of the picture taken at the same time, so no horizontal adjustment is required. Compare with Bob.

Web A computer network of a collection of internet sites that offer text, graphics and multimedia content through HTTP.

Web address A web address may consist of a unique domain name or of a name that is part of a subdirectory of a domain name. Every Web Page has its unique Web Address, technically known as a URI.

Example of a Domain Name web address:

http://www.google.com

Web archiving The process by which a class session is recorded on video and digitized on a computer for later playback through a web browser. The process typically includes video, audio, and the data projection materials from a course (including PowerPoint files) combined and presented on the web for viewing by students at any time. UCSC Media Services is the sole provider of this service on campus and more information may be found here.

Web browser Software that allows people to access and move between documents on the world wide web. Common browsers include Internet Explorer, Netscape Navigator, Opera and Lynx. One of the most challenging aspects of website design is making sure all of the pages in a website display properly in a variety of browsers, and in different versions of those browsers.

WebCam Camera that is typically connected directly to the computer for recording live-motion video or transmitting live-motion video over the Internet.

Webcasting Uusing the Web to deliver live or delayed versions of sound or video broadcasts.

Web client A computer or device running a web browser to request network resources.

Web crawler A system which trawls the WWW, generating all-encompassing Web indexes.

Web document Web document is a synonym of web page.

Web form A form on a Web site that enables visitors to communicate with the host by filling in the fields and submitting the information. Information recieved via a form can be received as public e-mail or processed through another kind of software, such as a correspondence management system. However it is received, e-mail sent via a Web form is formatted consistently, which can help ensure that certain information (name, address, e-mail address, etc.) is included. Formatted e-mail also makes it easier for other software programs to process the information. For these reasons, many congressional offices include Web forms on their Web sites to make processing incoming e-mail much more efficient.

Web mail This is the term we use to differentiate formtted Internet e-mail sent via a Web form from unformatted Internet e-mail (public e-mail).

Web page A web page is an HTML document, usually saved as an HTML file, although it may also be a temporarily created document that ceases to exist the moment the user agent or server session is closed. A web page may be the result from the input of many different files. Each object (ie image, video clip, sound clip, data or document) that is inserted into the web page most probably consists of a separate file. The web page or document thus serves as a container for all these different files. The size of a Web Page can be anything from a blank displayed page, to theoretically a document that would consist of many hundreds of printed pages. In practice it is unlikely that you will find such large web pages as they will take too long to load.

Web Page is a confusing name as it is not related at all to printed pages. A single web page may need many different paper sheets when printed. For the typical computer Web browser, a web page is the file(s) or document that loads from a unique address (URI). Every Web Page has its unique address, even though that address may only exist for the session that the document is used.

Cell phones and similar small devices cannot render traditional web pages. For such devices a traditional web pages is broken up into a deck of cards, where the "deck" would be the traditional web page, and the "cards" the small pieces of information making up the deck. This is technically achieved with c-HTML (Compact HTML), or alternatively with WML.

Web server A machine running server software such as Apache or IIS which has an assigned IP address and is connected to the internet.

Web site A Web Site is a collection of Web Pages or documents. The phrase is use indiscriminately for a few files residing in a subdirectory under some or other domain name, or more appropriately for all the documents that fall under a specific domain name.

Web site address An IP address of a web server.

WebTV Started as a general term for the whole gambit of technologies enabling people to surf the web with their TV by using a small box connecting the telephone line and television. The internet/web pages are transformed into a format that can be displayed on a regular TV.

WebDAV(World wide web distributed Authoring and Versioning) A platform-independent extension of HTTP defined by the Internet Engineering Task Force (IETF) that allows users to collaboratively manage files on Web servers.

Weighting When laboratory measurements are taken of audio gear, the literal, "true" figures obtained often do not reflect the anomalies introduced by human perception. In these cases, the measurements obtained may be mathematically modified, or "weighted" to take into account the peculiarities of human hearing. A common example is "A-weighting", a curve applied to sound pressure levels to more accurately reflect our loudness perception. Other types of weighting compensate for the ear's frequency response, distortion tolerance etc.

Well-made play (piéce bien faite) A type of play seen especially in England, France and the United States from 1825 to the present in which tight construction and careful, logical plotting are emphasized. Examples include Alexandre Dumas fils' La Dame aux Camellias, Gore Vidal's The Best Man and especially the plays of Eugéne Scribe and Victorien Sardou.

Whip pan (swish pan) An extremely fast pan, resulting in motion blur.

White balance A way of calibrating a camera's color response to take into account different color temperatures of light (i.e., fluorescent light is greenish; sunlight, more blue; incandescent light, yellowish). This calibration allows the camera to define what the color white is under any of these various lighting conditions. Failure to white balance could result in an unsightly, unnatural color cast. Many of the new higher-quality DV cameras on the market currently, such as the Sony VX-2000 or the Canon XL-2, have automatic white balancing features that are more reliable than were possible with previous cameras.

White level This part of the video signal electronically represents the white part of an image. It is a voltage of 1V peak to peak (assuming a sync of 0.3V) or 100 IRE whereas the black level is 0.3V peak to peak or 0 IRE.

White noise Random noise with equal energy per frequency is called white noise. It tends to sound very bright and "hissy" due to the unique characteristics of the human ear's frequency response curve. Each ascending octave contains twice as many frequencies as the next lower one, resulting in a significant "build up" of energy in the higher octaves.

Whiteboard Document-teleconference function that lets multiple users simultaneously view and annotate electronic documents with pens, highlighters and drawing tools.

Wide angle Camera lens with a short focal length and broad horizontal field of view.

Wide angle lens A lens that has a shorter focal length and a wider field of view than a normal lens

Wide area network A network of connected computers spread out over a large distance. All congressional offices operate wide area networks (WANs) that connect the LANs in their Washington offices with the LANs in their district or state offices. The World Wide Web can also be considered a WAN

Wideband A medium-capacity communications circuit/path. It usually implies a speed from 64Kbps to 1.544Mbps. (Contrast with broadband and narrowband).

Wide screen signaling WSS may be used on (B, D, G, H, I) PAL line 23 and (M) NTSC lines 20 and 283 to specify the aspect ratio of the program and other information. 16:9 TVs may use this information to allow displaying of the program in the correct aspect ratio. ITU-R BT.1119 and ETSI EN 300 294 specify the WSS signal for PAL and NTSC systems. EIA-J CPR-1204 and IEC 61880 also specify another WSS signal for NTSC systems.

Wide shot A camera shot with a short focal length that includes a large amount of the area in front of the camera; also called a long shot.

Wide-bit stream processing This technology maintains 20-bit precision through the recording process, for clearer reproduction of delicate, low-level music.

Widescreen Until the early 1950s nearly all movies used the Academy aspect ratio of 1.37:1. Under the assault of TV from that time on, most cinema released movies were filmed in a widescreen format where the aspect ratio was from 1.66:1 up to, in some cases, 2.7:1. The most common modern ratios are approximately 1.85:1 and 2.35:1.

Widescreen enhanced A picture format used for widescreen movies on DVD.

Widescreen TV Modern TVs (and other display devices) increasing support a display are with a 16:9 aspect ratio. This provides a much better experience when watching modern signal sources, such as DVDs and Digital TV.

WiFi (Wireless fidelity) Often referred to as Wireless Networking, WiFi refers to a local area network using high frequency radio signals to transmit and receive data.

Wild sound (wild track, wild sound, mos, mit out sound) Scenes that are filmed without the sound.

Windings The wire in a voice coil that is wound around the former (also called a bobbin) to create a coil. Generally, any coils in a transformer, motor, or as an inductor.

Window dubs The trick to off-lining is to always have access to the timecode for all of the source material. If the source medium is of professional quality, like Betacam SP, then viewing the material is expensive and complex. But it is also unnecessary: the material can be transferred to a more accessible medium, like 3/4-inch or VHS tape, with the timecode "burned in" on the picture, usually near the bottom. This is called a window dub. Each video frame is marked permanently with the exact timecode number. The advantage this offers is the ability to see the timecode on a VCR without a timecode reader. This assures frame accuracy during off-lining. Window-dubs are the video equivalent of workprints in film.

Windows media A media format developed by Microsoft for streaming and playing back media files.

.xls File extension that is associated with digital documents created in Microsoft Excel. If you have or are given a file with this extension on it (for example, Budget.xls), it is likely the document was originally created in Microsoft Excel.

Windows media player (WMP) An application developed by Microsoft to handle multimedia files such as audio, video and images.

Windows media video A Microsoft file format for encoding digital video files. Can be of any size compressed to match many different connection speeds, or bandwidths.

Wipe An editing technique in which images from one shot are fully replaced by the images of another, delimited by a definite border that moves across or around the frame.

Wireless application protocol (WAP) A protocol that defines the development and operating environment for handheld wireless devices such as mobile phones, pages or PDA's.

Wireless telephony The idea of replacing the conventional twisted pair telephone service to the home with a wireless RF connection. High-speed digital communications techniques would be utilized to allow enhanced telephone, multimedia, and data services to be transmitted over the airwaves to the home subscriber. In this scenario, the link to the information highway will be wireless.

WMA WMA stands for windows media audio.

WMA, an audio format owned by Microsoft, is a part of Microsoft's Windows Media technology, which includes Microsoft's Digital Rights Management tools, Windows Media Video encoding technology and Windows Media Audio encoding technology.

Windows Media Audio is one of today's most popular Net audio formats. Though not as popular as MP3, WMA tends to outperform MP3 in the area of sound quality, particularly with files encoded at lower bitrates like 64 or 96 Kbps. This performance advantage makes it handy for applications like portable digital audio players, where total play time is limited by a finite amount of internal memory.

WML(Wireless markup language) WML 1.1 16 June 1999. WML is not a W3C effort, but one by the WAF (Wireless Application Forum).

WML has the same aims as c-HTML, but does not adhere to several web standards. It should be regarded as a temporary solution until c-HTML and XHTML are implemented. WML runs on of WAP.

WMV WMV stands for Windows Media Video.

WMV, developed by Microsoft, is a generic name of Microsoft's video encoding solutions and doesn't necessarily define the technology what it uses. In WMV7, Microsoft has used its own flavour of MPEG4 video encoding technology. You can use a .wmv file either to download and play files or to stream content.

Windows Media Video is used for both streaming and downloading content via the Internet. Microsoft's Windows Media Player, an application bundled with Windows XP operating systems, lets you playback and manage a range of audio and video file types, including, of course, WMA and WMV.

Woofer (subwoofer) The bass and lower midrange sounds are reproduced by the woofer. To operate efficiently, a woofer's cone should be made of material that is stiff, yet lightweight. Cones made of polymers, polypropylene, light metals, or poly mixed with other materials including carbon strands and metals, provide excellent sound, and stand up to the heat, cold and moisture that car speakers face daily. Paper cones treated for moisture resistance also do a good job, and are usually very efficient. For car usage, untreated cones should be avoided.

The term "Subwoofer" came into common parlance as a result of the need for marketing departments to boost the "heavy hitting" image of their woofer products. Most such subwoofers are more dependent on the accompanying electronics than on the woofer itself. It was a campaign so successful, it is now as difficult to find a woofer as it is to find a "regular strength" antacid tablet. But as far as describing a particular type of Driver, the term is virtually worthless. The ludicrous extent to which the trend has gone is illustrated in the recent appearance of 4 inch "subwoofers." Study the ratings, specifications, and construction of any woofer you are considering, to see if will be appropriate for your system. In constructing your system, remember to start with the goal first, then the woofer and enclosure, and finally, the amplifier. Everything must work together, and fit together as one coherent system, if you are to be successful.

One area in which the term "subwoofer" does have some authentic application is in the popularity of dedicated low range speakers called powered subwoofers (usually incorporating an amplifier and Crossover) that are used with home-theatre systems to boost the low-end response.

Working title The name by which a movie is known while it is being made. This is sometimes different from the title with which it is released.

World system teletext BT.653 525-line and 625-line system B teletext.

World wide web consortium (W3C) Founded in 1994 as an internation consortium of companies to set standards on the web.

WORM (write once read many) CD's used for archiving/backing up catalogs, directories and other computerized paperwork.

Wow A defect affecting analogue audio signal sources that rely on rotating the medium, particularly LPs and compact cassettes. Wow is a slow, repetitive speed variation, typically repeating at less than once per second. If an LP or audio cassette undergoes this, it produces slow variations in the playback frequency. Wow is specified in per cent and specifications of more than around 0.1% are unacceptable. Digital sources such as CDs are immune to wow because they lock their playback speed to a solid-state timing device.

Wow and flutter Wow refers to low frequency variations in pitch while flutter refers to higher-frequency variations in pitch caused by variations in the tape-to-head speed of a tape machine.

WRAM (windows RAM) A memory format that allows direct access by both the computer and the video adaptor. This increases the speed at which video information is displayed. WRAM also allows for the addressing of larger blocks of video memory.

Wrap (windup) To finish shooting, either for the day or the entire production.

Wrap-arounds Opening and closing packaging for a program.

Write To copy data from the main memory to a storage device, such as a disk.

Writers guild The union representing writers, especially in television, cinema, and commercial radio.

WVGA(Wide video graphics array) A display resolution with 852 pixels horizontally and 480 pixels vertically. Frequently appears in entry level plasma displays.

W-VHS A new Wide-VHS standard proposed by JVC, featuring a high resolution format and an aspect ratio of 16:9.

WWW(world wide web) The World Wide Web was the name used by Time Berners-Lee for a project he envisaged in 1989 to make possible a universal document exchange by means of computer networks, particularly the Internet. The protocol he wrote for transporting documents is HTTP, and the Domain Name System uses WWW as the service name.

Originally only text documents (saved as HTML files) were accessed with browsers that could receive and display WWW documents. Nowadays a browser seemlessly integrates other services (such as mail, graphics, animation, scripts, video and music), and devices other than PCs can be used to access web documents.

WYSIWYG Editor A type of Web page editor that enables you to view and edit a Web page that looks exactly as it will look on the Web, rather than as HTML text, which is what a text editor does. WYSIWYG stands for What You See Is What You Get, and WYSIWYG editors were designed to enable people who do not know HTML code to create Web pages.

X

X and Y axis In a graph or chart showing the realtionship of one acoustical phenomenon or measurement relative to another, it is common to plot the ralionship on a chart with intersecting vertical and horizontal axis (X and Y) that graphicly shows the interaction between two or more elements, such as frequency and power in a given situation.

X.25 A data service using packet switching techniques. The X.25 standard is internationally recognised.

X.400 Electronic mail standard developed by the public service providers and the IT industry. An alternative to SMTP.

X-aiff Apple's Audio Interchange File Format. Well supported on the Macintosh and on Silicon Graphics.

XBM X bitmap N uncompressed black and white image format.

XDSL Generic term for an emerging technology for digital high speed access by home users to the Internet.

Related term: ADSL.

XGA (extended graphics array) A high-resolution graphics standard introduced by IBM in 1990. It provides 640 by 480 or 1024 by 768 and supports more simultaneous colors (65 thousand compared to 8514/A's 256 colors). In addition, XGA allows monitors to be non-interlaced.

XHTML Extensible Hypertext Markup Language (XHTML) is an industry standard language for building web pages that combines HTML and XML. Used properly XHTML means your pages will display correctly across different browsers, computers and mobile internet products such as PDAs.

Xlink W3C Candidate Recommendation 3 July 2000

XLink is a linking mechanism related to the HTML linking (with the <a> element), but it is much more powerful. In HTML linking is one-directional, while XLinks can be multidirectional. HTML links can only be made to one link resource at a time, while XLink makes possible links to multiple resources. XLink relates conceptually to XPath and XPointer.

XLR A professional audio connection standard in which the signal pins are not connected to the shielding earth. This allows them to carry balanced audio signals. Most commonly seen in three pin versions (for mono) although there are also five pin (stereo) versions. Sometimes called Canon plugs.

XLR connector A connector with three conductors used in professional audio applications, typically with a balanced signal. Compare RCA connector and BNC connector.

XM MPEG-7 Experimental Model sadasd.

Xmax A measure of a speaker cone's maximum Excursion (back and forth motion) in one direction while still maintaining a linear behavior (moving in a straight line with high precision). This factor is measured in inches or millimeters. Xmax is more precisely defined as the width of the voice coil that extends beyond the front plate plus 15%. This relates to how far the speaker can move in either direction without appreciable distortion.

XML Short for extensible markup language. XML is a programming language that enables designers to create their own tags to indicate specific information. The House of Representatives, for example, has recently issued a list of XML tags to be used for Web forms on Member Web sites and other Web sites that send e-mail to congressional offices. The purpose of these forms is to enable correspondence management systems (CMS) and other software to easily identify and process types of information — such as name, city, state, zip code, issue, etc. — which will help make the software more efficient and more effective. These tags will help CMS vendors that do not currently offer the ability to process incoming e-mail provide this feature.

When played quietly, this switched circuit allows fuller apparent sound from a system such that the tendancy for human hearing sensitivity to drop off at certain frequencies is compensated and the full range is heard.

X msvideo Microsoft's proprietary movie format.

Xpath W3C Recommendation 16 November 1999

XPath provides the syntax and data model to address segments of an XML document. Conceptually it relates to DOM as objects in a document are regarded to have family relationships such as parent, children and siblings. With XPath the nodes between family members can be accessed and manipulated. XPath can be thought of as the path that should be followed to reach a target. XPath relates conceptually to XLink and XPointer.

XPM X pixelmap An uncompressed color image format.

Xpointer Candidate Recommendation 3 July 2000

XPointer provides a standard manner for identifying document fragments. XPointer also relates to DOM by operating on the abstract document objects rather than on the XML syntax itself. XPointers can be thought of as points in the document that function as targets. XPointer relates conceptually to XLink and XPath.

X-ray Very short wavelength electromagnetic radiations. Very penetrating and used for photgraphing skeletal structures of people.

X-sgi movie Created by Silicon Graphics for use with X-Windows.

XSLT XSL transformations W3C Recommendation 16 November 1999

XSLT is a transformation language to change an XML document into another. It operates on the document tree (related to DOM) and is a sub-section of XSL, although it can operate independently from XSL. XSLT is obviously not as powerful as programming languages to change documents, but as it is an XML application, it follows the same rules as any XML-based application and can be created with a simple text-editor.

XSVCD XSVCD stands for extended SVCD.

XSVCD has same features as SVCD but it is possible to use higher resolution and higher bitrates to get higher video quality. XSVCD burned in "SVCD" Mode on a CD-R or CD-RW can be played on some hardware DVD players and many computers with appropriate software like a software DVD player or a media player with a MPEG-2 codec.

XviD XviD is an ISO MPEG4 compliant video codec. It's not a product but an open source project which is developed and maintained by people around the world. XviD, like many other MPEG4 formats, can be played with certain MPEG4 compatible, stand-alone DVD/DivX/XviD players.

X-wav Format that Microsoft uses for sounds.

X-Y pattern A method of taping in stereo using two mics with overlapping patterns.

Y

Y/C. A video format found in Super-VHS video recorders. Luminance is marked with Y and is produced separate to the C, which stands for chrominance. Thus, an S-VHS output Y/C requires two equal length coaxial cables for a perfect output.

Y cable or adapter A cable used to split a signal into two parts or combine two signals into one. The term, Y Cable is used because the cable has the appearance of the letter Y, where there are two parts joined into one, or one split into two, depending upon the purpose. Y Cables are common throughout audio as a simple and straightforward way to accomplish these two tasks.

The designation of impedance, as High Z, 47,000 ohms, or low Z, 4 ohms.

Y, C1, C2 A generalized set of CAV signals: Y is the luminance signal, C1 is the 1st color difference signal and C2 is the 2nd color difference signal.

Y, I, Q The set of CAV signals specified for the NTSC system: Y is the luminance signal, I is the 1st color difference signal and Q is the 2nd color difference signal.

Y, Pb, Pr A version of component video (Y, R-Y, B-Y) specified for the SMPTE analog component standard.

Y, R Y, B Y The general set of CAV signals used in the PAL system as well as for some encoder and most decoder applications in NTSC systems; Y is the luminance signal, R-Y is the 1st color difference signal and B-Y is the 2nd color difference signal.

Y, U, V The luminance and color difference components for PAL systems; simply the Y, B-Y, R-Y components with new names. The derivation from RGB is identical.

Y/C delay Lag of timing between the luminance (Y) and chrominance (C) signals.

Y/C Separator A Y/C separator is what's used in a video decoder to separate the luma and chroma in a NTSC or PAL system. This is the first thing that any video decoder must do. The composite video signal is fed to a Y/C separator so that the chroma can then be decoded further.

Y'CbCr Y'CbCr is the color space originally defined by BT.601, and now used for all digital component video formats. Y' is the luma component and the Cb and Cr components are color difference signals. The technically correct notation is Y'Cb'Cr' since all three components are derived from R'G'B'. Many people use the YCbCr notation rather than Y'CbCr or Y'Cb'Cr'.

4:4:4 Y'CbCr means that for every Y' sample, there is one sample each of Cb and Cr.

4:2:2 Y'CbCr means that for every two horizontal Y' samples, there is one sample each of Cb and Cr.

4:1:1 Y'CbCr means that for every four horizontal Y' samples, there is one sample each of Cb and Cr.

4:2:0 Y'CbCr means that for every block of 2 x 2 Y' samples, there is one sample each of Cb and Cr. There are three variations of 4:2:0 YCbCr, with the difference being the position of Cb and Cr sampling relative to Y.

Note that the coefficients to convert R'G'B' to Y'CbCr are different for SDTV and HDTV applications.

Y'IQ, YIQ Y'IQ is a color space optionally used by the NTSC video system. The Y' component is the black-and-white portion of the image. The I and Q parts are the color difference components; these are effectively nothing more than color placed over the black and white, or luma, component. Many people use the YIQ notation rather than Y'IQ or Y'I'Q'. The technically correct notation is Y'I'Q' since all three components are derived from R'G'B'.

Y'PbPr, YpbPr Y'PbPr is a scaled version of the YUV color space, with specific levels and timing signals, designed to interface equipment together. Consumer video standards are defined by EIA-770; the professional video standards are defined by numerous SMPTE standards. VBI data formats for EIA-770 are defined by EIA-805. Many people use the YPbPr notation rather than Y'PbPr or Y'Pb'Pr'. The technically correct notation is Y'Pb'Pr' since all three components are derived from R'G'B'.

Y'UV, YUV Y'UV is the color space used by the NTSC and PAL video systems. As with the Y'IQ color space, the Y' is the luma component while the U and V are the color difference components. Many people use the Y'UV notation when they actually mean Y'CbCr data. Most use the YUV notation rather than Y'UV or Y'U'V'. The technically correct notation is Y'U'V' since all three components are derived from R'G'B'.

YUV is also the name for some component analog interfaces on consumer equipment. Some manufacturers incorrectly label it YCbCr. THX certification will require it to be labeled YPbPr.

Yellow book Informal name given for the standard specification of the CD-ROM (compact disc, read-only-memory) developed by Philips and Sony. The standard defines the physical format of the CD-ROM.

YUV Also known as YCC, or analog YUV, or YCbCr

YUV is a color model that decomposes color in three components:

Y: Luminance (or chrominance)

U, Cb: Chroma channel, U axis, blue component

V, Cr: Chroma channel, V axis, red component

YUV is used in JPEG compression, as well as in the European TV standard, PAL.

YUV12 Intel's notation for MPEG-1 4:2:0 YCbCr stored in memory in a planar format. The picture is divided into blocks, with each block comprising 2 x 2 samples. For each block, four 8-bit values of Y, one 8-bit value of Cb, and one 8-bit value of Cr are assigned. The result is an average of 12 bits per pixel.

YUV9 Intel's 4:1:0 YCbCr format. The picture is divided into blocks, with each block comprising 4 x 4 samples. For each block, sixteen 8-bit values of Y, one 8-bit value of Cb, and one 8-bit value of Cr are assigned. The result is an average of 9 bits per pixel.

YUY2 Intel's notation for 4:2:2 YCbCr format.

YVU9C A bitstream format that converts the video signal from the RGB into the YUV color model, averages pixel colors so that the signal uses only nine bits per pixel, and then compresses the signal slightly. This format should only be used when compressing video with Indeo video 3.2. Newer Indeo video codecs provide the option to "Quick Compress" the source video.

Z

Z In electronics and television this is usually an abbreviation for impedance.

Z39.50 A network protocol which allows searching of (usually remote) heterogeneous databases and retrieval of data, most often used for retrieving bibliographic records.

Zero bit detection A circuit in a D/A converter that monitors the digital audio bit stream. upon encountering all bits low, or zero bits, the output of the D/A is disconnected from the preamp. This improves the signal-to-noise ratio specification.1

Zero crossing An analog waveform consists of two alternating voltage polarities (positive to negative to positive...etc.). The point where the polarity changes from positive to negative, or vice versa, is called the zero crossing. When looping a wave or editing two waveforms together, this is the ideal location for the splice as the levels of the two waves are both at zero. This eliminates the possibility of clicks or pops created by mismatched levels, and makes for a smooth sonic transition.

Zero length images Images without specified dimensions.

Zero output The absence of output signal or output power

Zip drives Removable, floppy-disk drive alternatives. Iomega's zip (low-end) and Jaz (high-end) disks accommodate 100MB and 1Gb of storage, respectively. The drives cost about $200 and $500, respectively, and individual cartridges cost $20. With speeds close to hard disk rates, zip/jaz cartridges/drives can replace hard disks for many uses, including large video file storage.

Zoom A zoom shot is made with a zoom lens, a lens of variable magnification properties that allows a continuous movement from a wide angle shot to a close shot without moving the camera. The same effect can be accomplished in reverse, from a close shot to a wide angle shot. The zoom shot can be accomplished either manually or by a motorized zoom lens.

Zoom lens A camera lens that can vary the focal length while keeping the object in focus, giving an impression of coming closer to or going away from an object. It is usually controlled by a keyboard with buttons that are marked zoom-in and zoom-out. The change in focal length of the lens does not result in a physical length of the lens.

Zoom ratio The ration of the shortest focal length to the longest in a zoom lens.

Zweiton A technique of implementing stereo or dual-mono audio for NTSC and PAL video. One FM subcarrier transmits a L+R signal, and a second FM subcarrier transmits a R signal (for stereo) or a second L+R signal. It is discussed in BS.707, and is similar to the BTSC technique.